The Sign Language Interpreting Studies Reader

Benjamins Translation Library (BTL)

ISSN 0929-7316

The Benjamins Translation Library (BTL) aims to stimulate research and training in Translation & Interpreting Studies – taken very broadly to encompass the many different forms and manifestations of translational phenomena, among them cultural translation, localization, adaptation, literary translation, specialized translation, audiovisual translation, audio-description, transcreation, transediting, conference interpreting, and interpreting in community settings in the spoken and signed modalities.

For an overview of all books published in this series, please see
www.benjamins.com/catalog/btl

EST Subseries

The European Society for Translation Studies (EST) Subseries is a publication channel within the Library to optimize EST's function as a forum for the translation and interpreting research community. It promotes new trends in research, gives more visibility to young scholars' work, publicizes new research methods, makes available documents from EST, and reissues classical works in translation studies which do not exist in English or which are now out of print.

Volume 117

The Sign Language Interpreting Studies Reader
Edited by Cynthia B. Roy and Jemina Napier

The Sign Language Interpreting Studies Reader

Edited by

Cynthia B. Roy
Gallaudet University

Jemina Napier
Heriot-Watt University

John Benjamins Publishing Company
Amsterdam / Philadelphia

The paper used in this publication meets the minimum requirements of
the American National Standard for Information Sciences – Permanence
of Paper for Printed Library Materials, ANSI z39.48-1984.

DOI 10.1075/btl.117

Cataloging-in-Publication Data available from Library of Congress:
LCCN 2015007148 (PRINT) / 2015013101 (E-BOOK)

ISBN 978 90 272 5857 1   (HB)
ISBN 978 90 272 5858 8   (PB)
ISBN 978 90 272 6851 8   (E-BOOK)

John Benjamins Publishing Co. · P.O. Box 36224 · 1020 ME Amsterdam · The Netherlands
John Benjamins North America · P.O. Box 27519 · Philadelphia PA 19118-0519 · USA

Table of contents

Preface

Bringing this Reader to fruition would not have been possible without the inspiration, encouragement, support and editorial suggestions of Franz Pöchhacker and Miriam Shlesinger for our idea to produce a Reader specific to Sign Language Interpreting Studies, based on their original *The Interpreting Studies Reader* (2002) which is a must read for any student in Interpreting Studies or related disciplines. We would like to recognize Miriam posthumously for her ongoing feedback and suggestions in reviewing our suggested papers for inclusion in the Reader.

We are also deeply indebted to Franz for his reviews of the entire manuscript; the Reader is truly a remarkable product. We are also grateful to Isja Conen for her willingness to take on this project with John Benjamins as well as her support and encouragement for the Reader.

We would like to acknowledge our colleagues who advised and encouraged our efforts for the Reader, in terms of supplying historical and biographical information, and these include: Dennis Cokely, Nadja Grbić, Alan Hurwitz, Robert Ingram, Betty Ingram, Carl Kirshner, Lorraine Leeson, Peter Llewellyn Jones, Marina McIntire, Christopher Stone, Laurie Swabey, and Anna Witter-Merithew. In particular we would like to thank Elizabeth "Betsy" Winston, whose advice, historical information and perspectives, suggestions, and editorial comments were extremely helpful. We also thank the two anonymous reviewers for their careful review and constructive suggestions that made this Reader a better book.

We were fortunate to have graduate students from the Department of Interpretation at Gallaudet University assist us with searching for copies of articles, references, and biographical information. Denise Mammen, a Masters student, assisted us for over a year and was especially helpful and brilliant. We also thank Emily Balzano, Mark Halley, Paul Harrelson, Ricardo Ortiz for their help with this project. Thank you to Dawn Wessling, who created and assisted with our index.

Two Ph.D. students at Heriot-Watt University, Lee Williamson and Marwa Shamy, made a significant contribution to the Reader by translating two of the papers that we wanted to feature, one originally composed in French and the other in German, into English. We acknowledge their efforts to produce these very good translations in a short timeframe.

In addition, we also want to thank Mayumi Shirasawa who found a Japanese paper written for the First National Conference of Japanese Sign Language Interpreters in 1968, and communicated with the National Research Association of Sign Language Interpretation for permission and their translation of this paper.

Gallaudet University Library staff generously gave their time and efforts to obtain obscure papers and help with reprint permissions. Our thanks to Sarah Hamrich, Elizabeth

Henry, Laura Jacobi, Jim McCarthy and Dianne Bowen. We also thank our respective university departments – the Department of Interpretation at Gallaudet University and the Department of Languages and Intercultural Studies at Heriot-Watt University for their support in this effort.

Finally, we thank our families, friends and colleagues who have watched and supported us throughout this undertaking. We have delighted in working together on this project as it has given us a long desired opportunity to work together, and we hope that you enjoy reading this volume as much as we have relished putting it together!

Cynthia B. Roy and Jemina Napier

December 1, 2014

Acknowledgments

We are indebted to the authors and copyright holders listed below for allowing us to reprint the papers that comprise this book. Where texts have been edited for reasons of space, we gratefully acknowledge authors' permission to use an abridged version of their work.

Quigley, Stephen. P. (ed). 1965. *Interpreting for deaf people: A report of a workshop on Interpreting*. Governor Baxter State School for the Deaf, Portland, Maine, July 7 27, 1965. U.S. Dept. of Health, Education, and Welfare, Vocational Rehabilitation Administration: U.S. Govt. Print Off.

The following articles are reprinted by permission of the Registry of Interpreters for the Deaf (RID), Alexandria, VA:

Hurwitz, Alan. 1980. "Interpreters' effectiveness in reverse interpreting: Pidgin Sign English and American Sign Language." In *A Century of Deaf Awareness in a decade of interpreting awareness: Proceedings of the 6th National Conference of the Registry of Interpreters for the Deaf*, ed. by Frank Caccamise, James Stangarone, Marilyn Mitchell-Caccamise, and E. Banner (eds.), 157–187. Silver Spring, MD: RID.

Flynn, John. 1985. "Accreditation of interpreters in Australia." *Journal of Interpretation* 2: 22–26.

McIntire, Marina and Gary Sanderson. 1995. "Bye-Bye! Bi-Bi! Questions of empowerment and role." In *A confluence of diverse relationships: Proceedings of the 13th National Convention of the Registry of Interpreters for the Deaf*, [no editor], 1993, 94–118. Silver Spring, MD: RID Publications.

Turner, Graham. H. 1995. "The bilingual, bimodal courtroom: A first glance." *Journal of Interpretation*, 7(1): 3–34.

Witter-Merithew, Anna. 1986. "Claiming our Destiny." *Views*, October, 12 and November, 3–4.

Zimmer, June. 1992. "Appropriateness and naturalness in ASL-English interpreting." In *Expanding Horizons: Proceedings of the Twelfth National Conference of Interpreter Trainers*, ed. by J. Plant-Moeller, 81–92. Silver Spring, MD: RID.

The following articles are reprinted by permission of David M. Feldman, Ph.D., Senior Editor of the *Journal of American Deafness and Rehabilitation Association*.

Brasel, Barbara Babbini, Dale. Montanelli, and Stephen P. Quigley. 1974. "The component skills of interpreting as viewed by interpreters." *Journal of Rehabilitation of the Deaf* 7 (3): 20–27.

Ingram, Robert M. 1974. "A communication model of the interpreting process." *Journal of Rehabilitation of the Deaf* 7 (3): 3–9.

Schein, Jerome. 1974. "Personality Characteristics Associated with Interpreter Proficiency." *Journal of Rehabilitation of the Deaf* 7 (3): 33–43.

The following two articles are reprinted by permission of the current copyright holder, Springer.

Ingram, Robert. 1978. "Sign Language Interpretation and General Theories of Language, Interpretation and Communication." In *Language Interpretation and Communication,* ed. by David Gerver & H. Wallace Sinaiko, 109–118. New York: Plenum Press.

Murphy, Harry. 1978. "Research in sign language interpreting at California State University Northridge." In *Language Interpretation and Communication,* ed. by David Gerver & H. Wallace Sinaiko, 87–97. New York: Plenum Press.

The following articles have been reprinted by permission of Gallaudet University Press, and the managing editor, Ivey Wallace:

Strong, Michael and Steven Fritsch Rudser. 1986. "The subjective assessment of sign language interpreters." *Sign Language Studies* 15(53): 299–314.

Davis, Jeffrey. 1990. "Linguistic transference and interference: Interpreting between English and ASL." In *Sign language research: Theoretical Issues,* ed. by Ceil Lucas, 308–321. Washington, DC: Gallaudet University Press.

Roy, Cynthia. 1992. "A sociolinguistic analysis of the interpreter's role in simultaneous talk in a face-to-face interpreted dialogue." *Sign Language Studies* 74: 21–61.

Akach, Philemon and Ruth Morgan. 1999. "Sign language interpreters in South Africa." In *Liaison interpreting in the community,* ed. by Mabel. Erasmus, 67–76. Hatfield, Pretoria: Van Schaik Publishers. Reprinted by permission of the publisher.

Bélanger, Danielle-Claude (1995). "Les spécificités de interprétation en langue des signes québécoise; première partie: Analyse à partir du modèle d'efforts et de l'équilibre d'interprétation", *Le Lien* 9(1): 11–16. "Deuxième partie: Comment préserver l'équilibre d'interprétation", *Le Lien* 9(2): 6–13. [Translated by Lee Williamson]. Reprinted by permission of the author.

Brasel, Barbara Babbini. 1976. "The effects of fatigue on the competence of interpreters for the deaf." In *Selected Readings on the Integration of Deaf Students at CSUN #1,* ed. by Harry Murphy, 19–22. Northridge, CA: CSUN. Reprinted by permission of the National Center on Deafness, California State University at Northridge.

Cokely, Dennis. 1982. "The interpreted medical interview: it loses something in the Translation." *The Reflector* 3: 5–10. Reprinted by permission of the author and publisher.

Grbić, Nadja 1997. "About Helpers and Experts: The changing social practice of sign language interpreting." In Text – *Kultur – Kommunikation: Translation als Forschungsaufgabe. Festschrift aus Anlaß des 50jährigen Bestehens des Instituts für Übersetzer- und Dolmetscherausbildung an der Universität Graz,* ed. by Nadja Grbić and Michaela Wolf, 293–305. Tübingen: Stauffenburg [Translated by Marwa Shamy]. Reprinted by permission of the publisher.

Llewellyn Jones, Peter. 1981. "Target language styles and source language processing in conference sign language interpreting." Paper presented at the *3rd International Symposium on Sign Language Interpreting,* Bristol, UK. Reprinted by permission of the author.

Locker, Rachel. 1990. "Lexical Equivalence in Transliterating for Deaf Students in the University Classroom: Two Perspectives", In *Issues in Applied Linguistics* 1(2): 167–195. Reprinted by permission of the publisher.

Nilsson, Anna Lena. 1997. "Sign Language Interpreting in Sweden." *Meta*, 42(3): 550–554. Reprinted by permission of the publisher.

Pollitt, Kyra. 1997. "The state we're in: Some thoughts on professionalization, professionalism and practice among the UK's sign language interpreters." *Deaf Worlds* 13 (3): 21–26. Reprinted by permission of the author.

Schulz, Andrea. 1997. "Sign language interpreting in Germany on the way towards professionalism." *Meta* 42 (3): 546–549. Reprinted by permission of the publisher.

Scott-Gibson, Liz. 1992. "Sign language interpreting: An emerging profession". In *Constructing Deafness*, ed. by Susan Gregory and Gillian Hartley, 253–258. London: Open University Press. Reprinted by permission of the publisher.

Shunsuke, Ito. 1968. "Interpreting to ensure the rights of deaf people: Interpreting Theory." In *Japanese Newspaper for the Deaf*, July 1, 1968. Translated by The National Research Association for Sign Language Interpretation and reprinted with their permission.

Tweeny, Ryan and Harry Hoemann. 1976. "Translation and Sign Languages." In *Translation: Applications and Research*, ed. by Richard Brislin, 138–161. New York: Gardner Press (John Wiley & Sons, Inc.). Reprinted by permission of the publisher.

Winston, Elizabeth. 1989. "Transliteration: What's the Message?" In *Sociolinguistics of the Deaf Community*, ed. by Ceil Lucas, 147–164. New York: Academic Press. Reprinted by permission of the author and editor.

Every effort has been made to obtain permission to reproduce copyright material. If any proper acknowledgment has not been made, or permission not received, we invite copyright holders to inform us of the oversight.

Introduction

The idea for this volume was inspired by Franz Pöchhacker and Miriam Shlesinger's (2002) edited volume, The *Interpreting Studies Reader*, which was, in turn, inspired by *The Translation Studies Reader* (2000) edited by Lawrence Venuti. Both volumes collected essays, articles, and book chapters that represented approaches to the study of translation and interpretation during the twentieth century. It is in the twentieth century that first translation and then interpretation emerged as new academic fields, separate and distinct from their related fields of psychology, linguistics, literary criticism, philology, rhetoric, and philosophy. In both volumes were featured classic and seminal texts about translation and then interpretation. In *The Interpreting Studies Reader* Pöchhacker and Shlesinger featured what they considered to be seminal theoretical and research texts in Interpreting Studies (IS), featuring a range of papers on conference and community interpreting reflecting various methodological and theoretical approaches to the study of interpreting. All the papers selected have made a major impact on our understanding of the socio-historical development of the interpreting profession worldwide, and our academic and scholarly investigation of interpreting processes, products and practices. In particular *The Interpreting Studies Reader* demonstrates how Interpreting Studies (including Sign Language Interpreting) has emerged as a discipline within its own right, which complements Translation Studies. Pöchhacker and Shlesinger's introductory essay covers the name and nature of IS, IS in relation to other disciplines, the evolution of IS, and what it means to define IS as a discipline in its own right. We urge our readers to take account of both volumes when studying translation and/or interpreting.

As Editors of this volume, we felt that it was time to document the same development of *Sign Language Interpreting Studies*, the Sign Language Interpreting (SLI) profession and the research that has contributed to the changing paradigms in our profession. In two relatively recent key articles in the field, Metzger (2006) and Grbić (2007) discuss the evolution of SLI research. In a chronological review of SLI research topics, Metzger analysed 97 published research papers sourced from two main databases, and tracked how the topics, methodologies and paradigms had shifted and expanded over four decades. In essence she noted that initially there were a narrower range of topics and methodologies produced mostly by researchers in the United States, to a broader range on both counts by contributors from all over the world. Grbić's bibliometric analysis of SLI research from 1970 to 2005 places SLI research in the context of wider translation studies. She analysed 908 SLI texts and found that there has been a significant increase in production over that time, with an acceleration in the mid to late 1990s. The majority of texts were published as journal articles or in collective volumes, and were distributed over various key themes.

The themes include discussions of settings and modes, professional issues, quality issues, ethics, role and socio-cultural issues, linguistic issues, cognitive issues and research issues.

Nevertheless, for the purposes of SLI Studies scholarship, there is a need for a volume devoted to both historical pieces and research pieces, some of which may be classic or seminal articles and essays dedicated to this specific domain of language interpreting. Students, educators, and practitioners can benefit from having access to a collection of influential articles that contributed to the progress of the global SLI profession.

In SLI Studies there is a long history of outstanding research and scholarship, and many of the older essays and articles are now out of print, or were published in obscure journals, or featured in publications that are no longer in print. Therefore our selection of papers follows the same philosophy as Pöchhacker and Shlesinger's Reader, in attempting to bring together inaccessible readings with those that are more available. The chosen readings are significant to the progression of SLI Studies as an academic discipline and a profession. As the years have gone by, many of these readings have been lost to students, educators, and practitioners because this audience simply does not know they exist. For example, a common practice in the profession is for conference interpreters to be relieved every twenty minutes. If you ask working interpreters the how or why behind this "rule," most have no idea that it resulted from a study conducted in 1976. The connection to past knowledge and research has been lost. Therefore this volume includes sections devoted to both perceptions and early research forming the study of SLI, observations of experienced practitioners, and investigations from a variety of disciplines in a proportion reflecting the nature of the field.

In putting together this Reader, we are focusing on two main objectives: (1) to share historical perspectives on the development and evolution of SLI, both as an object of study and as a professional practice; and (2) to follow the progress of SLI Studies research. Many of the early studies on SLI were conducted as masters theses or doctoral dissertations and then published in journals unrelated to SLI. Many of the thought-provoking essays were published in books or conference proceedings that are no longer in print and copies are difficult to locate. Many of the authors were practitioners who became interested in research, and several of these researchers are Deaf scholars who did some of the early work on SLI. Moreover, many of these researchers were trained in different disciplines and therefore each contribute different approaches, disciplinary perspectives, and methods to the development of SLI writing and research.

In order to cover a range of seminal texts we did try and source articles and papers from across the world. We recognize, however, that the Reader is dominated by texts that are written in English, and particularly that the majority of papers are from American authors. We did endeavor to include entries that we could get access to, or get permission to include, from non-English speaking countries, but we found them difficult to locate. We have featured three papers in this Reader (one Japanese, one German and one French), which have been translated into English. But we do acknowledge that there will be papers out there that are written in other languages that may have made an important impact on a national level in terms of development of the sign language interpreting profession in individual countries that we have not included in this Reader.

We also include seminal articles that are widely cited, as well as targeted papers that we think have been overlooked, forgotten, or disregarded by educators and practitioners. Along with each paper, we include biographies of the authors. Some are short as we could not find more information, whereas others are well-known authors in the Deaf/sign language studies fields and had extensive, accessible biographies. Wherever possible, we have contextualized the authors' backgrounds as researchers, or SLI practitioners, or both; and also provided information on their disciplinary backgrounds to inform readers (and primarily students) on the different people, approaches, disciplinary perspectives, and methods that have contributed to the development of SLI Studies writing and research. As noted by Shaffer (2013), the original disciplines and their respective influences on SLI Studies have changed over the course of time, which in turn has influenced the topics of SLI research.

While the progression through the articles in this Reader is somewhat chronological, the articles are also separated into sections by their focus at a particular time in SLI history, or their focus on professional practice. And, we excluded the literature on the teaching of professional skills knowing that it has a vast history of its own.

We know that SLI Studies is still an emerging and expanding research field (Leeson, Vermeerbergen & Wurm 2011), with many more publications produced post-2000, so we hope that this Reader will be a starting point for anyone wanting to delve into SLI education and research, to provide a foundation for understanding the development of our profession and for appreciating where we are at this point in time.

Our cut off point for inclusion in the Reader was 1999, as we felt that papers produced after 2000 are more accessible and widely available. As a consequence, some notable and prolific authors in SLI Studies do not have papers included in this volume, for example, Karen Bontempo, Robyn Dean, Lorraine Leeson, Christine Monikowski, Jemina Napier, Brenda Nicodemus, Debra Russell, Sherry Shaw, Laurie Swabey, and Christopher Stone. The publications of these authors have featured in the literature post-2000, but we would like to acknowledge their significant and continuing contribution to the research field of SLI Studies.

The structure of the book is as follows:

-   Chapter 1: Beginnings (late 1960s and early 1970s)
-   Chapter 2: Early Empirical Research (1975–1980)
-   Chapter 3: Practitioners Become Researchers (1980s)
-   Chapter 4: Insights into Practice (1990s)
-   Chapter 5: Challenging Perceptions of Profession and Role (1980s–1990s)

–   Chapter 6: International Perspectives on the Emerging Profession (1980s–1990s)

Preceding each chapter, there is an overview of the historical background of the chapter, why the papers have been selected as making a seminal contribution to SLI scholarship, followed by brief biographies of the authors.

Finally, we would like to recognize all the authors featured in this Reader for their contributions to development of the worldwide Sign Language Interpreting profession, and for producing such seminal work that inspired us to create this volume.

CHAPTER 1

Beginnings (1960s and early 1970s)

Introduction

Both Metzger (2006) and Grbić (2007) agree that, in the 1960s and 1970s, most known papers, studies, and handbooks about Sign Language Interpreting (SLI) were written in English and produced in the United States (U.S.). Thus the first three chapters of this reader are heavily American as we focus on the beginnings of the SLI profession and early empirical research. While the earliest records concerning sign language translation and interpretation found so far refer to a 'sign translator' in a court appearance in the Ottoman empire in 1612 (Stone 2012), and there are references to 'interpreters' for Deaf[1] people in London courts as early as 1725 (Stone & Woll 2008), early papers in other countries tend to be reports on SLI within that country. Our search for scholarly or research papers and monographs written in other countries and other languages is ongoing. As this search continues, it is likely that a richer, international perspective on SLI discussion and thinking will emerge.

SLI in the U.S. prior to 1964 was vastly different than it is today, and many other countries report the same progression, although begun more recently (Napier 2011). For many years and in most countries, sign language interpreters were family members, frequently the children of Deaf parents, who themselves were not deaf. Similar to immigrant families who move to countries where they do not speak the majority language, and the children learn that language and become informal interpreters for their parents and other family members (Valdes et al. 2003), 'hearing' children with Deaf parents often also function in this language brokering role in a range of settings (Napier in press). In the 1960s and 1970s, once they grew up, many of these children of Deaf adults typically worked full-time jobs in the deaf sector, such as teacher of the deaf, or rehabilitation counselor for the deaf, religious worker, social or welfare worker (Fant 1990). These people often volunteer interpreted as part of their job or as they could spare the time on nights and weekends. No one considered interpreting as full-time employment, or performed interpreting as a professional service (Fant 1990). In the United Kingdom (U.K.), for example, the Deaf Welfare

---

1. We use upper case 'D' to represent the linguistic and cultural identification of people who use a sign language as their natural and heritage language, and who want or require the use of a sign language interpreter to communicate with people who use a spoken language. We use lower case 'd' to indicate people with a hearing loss who may or may not want the services of sign language interpreters or where individual authors chose to use the lower case.

Workers Examination Board expected their candidates to undertake an interpreting test as part of their route to qualification as a welfare worker, but not as a stand-alone certification or license (Stone 2012). Moreover, there were few dedicated services for Deaf adults anywhere in the world at that time.

The early sixties, however, were the beginnings of change in the U.S., Japan, Sweden, and other countries regarding the language and status of Deaf people. As Napier (2011, 354) notes, "SLI was slower to emerge as a professional occupation because of its beginnings in welfare work and the lack of recognition of sign languages as authentic languages comparable to spoken/written language." In the Netherlands, Ben Tervoort's (1953) doctoral dissertation regarding the signing of Deaf children led to questions about the nature of the signs that the children were using and the fact that the signs seemed to have 'decomposable' parts. But it was William Stokoe's work, an English professor and a linguist at Gallaudet University, who published his first paper on American Sign Language (ASL) in 1960 in which he argued for its status as a language, not simply a gestural system, which was really the catalyst for change. Following Stokoe's initial publication, in 1965 the RID published its interpreting handbook, *Interpreting for Deaf People,* and Stokoe, Casterline, and Croneberg published *A Dictionary of American Sign Language on Linguistic Principles.* These publications were closely followed by Brita Bergman's (1973) publication (in Swedish) on the linguistic status of sign languages, and the first suggestion by Mary Brennan that the sign language used by Deaf people in the U.K. should be known as British Sign Language (Brennan 1975).

Thus began a transition from thinking that Deaf people needed communication assistance to manage their everyday lives to the idea that Deaf people were members of a linguistic minority, who, because they were denied access to the majority language, needed the assistance of a sign language interpreter. Interpreters as language specialists working between two languages and two cultures implied a greater status for both Deaf people and interpreters. The shift in perspective from ad-hoc helper to a professional language communication specialist was significant, and would eventually impact both interpreters and Deaf people worldwide.

In noting this transition, Jack Gannon (1981, 339), a Deaf historian, author, and educator at Gallaudet University in the U.S., began his Deaf history book with the following, "The sixties were the beginning." He was referring to the beginnings of Deaf organizations in the U.S., but included in that list was the national association of sign language interpreters that would organize and direct the professionalization of interpreters and interpreting services to American Deaf people.

Moreover, in the sixties in the U.S., began an era of expansive national laws and large national government grants, starting with the Kennedy (1960–63) and Johnson (1963–1969) administrations as a response to civil rights legislation, which included rights for 'handicapped' people. As these laws went into effect, and the grants were distributed through vocational rehabilitation services, funding became available to assist Deaf people in post-secondary education and the search for employment. This, in turn, fueled an urgent and immediate need for interpreters who could function effectively in those settings. Many of these forms of legislation occurred later in other countries, beginning in the 1980s and 1990s.

In the U.S., from 1965 through the 1970s, vocational rehabilitation services provided financial support for workshops to develop interpreter training curricula, certification examinations, and to write a handbook titled *Interpreting for Deaf People*, which was used as the primary interpreter training manual for over 20 years.

Interpreting for Deaf People

Dr. Boyce Williams, the first Deaf person to be employed at the U.S. federal government in Rehabilitation Services, was an active supporter of interpreting services for Deaf people. The Vocational Rehabilitation Administration (VR) began preparations for legislation that would authorize interpreting as a case service for Deaf clients throughout the vocational rehabilitation process whether they were training for employment or attending post-secondary institutions.

As Deaf leaders worked to make the legislation come about, VR funded a "Workshop on Interpreting for the Deaf" in June 14–17, 1964, at Ball State Teachers College, in Muncie, Indiana. "The major problem was the shortage of competent interpreters, so recruitment of interpreters and people to become interpreters were priority matters" (Fant 1990, 1–2).

One evening during this workshop it was suggested that a membership organization for interpreters could assist in establishing a registry, recruiting new interpreters, providing training, and promoting a code of behavior. An impromptu meeting was held and the National Registry of Professional Translators and Interpreters was formed, later to become the National Registry of Interpreters for the Deaf (RID). It is interesting to note that in 1964 this group was already identifying sign language interpreters as professionals in the first name selection.

In January 1965, Boyce Williams again facilitated, through VR, a second workshop that served as a planning meeting for the activities of the new organization. This group developed a constitution and by-laws, and recommended developing a manual on interpreting.

With yet another VR grant facilitated by Dr. Williams, a third workshop was held in July 1965, and the participants (listed in the appendix of the book) wrote a sign language interpreting manual, *Interpreting for Deaf People*, which was edited by **Stephen Quigley** and was published by the Heath, Education and Welfare Office (HEW) of the U.S. federal government in the same year. The introduction makes clear that this is not a manual on the language of signs and fingerspelling; it is, rather, a focus on specialized aspects of interpreting.

This book, then, like the first manuals or handbooks of spoken language conference interpreting (Herbert 1952; Rozan 1956), emphasized the professional rather than the academic, communicative or cognitive dimensions of interpreting. The manual was written to define interpreting issues, provide guidelines for a training curriculum, and to provide information to instructors and students about interpreting.

The manual included terminology, a code of ethics, and general aspects of interpreting: physical factors, platform, fingerspelling, idioms, and interpreting for oral deaf persons and people with severely restricted language skills. It also included a section about specialized settings in which interpreting frequently occurred, settings such as legal, medical, religious, job placement, and counseling and psychotherapeutic situations, along with an outline for training program and resources.

The first two chapters are included in this section as they address, firstly, the enduring issue of terminology, defining 'translation' as exact or literal rendering, 'interpretation' as more free rendering allowing for expansion, explanation, and paraphrasing, and, 'reverse interpreting' – the term used for interpreting from American Sign Language (ASL) to English. The second chapter presents the original RID Code of Ethics, a code of conduct that would become a frequently imitated model for both sign language interpreters in other countries and spoken-language community interpreters in later years.

This manual is a foundational document for SLI that carries a rich history and a lasting impact on SLI discussions everywhere. It is an historical accounting of its philosophical beginnings and adherence to a code of ethical practice. It was the primary textbook for sign language interpreting training programs in the U.S., until a newer version was published by the RID in 1980.

The next paper was first presented by **Ito Shunsuke** at the First National Conference of Japanese Sign Language Interpreters in 1968, and was later published in the newspaper for Deaf people that same year. In the first section of the paper Shunsuke argues for the need for SL interpreters, "For deaf people living in a democracy in order to become full members of society, interpreting plays an essential role." (1968, 1). In the second section, he gives examples of the responsibility of interpreters to Deaf people. He indicates that interpreters should not merely serve as neutral communicators between hearing and Deaf people, but that they shoulder responsibilities for accurate and equitable communication.

What is remarkable about the two papers above, American and Japanese, is that they were written around the same time expressing the similar thoughts about Deaf people and interpreting, while worlds away from each other.

Journal of Rehabilitation of the Deaf

By the early 1970s, the shift towards the recognition of ASL (and other sign languages) as a language and Deaf people as a cultural and linguistic minority group was embraced wholeheartedly by both Deaf people and interpreters. Both American and European linguists had begun to independently study their national sign languages (McBurney 2012) and interpreters were typically the first of professionals working with Deaf people to recognize the importance of these claims. Eventually, sign language interpreters and educators began to explore the nature of interpreting as a cognitive and linguistic process between two *languages* and cultures, and to recognize the value of researching this process. Robert Ingram was one of the first SLI scholars to write about the interpreting process in this way.

Because of the impetus and push from rehabilitation to support the development of a professional society for interpreters, and with the financial resources to pay for sign language interpreting services, the *Journal of Rehabilitation of the Deaf* decided to create a special issue on interpreting and sent out a call for papers. The papers in this edition represent, for the most part, the beginnings of scientific thinking and empirical research on sign language interpreting. While we would ideally have liked to include all the papers of that journal issue, we have selected three papers that we feel best encapsulate the discussions of the time in the U.S. and elsewhere shortly thereafter.

A Communication Model of the Interpreting Process

This article written by **Robert Ingram** is one of the first, if not *the* first, theoretical construct of the complex variables in interpretation. It is, certainly, the first model of interpreting as a communicative process, rather than a cognitive process. At the time, the Shannon & Weaver (1949) model of communication was a widely accepted model for the linear transfer of information, or messages from one person to another. Although overshadowed by the cognitive, information-processing models that would soon follow (Gerver 1976; Moser 1978), Ingram adapted and presented this model to encourage interpreters and emerging scholars in SLI to envision interpreting as a process that could be studied scientifically, and as a process that all interpreters, of spoken or sign languages, would encounter. As he notes, "Their purpose [the models of scientific renderings] is to describe processes, not personalities" (Ingram 1974, 7). He wrote this in reaction to a growing focus by psychologists on personality-linked aptitude characteristics of interpreters, rather than language fluency, and to separate interpreting from the 'handicap' label. He also considered interpreting a process that was unaffected by the language combination, rather it was a communicative and linguistic process that occurred no matter what language combinations were used.

More importantly, Ingram argued that models allow us to identify and isolate components of the interpreting process, an important first step. As he closes, he points to the need to scrutinize the communicative context, including but not limited to extra linguistic information as well as information about the surroundings, a scrutiny that the field did not address for another ten years after this publication. He posed questions about the impact of what we now call prosodic units and speech varieties, and about an interpreter's role that the profession is still debating in the 21st century.

The Component Skills of Interpreting as Viewed by Interpreters

Also in this 1974 issue, one of the first published research articles co-authored by **Barbara Babbini Brasel, Dale Montanelli, and Stephen Quigley**, appeared. Quigley's involvement in the planning and editing of the interpreter training manual led him to seek funding to research interpreting at his own university, the University of Illinois-Urbana/Champaign, and he hired Barbara Brasel as a researcher. This article presents the early findings of a four-year research program "designed to develop and refine methods of evaluating interpreters according to their levels of competence" (1974, 21).

They began by asking what differentiates the competent interpreter from the unqualified, the excellent from the mediocre, and so on. Responses from interpreters and Deaf people generated a list of skills, such as cognitive abilities, attitude, experience and others. Brasel decided to ask both groups to rank the various skills and then tested the proficiency of the interpreters to see if proficiency had an impact on the ranking.

The interpreters ranked accuracy, understanding and adaptability at the top of their lists, whereas Deaf participants ranked clarity of signing and professional behavior at the top of their lists. These findings would influence certification examinations that were being developed during these years (Carl Kirschner, personal communication, July 9, 2012). Over the years, surveys have remained a basic staple for research on interpreting and they continue to include many of the same basic questions asked by the questionnaire used in this study.

Personality Characteristics Associated with Interpreter Proficiency

Also, in this same journal **Jerome Schein** wrote up his research that combined psychological testing instruments with judgments of interpretations in an effort to link personality characteristics with interpreting skill. As he noted, not all fluent signers are good interpreters so there must be other variables that accounted for good interpreters, perhaps psychological ones. The first part of the research was to ask each interpreter to interpret an 'easy' text and then a 'hard' text. Their performances were filmed and later judged by six experts.

The six judges were two hearing females, two Deaf males, and two Deaf females, all of whom completed ratings on each interpreter for both passages. The factors considered were: sign-making skill, fingerspelling ability, expressiveness of face, general appearance, and accuracy of interpretation. The results showed that "Judges not only differed between themselves but also on their ratings of the same interpreter's performances on the easy and hard tasks." (1974, 34) So Schein used a simple sum measure as this showed less variance and thus a higher correlation.

Then the Edwards Preference Personality Schedule was administered to the same 20 interpreters who also took a battery of tests: test of musical ability, Otis-Lennon test of mental ability, reading comprehension, and a vocational interest inventory. The personality picture that emerged for the successful interpreter included: (1) desires to be the center of attention and to be independent, (2) is not overly anxious and does not seek sympathy for self, and (3) is not rigid and not afraid to make errors.

Because RID was tasked with determining who should be an interpreter, and evaluating interpreting skill, studies like Schein reflected the concerns of the time. Personality studies would fade away as concerns for fluency in ASL became the focus part of training.

However, questions about aptitude for SLI would re-surface in the 2000s (Bontempo & Napier 2009, 2011).

Editors' note

Much of the literature in English refers to the U.S. SLI profession as pioneering the development of the SLI field throughout the world. However, for further discussion of the history of sign language interpreting as a profession, see Napier (2011) and Stone (2012). For international examples of the development of sign language interpreter education see Napier (2009), or various conference proceedings of the World Association of Sign Language Interpreters (WASLI) which feature descriptions of the more recent, and ongoing, development of SLI in a range of countries.

1.1   Quigley, Stephen P. (ed.). 1965. *Interpreting for Deaf People.* Chapters 1 and 2. Washington, DC: Office of Health, Education and Welfare.

Born in Belfast, Northern Ireland, Stephen P. Quigley obtained his BA in 1953 in psychology from the University of Denver. He went on to earn both his MA in 1954 in speech and hearing disorders, and Ph.D. in 1957 in speech science and psychology at the University of Illinois. Prior to his retirement, Quigley was professor of education, speech, and hearing at the University of Illinois, Urbana-Champaign.

Quigley is best known for his work in the area of communication, language, and the improvement of education for children with hearing impairments (McNally, Rose & Quigley 1999). His investigations of Noam Chomsky's theory that careful manipulation of stimulus-response could produce more effective insights into language acquisition led to his development of the Test of Syntactical Abilities (Quigley, Steinkamp, Power, and Jones 1978), a standardized test for the diagnosis and assessment of syntactical abilities of deaf children.

Quigley noted the absence of a well-developed first language for deaf children entering school and the manner in which this deficit prevents the examination of language development. He conducted important research on the instructional use of ASL and English (Quigley & Paul 1984a, 1984b). Findings of these investigations suggest the benefits of teaching ASL to children with deafness and, as a second language, providing instruction in English.

Interpreting for Deaf People
Stephen P. Quigley (ed.)

I.   Introduction

Interpreting for Deaf People

This manual is designed to help meet several basic needs: (1) to define some interpreting problems and procedures that might be helpful to interpreters for deaf people; (2) to provide guidelines for a curriculum for the training of interpreters; (3) to provide information to help instructors of classes for interpreters; and (4) to provide information for students in classes on interpreting.

A.   What is interpreting?

It is important that the difference between interpreting and translating be clearly understood. In *translating,* the thoughts and words of the speaker are presented verbatim. In *interpreting,* the interpreter may depart from the exact words of the speaker to paraphrase, define, and explain what the speaker is saying. Interpreting requires adjustment of the presentation to the intellectual level of the audience and their ability to understand English.

The interpreter needs to be aware of the differences in the use of interpreting and translating. When translating, the interpreter is recognizing that the deaf person is a highly literate individual who prefers to have his thoughts and those of hearing persons expressed verbatim. Translating is not commonly used as highly literate deaf people frequently do not need the services of an interpreter unless they are in situations where misunderstanding might arise which could result in financial or personal loss. For deaf people who have been well educated but have difficulty with the common idioms of the English language, it may be necessary to do some explaining in the interpreting process. For many deaf people, it is necessary to paraphrase, define, and explain a speaker's words in terms and concepts which they can understand. This is interpreting. The lower the verbal ability, the greater is the need for simplification of the presentation. An interpreter must know when to interpret and when to translate and he can only know this when he has learned to recognize the type of deaf person or persons with whom he is dealing.

An interpreter should have proficiency in manual communication; however, it is recognized that such proficiency does not automatically qualify an individual as an interpreter. Expert users of the language of signs frequently need additional training to become interpreters. Not only must they be skilled at communicating the oral spoken words of an individual to a deaf person or persons, but they must be able to understand the manual communication usage of the deaf and interpret the ideas into the spoken word for hearing persons (reverse interpreting).

There are many classes in the United States for the teaching of manual communication. Although some instructors in these classes hope to try to prepare their students to become interpreters for deaf people, no formal systematic training programs for interpreters have yet been developed. Expert interpreters need experience as well as specialized training and the experience must come from frequent exposure to deaf people so that manual communication becomes second nature to the interpreter. It is hoped that the procedures discussed in the various sections of this report will contribute to the establishment of professional level programs for the preparation of highly qualified interpreters for deaf people.

B.   Need for interpreting

The need for interpreting is discussed by Roth (1964) who lists the many situations and occasions requiring the services of interpreters for deaf people. Because each of these situations involves detailed responsibilities several sections of this manual are devoted to specific areas of interpreting.

Legal problems in which people become involved require a sensitive and impartial interpreter to assist in courtroom procedures, witness testimony, and general legal transactions involving real estate, bank notes, wills, insurance, compensation, and domestic relations. Employment and job placement counseling require the services of interpreters at times, particularly in the areas of testing and counseling. The need for interpreters in areas involving medical and health problems is emphasized by Roth who discusses such intimate interpreting situations as visits to the physician's office, hospital and emergency cases, psychotherapy, and other aspects of psychiatric treatment. Other interpreting situations include religious affairs such as church services, marriages, funerals, Sunday School classes, and singing of prayers and hymns. Guidelines for the training of interpreters and a proper course of study are pressing needs. Recognizing that many experts in manual communication are not conversant with the specific needs of interpreting for deaf people, special guidelines and suggestions for proper courses of study and curriculum were included in Roth's list of urgent problems. Consideration needs to be given also to physical factors involved in interpreting, particularly in assemblies and group gatherings, conventions, lectures, workshops, and meetings.

C.   Registry of interpreters for the deaf

At a workshop on interpreting for the deaf conducted at Ball State Teachers College, June 14–17, 1964, in Muncie, Ind., a National Registry of Professional Interpreters and

Translators for the Deaf was organized. The purpose of the organization is to promote recruiting and training of more interpreters and to maintain a list of qualified persons. A code of ethics was taken under consideration for development and for presentation at a later date. Membership requirements were established and officers were elected.

A second meeting on interpreting for the deaf was held in Washington, D.C., on January 28–29, 1965. At that time, the name of the organization was changed to Registry of Interpreters for the Deaf and it has become further known as RID. A constitution was discussed and approved. The purposes of the organization were defined as follows:

1. To prepare, maintain, and distribute a registry of accredited interpreters and translators for deaf people.
2. To establish certification standards for qualified interpreters and translators.
3. To recruit qualified interpreters and translators.
4. To work for the advancement and training of qualified interpreters and translators.
5. To prepare literature dealing with methodology and the problems of interpreting and translating.
6. To prepare a guideline of terminology applicable to the various aspects of interpreting and translating.
7. To work within the framework of organizations of the deaf insofar as possible.
8. To adopt and promote a code of ethics.

Other sections of the constitution involved election of officers, fees, and amendments.

Officers who were elected to 4 year terms of office at the Muncie, Ind., meeting are:

> President – Kenneth Huff, Superintendent, Wisconsin School for the Deaf, Delavan, Wis.
> Vice president – Dr. Elizabeth Benson, Dean of Women, Gallaudet College, Washington, D.C.
> Secretary-treasurer – Mrs. Virginia Lewis, Associate in Anesthesiology, Youngstown, Ohio.
> Board members at large – Frank B. Sullivan, Grand Secretary-Treasurer, National Fraternal Society of the Deaf, Oak Park, Ill., Mrs. Lillian Beard, Second Baptist Church, Houston, Tex.

A steering committee has been appointed and boards of examiners have been established in various regions in the United States:

Steering Committee:
Louie J. Fant, Jr., *Chairman,* Associate Professor of Education, Gallaudet College, Washington, D.C., 20002.
Dr. Elizabeth Benson, Dean of Women, Gallaudet College, Washington, D.C., 20002.
Mr. Edward C. Carney, Specialist, Distribution, Captioned Films for the Deaf, U.S. Office of Education, Washington, D.C., 20202.
Rev. H. H. Hoemann, Lutheran Missionary to the Deaf, 1103 Lamberton Dr., Silver Springs, Maryland.

Region I – (Connecticut, Maine, Massachusetts, New Hampshire, Rhode Island, and
    Vermont)

Board Members
Joseph P. Youngs, Superintendent, Chairman, Governor Baxter School for the Deaf, Portland, Maine.
Gordon Clarke, American School for the Deaf, West Hartford, Conn.

Region II – (Delaware, New Jersey, New York, and Pennsylvania)

Board Members
Mrs. Frances Lupo Celano, Chairman, Lexington School for the Deaf, 904 Lexington Avenue, New
    York, N.Y.
Miss Fannie H. Lang, Publicity Director, Pennsylvania Society for Advancement of the Deaf, 45 Betsy
    Lane, Ambler, Pa.

Region III – (District of Columbia, Kentucky, Maryland, North Carolina, Virginia, West
    Virginia and Puerto Rico)

Board Members
Miss Anne Davis, Chairman, Mary-land School for the Deaf, Frederick Md.
Charles B. Grow, Superintendent, Kentucky School for the Deaf, Danville, Ky.

Region IV – (Alabama, Florida, Georgia, Mississippi, South Carolina, and Tennessee)

Board Members
Fred R. Sparks, Jr., Superintendent, Chairman, Georgia School for the Deaf, Cave Spring, Ga.
Miss Marie Horn, 4306 Stein Street, Mobile, Ala.

Region V – (Illinois, Indiana, Michigan, Ohio, and Wisconsin)

Board Members
David O. Watson, Chairman, Route 1, Winneconne, Wis.
Hilbert C. Duning, 1188 Cryer Avenue, Cincinnati, Ohio.

Region VI – (Iowa, Kansas, Minnesota, Missouri, Nebraska, North Dakota, and
    South Dakota)

Board Members
Melvin H. Brasel, Educational Director, Chairman, Nebraska School for the Deaf, Omaha, Nebr.
William Marra, Kansas School for the Deaf, Olathe, Kans.

Region VII – (Arkansas, Louisiana, New Mexico, Oklahoma, and Texas)

Board Members
Mrs. Lillian Beard, Chairman, 8217 Wier Drive, Houston, Tex.
Edward L. Scouten, Principal, Louisiana State School for the Deaf, Baton Rouge, La.

Region VIII – (Colorado, Idaho, Montana, Utah, and Wyoming)

Board Members
Jack D. Downey, Chairman, 7006 Brookover Drive, Boise, Idaho.
Eula R. Pusey, 128 L Street, Salt Lake City, Utah.

Region IX – (Alaska, Arizona, California, Hawaii, Nevada, Oregon, and Washington, Guam)

Board Members
Mrs. T. R. Babbini, Chairman, 14607 Huston Street, Sherman Oaks, Calif. Ralph Neesam, California
   School for the Deaf, Berkeley, Calif.

Information regarding the Registry of Interpreters for the Deaf may be obtained by writing
to Mr. Kenneth Huff, Superintendent, Wisconsin School for the Deaf, Delavan, Wis.

   After January 1, 1965, and until definite accreditation procedures can be developed
and put into effect, any person interested in becoming a member may do so by obtaining
sponsorship of two other active or sustaining members of the Registry of Interpreters for
the Deaf and by paying a membership fee of $4.

D.   Manual on interpreting

The present manual on interpreting is the direct result of a meeting of members of the
board of the Registry of Interpreters for the Deaf sponsored by the Vocational Rehabilitation Administration in Washington, D.C., in January 1965. The manual is the result
of the combined efforts of the participants in a workshop sponsored by the Vocational
Rehabilitation Administration at the Governor Baxter State School for the Deaf in
Maine, July 7–27, 1965. It should be emphasized that the various areas of interpreting as
expressed in the section headings are based largely on the experience and knowledge of
the participants as interpreters rather than on their particiular knowledge of the specific
fields of interpreting such as law and medicine. The participants at this workshop were
selected mostly because of their skill and experience as interpreters. It is quite likely,
however, that errors have been made in sections of the manual and there may be some
serious omissions. As the readers note errors or have suggestions for improvement of
the manual it is suggested that they communicate with the President of the Registry of
Interpreters for the Deaf.

E.   Terminology

The following list defines some terms peculiar to manual interpreting which are used
throughout this booklet.

1.   Esoteric manual communication: A secretive gesture language employing only mini-
     mal hand movements and maximum use of facial expression that deaf persons some-
     times employ when they do not wish their conversation observed by others present
     who know the language of signs.

2. Interpreting: (Often used to indicate both interpreting and translating as well as the reverse of both.) An explanation of another person's remarks through the language of signs, informal gestures, or pantomime.

3. Manual alphabet: The 26 different single hand positions that represent the 26 letters of the alphabet. Use of these hand positions to form a word or sentence is called fingerspelling.

4. Manual communication: Communication in both language and concept between two or more people through the use of the language of signs.

5. Manual, manual-training: A method of training or educating a deaf person through fingerspelling and the language of signs. Manual classes generally are instituted for those children who have been determined to be nonoral.

6. Oral, oral-training: A method of training or educating a deaf person through speech and speechreading without employing the language of signs or fingerspelling.

7. Receptive, comprehension skills: The ability to understand what is expressed in both fingerspelling and the language of signs.

8. Reverse interpreting: Transmittal of the language of signs into an approximate oral representation in proper English syntax.

9. Reverse translating: Transmittal of the language of signs into an exact oral representation of the manually signed and fingerspelled statement.

10. Rochester method: An oral multisensory procedure for instructing deaf children in which the receptive medium of speechreading is simultaneously supplemented by fingerspelling and auditory amplification. The language of signs is wholly excluded from this procedure of instruction.

11. Sign language, language of signs: An ideographic language which uses manual symbols apart from the manual alphabet. This is commonly used to describe the language of the deaf in which both manual signs and fingerspelling are employed.

12. Simultaneous delivery: The rendering of a message into the language of signs at the same time the message is being delivered orally, or rendering of a message into an oral interpretation at the same time the message is being delivered in the language of signs (simultaneous reverse delivery).

13. Simultaneous interpreting or translating: Simultaneous use of the language of signs and silent oral presentation.

14. Simultaneous method: A method of training or educating a deaf person through use of *both* manual and oral methods simultaneously.

15. Speechreading, lipreading: The ability to understand the oral language or speech of a person through observation of his lips and facial movements.

16. Translating: A verbatim presentation of another's remarks through the language of signs and fingerspelling.

17. Transmissive, expressive, performance skills: The ability to express oneself in the language of signs and fingerspelling.

II.   Registry of interpreters for the deaf code of ethics

PREAMBLE

Recognizing the unique position of an interpreter in the life of a deaf person, the Registry of Interpreters for the Deaf sets forth the following principles of ethical behavior which will protect both the deaf person and the interpreter in a profession that exists to serve those with a communication handicap.

In the pursuit of this profession in a democratic society it is recognized that through the medium of interpreters, deaf persons can be granted equality with hearing persons in the matter of their right of communication.

It is further recognized that the basic system for self-regulation governing the professional conduct of the interpreter is the same as that governing the ethical conduct of any business or profession with the addition of stronger emphasis on the high ethical characteristics of the interpreter's role in helping an oftentime misunderstood group of people.

The standards of ethical practice set forth below encourage the highest standards of conduct and outline basic principles for the guidance of the interpreter.

CODE OF ETHICS

1.   The interpreter shall be a person of high moral character, honest, conscientious, trustworthy, and of emotional maturity. He shall guard confidential information and not betray confidences which have been entrusted to him.
2.   The interpreter shall maintain an impartial attitude during the course of his interpreting avoiding interjecting his own views unless he is asked to do so by a party involved.
3.   The interpreter shall interpret faithfully and to the best of his ability, always conveying the thought, intent, and spirit of the speaker. He shall remember the limits of his particular function and not go beyond his responsibility.
4.   The interpreter shall recognize his own level of proficiency and use discretion in accepting assignments, seeking for the assistance of other interpreters when necessary.
5.   The interpreter shall adopt a conservative manner of dress upholding the dignity of the profession and not drawing undue attention to himself.
6.   The interpreter shall use discretion in the matter of accepting compensation for services and be willing to provide services in situations where funds are not available. Arrangements should be made on a professional basis for adequate remuneration in court cases comparable to that provided for interpreters of foreign languages.
7.   The interpreter shall never encourage deaf persons to seek legal or other decisions in their favor merely because the interpreter is sympathetic to the handicap of deafness.

8. In the case of legal interpreting, the interpreter shall inform the court when the level of literacy of the deaf person involved is such that literal interpretation is not possible and the interpreter is having to grossly paraphrase and restate both what is said to the deaf person and what he is saying to the court.

9. The interpreter shall attempt to recognize the various types of assistance needed by the deaf and do his best to meet the particular need. Those who do not understand the language of signs may require assistance through written communication. Those who understand manual communication may be assisted by means of translating (rendering the original presentation verbatim), or interpreting (paraphrasing, defining, explaining, or making known the will of the speaker without regard to the original language used).

10. Recognizing his need for professional improvement, the interpreter will join with professional colleagues for the purpose of sharing new knowledge and developments, to seek to understand the implications of deafness and the deaf person's particular needs, broaden his education and knowledge of life, and develop both his expressive and his receptive skills in interpreting and translating.

11. The interpreter shall seek to uphold the dignity and purity of the language of signs. He shall also maintain a readiness to learn and to accept new signs, if these are necessary to understanding.

12. The interpreter shall take the responsibility of educating the public regarding the deaf whenever possible recognizing that many misunderstandings arise because of the general lack of public knowledge in the area of deafness and communication with the deaf.

1.2   Shunsuke, Ito. 1968. "Interpreting to ensure the rights of deaf people: Interpreting Theory." In *Japanese Newspaper for the Deaf*, July 1, 1968. [Translated by The National Research Association for Sign Language Interpretation]

Ito Shunsuke was born in Fukuchiyama, Kyoto in 1927. After his graduation from Kyoto teacher's school (current Kyoto University) and Ritsumei-kan University in Kyoto, he was served as an instructor at Kyoto School for the Deaf in 1949–1988. While he was working as an instructor, he was involved in SLI as one of the first interpreters. His efforts brought about the founding of the National Association of Sign Language Interpreting for which he served as its first director. During his time as director, he supported, educated, and trained many interpreters in Japan and was awarded a position as honorary director after his retirement. In 2006, he passed away and is highly regarded in both the Japanese Deaf community and the community of sign language interpreters.

"Interpretation theory"

Interpretation defending the rights of deaf people

Ito Shunsuke

In the history of deaf education and of the Deaf Movement, Interpretation Theory has never been discussed. But when you want to discuss both deaf people and sign language, or the Deaf Movement, I think Interpretation Theory plays a very important role.

I would like to explain what I mean by Interpretation Theory, based on the discussion among the members of the interpreters' group known as Mimizuku, located in Kyoto, Japan. I hope this will be read by lots of people, and that you will give us your opinions.

A.   The necessity and Significance of Interpretation

Why is interpretation, including sign language, necessary for deaf people? Before starting a discussion of this issue, I want to bring up two real-life cases. The first case is that of Mr. A, a deaf man.

Mr. A had been educated diligently in the Oral Method. In other words, he had been taught by his eager parents and teachers to lip-read and speak, both in his house and in his workplace. He also learned to read and write Japanese.

Now, Mr. A had a problem in his house and he filed suit in a family court. All of the problems in his house were revealed to the judge and the member of an arbitration board. The problems were discussed, and, in the end, the secretary of the court wrote an arbitration proposal. The proposal was shown to Mr. A. It was not to his liking. In fact, it was completely different from what he had been insisting upon for a long period. But he was unable to make his objections known, and, therefore, everyone thought he had found the proposal acceptable.

In my opinion, a meeting is of value only if its members can express themselves and exchange opinions on the spot. In the case of Mr. A., he was not offered this opportunity, and he was forced to accept a proposal not to his liking. At that time, there were no interpreters present.

The second case revolves around a government official and a group of deaf people. The group had requested a sign-language interpreter. The official said the following:

---

* This is a report on which current Japanese Sign-Language Interpretation theory is based.

"I fail to understand why sign-language interpreters are necessary for deaf people. Whether interpreters are a temporary necessity because deaf adults are not educated in the Oral Method, or whether interpreters will always be needed is beyond me. Will all of the civil servants in the ward offices, city offices and employment offices have to learn sign language? That's asking too much. I think deaf people who can communicate by writing have no problem wherever they go. Then there is no need for interpreters. Requesting an interpreter any time and anywhere, despite the level of education among deaf people, is a step backward, is it not?"

These two cases are very important when you consider the problems of deaf people and the problem of Interpretation Theory. The opinion of some people can be summed up as follows: "Education for deaf people is improving, both in matters of substance and technique. When all deaf people can understand spoken language perfectly, and deaf people can communicate well with hearing people by writing, lip-reading, and speaking, sign language interpreters will no longer be necessary." This is currently the view of legislators and others in the law profession.

Article 134 of the Civil Procedure Code and Article 175 and 176 of the Criminal Procedure Code all state the following: "If a deaf defendant is unable to communicate by reading and writing while in court, an interpreter should be provided. However, if the defendant can read and write, his responses can be elicited in writing." These statements correspond to the actions of the court mentioned in the first case, and to the statement of the government official mentioned in the second case. If deaf people were in agreement with these statements there would be no need to discuss this issue.

But this is not the case. Without interpreters, deaf people are at a disadvantage. For example, if Mr. A. in the case above had had access to an interpreter, he could have objected immediately to proposal that he had been given. Likewise, deaf people at the unemployment office might be introduced to better jobs. After all, in encounters with other people it is normal to be able to offer one's opinions and objections right away. By means of an interpreter, deaf people are able to understand the contents of a conversation immediately. Thus, they are able to speak up instantly.

The foundation of a democracy is the freedom of speech. For the deaf people living in a democracy, in order to become full members of society, interpreting play an essential role.

B.   The standpoint of the interpreter

Interpreters are needed by deaf people during lectures, speeches, lessons, meetings, workshops and conversations–in short, any time there is spoken communication. And interpreters should be good at sign language as well as writing and finger-spelling, and should also be able to do the following: (1) grasp accurately what the speaker thinks, and (2) be able to express in sign language that which has been expressed in spoken language.

An interpreter may encounter any number of difficult situations. For example, an interpreter will need to adjust his or her sign-language technique to the interest, way of thinking, and linguistic level of the individual or group for whom he or she is interpreting. It is also up to the interpreter to encourage deaf people to offer their opinions and participate in the meeting or discussion. Furthermore, interpreters must refrain from expressing their own opinions, and, of course, they are unable to take written notes.

While interpreting, sometimes we get confused and it becomes difficult to interpret properly. For example, it would be extremely difficult to interpret in court on behalf of a deaf individual who has neither the ability to write nor the ability to use sign language. It may also be difficult to interpret in matters concerning complicated human relationships. Unfortunately, sometimes interpreters go beyond their duties as interpreters and align themselves with hearing people in opposition to deaf people. As almost of interpreters are hearing, they are apt to have this tendency.

The duty of interpreters to deaf people is not merely to serve as a neutral communicator between hearing and deaf people, nor to support the status quo. It is not accurate to look at hearing people as rulers and deaf people as the oppressed. But we hearing people impose our opinion on deaf people so often that sometimes it does seem that deaf people are oppressed. This is unacceptable. The fundamental duty of interpreters should be to ensure the livelihood of deaf people and to stand by them as they assert their human rights.

Sometimes interpreters have to observe deaf people and imbue in them a sense of human rights. Other times, interpreters must hone their skills as interpreters in order to properly convey the meaning of spoken Japanese via sign language. And to do this interpreters may have to learn from the requests and assertions of deaf people. Whether or not the interpreter did his or her job well or not should be determined only by these criteria.

For example, if you, as an interpreter, got a call from a factory boss and were told, "A deaf worker here often takes vacations in order to participate in events for deaf people. His colleagues are annoyed. He lacks common sense. Please scold him!" you may find yourself in a bind. But you must ask yourself why vacation with pay is not allowed at this company, and why this deaf man is not allowed to participate in events for deaf people with the assistance of a colleague.

In situations such as these, it is the duty of the interpreter not just to serve as a messenger between the company and deaf worker, but to comprehend the situation and to try to find a solution that would suit both the company and the worker.

Above, I wrote about the duties of interpreters to deaf people. Now I want to ask for your opinions on whether interpreters have the duties listed below.

1. To defend the rights of deaf people, and to adopt those rights as their own.
2. To understand, accept, and research not only the general problems of deaf people but also problems of each deaf individual.

3. To participate in the aims of deaf people to develop and enhance their livelihood, to participate in the similar aims of people with other disabilities, and to participate in the national democratic movement.
4. To act as counselors to deaf people who have problems in regard to their living arrangements or vocations, learning from the problems and requests of deaf people and acting accordingly.
5. To continue studying sign language, finger-spelling and writing, with a view to enhancing one's skills.

1.3   Ingram, R.M. 1974. "A communication model of the interpreting process." *Journal of Rehabilitation of the Deaf*, 7: 3–9.

Robert "Bob" Ingram, a child of Deaf parents (Coda), was active in SLI in the 1970s and 1980s. Ingram wrote many articles about American Sign Language and SLI, was one of the first authors to promote linguistic research on SLI, and was active in international SLI. Ingram has an MA in linguistics and intercultural communication from Brown University in Providence, Rhode Island, and was enrolled in the Ph.D. program in linguistics at Brown when he wrote and published this paper on the communication model. When his model was published, SLI was just beginning to emerge as a full-time occupation and was often regarded as a sub-branch of deaf education and rehabilitation. In a later publication, he addresses the intercultural context of interpretation more explicitly, but the origins of that paradigm can be traced directly to this paper.

While a student at Brown, Ingram was the George C. Marshall Research Associate at the University of Copenhagen, Denmark, from 1976–1977, and with his wife Betty, edited the proceedings of *Hands Across the Sea,* the first international conference on SLI. An early proponent of terminology and attitudes that reflect equal consideration of the source language and the target language, Ingram was an instructor and curriculum specialist at Madonna College in Livonia, Michigan, in sign language and interpreting, and wrote several articles on teaching sign language interpreting. He was instrumental in promoting collaboration with spoken language interpreters, researcher and educators.

A communication model of the interpreting process

Robert M. Ingram

The process of interpreting for deaf persons has been viewed from various perspectives with varying degrees of scientific credibility. The communication models presented in the following discussion propose to define the interpreting process in a scientific manner and suggest implications for examining various aspects of interpreting within the framework of that model.

A simplistic model of any direct one-to-one communication would be that represented by Figure 1. In this model the speaker (source) states (encodes) the message, which is carried through the air (channel) and picked up by the listener (receiver). For the message to register with the receiver, the message must be decoded from sound to thought. The listener then responds to the message, setting in motion another communication.

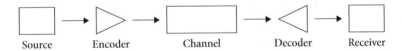

Source   Encoder   Channel   Decoder   Receiver

Figure 1

When one of the principals in the communication process is a deaf person relying on the language of signs as his prime method of communication, and the other principal is a hearing person with limited or non-existent command of the language of signs, an interpreter must function as the channel for communication to be effective. An elaboration of our simplistic communication model is necessary to explain these additional complications.

Figure 2 illustrates the interpreting process. When the hearing person speaks his message in English, the interpreter must decode the message from its spoken symbols to determine the thought embodied in those symbols and then encode the message once more into the visual symbols of the language of signs. The deaf person must then decode these visual symbols to arrive at the meaning of the communicated message.

Figure 2 fails to show that two different communication forms and language systems are involved in the communication process when an orally communicating hearing person and a manually communicating deaf person are communicating via an interpreter. Figure 3 adds these dimensions.

---

*Mr. Ingram is consultant with the deaf and partially hearing, Detroit, Michigan Speech and **Hearing Center.***

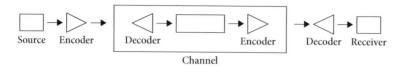

Figure 2

Communication may be in the *form* of any of the five senses – taste, touch, smell, sound or sight – or any combination of these. When we discuss *systems* we are talking about *language*. All languages are composed of three systems: lexical (words or signs), syntactic (grammar) and semological (meaning) (Gleason, 1965). American Sign Language (ASL), the method of manual communication used by most deaf adults in the United States, is a linguistically distinct language. Therefore it has lexical, syntactic and semological systems. Manual English and Signed English are not distinct languages but rather manual-visual codes of English. Manual English and Signed English follow the lexicon and semology of American Sign Language but rely on the syntax of English. The Seeing Essential English (SEE) method and variations of it utilize only the lexicon of American Sign Language, albeit in a drastically revised composition. The SEE method does follow the form of American Sign Language – visual – but form, remember, is an element of communication, not a system of language (Fant, 1972).

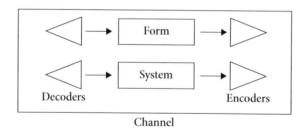

Figure 3

Given three different situations with speakers who use only English and receivers who understand different ones of the methods of manual communication, we have three different communication models. The source, encoder, decoder and receiver remain the same, but the channel expands from that shown in Figure 3 to illustrate the three language systems.

Example A (Figure 4) – Interpreting from English to American Sign Language
Source: Orally communicating hearing person using English
Channel: Interpreter
Receiver: Manually communicating deaf person using American Sign Language.

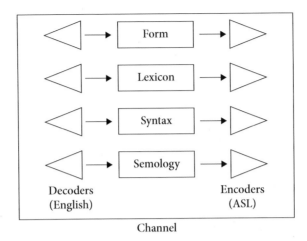

Figure 4

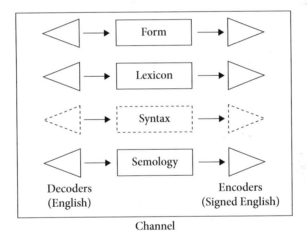

Figure 5

The interpreter, as channel, must decode the form of the communication (aural) before encoding the message into the visual form understood by the receiver. The interpreter must also decode the lexicon, syntax and semology of the message as that message appears in English before encoding the message in the corresponding systems of American Sign Language.

Example B (Figure 5) – Transliterating (Fant, 1972: 56–57) from English to Signed English or Manual English

Source: Orally communicating hearing person using English

Channel: Interpreter

Receiver: Manually communicating deaf person using Signed English

In Example B the process by which the interpreter decodes and encodes the syntactic system of the message is represented by broken lines, because only one syntax is involved – the syntax of English.

Example C (Figure 6) – Transliterating from English to SEE

Source: Orally communicating hearing person using English

Channel: Interpreter

Receiver: Manually communicating deaf person using SEE

Example C shows both the semological and syntactic decoding-encoding processes within the channel in broken lines to illustrate that only one syntax and one semology are involved. The lexical system is shown in solid lines, but the arrows designating the communication flow are curved to show that while the SEE method does rely on the lexicon of American Sign Language, considerable lexical adjustments are made.

Oral interpreting can also be represented by a communication model (Figure 7). The three language systems, while still extant and separate, are shown in one broken component, because there is only one language used throughout the process – English. Form is illustrated in solid lines, because the interpreter decodes the message aurally (speech) and encodes the message visually (lip movements). The same model may be used to illustrate interpreting in the Rochester Method – fingerspelling.

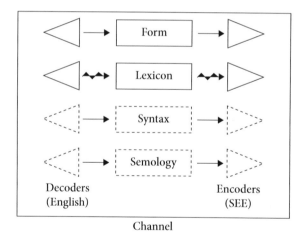

Figure 6

By expanding our communication model as in Figure 8 we get an even broader perspective of the interpreting process. We can now examine the communication environment scientifically. The environment consists of such items as clothing, lighting, backgrounds, visual barriers and auditory barriers. Those environmental items which directly inhibit the effectiveness of the channel (or interpreter) are known as channel noise, be they auditory or not.

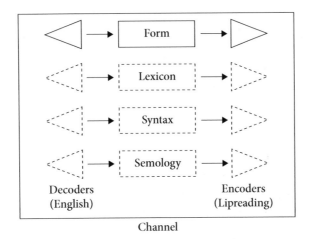

Figure 7

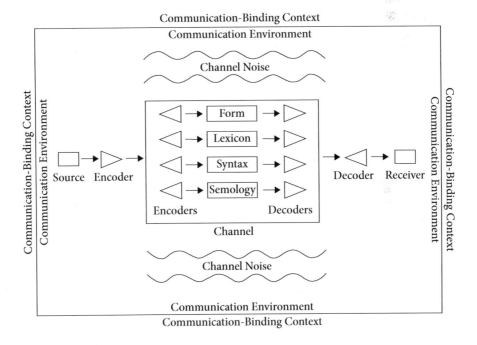

Figure 8

An additional factor in the communication process is the communication-binding context. This factor is an attempt to explain why the communication exists in the first place and why it exists in the form in which it exists. The communication-binding context exists in any communication process; when an interpreter is involved the communication-binding context may be altered (Anderson, 1971).

Communication models such as those offered here provide several advantages for examining the interpreting process. Among those advantages are:

1. Communication models are scientific. Their purpose is to describe processes, not personalities. Even ethical questions may be examined through communication models with greater objectivity.
2. Communication models may be used to point out objectively differences and similarities of various communication methods. Such analyses may be valuable in determining the most effective method to use in a given situation.
3. Models allow us to consider the environment as an integral part of the interpreting process inseparable from the actual interpreting.
4. Models allow us to identify and isolate components of the interpreting process. With a model, we can specifically locate a malfunction in the interpreting process rather than saying simply, "You interpreted that wrong." An interpreter who can see a mistake he has made as simply a malfunction of one component in the interpreting process is encouraged to correct or improve that component rather than be totally discouraged.

Each of the advantages of communication models suggested here should be further scrutinized. Attention needs to be given to the communication-binding context. Is the communication-binding context altered and how by the interjection of an interpreter into the communication process? McLuhan (1964) says, "The medium is the message." Is the interpreter the message? There can be no question but that the three language systems are interrelated but to what extent? What is the interrelationship of system and form in the interpreting process? Where do we account for those slight inflections of voice or signs, known as suprasegmentals, that can greatly alter communication? What is the role of the interpreter in conveying those suprasegmentals, and how is this process carried out? How does the interpreter cope with various dialects and idiolects of speech or signs? All of these questions merit attention. All of these questions can be examined in the framework of a communication model of the interpreting process.

References

Andersen, K.E. *Persuasion: Theory and Practice.* Boston: Allyn and Bacon, 1971.
Fant, L.J. The CSUN approach to the training of sign language interpreters. *The Deaf American,* 1972, *24,* 56–57.
Gleason, H.A. *Linguistics and English Grammar.* New York: Holt, Rinehart and Winston, 1965.
McLuhan, M. *Understanding Media: The Extensions of Man.* New York: McGraw-Hill, 1964.

1.4   Brasel, Barbara. B., Dale Montanelli, and Stephen P. Quigley, S.P. 1974. "The component skills of interpreting as viewed by interpreters." *Journal of Rehabilitation of the Deaf* 7: 20–27.

Barbara Babbini Brasel was a Deaf woman whose influence and work continues to impact the field of SLI. Barbara attended the Utah School for the Deaf, skipping grades, and graduated at 14. She took the admission exams for Gallaudet College and was eventually admitted in spite of her young age, through the efforts of her brother Robert Sanderson who would later become a president of the National Association of Deaf People. Brasel left Gallaudet before graduating, and later enrolled at California State University at Northridge (CSUN) and graduated with BA in psychology and an MA in administration and supervision. She was a founding member of the Registry of Interpreters for the Deaf and served on the Board of Directors from 1982–1987. She maintained a life-long interest in interpreters and the interpreting process and did her Masters thesis study on interpreters (see Chapter 2).

After finishing her MA, she worked at the University of Illinois, Champagne-Urbana, at the Institute for Research on Exceptional Children under the direction of Stephen P. Quigley. Quigley received a five-year grant to study interpreters. He recruited Brasel to work on this grant and was instrumental in teaching her advanced research skills and academic writing. This paper reports the results of one of the first projects of this grant that had its funding cut after two years. Brasel moved to Connecticut, taught for a few years at the American School for the Deaf, and, in 1975, became the Executive Director of the Connecticut State Commission on the Deaf and Hearing Impaired.

The Interpretation Department at Gallaudet University has recognized Brasel's contribution to interpreting research by naming their graduate research award in her honor.

Dale S. Montanelli is Associate Professor Emeritus in the Department of Human and Community Development at the University of Illinois at Urbana-Champaign. She received her Ph.D. from the University of Illinois in 1970, with a major in psychology and a minor is special education. Her early research concerned how children learned to use multiple cues to make sense of their environments. As a result of that work she was asked to serve as Assistant Project Director of the "Interpreters for Deaf People" and the "Development and Description for Syntactic Structure in the Language of Deaf Children" projects, led by Stephen Quigley in the Institute for Research on Exceptional Children. The Bureau of Education funded these projects for the Handicapped.

Stephen P. Quigley (see above).

The component skills of interpreting as viewed by interpreters

Barbara Babbini Brasel, Dale S. Montanelli, & Stephen P. Quigley

A competent interpreter may be defined as a person with normal hearing who is skilled in the language of signs and fingerspelling, who can either *translate* the spoken message verbatim into the language of signs for literate, well-educated deaf persons, or can *interpret* the spoken message in the sense that the interpreter paraphrases, defines, simplifies, condenses, or explains to the language-handicapped deaf person what is meant by the spoken message; and who can also reverse either process by verbally translating the usually grammatical signed and fingerspelled message of the well-educated deaf person, or reverse-interpreting the often ungrammatically structured sign language of the language-handicapped deaf person into grammatically correct spoken language. Just how an individual manages the task of transforming auditory stimuli into bodily movement, facial expression, and structured gestures; or transforming visual stimuli into comprehensible spoken language – has been the subject of much interest and discussion but very little research.

Part of the reason for the lack of research has been the difficulty of describing exactly what a competent interpreter does with his hands, face, and body, let alone the cognitive processes he employs, that sets him apart from the user of sign language who may be able to employ sign language effectively when expressing his own thoughts or his own message – but cannot function effectively when trying to relay other-generated thoughts or messages. In other words, just what is it that discriminates between the competent and the unqualified; between the excellent and the mediocre; or between the mediocre and the unacceptable?

The question just asked, when asked of nearly any expert on interpreters and interpreting, rarely elicits a quick and simple response. Instead, the individual will usually begin listing the component skills a good interpreter must have – but nearly always he will qualify his remarks by statements to the effect that no one skill is all-important; that above-average ability on several skills does not necessarily make one a competent interpreter; nor does mediocre ability on one or two skills make one an incompetent interpreter. What it all boils down to is that interpreting is a conglomerate of skills, some more important than others, and that these skills are partly technical, partly psycho-motor, partly cognitive, partly attitudinal, and partly experiential. Before any meaningful research could be conducted in

Ms Brasel is Volunteer Coordinator, staff-in-service communication training. American School for the Deaf: Dr. Montanelli is on the staff of the Institute for Research on Exceptional Children and Dr. Quigley is Professor of Speech and Hearing, University of Illinois.

the area of interpreting, therefore, a list of component skills had to be compiled, and, in addition, a set of standards for performance had to be developed which would reflect the relative importance of each component skill with respect to all of the other component skills as well as to the overall performance.

Method

As a preliminary step in a four-year research program designed to develop and refine methods of evaluating interpreters according to their levels of competence, the Institute for Research on Exceptional Children at the University of Illinois conducted a questionnaire survey of approximately 300 interpreters in attendance at the National Registry of Interpreters for the Deaf (R.I.D.) convention in Long Beach, California in August, 1972. Along with questions designed to elicit information about the respondents' familiarity with interpreting and the interpreting process, the questionnaire asked that the respondents rate the importance of fourteen skills which had previously been identified by experts as being component skills or aspects of interpreting.

The respondents

Distribution and sex: From the approximately 300 questionnaires that were distributed, responses were subsequently received from 109 individuals, 43 (39.5%) of whom were males and 66 (60.5%) of whom were females. All but 11 of the respondents were members of the R.I.D. Although the largest percentage (34.9%) were from California, the remainder represented a fairly even distribution from all sections of the country. Among the 109 respondents there were four who identified themselves as deaf consumers of interpreting services, and fifteen who classed themselves as both deaf consumers of interpreting services *and* intermediary interpreters who acted as liaison agents between regular interpreters and deaf people with minimal language skills. The hearing group was composed as follows:

	Number	Per cent
Interpreter for deaf people	79	72.5
Employer of interpreters	2	1.8
Teacher of deaf children	2	1.8
Teacher of Manual Communication	1	0.9
Student Interpreter (beginner)	1	0.9
Other (counselor, researcher, etc.)	5	4.6

Age and education: A composite picture of the group revealed that the average age was 38.0 years, although the group was fairly evenly distributed in four age categories between age 16 and 55. As was found in the survey of Illinois interpreters conducted by Quigley, Brasel, and Wilbur (1972), the group was better educated than average. Among the 57.0 per cent having had at least some college, 53.0 per cent had gone on to obtain bachelors degrees, and 32.0 per cent had also obtained graduate degrees.

Amount of interpreting: The group reported interpreting an average of 39.3 hours per month, although 19.2 per cent reported interpreting more than 80 hours per month. Among those who reported having done any interpreting during the preceding year, 58.7 per cent reported they were paid for their services an average of 65.4 per cent of the time, with the remainder of their interpreting being done on a voluntary (unpaid) basis.

Interpreting as a part of regular job duties: Interpreting for deaf co-workers or clients was part of the regular duties on the job for 55.0 per cent of the respondents, and an additional 40.0 per cent reported that while they were not specifically required to interpret as part of their regular duties, they worked with deaf people for whom they interpreted at least occasionally. Most of the respondents had, at one time or another, worked in jobs where interpreting for deaf people was part of their job duties (54.1%) even though interpreting might not be required in their present jobs.

Contacts with deaf people: It was also found that 34.0 per cent of the group either live with or have regular close social or familial contacts with deaf persons for whom they frequently interpret. This may be related to the percentage of respondents who reported having had deaf parents (38.9%) and/or deaf relatives (14.7%). In addition, the majority had learned their manual communication skills at home from deaf relatives and deaf friends of the family (51.4%). Surprisingly enough, a considerable number had learned from deaf friends at work or at school (42.2%), and 73.4 per cent had taken classes in sign language or interpreting (or both).

Self-evaluation of interpreting skills: When asked to rate themselves on their own *expressive* interpreting skills, 75.0 per cent of the respondents rated themselves "above average", but the percentage of "above average" ratings of their own competence fell to 54.1 per cent when they were asked about their *receptive* interpreting skills (i.e. "reverse interpreting" skills). Apparently the respondents were not quite as confident of their receptive abilities as they were of their expressive abilities.

Types of interpreting experience reported: Table 1 shows the percentage of respondents reporting experience in specific types of interpreting situations, both as interpreters and as observers of other interpreters performing in similar situations. As can be seen, the majority of the respondents reported having frequent experience in person-to-person interpreting, with educational interpreting, religious interpreting, and workshop and conference interpreting following in that order. Interpreting for deaf-blind persons, followed by interpreting in psychiatric or psychological counseling situations and vocational training situations were the areas in which the group reported the least frequent experience; however, from Table 2 it can be seen that the majority of the respondents had at least some experience in most of the interpreting situations listed.

Table 1. Percentage reporting interpreting experience in specific situations; and observation of other interpreters in the same situations: All respondents (N = 109)

Interpreting situation	Percentage reporting experience			Percentage reporting having observed others interpreting		
	Often	Some-times	Never	Often	Some-times	Never
Legal	10.1	50.5	39.5	3.7	33.0	63.3
Medical	13.8	54.1	32.1	3.7	11.9	84.4
Religious	31.2	25.7	43.1	27.5	51.4	21.1
Educational	45.0	32.1	22.9	42.2	35.8	22.0
Counseling (Psychiatric or Psychological)	5.5	36.7	57.8	2.8	20.2	77.1
Counseling (Vocational)	17.4	26.6	56.0	7.3	27.5	65.1
Vocational training	17.4	29.4	53.2	8.3	36.7	55.1
Workshop or conference	26.6	41.3	32.1	50.5	41.3	8.3
Platform (large mixed audiences)	28.4	40.4	31.2	58.7	36.7	4.6
Person to person	60.6	34.0	5.4	53.2	42.2	4.6
For deaf-blind	1.8	26.6	71.6	3.7	39.4	56.9
Other	15.6	4.6	79.8	2.8	11.0	86.2

Amount of experience in observing other interpreters in action: When one compares the percentage of the respondents reported experience with the percentage reporting having observed other interpreters in similar situations (Table 2), however, some interesting differences are found. Although 60.6 per cent of the respondents had reported having at least some experience in legal situations, only 36.7 per cent had observed other interpreters interpreting in court. By the same token, while 67.9 per cent had medical situation interpreting experience, and 42.2 per cent had at least some experience in psychological counseling situations, only 15.6 and 22.9 per cent respectively had ever observed other interpreters functioning in like situations. The confidential nature of the medical and counseling situations would probably explain the lower incidence of the latter types of observation, but one would think that observing an experienced legal interpreter in an open courtroom situation would be a valuable learning experience for other interpreters, and that this type of situation would attract observers who hope to enter legal interpreting.

Table 2. Comparison of the percentages of reported experience versus reported observation of other interpreters (rank ordered): All respondents

Own experience	At least some exper.	Observation of others	At least some exper.
Person to Person	94.6	Person to Person	95.4
Educational	77.1	Platform	95.4
Platform	68.6	Workshop	91.7
Medical	67.9	Educational	88.0
Workshop	67.9	Religious	78.9
Legal	60.6	Vocational training	44.9
Religious	56.9	Deaf-blind	43.1
Vocational training	46.8	Legal	36.7
Vocational counseling	44.0	Vocational counseling	34.9
Psychol. counseling	42.2	Psychol. counseling	22.9
For deaf-blind	28.4	Medical	15.6
Other	20.2	Other	13.8

Rating of component skills

Procedure: In order to determine how important each component skill was when compared with all of the others, the respondents were presented with a list of fourteen skills or aspects of interpreting, and were asked to rate each one on a scale of one (least important) to nine (most important). Space was also provided for additions to the list (as well as for listing the skills the respondents did not feel should have been included in the original list of 14), and respondents were asked to rate any additions to the list in the same way they had rated the original 14 skills listed in the questionnaire.

Instructions to the respondents included a request that they read through the entire list first, select the skill they deemed most important and circle the number nine (9); then select the skill they deemed least important and circle the number one (1); then to rate the other skills anywhere from one through nine. This was done in an effort to force respondents to use the extreme ends of the scale – which most questionnaire respondents are reluctant to do – as well as to identify if possible the most and least important skills.

The ratings were then analyzed, using Thurstone's Law of Categorical Judgement, to determine an importance value (or weight) for each skill.

Results

Table 3 gives the results of the analyses of the ratings, with the total sub-divided to compare the responses of the hearing respondents with those of the deaf respondents. As can be seen from the table, there were some striking differences between the groups in their opinions of the relative importance of specific skills, and between the overall ratings obtained from both groups combined and the individual sub-groups. (These differences will be discussed in the discussion section.) Whereas the combined ratings showed that *accuracy in transmission of concepts* was of primary importance to good interpreting, the hearing respondents felt it was more important for an interpreter to be able to adjust his interpretation to the language level of his deaf audience than to be accurate; and the deaf respondents felt it was more important to be able to sign clearly and understandably than to be accurate or adaptable. Both groups felt that fast fingerspelling was of minimal importance, perhaps because of a misapprehension that resulted from the use of the term "fast fingerspelling" in the questionnaire instead of "fingerspelling speed" – which, if used, might have elicited different responses. From the comments written on many of the questionnaires, it appeared that many of the respondents equated "fast fingerspelling" with "slurred fingerspelling" – the result of too-fast fingerspelling.

Suggestions from respondents for additions or deletions to the list of skills: In response to the invitation to suggest additions to or deletions from the questionnaire list of 14 skills, most of the respondents wrote that the list appeared to be comprehensive (or left it blank, which implies the same thing). A few, however, suggested that "understanding of deafness and deaf people" should be added to the list, apparently not considering this to be a sub-skill of the listed "Adaptability". Understanding deaf people with minimal language ability was another suggestion from a few respondents, as was the ability to maintain emotional detachment. While not offered as a specific skill, several respondents commented that the educational level of the interpreter should be sufficient for him to understand the material he was to interpret. Emotional warmth, while a personality trait rather than a skill, was mentioned by several as being a desirable quality for an interpreter to have; and several also mentioned that appropriate dress and appearance were important. As was mentioned earlier, several respondents felt that fast fingerspelling was not a component skill, but their explanatory comments made it clear that they were referring to fingerspelling that was so fast that it was slurred and unreadable rather than fast enough to enable the interpreter to keep up with the speaker.

Discussion

Perhaps the most interesting finding in the analyses of the ratings of the component skills was the difference found between the deaf and the hearing respondents. It would seem

Table 3. Ranking of the component skills, by deaf and by hearing respondents, and computed weights based on rated importance

Skills or aspect	Total group n = 109		Hearing respondents n = 86		Deaf respondents n = 23	
	Rank	Weight	Rank	Weight	Rank	Weight
Accuracy in transmission of concepts	1	16.79	2	6.03	4	2.37
Adaptability (ability to adjust interpretation to the language level of the deaf audience)	2	14.50	1	6.69	4	2.37
Clear and readable signs (easily understood, appropriate in size and correctly positioned)	3	14.31	3	5.80	1	2.60
Reverse interpreting	4	12.57	4	5.22	8	2.28
Mood transmission (appropriate use of facial expression and body movement to convey speaker's mood and feelings)	5	12.41	7	4.92	9	2.27
Smoothness (smooth flow of signs and fingerspelling, with appropriate rhythm, pauses, and emphasis)	6	12.13	5	4.95	5	2.35
Clear and readable fingerspelling	7	11.89	6	4.93	2	2.42
A large vocabulary of signs	8	10.86	10	4.51	3	2.42
Professional behavior and attitude	9	10.61	9	4.61	7	2.29
Classical interpreting (ability to transmit concepts by paraphrasing, defining, explaining and condensing)	10	10.47	8	4.66	10	1.85
Overall interpreting speed	11	7.71	11	3.56	12	1.83
Verbatim translation (word for word translation of speech into signs and fingerspelling)	12	7.24	12	3.44	13	1.75
Oral interpreting (ability to convey speaker's words silently but clearly on the lips with or without simultaneous manual interpretation)	13	6.26	13	3.00	11	1.83
Fast fingerspelling	14	2.03	14	0.26	14	0.96

that accuracy and adaptability are of primary concern to the hearing respondents, while the deaf respondents felt that clarity of signs and fingerspelling were more important. This difference in opinion probably reflects a difference in orientation between the two groups which might be more understandable when one remembers that a deaf person has to be able to understand the signing and fingerspelling before he can even begin to understand the concepts being signed and fingerspelled. It may be that the hearing respondents assumed that accuracy in transmission of concepts would be possible only if accompanied by clarity in signing and fingerspelling, and by an awareness of the language level of the deaf audience, and therefore responded on the basis of this assumption; but it would seem that the deaf respondents made no such assumption. They appear to feel that *technical* understanding had to precede *cognitive* understanding – and responded on that basis.

Also interesting was the difference between hearing and deaf respondents on the rating of reverse interpreting. The hearing respondents felt that the ability to understand the deaf speaker was high in importance – ranking along with adaptability, accuracy and clarity – while deaf respondents felt it was of secondary importance, rating eighth behind all of the expressive skill factors and professional behavior and attitude. This probably reflects the deaf respondents' experience with interpreting as a whole, for most of the interpreting that deaf persons have experience with has been expressive interpreting of the platform or conference type; and reverse interpreting usually takes place in the comparative seclusion of person-to-person or small group situations. The deaf respondents, therefore, would tend to minimize the importance of something they rarely encounter or do not personally have need of – whereas the hearing respondents, having frequently had the experience of person-to-person interpreting, legal interpreting, etc., with, perhaps, deaf people of limited language ability, would tend to recognize that reverse interpreting ability is an important skill for an interpreter to have even though he may not be called upon to uitilize it to the extent that he is called upon to use his expressive interpreting skills.

References

Quigley, Stephen P., Brasel, Barbara E., and Wilbur, Ronnie, "A survey of interpreters for deaf people in the state of Illinois." *Journal of Rehabilitation of the Deaf* 1972, 6(1), 7–10.

1.5   Schein, Jerome. 1974. "Personality characteristics associated with interpreter proficiency." *Journal of Rehabilitation of the Deaf, 7*, 33–43.

Jerome D. Schein was an international authority in Deafness studies. He was the only person to have held both of the only two endowed chairs of Deafness research in the world – the P.V. Doctor Chair at Gallaudet University and the David Peikoff Chair at the University of Alberta, Canada. He published 25 books and more than 200 refereed papers on sensory disorders and has received numerous awards and honors. His most recent book, *Hearing Disorders Handbook*, with Maurice H. Miller was published in 2008. Schein joined the faculty of Gallaudet College (now University) as a professor of psychology and director of the Office of Psychological Research. While at Gallaudet, he was also the editor of Deafness, Speech and Hearing Abstracts (1961–1965) as well as holding various offices in the District of Columbia Psychological Association, including the presidency. He was elected a Fellow of the American Psychological Association in 1976. In 1968, he accepted the position as Dean of Education and Home Economics at the University of Cincinnati. While there he wrote the *The Deaf Community Studies in the Social Psychology of Deafness*.

From 1970 to 1986 he was professor of sensory rehabilitation at New York University, and then emeritus. At NYU, he was also the director of the Deafness Research and Training Center. While there, Schein did the first national study of the Deaf population in the United States and the first national study of the Deafblind population of the US. When he retired from NYU, he accepted the P.V. Doctor Chair at Gallaudet, and later held the David Peikoff Chair from 1989–1993.

Personality characteristics associated with interpreter proficiency

Jerome D. Schein

In the search for predictors of interpreter proficiency, assessments of personality appear at the outset to have potential as contributors to valid variance. Mastery of sign language alone is unlikely to account for differences between those who elect to interpret for deaf people and those who do not, and between those who perform well and those who do poorly. Assuming equal competency in manual communication, then, what distinguishes the interpreter from the casual sign maker may be, in part, personological. Other factors – intelligence, general language facility, physical makeup – obviously contribute to the quality of interpreting. In this research, however, the investigation focuses on personality: specifically on those aspects measured by the Edwards Personality Preference Schedule (EPPS).

Procedures

A sample was drawn consisting of 34 interpreters living in Hartford, Connecticut, New York City and Rochester, New York. The geographic bias was dictated by practical considerations. Each interpreter signed two brief passages, one judged to be difficult and one easy. Their performances were filmed and later judged by 6 experts.

Only 20 of the 34 interpreters completed enough of the test battery to warrant their inclusion in the study. The correlation analysis is based on an N of 20 for the Pearson r's and 17 for the stepwise multiple-regression analysis, as three additional cases were lost because of incomplete data.

The Assessment. The judges completed a rating form for each interpreter on the two test passages. The factors considered were sign-making skill, fingerspelling ability, expressiveness of face, general appearance, and accuracy of interpretation. These ratings on a five-point (1 = poor to 5 = very good) scale were summed to provide a score ranging from 15 (poor in every category) to 75 (very good in every category). An intuitively weighted sum to emphasize quality of signs, level of interpretation and concept presentation yielded results similar, though not identical, to the simple sum. Analyses using both scores will be discussed under Results.

Dr. Schein is Director, Deafness Research & Training Center. New York University.

Interpreter Variables. In addition to the EPPS, each interpreter completed a biographical form, the Seashore Test of Musical Ability, the Cooperative Reading Comprehension Test, the Otis-Lennon Test of Mental Ability, and the Strong Vocational Interest Inventory.

The Test. Two paragraphs of approximately 150 words were tape-recorded to standardize administration. The "easy" passage approximated a fourth-grade reading level and the "hard" passage twelfth-grade. The former dealt with the uses of cork, and the latter with education.

Interpreters had no prior knowledge of the nature of the test passages. The instructions were to interpret for a deaf audience with a high-school-level education. The passages were presented in a counter-balanced order, half of the interpreters receiving the easy and half the hard passage first. Their performances were filmed against a plain background, using a 16 mm motion-picture camera and black-and-white film. The camera-to-interpreter distance was about 18 feet, and the film frame included the body from the knees to above the head.

Judging. Prior to viewing the films, the judges familiarized themselves with the test passages and the rating forms, and they discussed the intent of the assessment, noting that both accuracy and technique were to be considered. The judging was done at a single sitting, with each judge given as much time as desired to rate. Interpreters were identified on the film by code number only.

The Judges. Four judges were initially chosen: two normal-hearing females (HF-1,2) and two deaf males (DM-1,2). Each had nearly a life-long association with interpreting. As will be seen in Table 1, the four judges' ratings did not correlate highly. Suspecting that either sex or hearing status might be involved, two deaf female judges (DF-1,2) were added. Their ratings failed to clarify the underlying reasons for the discrepant assessments. The statistical analyses for all six judges, then, were limited to the weighted-sum criterion as it provided the best results.

Results

Because this research is exploratory in nature, the results are presented in detail intended to convey the complexity of the mensurational problem. Judges not only differed between themselves but also on their ratings of the same interpreter's performances on the easy and hard tasks. The latter differences may, of course, reflect valid variance; i.e. the interpreting characteristics associated with easy tasks may not be identical to those associated with difficult tasks. As will be seen, however, the emerging picture has more consistency than inconsistency about it.

Interjudge Reliability. The interjudge reliability, as illustrated by the intercorrelations shown in Table 1, appeared low enough to warrant separate analyses of each judge's ratings to detect generalized patterning. Note that the incomplete design (two normal-hearing males would be needed to complete it) suggests that neither sex nor hearing ability determines the discrepancies in ratings between these judges.

Table 1. Correlations[a] between judges' ratings (simple sum) of interpreters on easy and hard passages

	HF-1	HF-2	DF-1	DF-2	DM-1	DM-2
Easy						
HF-1	100	76	51	72	31	35
HF-2	76	100	57	75	42	60
DF-1	51	57	100	60	40	37
DF-2	72	75	60	100	22	53
DM-1	31	42	40	22	100	71
DM-2	35	60	37	53	71	100
Hard						
HF-1	100	53	40	52	44	20
HF-2	53	100	58	83	21	60
DF-1	40	58	100	66	41	43
DF-2	52	83	66	100	17	48
DM-1	44	21	41	17	100	62
DM-2	20	60	43	48	62	100

[a]Decimal point not shown.
H = Hearing, D = Deaf, F = Female, M = Male

The correlations between each judge's ratings of interpreter performances on easy and hard passages range from .79 to .95. These corresslations suggest the possibility of somewhat different criteria being applied to judging the two levels of difficulty, at least by Judges HF-1 and 2 and DM-1 and 2; hence the results were separately analyzed for the two levels of interpreting difficulty.

Correlation Analysis: Simple-Sum Criterion. The correlation matrix was examined for variables having at least 3 significant r's out of 8 possible (2 passages × 4 judges). Five scales of the EPPS – Exhibition, Autonomy, Succorance, Endurance, Abasement – met this requirement, along with the interest pattern for Social Studies Teacher on the Strong, and self-ratings of communication proficiency with highly educated, low-verbal and nonverbal deaf audiences.

Fewer than 3 significant r's emerged for EPPS Order and Dominance, Strong Literary Vocational interests, years of experience with sign language, and reading comprehension. No significant correlation with the simple-sum criterion was found for the Seashore test, Otis IQ, education, age, or RID membership.

Table 2. Correlations between each judge's ratings (simple sum) of interpreter performance on hard versus easy passage

Judge	Correlation between easy and hard ratings[a]
HF-1	79
HF-2	85
DF-1	90
DF-2	88
DM-1	86
DM-2	95

[a]Decimal point not shown.
H = Hearing, D = Deaf, F = Female, M = Male

Correlation Analysis: Weighted-Sum Criterion, Using the same selection procedure as in the simple-sum case, a similar pattern of relations appeared: the same five EPPS scales, the single Strong interest pattern, and self-ratings of proficiency. In addition, small but significant correlations did appear with EPPS Aggression, RID membership, and self-rating of proficiency in a rehabilitation-counseling setting.

Multiple Regression: Simple-Sum Criterion. Stepwise multiple-regression analyses were performed for each judge separately for the easy and hard passages. The F level for inclusion was set at.01; for deletion.005; tolerance level,.001. These severe levels were chosen out of respect for the small sample size (N = 17). To further avoid error variance, the self-rating of interpreter proficiency with highly educated deaf persons was eliminated, leaving eight factors.

Inspection of Table 3 reveals that, except for Judge HF-1, the eight variables account for substantial simple-sum variance. Even for Judge HF-1, three variables – Exhibition, Succorance, Social Studies Teacher – accounted for 40 percent of the variance for the easy passage and 21 percent for the difficult passage. For Judge DM-2, on the other hand, the combined predictors accounted for a remarkable 89 percent of easy and 84 percent of difficult variance.

Multiple-Regression: Weighted-Sum Criterion. Table 4 summarizes the analysis of the eight variables, using the weighted-sum criterion and adding a ninth variable, the self-rating of ability to interpret for highly educated deaf persons. The results yield higher R's for the normal-hearing female judges and slightly lower for the two males. The analyses for the deaf female judges are also given. The weighted criterion appears clearly preferable

Table 3. Summary of stepwise multiple-regression analyses of simple-sum criterion of inter-preter skill versus eight variables

Judge HF-1					
Easy passage			Difficult passage		
Variable	Multiple R[a]	% Variance	Variable	Multiple R[a]	% Variance
Exhibition	46	21	SS Teacher	34	12
SS Teacher	58	33	Succorance	44	19
Succorance	63	40	Exhibition	46	21
Profic. Nonverbal	64	40	Profic. Low Verbal	48	23
Abasement	64	41	Endurance	49	23
Endurance	68	46	Abasement	53	28
Profic. Low Verbal	68	47	Profic. Nonverbal	54	29
Autonomy	69	47			
Judge HF-2					
Profic. Low Verbal	47	22	Exhibition	40	16
Endurance	62	39	Abasement	51	26
Exhibition	71	50	Profic. Low Verbal	58	34
Succorance	74	55	SS Teacher	65	42
Abasement	75	56	Succorance	72	51
SS Teacher	78	60	Autonomy	76	57
Profic. Non Verbal	78	60	Endurance	78	60
Autonomy	78	61			
Judge DM-1					
Profic. Nonverbal[b]	48	23	Profic. Nonverbal	44	19
Autonomy	60	36	Abasement	52	27
Profic Low Verbal	63	40	Endurance	57	33
Exhibition	68	46	SS Teacher	67	46
Succorance	70	49	Profic. Low Verbal	69	48
SS Teacher	71	51	Succorance	70	48
Abasement	74	54	Autonomy	70	49
Endurance	81	66	Exhibition	70	49
Profic. Nonverbal	84	70			

(Continued)

Table 3. (Continued)

			Judge DM-2		
	Easy passage			Difficult passage	
Variable	Multiple R[a]	% Variance	Variable	Multiple R[a]	% Variance
Abasement	60	37	Abasement	66	43
Exhibition	72	52	Exhibition	69	48
Succorance	75	56	Endurance	73	54
SS Teacher	80	64	SS Teacher	78	60
Endurance	87	75	Succorance	82	67
Profic. Nonverbal	90	81	Autonomy	84	71
Autonomy	94	89	Profic. Nonverbal	87	75
Profic. Low Verbal	94	89	Profic. Low Verbal	92	84

[a]Decimal point not shown.
[b]Proficiency Nonverbal removed at Step 6 and reintroduced at Step 9.

overall, since the losses for the deaf male judges is small (2 to 12 percent, with a 4 percent gain in one instance) and the gains for the normal-hearing female judges substantial. The two deaf females' results are excellent, with R's ranging from.85 to.93.

Discussion

Despite differences between judges' and within judges' ratings of the same interpreter on tasks at two levels of difficulty, a consistent pattern emerges. The clusters are made up of (a) EPPS scales, (b) self-ratings of interpreting ability, and (c) Social Studies Teacher interest profile on the Strong.

The EPPS scales form a logical cluster at the intersection of exhibitionist and independence needs. Consider Edwards's descriptions of the five traits (the plus or minus in parentheses after the trait name indicate the direction of the correlation with interpreter ratings):

> *Exhibition* (+): To say witty and clever things, to tell amusing jokes and stories, to talk about personal adventures and experiences, to have others notice and comment upon one's appearance, to say things just to see what effect it will have on others, to talk about personal achievements, to be the center of attention, to use words that others do not know the meaning of, to ask questions others cannot answer.

> *Autonomy* (+): To be able to come and go as desired, to say what one thinks about things, to be independent of others in making decisions, to feel free to do what one wants, to do things that are unconventional, to avoid situations where one is expected

to conform, to do things without regard to what others may think, to criticize those in positions of authority, to avoid responsibilities and obligations.

Succorance (–): To have others provide help when in trouble, to seek encouragement from others, to have others be kindly, to have others be sympathetic, and understanding about personal problems, to receive a great deal of affection from others, to have others do favors cheerfully, to be helped by others when depressed, to have others feel sorry when one is sick, to have a fuss made over when hurt.

Abasement (–): To feel guilty when one does something wrong, to accept blame when things do not go right, to feel that personal pain and misery suffered does more good than harm, to feel the need for punishment for wrong doing, to feel better when giving in and avoiding a fight than when having one's own way, to feel the need for confession of errors, to feel depressed by inability to handle situations, to feel timid in the presence of superiors, to feel inferior to others in most respects.

Endurance (–): To keep at a job until it is finished, to complete any job undertaken, to work hard at a task, to keep at a puzzle or problem until it is solved, to work at a single job before taking on others, to stay up late working in order to get a job done, to put in long hours of work without distraction, to stick at a problem even though it may seem as if no progress is being made, to avoid being interrupted while at work.

The interpreter pattern of needs suits a description of someone who is desirous of being the center of attention, wants to be independent, is not expecting help from others, is not afraid to make errors, and is not perseverative. The negative correlation between interpreter proficiency and Endurance may at first seem incongruous, but a person who is overly persistent, perhaps rigid, is not apt to adjust well to the rapidly shifting demands of interpreting. The high need for attention (Exhibition) and low need for guilt (Abasement), fit well, as do the high need for independence (Autonomy) and low need for sympathy (Succorance).

The self-ratings of interpreting ability appear to have validity – a not surprising finding. They likely measure the individual's confidence in his own ability, as much as being an objective appraisal of performance: note that years of signing did not correlate significantly with the judges' assessments. More attention might be devoted to understanding why interpreters' estimates of their effectiveness with some deaf groups were significantly correlated with the criteria while others were not. Careful development of a self-rating scale of interpreter ability would seem valuable.

The contribution of the single scale from the Strong does not seem worth the heavy investment of time in obtaining and scoring it. An analysis of the scale may lead to preparation of a version which would add to the predictive account of interpreter personality.

The criterion problems deserve further discussion. The relatively low relations between six expert judges' ratings provides an important point of departure for research. Now that certification for interpreters is at hand the necessity for establishing judgmental integrity grows acute. The limited study done here with 6 judges leaves the issues in doubt.

Is film an adequate medium for recording interpretation? To what extent does sex of judge influence the ratings? To what extent does hearing status affect interpreter assessments? What factors should enter such assessments? How should they be weighted? The data gathered for this investigation show that the judges tend to assess specific aspects of interpreting behavior in idiosyncratic ways. That this finding will hold over a large number of judges should be tested. Clearly, any sample of interpreter performance to be used for determining proficiency should include more than one level of difficulty and extend over a sufficient period of time to allow variations in technique and degree of skill to be manifested. The use of two test passages of widely divergent difficulty proved advantageous in illustrating the need for an adequate behavioral sample.

Table 4. Summary of stepwise multiple-regression analyses of weighted sum criterion of interpreter skills versus nine variables

Judge HF-1					
Easy passage			Difficult passage		
Variable	Multiple R^a	% Variance	Variable	Multiple R^a	% Variance
Succorance	68	47	Succorance	56	32
Abasement	84	71	SS Teacher	68	46
Profic. Hi Ed.	86	74	Abasement	70	50
SS Teacher	88	77	Profic. Hi Ed.	72	52
Exhibition	88	78	Exhibition	74	54
Autonomy	89	79	Autonomy	74	55
Profic. Nonverbal	89	79	Profic. Nonverbal	74	56
Profic. Low Verbal	89	80	Profic. Low Verbal	75	56
Endurance	90	80	Endurance	75	56
Judge HF-2					
Abasement	73	54	Abasement	67	44
Succorance	84	71	Exhibition	79	63
Exhibition	87	75	Succorance	84	70
Profic. Low Verbal	89	79	Endurance	86	74
Profic. Nonverbal	90	80	SS Teacher	89	79

Table 4. (Continued)

Endurance	91	82	Profic. Low Verbal	89	80
SS Teacher	91	83	Profic. Nonverbal	90	80
Profic. Hi Ed.	91	83	Autonomy	90	81
Autonomy	92	84			

	Judge DM-1				(*Continued*)
	Easy passage			**Difficult passage**	
Variable	**Multiple R**[a]	**% Variance**	**Variable**	**Multiple R**[a]	**% Variance**
Profic. Low Verbal	41	17	Profic. Hi Ed.	44	20
Autonomy	53	28	Profic. Nonverbal	51	26
Exhibition	56	32	Abasement	56	32
Profic. Hi Ed.	57	33	Endurance	61	37
SS Teacher	58	34	SS Teacher	69	48
Abasement	61	37	Profic. Low Verbal	72	52
Endurance	70	49	Succorance	73	53
Succorance	74	54	Exhibition	74	54
Profic. Nonverbal	76	58	Autonomy	74	55

	Judge DM-2				
Abasement	56	32	Abasement	61	37
Exhibition	68	46	Endurance	65	43
SS Teacher	71	50	Exhibition	70	49
Succorance	76	58	SS Teacher	74	55
Endurance	83	70	Succorance	77	60
Profic. Nonverbal	87	76	Autonomy	80	63
Autonomy	91	83	Profic. Nonverbal	82	68
Profic. Hi Ed.	93	87	Profic. Low Verbal	89	79
Profic. Low Verbal	93	87	Profic. Hi Ed.	90	81

	Judge DF-1				
Profic. Hi Ed.	49	24	Prof. Hi Ed.	58	34
Succorance	67	44	Autonomy	77	59
Endurance	71	51	Succorance	80	64
Profic. Low Verbal	74	55	Profic. Nonverbal	81	65
Profic. Nonverbal	82	67	Profic. Low Verbal	86	74

Table 4. (Continued)

Exhibition	83	70	Abasement	86	75
Abasement	84	70	SS Teacher	87	75
SS Teacher	85	72	Endurance	87	76
Autonomy	85	72	Exhibition	87	76

	Judge DF-2				(Continued)
	Easy passage			**Difficult passage**	
Variable	**Multiple R^a**	**% Variance**	**Variable**	**Multiple R^a**	**% Variance**
Abasement	69	48	Abasement	69	48
Succorance	83	69	Succorance	81	66
Exhibition	85	72	Exhibition	83	69
Endurance	86	73	Autonomy	84	71
Profic. Hi Ed.	87	75	Endurance	86	74
Autonomy	88	77	Profic. Nonverbal	88	77
Profic. Low Verbal	89	78	Profic. Low Verbal	90	81
Profic. Nonverbal	92	84	SS Teacher	91	83
SS Teacher	93	86			

[a]Decimal point not shown.

An obvious alternative to subjective ratings would be to have viewers write down the message they perceived the interpreter to be transmitting. This "simple" solution, however, raises many other problems: A message may be misunderstood because the receiver was inept, not the sender; the same message cannot be used more than once with each receiver, etc. What is more, beyond a minimum level of proficiency, preferences for interpreters involve matters of style. These factors probably account for much of the differences in judges' ratings and in deaf persons' satisfaction with interpreters.

Despite the generally encouraging results, these findings should be looked upon with caution, both as to the factors achieving statistical significance and those which did not. The sample size is very small. The criterion measures, though considered separately for each judge, seem to contain a large component of error. Because all of the subjects were active interpreters, the range of talent is reduced and correlations thereby attenuated. Intelligence, for example, would undoubtedly contribute valid variance, but the narrow range of IQs with the conjoint restriction in interpreter proficiency obscured this logical relationship. Other factors may have been similarly undervalued.

Finally, it should be noted that the personality factors adduced are associated with interpreters presently in the field. To determine the predictive efficacy of these factors, interpreter candidates' scores on each should be determined and the results related to the success of the candidates after training. Such cross validation is essential before much confidence can be placed in their value for interpreter selection.

Summary

Twenty manual interpreters completed a battery of psychological tests and interpreted two tape-recorded selections. A correlational analysis of the test data and ratings of interpreter proficiency yielded significant r's for five scales of the Edwards Personal Preference Schedule, one scale from the Strong Vocational Interest Inventory, and self-ratings of interpreting ability under various conditions. A personality picture emerged for the successful interpreter: desires to be the center of attention and to be independent, is not overly anxious, does not seek sympathy for self, and is not rigid. This research also aroused questions about judging interpreter ability. The need for cross-validation of results was emphasized.

Acknowledgments

This research was supported, in part, by grants from the Social and Rehabilitation Service, Department of Health, Education and Welfare. Dr. William Schiff was responsible for gathering the data and preparing the initial data analysis. Others who contributed substantially to this project cannot be listed without violating their rights of privacy. It should be apparent, however, that the interpreters and their judges deserve the author's deepest gratitude.

CHAPTER 2

Early empirical research (1975–1980)

Introduction

As we pointed out in the first chapter, in the sixties and seventies, most known papers, studies and handbooks about Sign Language Interpreting (SLI) were written in English and produced in the United States (Metzger 2006; Grbić 2007); this remains true for this chapter. This chapter includes more examples of early empirical research, mostly experimental studies, produced in the U.S., which are pioneering but were published in books or monographs that are now out of print or unavailable.

We also provide a quick overview of the historical background for SLI research in the U.S. We provide this background information for two reasons: (1) it describes the history of the development of writings and scholarship about SLI that would later be paralleled by other countries and their sign language communities as they drew on developments in the U.S., and (2) and two, it describes a path to academia and research that informs the history of community interpreting scholars and practitioners worldwide.

By the mid-1970s and early 1980s, the rising awareness of Deaf people with language needs, and legislation, such as the Education for All Handicapped Children Act of 1975 (Public Law 94–142) which required providing interpreting services to Deaf children in public schools, and the Vocational Rehabilitation Act of 1973, Section 504, that created an increasing enrollment of Deaf students in post-secondary and vocational programs, all of which, in turn, spurred the demand for interpreters. The number of deaf persons in the U.S. earning advanced degrees during this time tripled (Gannon 1981). The increased number of Deaf students in mainstream/public education and the increased need for interpreters in vocational rehabilitation work (both post-secondary education and employment opportunities) throughout the 1970s created such a demand for interpreters that the U.S. government once again provided funding to support ten, community college, interpreter training programs throughout the U.S. and grouped them into a consortium, the National Interpreter Training Consortium (NITC).

By the late 1970s, educators in these programs began to share training materials, teaching methods, and evaluation processes. The need for research to inform educational practice prompted Gallaudet University's National Academy to convene a conference in Atlanta, Georgia, in 1979, of 47 individuals, all nationally recognized educators and researchers. Participants were asked to suggest discussion topics for the conference and one of the major topics was research. Conference participants identified potential research topics such as: attitudes, entry level requirements, teaching methodology, bilingualism, language processing models, environmental factors, educational interpreting, the needs of special groups and more. They noted that little research had been conducted to date and much more was needed. The final report is gathered in a document *Interpreter Training: the state of the art*, (Yoken 1979), published by the National Academy. All the authors cited in this chapter of the Reader appear in the list of research studies that were available at that time.

Later that same year, Anna Witter-Merithew from the National Technical Institute for the Deaf (NTID) and Rebecca Carlson of the Technical-Vocational Institute of St. Paul/Minneapolis received funding from their universities to bring together interpreter educators. At this meeting in St. Paul, Minnesota, the group voted to establish the Conference of Interpreter Trainers (CIT) which has become an organization for presenting research studies and pedagogical strategies for educating sign language interpreters and now attracts many international SLI participants as well. Many in the group that formed CIT were present at the 1979 Atlanta conference on interpreter training and would also attend a second conference in 1980, thus the call for research about interpreting became a theme in these gatherings. Deconstructing the task of interpreting, as a research venture, became a necessary first step that was undertaken by CIT in the 1980s.

At the 1979 conference, the participants pooled their knowledge of research studies and academic writings. Afterwards, the National Academy at Gallaudet College conducted a more extensive search for research studies, which revealed that a large number of papers were opinion papers, only a few were empirical studies and they tended to be linguistic studies of ASL.

> It [the search] uncovered no hard research that was systematically feeding into the overall long-range development of the area of interpreter training and the effective utilization of interpreters by deaf people.　　　　　　　　　　(Per-Lee 1980, 1)

The U.S. Office for Handicapped Individuals and the National Institute for Handicapped Research decided to hold a follow-up conference to prioritize research needs and develop plans for specific research projects. At this 1980 Conference, "*Interpreter Research Targets for the Eighties,*" were many participants from the initial meeting, who were now joined by acknowledged researchers, linguists, and educators of the time. The participants selected five priority topics for research, created proposal outlines for each project, and, as another priority, called for a national research center on interpreter training to move forward on these research projects. Although a national research center was never created, this conference and the publications included were an early call for more studies into the processes of SLI.

One of the studies highlighted at both these conferences was a study conducted by **Barbara Babbini Brasel** that was published in 1976 in the first issue of the Center on Deafness Publication series at California State University Northridge (CSUN). Brasel found that interpreting errors began to increase in a statistically significant way after 20–30 minutes and then deteriorated rapidly after 60 minutes. Although her study reported the results of interpretations generated by only two interpreters, her findings have been the basis for the "20-minute" working condition that has become a consistent and common practice for sign language interpreters working in classrooms and with teams. This paper is actually a condensed version of her Masters research that was finished in 1969 (Cerney 2013). The thesis in its entirety is still available at the National Center on Deafness at California State University, Northridge. We include the 1976 publication here because this paper and its date are well known, and had a lasting impact on the working conditions of sign language interpreters.

Ryan Tweney and Harry Hoemann's paper appeared in a seminal collection, *Translation: Applications and Research*, edited by Richard Brislin, a cross-cultural communication scholar, who was also the keynote speaker at the 1985 RID Conference. Citing linguistic studies of ASL, they asserted that there was no evidence that sign languages are inferior, nor are they different in their linguistic organization, thus the translation of sign languages is no different from the translation of spoken languages. While they did mention the lack of dictionaries of ASL and that film was a better medium than print (as ASL has no written form), many of the same strategies used by translators of spoken languages could be used with sign language. For example, *back translation* is not only a strategy for translation, but can be used to investigate the properties of a language. At that time, many of the linguistic features of ASL were yet to be described so Tweney and Hoemann suggested that back translation might provide insight as to how a specific feature functioned or might be labeled. They described their own studies using back translation to identify linguistic features of ASL and encourage its use for further investigation of ASL.

Language Interpretation and Communication

David Gerver was a psychologist "whose 1971 doctoral dissertation can be regarded as the most comprehensive and influential piece of psychological investigation into simultaneous interpreting today." (Pöchhacker 2004, 26). Gerver formulated the first information-processing model of simultaneous interpreting which informed most models developed thereafter. He is also recognized for organizing a pioneering conference on interpreting and editing the proceedings of that conference:

> In 1977, Gerver co-organized an interdisciplinary symposium on interpreting research in Venice which brought together experts from a variety of scientific disciplines (including linguistics, cognitive psychology, sociology, and artificial intelligence) as well as interpreter personalities such as Herbert and Seleskovitch. The proceedings volume [*Language Interpretation and Communication*] of that milestone event (Gerver & Sinaiko 1978), though long out of print, remains one of the richest and most comprehensive collections of papers on interpreting to date and the discipline's most important 'classic'. (Pöchhacker 2004, 34).

Until the NATO conference, most researchers were looking for ways either to predict who would make a good interpreter (candidate screening) or to identify the most effective methods to train interpreters. At this conference interpreting was discussed as an object of scientific inquiry by a variety of disciplines and without a focus on the specific languages; moreover, there were seven papers by sign language and interpreting researchers, bringing spoken and SLI interpreters and researchers together for the first time. We include two papers from Gerver & Sinaiko's 1978 publication titled *Language Interpretation and Communication*.

Robert Ingram's paper in this volume "Sign Language Interpretation and General Theories of Language, Interpretation and Communication," begins by citing studies, including Tweney and Hoemann, demonstrating that sign languages are natural languages, and concluding that this should alter our thinking about language and interpretation. He argued that all the SLI presenters were saying essentially the same thing, that SLI is a part of interpretation in general and descriptions that ignore sign language interpreting would be incomplete. It was a pioneering statement that would resonate with SLI researchers and encouraged many to collaborate with spoken language interpreting scholars and researchers.

While Ingram agreed that sociolinguistics offered a suitable methodological approach to the study of interpreting (as Nida suggested in 1976), he proposed that semiotics was even more appropriate as it potentially captured all the variables of human communication (for the potential of semiotic studies see Poyatos 1987/2002). He cited Eco (1976) in noting that messages are texts whose content are multi-layered discourse, and thus all the layers are open for investigation in interpreting. He also appealed for studies in sociology and social psychology, areas that, while it took almost thirty years, have since been rich sources of informing our understanding of interpreters and their role, e.g. Brunson (2011).

Harry Murphy's paper "Research in sign language interpreting at California State University, Northridge (CSUN)," includes a discussion of three completed research studies at CSUN, including Brasel's 1976 study, and then presents the findings of his own SLI project. CSUN was one of the first public universities to accept Deaf students and provide interpreters. In providing interpreters, there was a growing recognition of the difficulty of post-secondary education with young Deaf people who may not have had adequate preparation. The overall project goal was to determine how well Deaf students received information through sign language via an interpreter.

The body of his paper is in two parts: (1) a review of previous research (three small studies, including Brasel's 1976 paper), and (2) the research that was being conducted at CSUN at the time. One study focused on interpreters' ability to sign when they heard a spoken lecture, another study tested the interpreters' ability to understand sign language, and a third study quizzed both students who could hear and Deaf students about information from the same lecture. When quizzed about this information, Deaf students scored 16% less well than students who could hear, but it was determined that it was not because of sign language or the interpretation, but likely because of the lesser fluency in English, and other educational factors.

Murphy's paper covers several lesser-known studies of SLI as well as the Brasel study, and the question of what and how much Deaf people understand through interpreters is an on-going question in SLI research.

Lastly, we include another study highlighted at the research conferences that was **Alan Hurwitz**'s paper about his dissertation research. Hurwitz is Deaf and, at the time, was an Associate Dean for Educational Support Services at the National Technical Institute for the Deaf (NTID), which entailed the responsibility for providing interpreting services to Deaf students who attended NTID and the Rochester Institute of Technology (RIT). His research, carried out in the 70s, was influenced by the need to improve interpreting skills, and provide quality services for Deaf students.

Hurwitz analyzed experienced and less experienced interpreters interpreting into English from ASL or a sign code for English, and ASL to English. He used the term 'reverse interpreting' that, at the time, meant interpreting from ASL into English, a term that was to soon become redundant in the literature. He provided narrative texts in both English and ASL, and then analyzed the accuracy of the interpretations. He found that experience improved the quality of interpreting from ASL into English, but that both experienced and novice interpreters have equal difficulty comprehending an ASL message and producing an accurate message in English.

Aftermath

As Pöchhacker (2004) notes, in spite of these calls for studies and collaboration with spoken language interpreting, collaboration came about only gradually in the 1980s, and the papers that we feature here seem to have made little impact at the time. However, texts such as *Language Interpretation and Communication* and *Translation* became rich sources for the writers and scholars who conducted research in 1980s. Now these volumes are out of print and largely forgotten, while the papers they contain are forward thinking and predictive of the progress of the field. Quigley, Schein, Murphy, Tweney and Hoemann were all psychologists or specialists in deafness who did not persist in this line of research. Ingram, Hurwitz and Brasel, however, a practitioner and consumers respectively, continued in SLI for some time to come.

2.1   Brasel, Barbara B. 1976. "The effects of fatigue on the competence of interpreters for the deaf." In *Selected Readings on the Integration of Deaf Students at CSUN #1*, ed. by Harry Murphy, 19–22). Northridge, CA: California State University at Northridge.

Barbara Babbini Brasel was a deaf woman whose influence and work continues to impact the field of SLI. Barbara attended the Utah School for the Deaf, skipping grades, and graduated at 14. She took the admission exams for Gallaudet College and was eventually admitted in spite of her young age, through the efforts of her brother Robert Sanderson (also the father of Gary Sanderson, see Chapter 5) who would later become a president of the National Association of Deaf People. Brasel left Gallaudet before graduating, and later enrolled at California State University at Northridge (CSUN) and graduated with BA in psychology and an MA in administration and supervision. She was a founding member of the Registry of Interpreters for the Deaf and served on the Board of Directors from 1982–1987. She maintained a life-long interest in interpreters and the interpreting process.

After finishing her MA, she worked at the University of Illinois, Champagne-Urbana, at the Institute for Research on Exceptional Children under the direction of Stephen P. Quigley. Quigley received a five-year grant to study interpreters and interpreting. He recruited Brasel to work on this grant and was instrumental in teaching her advanced research skills and academic writing. This paper reports the results of one of the first projects of this grant that had its funding cut after two years. Brasel moved to Connecticut, taught for a few years at the American School for the Deaf, and, in 1975, became the Executive Director of the Connecticut State Commission on the Deaf and Hearing Impaired.

The Interpretation Department at Gallaudet University has recognized Brasel's contribution to interpreting research by naming their graduate research award in her honor.

The effects of fatigue on the competence of interpreters for the deaf

Barbara Babbini Brasel

With increased recognition of the rights of deaf persons to function effectively in a world composed of those with normal hearing has come an increased emphasis upon educational and economic betterment of the deaf. This has resulted in an increased demand for skilled interpreters for an ever-increasing variety of roles – from platform interpreting at a conference or workshop, through interpreting in psychological or psychiatric settings, to verbatim translating of classroom lectures for deaf adults attending colleges for those with normal hearing.

This has not been an unmixed blessing insofar as professional interpreters for the deaf are concerned. Along with the increased demand for their services has come an increased workload for those highly competent interpreters who have chosen to accept full-time employment with programs which include deaf individuals as co-workers, students, or participants. Also there are few guidelines for the employers of these interpreters, most of whom are not familiar with the language of signs themselves and have only a limited knowledge of the strain, physical and mental, that such work imposes upon those who must translate auditory stimuli into physical movement, facial expression, and pantomime.

With no concrete guidelines established by empirical research, it is perhaps understandable that employers of interpreters on a full-time basis feel that an interpreter, who may be paid as much if not more than a full-time secretary or clerical worker who works 40 hours a week, should fill in his/her time when not actually interpreting by performing other chores such as typing, bookkeeping, filing, or even tutoring. While it is generally recognized that few interpreters can interpret for 30 or more hours a week, there have been no studies to discover exactly how long, how many hours, an interpreter *can* interpret at a time and still retain efficiency in both interpreting and clerical/secretarial tasks.

There have been many educated guesses as to how long an intepreter can interpret before fatigue begins to affect his interpreting competence, yet to the writer's knowledge no systematic study has been done in this area. In addition, it is suspected that the demands of an interpreter's physical and mental capacities imposed by sustained interpreting cannot help but have an effect upon his ability to perform other physical and intellectual chores. Interpreting for deaf persons requires that an individual, in addition to being able to sign and fingerspell fluently, have excellent recall and short-term memory ability. An interpreter must, while translating or interpreting what *has* been spoken, be able to listen to, store in his memory, and subsequently recall what *is* being spoken. Depending upon the interpreter's ability and speed of translation into the language of signs, the interpreter may be anywhere from three to seven or eight (or more) words behind the speaker. Short-term memory and recall are also important in clerical/secretarial work, for the ability to take dictation in shorthand also depends upon the same faculties as does interpreting for the deaf. Remembering spoken and written orders is also a function of short-term memory, although long-term memory faculties are also involved in the latter. Therefore, what affects short-term memory in one situation will undoubtedly affect short-term memory in a similar but unrelated situation.

Fingerspelling utilizes many of the same muscles in the hands and arms that are utilized in typing, and fatigue affecting the fingerspelling muscles should also affect the typing muscles. There may also be interference with the ability to concentrate after sustained intellectual and auditory bombardment such as takes place during the task of interpreting for a lecture, and it was decided to test this ability along with short-term memory and typing skill in a controlled experiment to elicit information on just when fatigue begins to affect physical and intellectual functioning during the task of interpreting.

A pretest-posttest design was selected to test the following hypotheses:

1. Interpreters for the deaf can interpret for 20 to 30 minutes without significant loss in interpreting competence as measured by error rate per minute and quality of interpreting performance as measured by ratings given the interpreter by competent judges before and after an interpreting task.
2. Interpreters can interpret for 20 to 30 minutes without significant deterioration in intellectual or physical skills as measured by typing speed and accuracy, ability to add a column of figures rapidly, and ability to memorize and recall five out of ten nonsense syllables (trigrams) exposed for three seconds per trial.
3. After 30 minutes of sustained interpreting, interpreting error rate will increase in proportion to increase in sustained interpreting time.
4. After 30 minutes of sustained interpreting, interpreting quality will deteriorate, and this will be evident in lower ratings given by a panel of competent judges.
5. After 30 minutes of sustained interpreting, typing speed will decrease, and typing error rate will increase in proportion to increase in time.
6. After 30 minutes of sustained interpreting, time required to add a three-digit column of numbers will increase as a function of increase in time.
7. After 30 minutes of sustained interpreting, short-term memory and recall functions, as measured by the number of trials required to correctly write down five out of ten trigrams, will deteriorate as a function of time spent in sustained interpreting.

Method

Subjects: The subjects were two male and three female interpreters selected for their recognized competence from a pool of available interpreters at California State University,

Northridge. Partially successful attempts were made to select interpreters of at least acceptable ability. Of the five, four met this criterion, three being rated as either good or outstanding and one as acceptable. The fifth interpreter, while of above average ability in his command of conversational sign language, proved to be too inexperienced and slow to rate higher than high unacceptable. Although he was tested, his scores were not included in some of the statistical computations for reasons that will be discussed later in this paper.

The subjects drew straws for the length of time of their task prior to any testing.

Apparatus: A Wollensak tape recorder was utilized, with two hour-long tapes made by the same speaker, William Glasser, with the topic being the same for both tapes. Typing tests of approximately equal difficulty, length, and content were presented on an 8×10 sheet of paper. Two separate but equivalent tests in addition were used, each test consisting of a column of 10 three-digit numbers. Two decks of 3×5 cards were used. On each deck was printed a three-letter trigram. Both decks were matched (5) on numbers of high and low similarity trigrams. Also used was a Benrus stopwatch.

The testing took place in a regular classroom, each subject being tested separately. Positioned behind the interpreter, and out of his range of vision was a floodlight of moderate intensity, which was operated by a wall switch directly underneath the floodlight at about waist height. The interpreters could not tell when the floodlight was turned on or off because the room was brightly lit.

Procedure: As each subject arrived, he was presented with straws from which he drew one which had his interpreting interval time written on it. (The last interpreter, unavoidably, was *assigned* to the one remaining interval time.) He was then given the following tests, with the order randomized for each subject:

1. Trigram test: Each trigram in the first deck was exposed by the experimenter for approximately three seconds, with the experimenter holding each card upright for the mental count of "thousand one, thousand two, thousand three" before laying it down and exposing the next card. Three trials were given each subject before he was asked to write down as many of the trigrams as he could recall, in any order. All subjects were told at the beginning of the test that they were expected to use the first trials for learning and then to try to recall at least five out of ten trigrams they were shown. A maximum of ten trials was imposed.

2. Math test: The subjects were given the first math test and instructed to add the column of figures as rapidly as they could. An assistant experimenter checked their time with the stopwatch.

3. Typing test: The first typing test was then administered, each subject being given five minutes in which to type as much of the test material as possible and instructed not to attempt to correct or strike over errors.

4. Interpreting evaluation pretest: The subjects were then evaluated on a 13-item form (3) during the first five minutes of their interpreting stint, each subject being told that the first five minutes was a "warm-up" period. According to the straw drawn,

the subject had to interpret for 20, 30, 60 or 90 minutes, with one subject drawing the 0-minute (control) straw. The control subject did no interpreting whatsoever and was thus not evaluated at the time of the study, evaluation of her skills having taken place by the same judges during a separate but similar study (3).

5.   Interpreters were then observed by four judges, two deaf persons (including the experimenter) and two outstanding interpreters, both skilled in reverse interpreting. An additional assistant sat behind the interpreter, within reach of the switch that controlled the floodlight, and every five minutes turned the light on and off quickly so that the judges could mark the passage of each five-minute block of time.

The deaf judges concerned themselves with tallying each and every time they observed an interpreting error (slurring of fingerspelling, use of the wrong sign for a word, failure to keep up with the speaker, "bootleg rests," or any time the deaf person found himself baffled or confused or did not understand a fingerspelled or signed word). The interpreter-judges were instructed not only to listen to the tape recording but also to watch the interpreter for concepts he failed to convey or misinterpreted.

At the end of the assigned time, the subjects were given, again in randomized order, second trigram, math, and typing tests, all of which were different from but equivalent to the pretests mentioned earlier.

Results

Hypothesis 1 would seem to be supported in that the majority of the significant differences were found when subjects 4 and 5 (60 and 90 minutes) were compared. This would indicate that for up to 30 minutes, there are no significant differences in interpreting competence, errors, or quality – although a deterioration can be noted beginning at about 25 minutes. After 30 minutes, there is a slow but steady increase in error rate, and after 60 minutes this increase becomes significant.

Hypothesis 2 is partially supported in that there were no significant differences in any of the clerical skills dimensions *except* the typing error rate, which increased for all subjects regardless of the amount of time spent interpreting. Subject 2, in particular, was interesting in that while he did very poorly on the interpreting evaluation pretest, he alone of the four interpreters evaluated was judged to have improved slightly in his interpreting skill at the end of his 20-minute interpreting task. In addition, as was noted earlier, he completely failed the trigrams pretest, but managed to score better on the posttest than three out of the other four interpreters. Yet on the typing test he lost only one word per minute in speed, while his error rate more than doubled (from nine to 22). Questioned after the experiment, he stated that he had been so nervous about the prospect of interpreting in the test situation that he could not concentrate during either the math or the trigrams test. He also stated that once the interpreting task was completed, he felt much more relaxed and able to concentrate.

The fact, however, that after only 20 minutes of interpreting, his typing error rate rose to double its former level may indicate that the impact of interpreting, in a physical sense, falls hardest upon those who are relatively inexperienced or incompetent.

Hypotheses 3 through 5 and hypothesis 7, therefore, are apparently fully or at least partially supported, but hypothesis 6 was not supported by the data in this study. Part of the problem may be that different intellectual abilities are required for mathematical computations than are required in interpreting. The standard deviation of the pretest indicates a wide range of mathematical ability, and those subjects who scored low on the pretest tended to score higher on the posttest, while those who scored high on the pretest scored lower on the posttest – and this apparently had no connection with the length of time spent in interpreting.

It is recognized that there are many variables which may have influenced the results found in this study. One variable may have been knowledge of the time the interpreters would have to interpret, for when a subject is aware of the amount of time he will have to spend doing a chore, he tends to automatically "pace" himself so as not to overtax himself. Consideration was given to keeping subjects unaware of how long they would be required to interpret for the study, but it was abandoned as unfeasible because of the necessity to inform the subjects, who all had tight schedules, exactly how long their services would be required. They all asked immediately upon, arrival, and in the interests of keeping peace with an overworked group of persons, it was felt wiser to let them know immediately after they had drawn their straws. This probably influenced the results, for the two interpreters (subjects 4 and 5) who drew the longest stints (the 60 and 90 minute chores) were both veteran interpreters who had learned how to pace themselves. If they had not known how long they were to interpret, it is possible the results would have been even more significant, but perhaps of limited validity because most interpreters in the field today know approximately how long they will be required to interpret in any given situation.

Subjects 4 and 5 both began interpreting with a relatively high error rate (when compared with their scores a few minutes later), then seemed to settle down and make fewer errors for the next five or 10 minutes. Then their error rates began a slow but steady climb, only to drop suddenly when the speaker on the tape paused several times, thus giving them a brief rest. This respite seemed to help only temporarily, for the error rate immediately began to climb sharply before leveling off at a high rate. Subject 5, between 60 and 75 minutes, stabilized as to error rate increase, but the judges, on their tally sheets, all commented upon the deterioration in the quality of her interpreting. Sample comments were "All life gone," "Expressionless," "Facial expression deadpan." In addition, the deaf judges also commented upon "slurring of lip movements. Can no longer understand her silent speech." Also, she kept taking "bootleg" rests, omitting increasing numbers of "non-essential" words from her verbatim translation, in other words, reverting to shorthand sign language, understandable, but far from as interesting or as accurate as verbatim translation.

Subject 4 was guilty of all these interpreting flaws as well, but to a less marked degree when compared to her pretest performance. Regardless, her evaluation on the posttest dropped from 4 (good) to 2 (marginal – borderline unacceptable), while subject 5 dropped from 5 (outstanding) to 3 (unacceptable).

Conclusions

The general conclusion to be drawn from the study is that interpreters for the deaf have a demanding job that has a significant effect upon other skills they may have, and this effect increases as the length of sustained interpreting time increases. In addition, the longer an interpreter interprets past the 30-minute mark without intervening rest periods, the more his interpreting skills will deteriorate. No assumptions can be made on the basis of this study as to what the cumulative effects of three, four, or more hours of daily interpreting will be, with or without intervening rest periods. It might be well to note at this point that most college and university lecture periods are from one to three hours in length. Little can be done to shorten them, and it would be awkward to attempt to switch interpreters in mid-lecture, but at least employers of full-time interpreters can see that their interpreters get plenty of rest in between three-hour classes – rest that is free of other duties, which they would probably perform inefficiently anyway if the results of this study are any indication.

Recommendations

It is suggested that this study be replicated with a larger number of subjects, with screening procedures set up to match subjects on ability, experience, and educational background. In addition, research should be undertaken to discover what the recovery rate is once the interpreting chore is completed. It would be interesting and helpful to know exactly how much resting time an interpreter needs to recover his baseline skills after interpreting for a given period of time without rest. Guidelines are needed in this area, for opinions vary. Some feel that an interpreter is "resting" when engaged in non-interpreting chores, while others feel that an interpreter can interpret only 20 minutes at a time with an hour's rest in between.

Another area that needs study is that of the cumulative effects of daily interpreting without sufficient rest periods intervening. What are the effects of accumulated fatigue upon the interpreter's ability to function in non-interpreting work situations? What are the effects upon his mood and outlook? What are the effects upon his family life? These and other questions need answering in these times of increasing professionalism in the area of interpreting for the deaf, and answering them and implementing the answers into practice by those who employ interpreters can only result in upgrading the profession of interpreting for the deaf and increasing the quality of the services provided to those members of the "deaf world" who, without the services of interpreters, would find many doors into the world of the hearing closed very tightly to them.

References

Aborc, M., and H. Rubenstein, "Information Theory and Immediate Recall," *Journal of Experimental Psychology,* 44 (1952), 260–66.

Brasel, K.E., "Needed: Qualified Interpreters," *The Illinois Advance,* January, 1969, pp. 1–2.

Brasel, K.E., and J. Shipman, "Expressive Translation," an evaluation form for use in rating interpreters for the deaf, San Fernando Valley State College, n.d.

Gibson, E.J., "A Systematic Application of the Concepts of Generalization and Differentiation to Verbal Learning," *Psychological Review,* 47 (1940), 196–229.

Horowitz, L.M., "Free Recall and the Ordering of Trigrams," *Journal of Experimental Psychology,* 62 (1961), 51–57.

Huff, K.E., "The Best is None Too Good," an address made at the Conference of Interpreters for the Deaf at San Fernando Valley State College, April 3, 1965.

Quigley, Stephen, and Joseph Youngs, eds., *Interpreting for Deaf People,* Washington, D.C.: Department of Health, Education and Welfare, 1965.

Smith, J.M., ed., "Workshop on Interpreting for the Deaf," proceedings of a workshop held at Ball State Teachers College, June 1964.

Underwood, B.J., *Experimental Psychology,* 2nd ed., New York: Appleton-Century-Crofts, 1966, Ch. 8.

2.2   Tweney, Ryan and Harry Hoemann. 1976. "Translation and Sign Language." In *Translation: Applications and Research,* ed. by Richard Brislin, 138–161. New York: Gardner Press.

Ryan Tweney received his Ph.D. from Wayne State University in 1970 specializing in cognitive-experimental psychology, with an emphasis on psycholinguistics. He went to Bowling Green State University, Ohio, and remained there his entire career as a professor of psychology. Shortly after his arrival at Bowling Green, he began collaborating with Harry Hoemann on a series of studies on ASL. Tweney contributed the psycholinguistic theory and knowledge of how to design and conduct studies in that field. Tweney actually had little contact with deaf people but did assist with gathering data at Gallaudet University and visited Ursula Bellugi's laboratory at the Salk Institute in California. His last active research with deaf people and ASL was in the 1970s.

For over 30 years at Bowling Green State University, Dr. Harry Hoemann was a psychology professor, best known for teaching American Sign Language (ASL). He was educated as a theologian and became a Lutheran minister for the deaf, and was responsible for a large deaf parish for 9 years in Washington D.C. He subsequently turned his focus to education and psychology, earning his Ph.D. under Hans Furth at Catholic University in 1969. Hoemann was hired as an assistant professor in the Psychology department at Bowling Green State University, and was named Professor Emeritus by the time he retired in 2000. During his career he received several important research grants in developmental psychology of deaf children, published his findings in notable journals and presented his work at international conferences. With his wife Shirley, he created sign language playing cards and flash cards, published by the National Association of the Deaf, and collaborated on an educational video for Brazilian sign language after spending a summer in Brazil with the deaf community. Later on he and his wife incorporated a publishing company and sold their educational materials worldwide.

Translation and sign languages

Ryan D. Tweney & Harry W. Hoemann

A significant fraction of the world's population does not possess a vocally encoded linguistic system as a first language. For most congenitally deaf individuals, and for those who become profoundly deaf prior to the acquisition of spoken language, some form of sign language will constitute the earliest linguistic system, and it will be the one most likely to be utilized in ordinary social interaction. It thus becomes of great practical interest to consider the unique problems of translation when a sign language is the source language, the target language, or both.

Furthermore, much recent attention has been directed toward sign languages because of their intrinsic interest as semiotic systems (Stokoe, 1974). As a natural extension of that interest, "intersemiotic translation" (Jakobson, 1959), involving sign language to spoken language conversion and vice versa, is deserving of study, both for its intrinsic value and for the light it can shed on intersemiotic relations in general.

The process of translation is one in which meaningful utterances in one linguistic system are converted into related meaningful utterances in another system. Most research on translation has involved conversion among spoken linguistic systems, in spite of the fact that definitions of translation generally fail to restrict the domain to that of speech. Intersemiotic translation, however, has not generally been considered by researchers in translation or in linguistics. The restriction of translation interest to spoken languages is doubly unfortunate because it has eliminated certain theoretical and empirical issues from consideration.

In the case of spoken languages, a number of empirical studies of simultaneous translation have shown that interpreters lag behind speakers, and tend to fill in pauses in the speaker's utterances with "bursts" of translated material (Oléron and Nanpon, 1965; Barik, 1973). It is not known, however, whether the phenomena observed result from the necessity of an ordered, linear sequence in the transmission of speech or whether they result from constraints on the ability of the translator to simultaneously encode utterances in one speech code while decoding utterances in another. This issue could be approached by careful consideration of the behavior of simultaneous translators encoding sign into speech, speech into sign, and sign into sign, and comparing the results with the more commonly studied speech-into-speech encoding. Further, only in sign language can true simultaneous production of two languages occur. Because sign languages are generated manually, they are unique in permitting simultaneous generation of a spoken and a signed message.

A clergyman addressing a mixed group of deaf and hearing individuals might simultaneously *say* "The congregation will please rise" and *sign* "church group please stand" (where each word is a gloss for a single sign). Similar phenomena can be observed in deaf educational institutions, where lecturing activity may present a simultaneous sign translation. Study of this activity should be rewarding for the light it can shed on the cognitive processes related to encoding in language.

The neglect of consideration of sign languages by translation research can be seen as part of a much wider general neglect of sign systems by language scientists and educators. Because the approach to deaf education in the Anglo-Saxon countries has, until very recently, emphasized the acquisition of oral language skills, research on deafness has also ignored the properties of sign languages. The same orientation has assumed that prior acquisition of a sign system can interfere with the acquisition of oral skills. The first point is dealt with later. The second point has never been put to adequate empirical test. It is worth nothing, however, that Charrow and Fletcher (1974) found that deaf adolescents whose first language was sign performed better on the Test of English as a Foreign Language than comparable deaf adolescents who lacked sign as a first language. If anything, then, prior sign useage may facilitate rather than hinder acquisition of an oral code.

A number of misconceptions about the nature of sign are current. Two deserve special mention: (1) the belief that sign languages are pantomimic and therefore understandable by anyone regardless of their native tongue, and (2) the related belief that sign languages are not really languages at all but simply an extension of such nonlinguistic gesture systems as the use of finger-pointing to represent objects. Of course, the acceptance of either point of view would radically alter the conceptualization of translation issues involving manual language. The first myth, in fact, suggests that there are *no* issues for translation theory, because any human being ought to be able to "translate" a manual representation into its meaning. The second myth, that sign systems are trivially deictic, need not lead to the same radical conclusion, but it does suggest that some aspects of manually encoded communications may be difficult or impossible to translate, because they derive from nonlinguistic expressive gestures.

Recent research in the linguistic and psycholinguistic properties of sign languages makes it possible to present evidence suggesting that sign languages are functional linguistic systems. The first part of this chapter summarizes some of the relevant evidence, and serves as the basis for the second part, which examines the application of the findings to existing sign language translation issues.

The nature of sign languages

A sign language is any linguistically structured communication system in which meanings are mapped primarily onto gestures made by the arms, hands, torso, and face of the communicator. Such systems need to be carefully distinguished from gestural encodings of vocal languages (Stokoe, 1974). Thus finger spelling, the representation of an alphabet by hand gestures, is not a manual language, but a manual encoding of a vocal language. For people with knowledge of English, finger spelling is exactly analogous to the transmission of English texts by writing. In both finger spelling and reading, the receiver's ability to decode the sender's message is wholly dependent on his knowledge of another language system, together with a set of arbitrary correspondence rules. True sign languages, on the other hand, can be correctly decoded only if knowledge of the internal structure of the manual language is possessed by the receiver; knowledge of English is irrelevant. Clearly, the use of finger spelling involves no important issues of translation. Manual languages are generally used, however, in conjunction with finger-spelled terms from the dominant spoken language. Such variation means that "pure" sign language is not often observed, and that the relationship between sign language and the dominant system needs to be taken into account. Sign languages must also be distinguished from pantomimic communication systems, in which a gesture is a kind of acting out of the meaning. Very few signs possess pantomimic quality to a sufficient degree to allow meaning to be apprehended directly. Rather, nearly all signs represent meanings conventionally, like spoken words (Hoemann, in press; Stokoe, 1972).

A variety of manual language systems exist and are in contemporary use. As with vocal languages, geographical differences are found, and historical change is known to occur. Thus, although French sign language and American sign language (ASL) are related historically, they differ greatly today. British sign language also differs substantially from ASL. Manual languages show considerable variation within national borders. The relative social isolation of deaf children in residential schools in the United States has lead to a proliferation of local dialects. In fact, dialect variants peculiar to a single residential school for the deaf are not unusual and may persist within the surrounding adult deaf linguistic community.

The use of manual languages is affected by constraints of social acceptability. Stokoe (1972) has applied Ferguson's (1959) notion of diglossia to the description of manual language useage. Two variants, H (high, or formal) and L (low, or conversational), are easily identified. In America, the H sign order corresponds closely to English word order, and extensive finger spelling may be utilized to encode English articles and prepositions. Such devices are not generally found in L variants, although finger spelling may be utilized for particular words without conventionalized manual equivalents. Differentiating only two categories is, in a sense, artificial, because a continuum of useage exists. Further, the use of H and L depends not only on the particular social demands of the situation, but also on the background of the signer – for example, whether he or she has attained command over English syntax. Similar differences as a function of sociolinguistic variables have been described (for spoken languages) by Labov (1972b) and Bailey (1973). The differentiation of H and L sign useage in America is similar to the differentiation of vernacular Black

English from Standard English among Black Americans (see, e.g. Houston, 1969; Labov, 1972a). It is now quite clear from the evidence that variation in the useage of particular phonological rules is a characteristic feature of speech systems. Thus the use of "are-less" constructions (e.g. "They going to the store") among Black American speakers is related in a lawful fashion to situational constraints and to the perceived formality of the situation (Labov, 1972a). That a similar situation exists within ASL has been argued by Woodward (1973, 1974) who has shown that systematic variation exists among deaf adult signers in Washington, D. C, and Montana.

Manual languages have been subjected to repeated attempts to modify, or to create anew, lexicons and syntactic mechanisms. Deaf educators have generally made such attempts with an educational purpose in mind. Because the social communities of deaf individuals are relatively isolated and more-or-less segregated from speaking communities and because of the prevalence of residential schools for the deaf, these attempts have been surprisingly successful. The earliest (and the most successful) was that of the Abbe Charles Michel de l'Épee, who in 1776 published an extensively elaborated systematic sign language he had developed while working in the Institution des Sourds et Muets in Paris, France (Bender, 1970). This system was later modified by his successor, Roch Ambroise Sicard, who decided that the original system was overly methodical and overly burdened with irrelevant syntactic devices derived from French. Sicard thus eliminated certain regular structures in de l'Épee's version and incorporated many naturally occurring sign structures found among deaf individuals. The result was an easily learned and transmitted language that eventually evolved into the contemporary American and French sign languages. Sicard's system was brought to the United States by Thomas Hoplins Gallaudet in 1816.

In recent years several attempts have been made to modify ASL for educational purposes (Bornstein, 1973). All share a common goal, that of making the learning of English easier. As just one example, Anthony's "Seeing Essential English" (SEE) provides a system that closely parallels English structure. Analogs of English articles, function words, prepositions, and conjunctions are included. The utility of such systems is still an open question. To the extent they become utilized in future educational settings, however, it is probably safe to predict that they will influence the structure of vernacular ASL in the direction of greater similarity to English. This, in turn, would have clear implications for the translatability of signed utterances and for the assumptions that a translator can safely bring to the translation process.

Brief mention is necessary for certain special-purpose manual languages. The best known, American Indian sign language, is now extinct but once served widely as a form of intertribal communication. Extensive descriptions of its lexicon were made by Mallery (1881) and Clark (1885). The origin of the system is unknown. Kluge (1885) described a monasterial sign language used by monks who observe silence for religious reasons. Cistercian sign language is now undergoing rapid change and may soon become extinct

(Barakat, 1969). Formal descriptions do not yet exist for any of these systems. Although translation involving such languages was at one time of great practical importance, the need for translation has disappeared almost completely.

The linguistic structure of sign

Surprisingly little attention has been paid by linguists to the formal description of the linguistic properties of sign. Until Stokoe's work appeared in the early 1960s, the Indian sign language descriptions of Mallery and Clark provided the only discussion of sign linguistic structure (their work was at the level of an informal "school grammar," rather than in terms of a formalized descriptive approach).

The seminal application of modern linguistic analysis was due to Stokoe (1960), who first described ASL in terms of the contrastive categories of structural linguistics. In looking for minimally contrastive formatives in sign, Stokoe isolated combinatorial units, called *cheremes* (after the Greek *chéir, cheirós* – hand), which are analogous to phonemes in vocalic languages. Three types of cheremes can be described, a place marker, or *tab*, a hand configuration marker, or *dez*, and a movement marker, or *sig*. The sign for girl, for example, consists of moving (sig) the ball of the thumb (dez) along the signer's cheek (tab). If a different dez were used, say, the outstretched palm instead of the ball of the thumb, then the meaning of the sign would differ (in this case, the result would be the sign for brown).

Complete description of the cheremics of ASL would consist of a list of all cheremes, together with an indication of the range of allocheric variation and the distributional constraints imposed on cheremes. Sign cheremes represent conventionalized structural patternings of the total set of produceable gestures (Stokoe, 1974). Although no complete description has been attempted for any sign language, Stokoe has supplied a fairly complete list of cheremes for ASL, together with at least some information on allocheric variation and on distributional constraints. Morphocheremic description, that is, description of the interaction of cheremic units within signs, has, however, barely been started.

Stokoe's classification does present certain problems. In the first place, the elaboration of three types of cheremes appears a priori, and has less linguistic motivation than one would like. To be sure, phonemes can be divided into two classes, vowels and consonants, in much the way cheremes have been divided into three (cheremes, however, represent simultaneously cooccurring features). The analysis of a particular phoneme as a vowel can be done on the basis of several criteria, all of which are known to be relevant to the production of speech (e.g. presence of vocal tract resonance). For cheremes, however, no such rationale can yet be provided. One can imagine a classification of speech sounds based on tab, dez, and sig components involving the tongue, lips, and vocal cords. All speech could be described in this fashion, but the description would not be directly related to the linguistically relevant parameters. The necessity of relating *acoustic* distinctive features to *articulatory* distinctive features has been much discussed in the speech perception litera-ture (e.g. Stevens, 1971). Some support for the adequacy of Stokoe's system can be derived from the results of short-term memory studies. Bellugi, Klima, and Siple (1975) found that errors in memory for signs occurred along dimensions predicted by a cheremic analysis. Thus the sign for noon was mistakenly recalled as tree, a sign that differs only in the type of movement (i.e. along the sig dimension). Other errors occurred along dez or tab dimen-sions, or along some combination of more than one dimension.

The lack of linguistic motivation is especially evident for the distinction between dez and tab. Whereas some tabs (the forehand, say) are never used as dez, others (the hand turned palm up, with the fingers held together) can be used as tab or as dez. Stokoe has attributed this problem to the inadequacy of morphocheremic description, a full account of which would, presumably, deal with such difficulties. The problem may, however, be more basic. If the analysis of signs into three dimensions is insufficient (i.e. if a different categorization is required), then no amount of morphocheremic description is likely to clarify the difficulty. It is apparent, for example, that a fourth dimension will be needed to represent the relative orientation of the dez hand in a given sign. The possible inadequacy of the cheremic description system goes beyond the need for such straightforward supple-mentation, however. Clearly, future research needs to be directed to this issue.

ASL syntax still awaits its Stokoe. Few serious attempts using the techniques of modern linguistic analysis have been made to describe fully the syntactic mechanisms found in ASL. McCall (1965) provided a "grammar" of ASL based on the generative-transformational principles of Chomsky's (1957) model. McCall's corpus consisted, how-ever, of English glosses of all of the filmed utterances of a number of signers at a social gathering. No use was made of signer's intuitions about grammaticality, nor, in fact, was any attempt made to separate well-formed from ill-formed utterances. Further, McCall's grammatical rules derived sentences from other, kernel sentences, rather than from deep structures. As a result, McCall's grammar provided only the most superficial description of ASL syntax. Woodward (1972) has provided a very small fragment of a transformational grammar of ASL which avoided the difficulties associated with McCall's work. Only 11 rules were formally described, however, making Woodward's grammar little more than a demonstration of what might be possible.

Stokoe (1972) has described a number of possible approaches to the linguistic descrip-tion of sign syntax, of which two deserve comment here. He is, first of all, very negative about the possibility of applying generative transformational principles to the description of manual systems. According to Stokoe, the fundamental assumption that a grammar relates *sounds* and meaning makes generative theory useless, unless one is willing to say that sign languages are derivative from spoken languages. It does not seem to us, however, that this is a necessary assumption within generative theory. Were a generativist interested in describing sign using transformational principles, there is no reason why the fundamen-tal principle could not be modified to involve relations between *gestures* and meaning. The point seems to have little force. Stokoe is also critical of the need for sequential ordering of phonological elements which he claims are necessary for the operation of transformational rules on the phonological level. The simultaneous production of sign elements, however, renders such a scheme unworkable, according to Stokoe. Again, however, we do not feel that this is a necessary characteristic of a generative account, since only terminal-level rules need be involved in the ordering of elements in an utterance. Of course, Stokoe is correct in asserting that generative accounts have not been developed. We can look forward to the day when they do become available.

Stokoe is more favorable about the possibilities of applying Ceccato's (1961) operational model of syntax to the analysis of sign. This approach, developed for use in computer applications, utilizes a lattice or network of relationships between the fundamental content-elements of a sentence. The model operates by elaborating links between elements, links between sets of linked elements, and so on. Unlike generative systems, there is no need for the principal relationships to be hierarchically related. Generative grammars handle sentence embedding processes by first deriving hierarchial trees with incorporated S nodes, followed by the application of transformational processes to provide ordering, inflections, and specific lexical interpretations. Operational grammars, however, provide for ordering of only major segments, whereas elements within segments can remain unordered. This feature, according to Stokoe, permits the lack of syntactic ordering constraints in sign language to be easily represented. Of particular interest in Stokoe's discussion is his claim that operational analysis of sentences in both ASL and English reveals, greater intertranslatability than would be expected from a generative analysis. The underlying lattice for an utterance may be the same in both languages, even though the realization of each lattice element in the ASL utterance may be very different from its realization in English. As interesting as the suggestion appears, however, it is speculative until such time as formalized operational grammars of a sign language become available.[1]

Can anything definite be said about the nature of syntax in sign languages? In fact, the emergence of sign language research is so recent that very little has been done. The relative lack of order constraints has been referred to. Although this characteristic is shared by some spoken languages, ASL lacks, to a very great degree, not only order constraints but sign-level inflection markers to indicate grammatical role. The absence of both ordering and morpological inflection has been used to argue that sign languages lack linguistic structure (Tervoort, 1968). Yet, in ASL, grammatical role is indicated using a number of inflectionlike devices. Thus deictic reference to agents and patients in ongoing discourse is provided by the manual indication of a kind of stage in front of the signer. Particular

---

1.   Advances in the computer processing of language have, however, gone in a somewhat different direction. Instead of focusing on syntactic relationships, the most successful (e.g. Winograd, 1972) rely on semantic and logical interpretation of syntactic structure.

individuals are located on the "stage" initially by pointing, and can later be referred to by reference to the particular location. This device reduces need for personal pronouns in ASL (though finger-spelled pronouns sometimes occur in ASL as importations from English).

Psycholinguistic Properties of Sign Languages Several lines of research have been initiated by psycholinguists interested in the functional properties of sign language. The work is indirectly relevant to issues of translation insofar as any finding which indicated a functional deficiency relative to spoken languages would need to be considered in translation programs. To date, however, evidence for deficiencies, except in very specific circumstances, has not been found. The account given here must be brief – a fuller review is given by Bonvillian, Charrow, and Nelson (1973).

The most basic psycholinguistic question involves communicability. Can sign languages serve as an effective channel for the transmission of messages from a sender to a receiver? Hoemann (1972) taught young deaf children a simple competitive game, and then required that the children in turn teach the game to another child. Deaf children communicating in ASL and finger-spelled English were not as effective as comparable hearing children using English. Specific problems included a tendency of deaf children to explain in detail some single feature of the game, such as rolling the die or moving a counter, without indicating the way in which the game was to be won. The finding thus may be due to deficiencies in social or in cognitive development rather than to a characteristic of the language medium. Using deaf adolescents, Jordan (1974) found that ASL was *more* effective than English used by hearing adolescents. Jordan used a picture-description task in which the sender was required to describe one picture out of a multiple array and the receiver was required to choose the correct target picture from an identical array. Together with the Hoemann study, the results suggest that relative communicative effectiveness may be content-specific. It is possible that highly visualizable arrays are more readily encoded in a sign language than in a spoken language, whereas abstract material (like game rules) are more readily encoded by a spoken language. The hypothesis has never been directly tested.

Schlesinger (1971) required deaf adult users of Israeli Sign Language (ISL) to describe simple actor-action-object-indirect-object pictures to another deaf adult. Performance was surprisingly poor, even when multiple sentences in ISL were used to describe each picture. Schlesinger suggested that the grammatical encoding of object-indirect-object relationships may not be a linguistic universal, since it appears not to be found in ISL. The conclusion is, however, premature since ISL may rely heavily upon deictic mechanisms which were not available in the experimental situation used. Thus, if ISL distinguishes object from indirect object by relative location on an imaginery stage, rather than by order relationships or inflections, then Schlesinger's task may have worked against his subjects. This conjecture is supported by the results of a study by Bode (1974) in which deaf ASL users performed at a very high level on a task similar to Schlesinger's. Bode's subjects were matched for their knowledge of ASL, thus ensuring use of a mutually understood code by her subjects – a precaution not utilized by Schlesinger.

Few studies have been conducted of the perception of sign languages. Tweney, Heiman, and Hoemann (in preparation) studied the effect of temporal interruption of a signed message on intelligibility of the message. The rate of interruption and the degree of linguistic structure in the message were varied. A high degree of resistance to such disruption was found. Further, well-formed strings of signs were more resistant than syntactically well-formed but meaningless strings or random strings, suggesting that syntactic and semantic structure play a functional fole in sign as in speech (Heiman & Tweney, 1975). Sign language, like spoken language (Miller, 1951), appears to utilize linguistic structure to add redundancy, thereby increasing the ease of transmission of messages (Fodor, Bever, and Garrett, 1974). Future research is needed to determine the exact mechanisms used by sign language to achieve this result.

Translation of sign languages

From what has been said about the nature of sign languages, there is no reason to expect translation involving sign languages to be radically different from translation involving spoken languages. This conclusion follows because there is no linguistic or psychological evidence that sign languages are functionally inferior to spoken languages or that they rely on different principles of linguistic organization. Research on this issue is still very limited, to be sure, but it seems unlikely to us that major surprises are to be expected. The specific linguistic characteristics of sign language still need to be detailed, along with specific psycholinguistic properties. But the evidence to date suggests that all language rests on the same set of universal cognitive capabilities whether it is based on manual encodings or on acoustic encodings.[2] Research on translation of sign languages should, therefore, be able to build on prior findings in translation theory and research.

The general conclusion receives pragmatic support from the fact that sign language interpreting is widespread. Large numbers of adult deaf persons rely on manual systems of communication and need interpreters to render the spoken language into signs and vice versa. Such services have traditionally been rendered on a volunteer basis by persons whose parents were deaf or who learned sign language from professional contact with deaf persons. In the past decade there has been a concerted effort to professionalize interpreter services for the deaf. In 1964 a registry of interpreters for the deaf was organized (Quigley, 1965). Its constitution calls for publication of a registry of persons qualified to serve as interpreters and the development of standards of certification. Examination and certification procedures were implemented at a national evaluation workshop held in Memphis,

---

2. This issue is treated at more length in Bellugi (1974); Tweney, Hoemann, and Andrews (1975); and Tweney, Heiman, and Hoemann (in preparation).

Tennessee in 1972. Persons seeking certification are now required to take an examination in expressive translating (verbatim signing of an English presentation), or in expressive interpreting (freely rendering an English presentation in colloquial sign language with freedom to paraphrase), or in reverse interpreting (rendering a colloquial sign language presentation into spoken English). An examination in comprehensive interpreting skills (translating, interpreting, and reverse interpreting) is also available. Professional training for interpreters is available at several educational institutions in the United States. It is interesting to note that professional training for interpreters has been available in the USSR for many years (Godin, 1967).

Interpreting from one sign language to another is infrequent but is manifested at international conferences, such as the annual meetings of the World Federation of the Deaf. In international dealings some unusual circumstances can occur. A perhaps apocryphal story concerns a noted American educator of the deaf who wished to converse with a French colleague. A deaf person served as the educator's interpreter by speech-reading French and translating into sign, and by translating the educator's signs into spoken French!

Translations intended to be relatively permanent (as distinguished from the immediate and ephemeral interpretation of conversation) are beginning to emerge for sign languages. Literary works, particularly drama and poetry, are being translated into sign language in several centers. Particularly notable are the efforts of the National Theater of the Deaf in New York City and the efforts of the Drama Department of Gallaudet College, which has been in existence since 1892 (Newman, 1971). Although most of the translation has been from spoken language to sign, original dramatic works scripted in sign language have appeared. Most notable is Gilbert Eastman's *Sign me Alice* (1974), which has been translated into an annotated, glossed version of written English.

Translation of dramatic works has revealed the same difficulties that are well known in spoken translation. As Jakobson (1959) has indicated, the lack of grammatical correspondence between one language and another does not prevent translation (although unit-by-unit equivalence may not be possible). But if particular grammatical categories (genders, say) carry semantic impact in one language, then translation may not be possible: "Only creative transposition is possible" (Jakobson, 1959, p. 238). This difficulty may be especially characteristic of sign-to-spoken translation. George Detmold, in the introduction to the English translation of Eastman's play, indicated that "the play makes clear sense as an English script; but the thousand little jokes, puns, and word-plays are missing, as well as the lyric beauty of some passages, if the play is read simply as English" (Eastman, 1974, p. vii).

Sign languages possess limitless possibilities for the expression of emphasis and emotion, perhaps to a greater degree than for spoken languages. Thus body movements, elements of dance, and facial expressions can be combined with a signed message in a way not possible in most spoken languages. Further, the articulation of particular signs can be extended over longer or shorter distances, stretched out or shortened temporally, or delivered simultaneously with other messages. The use of such mechanisms in sign can be seen not only in drama but in the modern dance performances of Gallaudet College students and in signed hymns in religious services for the deaf. Formal, group signing of a hymn lacks acoustic melody, but substitutes expressiveness and beauty of an entirely different sort.

All interpretation and translation activity involving sign language suffers from a fundamental practical problem: no true dictionaries or grammars exist for any sign language. The importance of this factor is suggested in the following comment by Bates:

> Translators may be divided into four kinds: those who neither use nor need dictionaries; those who need them and use them; those who need them but don't use them; those who would like them but have to do the best they can without.
>
> (1936, p. 99)

All sign language translators are, of necessity, in the fourth category. The importance of the problem is suggested by the late historical appearance of adequate translations of Greek and Latin works into English (Amos, 1920). Until appropriate dictionary materials were available, nearly all translations left a good deal to be desired (see Tytler, 1791, for an early consideration of some of the problems). Dictionaries do not, of course, provide more than word-level translation, and so capture only one level of meaning (Nida, 1964). Nevertheless, they can provide a translator with helpful guides to the rendering of passages at all stages of translation, and are especially helpful when the translator is himself not a native user of both of the languages. The relation of dictionaries to translation activity is reciprocal – just as dictionaries assist in translation, the knowledge gained by translators is important and useful in the preparation of dictionaries. In fact, the basis of modern dictionaries can be found in Renaissance times when interlinear glosses of classical texts were common (Amos, 1920). It was then a short step to the preparation of lists of frequently used terms from the gloss (Starnes & Noyes, 1946).

A number of bilingual sign language-English dictionaries have been produced in recent years (as well as dictionaries in other languages – see Bornstein and Hamilton, 1972), and are, of course, helpful in translating. They are not true dictionaries, because all relate a sign to its closest English equivalent. Multiplicity of meaning is rarely indicated, and the total number of signs indexed is still very small. Stokoe, Casterline, and Croneberg (1965) have provided the most extensive and the most widely used such dictionary, a work which is currently under revision. Signs are described using a cheremic notational system, supplemented with articulation notes and photographs. Some hints on usage are provided. Signs are grouped on the basis of the locus of execution. The listing within each tab group is alphabetical in the sense that entries for particular signs are arranged in an order based in part on the closest finger-spelled letter that is equivalent to some part of the sign. Thus if a sign is formed with an extended index finger, it is listed under G, because the finger-spelled letter G is similarly formed. This method of organization is external to sign language as such, although it makes the dictionary more useable for beginning signers who already know a spoken language.

Can true sign language dictionaries be created? In theory, there is nothing to prevent this, but substantial practical difficulties exist. Film or video tape is the obvious medium, but would clearly be an awkward way to record entries. Imagine the difficulty of using a tape-recorded dictionary of a spoken language! What is called for, obviously, is a notational system that permits the rapid and clear recording of sign language utterances. No such conventionalized and accepted notational system is in existence, although attempts to create one have been made (with only limited success).

Bébian (1825) developed a system of conventionalized symbols to represent hand shapes, body parts, movements, and "Points physionomiques" to indicate different methods or styles of articulation. The system was able to represent most sign language gestures in written form, but it suffered from the intrinsic limitation that the dimensions chosen for written representation were not motivated by linguistic considerations. The approach of Stokoe, Casterline, and Croneberg (1965) is far superior in this regard because it used dimensions that do have linguistic importance. This does not, of course, completely describe any one sign, but it does allow all of the critical aspects to be captured – the rest is allocheric variation and need not be represented. (Of course, this assumes the descriptive adequacy of the system – a point which has been challenged earlier.)

All notational systems suffer from a lack of clear representation of the dynamic characteristics of signs. This is true even for those systems that have relied on pictorial representation of signs. Thus Fant's (1972) introductory text used photographs of signs. Hoemann and Hoemann (1973) used line drawings in a set of flash cards for student use. Klima and Bellugi (1972) attempted to capture some of the dynamic aspects of signing by using multiple-exposure photographs. None of the systems of representing signs is completely adequate, however. All require extensive verbal descriptions of each sign to supplement the visual, pictorial representations. Although one picture may be worth a thousand *words,* one *sign* may need a thousand pictures!

An interesting notational problem emerges when English glosses of signed messages are prepared. There is, of course, the expected difficulty arising from the lack of single word equivalents for particular signs – a difficulty found in preparing glosses for any language. In addition, most ASL useage in the United States involves varying amounts of interpenetration from English. Thus, as a result of classroom instruction, deaf individuals are able to rely on finger-spelled English words to supplement lexical deficiencies in ASL. This is especially necessary when technical matters are being discussed; ASL lacks technical vocabulary, and makes up for it by finger-spelling (or in some cases, by pantomime). Such variation needs to be clearly represented in the preparation of textual glosses.

A particular research tool that relies heavily on translation has been utilized to shed light on the nature of sign language. The method, known as back translation (Brislin, 1970; Werner and Campbell, 1970), uses two bilingual translators and a text in a source language (SL) which is to be translated into a target language (TL). One translator prepares an initial

TL version of the SL text. The other translator then retranslates the TL version into the SL. The two SL versions can be compared, and the differences taken into account in the preparation of a new TL version. The cycle (SL to TL to SL) can be repeated until both SL versions are equivalent. The procedure provides evidence for the adequacy of translations of the TL version and an operational method for achieving an adequate translation of any text. Furthermore, inspection of the kinds of SL constructions that are difficult to translate can be used to formulate recommendations for the preparation of easily translated text (Sinaiko & Brislin, 1973).

Back-translation procedures can also be useful for investigating the properties of particular languages, because they provide a means of evaluating the extent to which meaning is preserved in translation and the strategies by which meaning is encoded. Two studies have been reported in which back translation procedures were applied to the investigation of the properties of ASL. In the first (Tweney & Hoemann, 1973), lists of complex English sentences were presented to adult deaf subjects who were required to generate an ASL version for each sentence. The videotaped ASL statements were presented to another set of subjects who were required to prepare English-language versions. The meaning of the original sentences was preserved in 63 percent of the observations. The original grammatical structure remained unchanged in only 27 percent of the back translations, however. The results tentatively suggest that ASL may serve as an adequate system for encoding the meaning of a variety of English sentence types even when complex grammatical constructions with no ASL counterparts are involved.

The second study introduced modifications in the back-translation procedure (Hoemann & Tweney, 1973). The target-language version was prepared by a hearing informant who had learned ASL as a first language from deaf parents. The informant was instructed to use colloquial ASL and to avoid literal translations of the English original. Finger spelling was prohibited. Relatively long English texts of 150 to 200 words were used to ensure presence of a meaningful context. Videotaped ASL translations were shown to adult bilingual subjects, who were instructed to write down in English the gist of the text. Because memory for details was not of primary interest, subjects were allowed to view the tape as many times as they desired and to make changes in their translations after each viewing. The results of the second study clearly showed that ASL was an adequate linguistic medium for transmitting many kinds of complex information. The meaning losses that did occur were in all cases either trivial details or obvious from the context.

Whether ASL is equally able to encode technical prose for which specialized vocabulary may be lacking remains a question for further research. A ban on finger spelling for such material may prove to be inappropriate. Thus translators in a back-translation experiment involving English and Vietnamese often left a technical English word intact or transliterated the word using Vietnamese characters (Sinaiko & Brislin, 1973). Finger spelling is the only comparable strategy available to translators working in a sign language.

At the present time the body of data from back translation of sign language is relatively small; however, additional applications of back-translation procedures to the study of sign languages offer numerous possibilities for further research. It is interesting that translation may help elucidate the nature of sign language. It is hoped that the results will, in turn, aid translation efforts.

Conclusion Sign languages have only recently become the object of scientific research. This chapter has, as a result, ranged fairly widely to represent the work that has been done. For the same reason, we have attempted to point out some areas in which more research appears to be needed. At present, very little can be said with certainty about the specific translation problems encountered in dealing with sign languages. Much of what we have presented amounts to common wisdom rather than demonstrated fact. Nevertheless, two conclusions are, we feel, particularly clear: (1) sign languages, insofar as they possess the functional properties of language in general, present no inherently unsolvable problems for translation theory, and (2) sign languages do have unique properties that must be taken into account in translation activity. Future work must delineate the phenomena that fall under each heading. Translation of sign languages, like translation in general, can be completely effective only when it is based on linguistic and psycholinguistic knowledge concerning each language involved.

References

Amos, Flora Ross. *Early theories of translation.* New York: Columbia University Press, 1920.

Bailey, Charles-James N. The patterning of language variation. In Richard W. Bailey and Jay L. Robinson, Eds. *Varieties of present-day English.* New York: Macmillan, 1973, pp. 156–186.

Barakat, Robert A. Gesture systems. *Keystone Folklore Quarterly,* 1969, *14,* 105–121.

Barik, Henri C. Simultaneous interpretation: temporal and quantitative data. *Language and Speech,* 1973, *16,* 237–270.

Bates, E. Stuart. *Modern translation.* London: Oxford University Press, 1936.

Bébian, R.A. *Mimographie, ou essai d'écriture mimique, proprea regulariser le language des sourds-muets.* Paris: Louis Colas, 1825.

Bellugi, Ursula. Some aspects of language acquisition. In Thomas A. Sebeok, Ed. *Current trends in linguistics: Volume 12, Linguistics and adjacent arts and science.* The Hague: Mouton, 1974, pp. 1135–1158.

Bellugi, Ursula; Klima, Edward S. and Siple, Patricia. Remembering in Signs. *Cognition: International Journal of Cognitive Psychology,* 1975 (In press).

Bender, Ruth E. *The conquest of deafness: A history of the long struggle to make possible normal living to those handicapped by lack of normal hearing.* Revised Edition. Cleveland: Case Western Reserve University Press, 1970.

Bode, Loreli. Communication of agent, object, and indirect object in signed and spoken languages. *Perceptual and Motor Skills,* 1974,39, 1151–1158.

Bonvillian, John D., Charrow, Veda, R., and Nelson, Keith E. Psycholinguistic and educational implications of deafness. *Human Development,* 1973, *16,* 321–345.

Bornstein, Harry. A description of some current sign system designed to represent English. *American Annals of the Deaf,* 1973, *118,* 454–463.

Bornstein, Harry, and Hamilton, Lillian B. Recent national dictionaries of signs. *Sign Language Studies,* 1972, *1,* 42–63.

Brislin, Richard W. Back-translation for cross-cultural research. *Journal of Cross-Cultural Psychology,* 1970, *1,* 185–216.

Ceccato, Silvio. *Linguistic analysis and programming for mechanical translation.* Milan: Giangiacomo Feltrinelli, Editore, Undated (1961). (Technical Report No. RADC-TR-60-18, United States Air Force).

Charrow, V.R., & Fletcher, J.D. English as the second language of deaf children. *Developmental Psychology,* 1974, *10,* 463–470.

Chomsky, Noam. *Syntactic structures.* The Hague: Mouton and Co., 1957. "Janua Linguarum, Series Minor, No. 4".

Clark, W.P. *The Indian Sign Language, with brief explanatory notes of the gestures taught deaf mutes in our institutions for their instruction …* Philadelphia: L. R. Hamersly & Co., 1885.

Eastman, Gilbert C. *Sign me Alice: A play in sign language.* Washington, D.C.: Gallaudet College Bookstore, 1974.

Fant, Louis J. *Ameslan: An introduction to American Sign Language.* Silver Springs, Md.: National Association of the Deaf, 1972.

Ferguson, Charles A. Diglossia. *Word,* 1959, *15,* 325–340.

Fodor, J.A., Bever, T.G., and Garrett, M.F. *The psychology of language: An introduction to psycholinguistics and generative grammar.* New York: McGraw-Hill, 1974.

Godin, Lev. Interpreters for the deaf in Russia. *American Annals of the Deaf,* 1967, *112,* 595–597.

Heiman, Gary W., and Tweney, Ryan D. The intelligibility of temporally interrupted American Sign Language as a function of linguistic organization. Paper presented at the 55th Annual Meeting of the Western Psychological Association, Sacramento, California, April 26, 1975.

Hoemann, Harry W. The development of communication skills in deaf and hearing children. *Child Development,* 1972, *43,* 990–1003.

Hoemann, H.W. The transparency of meaning of sign language gestures. *Sign Language Studies,* 1975, In press.

Hoemann, Harry W., and Hoemann, Shirley A. *Sign Language Flash Cards.* Silver Spring, Md.: National Association of the Deaf, 1973.

Hoemann, Harry W., and Tweney, Ryan D. Is the Sign Language of the deaf an adequate communicative channel? *Proceedings of the American Psychological Association,* 1973, 801–802.

Houston, Susan H. A sociolinguistic consideration of the Black English of children in northern Florida. *Language,* 1969, *45,* 599–607.

Jakobson, Roman. On linguistic aspects of translation. In Reuben A. Brower, Ed. *On translation.* Cambridge: Harvard University Press, 1959. Harvard Studies in Comparative Literature, pp. 232–239.

Jordan, I. King, Jr. A referential communication study of linguistically adult, deaf signers. Paper presented at the First Annual Sign Language Conference, Gallaudet College, Washington, D.C., April 27, 1974.

Klima, E.S., and Bellugi, U. The signs of language in child and chimpanzee. In T. Alloway, L. Krames, and P. Pliner, Eds. *Communication and affect: A comparative approach.* New York: Academic Press, 1972.

Kluge, F. Zur Geschichte der Zeichensprache. Angelsächsische indicia Monasterialia. *Internationale Zeitzschrift für Allgemeine Sprachwissen-schaft,* 1885, *2,* 116–137.

Labov, William. *Language in the inner city: Studies in the Black English vernacular.* Philadelphia: University of Pennsylvania Press, 1972 (a).

Labov, William. *Sociolinguistic patterns.* Philadelphia: University of Pennsylvania Press 1972 (b).

Mallery, Garrick. Sign language among North American Indians, compared with that among other peoples and deaf-mutes. In J. W. Powell, Ed. First Annual Report of the Bureau of American Ethnology, 1881, pp. 263–552. (Reprinted 1972, The Hague: Mouton & Co.).

McCall, Elizabeth A. A generative grammar of Sign. Unpublished Master's Thesis, Department of Speech Pathology and Audiology. University of Iowa, 1965.

Miller, George A. *Language and communication.* New York: McGraw-Hill, 1951.

Newman, Pat. Gallaudet on stage. *Hearing and Speech News,* 1971, 39(1), 12–15.

Nida, Eugene A. *Toward a science of translating.* Leiden: E. J. Brill, 1964.

Oléron, P. & Nanpon, H. Recherches sur la traduction simultanée. *Journal de Psychologie Normale et Pathologique,* 1965, 62, 73–94.

Quigley, Stephen P., Ed. *Interpreting for deaf people: A report of a workshop on interpreting.* Washington: U.S. Department of Health, Education, and Welfare, 1965.

Schlesinger, I.M. The grammar of Sign Language and the problems of language universals. In J. Morton, Ed. *Biological and social factors in psycholinguistics.* London: Logos Press, 1971.

Sinaiko, H. Wallace, and Brislin, Richard W. Evaluating language translations: Experiments on three assessment methods. *Journal of Applied Psychology,* 1973, 57, 328–334.

Starnes, DeWitt T., and Noyes, Gertrude E. *The English dictionary from Cawdrey to Johnson 1604–1755.* Chapel Hill, N.C.: The University of North Carolina Press, 1946.

Stevens, Kenneth N. Perception of phonetic segments: Evidence from phonology, acoustics, and psychoacoustics. In D. L. Horton and J. J. Jenkins, Eds. *Perception of Language.* Columbus, Ohio: Merrill Publishing Co., 1971.

Stokoe, William C, Jr. Sign Language structure, an outline of the visual communications systems of the American deaf. *Studies in Linguistics,* Occasional Paper #8, Buffalo, N.Y., 1960.

Stokoe, W. C, Jr. *Semiotics and human sign languages.* The Hague: Mouton, 1972.

Stokoe, William C, Jr. Classification and description of sign languages. In Thomas A. Sebeok, Ed. *Current trends in linguistics, Vol. 12: Linguistics and adjacent arts and sciences.* The Hague: Mouton, 1974, pp. 345–372.

Stokoe, William C, Jr., Casterline, Dorothy, and Croneberg, Carl. *A dictionary of American Sign Language.* Washington: Gallaudet College Press, 1965.

Tervoort, B.T. You me downtown movie fun? *Lingua,* 1968, 21, 455–465.

Tweney, Ryan D., Heiman, Gary W., and Hoemann, Harry W. Psychological processing of sign language: The functional role of syntactic and cheremic structure. In preparation.

Tweney, Ryan D. & Hoemann, Harry W. Back translation: A method for the analysis of manual languages. *Sign Language Studies,* 1973, 2, 51–80.

Tweney, Ryan D., Hoemann, Harry W., and Andrews, Carol E. Semantic organization in deaf and hearing subjects. *Journal of Psijcholinguistic Research,* 1975, 4, 61–73.

Tytler, Alexander Fraser (Lord Woodhouselee). *Essay on the principles of translation.* London: J. M. Dent & Co., no date (First published 1791).

Werner, Oswald, and Campbell, Donald T. Translating, working through interpreters, and the problem of decentering. In R. Naroll and R. Cohen, Eds. *A handbook of method in cultural anthropology.* Garden City, N.Y.: Natural History Press, 1970.

Winograd, Terry. Understanding natural language. *Cognitive Psychology,* 1972, 3, 1–191.

Woodward, James Clyde, Jr. A transformational approach to the syntax of American Sign Language. In William C. Stokoe, Jr. *Semiotics and human sign languages.* The Hague: Mouton, 1972.

Woodward, James C, Jr. Inter-rule implication in American Sign Language. *Sign Language Studies,* 1973, 3, 47–56.

Woodward, James C, Jr. A report on Montana-Washington implicational research. *Sign Language Studies,* 1974, 4, 77–101.

2.3   **Ingram, Robert. 1978. "Sign language interpretation and general theories on language, interpretation and communication." In** *Language Interpretation and Communication*, **ed. by David Gerver and H. Wallace Sinaiko, 109–118. New York: Plenum Press.**

Robert "Bob" Ingram, a child of deaf parents (Coda), was active in SLI in the 1970s and 1980s. Ingram wrote many articles about American Sign Language and SLI, was one of the first authors to promote linguistic research on SLI, and was active in international SLI. Ingram has an MA in linguistics and intercultural communication from Brown University in Providence, Rhode Island, and was enrolled in the Ph.D. program in linguistics at Brown when he wrote and published this paper on the communication model. When his model was published, SLI was just beginning to emerge as a full-time occupation and was often regarded as a sub-branch of deaf education and rehabilitation. In a later publication, he addresses the intercultural context of interpretation more explicitly, but the origins of that paradigm can be traced directly to this paper.

While a student at Brown, Ingram was the George C. Marshall Research Associate at the University of Copenhagen, Denmark, from 1976–1977, and with his wife Betty, edited the proceedings of *Hands Across the Sea,* the first international conference on SLI. An early proponent of terminology and attitudes that reflect equal consideration of the source language and the target language, Ingram was an instructor and curriculum specialist at Madonna College in Livonia, Michigan, in sign language and interpreting, and wrote several articles on teaching sign language interpreting. He was instrumental in promoting collaboration with spoken language interpreters, researcher and educators.

Sign language interpretation and general theories of language, interpretation and communication

Robert M. Ingram

The practice of interpretation of sign languages dates back many, many years, though the practice is just now struggling to achieve the status of a profession – shifting from a more-or-less clinical focus to a more-or-less linguistic one. Research on sign languages, which is itself very recent, has convincingly demonstrated that at least some sign languages are indeed languages in the linguistic sense, thereby forcing us to expand our conceptions of the nature of language and to re-examine our approaches to the study of language. Experiments on the simultaneous interpretation of sign languages are contributing to our knowledge and understanding of language and communication in general as well as to the resolution of problems dealing specifically with sign language interpretation. These are the major points that we have gained from the presentations by Domingue and Ingram, Tweney, and Murphy. The relevance of their discussions of sign language interpretation to the general subject areas of language, interpretation, and communication is largely self-evident. Essentially, we are all saying that the interpretation of sign languages is an integral part of the general study of interpretation and that no description (practical or theoretical) of interpretation which fails to take account of sign language interpretation can be regarded as complete. I have set myself the task of demonstrating this point beyond any doubt. The papers by Domingue and Ingram, Tweney, and Murphy have called attention to a number of problems in interpretation of sign languages. My approach will be to explore some of these problems further in relation to language, interpretation and communication in general.

Linguistic versus semiotic translation

In his opening remarks, Tweney alludes to Jakobson's (1959) distinction between linguistic translation and semiotic translation (or transmutation), and, in an earlier paper with Hoemann, he refers to sign languages as 'semiotic systems' (after Stokoe, 1972) and to sign language interpretation as a type of 'intersemiotic translation' (Tweney and Hoemann, 1976, p. 138). But when Jakobson speaks of semiotic translation, he is speaking of the translation of one non-linguistic code to another, such as the translation of painting to music, or of a linguistic code to a nonlinguistic code, as in the translation of a verse to a series of drawings. If we regard sign languages as 'the drawing of pictures in the air', then we might conclude that sign language interpretation does belong to Jakobson's category of semiotic translation. However, Tweney cites considerable evidence to support the conclusion that sign languages are not 'pictures in the air' but are, in fact, linguistic systems, thus establishing sign language interpretation under the category of linguistic translation rather than semiotic translation. What appears to be a dilemma here is, in fact, no different from the problem that we face in characterizing the interpretation of spoken languages. That sign languages are indeed languages in the linguistic sense is a point which has been well established. Lest there be any equivocation on this point, consider the conclusion of Klima and Bellugi (1976, p. 46).

"When we refer to sign languages as "languages", we mean that they have sentential units which have a strict semantic-propositional interpretation (providing among other things for the possibility of paraphrase); that they also have a hierarchically organized syntax – open-ended in terms of possible messages – and furthermore, that at the formational level of the individual lexical units (the individual signs) as well as the syntactic level, there are specific constraints as to well-formedness. What is more, there is a definite sense among those with a sign language as a native language (for example, the offspring, deaf and hearing, of deaf parents – offspring who learned sign language as their first language) that the sign decidedly has a citation form – a form which exists out of any specific real-life context. That is, the sign is not situation-bound as are some affective units of communication. (We presume, for example, that a scream does not have a citation form in this sense; nor presumably would an element of free pantomime). Thus, an ASL sign as such is no more bound to a particular context than is a word of spoken language."

Given this view of sign languages as linguistic systems, we can only conclude that sign languages belong with spoken languages within the category which Jakobson calls linguistic translation.

There is, on the other hand, a sense in which sign language interpretation can be regarded as semiotic, but that is a sense in which all simultaneous interpretation – indeed all use of language – is semiotic. Rather than establishing language in opposition to other semiotic systems, Jakobson (1975) has more recently argued for a view of language as a type of semiotic system, a position also taken by Eco (1976). From this perspective, we see linguistic translation, including the simultaneous interpretation of sign languages as well as of spoken languages, not as distinct from semiotic translation but as a subset of the more general category of semiotic translation.

Limitations to a linguistic point of view

Recent findings about sign languages are but one entry in a growing list of factors pointing to the inadequacy of contemporary linguistics to describe human languages. Says one prominent anthropological linguist (Hymes, 1973, p. 60): 'Thus, one of the problems to be overcome with regard to language is the linguist's usual conception of it. A broader, differently based notion of the form in which we encounter and use language in the world ... is needed.' To Hymes, this broader view is represented by the term 'ways of speaking', or 'the ethnography of communication'. To others, the answer lies in the study of speech acts, ethnomethodology, or the intersection of linguistics with other disciplines, e.g. sociolinguistics, psycholinguistics, or neurolinguistics. Semiotics incorporates contributions from all of these approaches and others besides and, in my view, represents the most productive platform from which to study language in general and simultaneous interpretation in particular.

Seleskovitch (1976) takes a similar view of the insufficiency of linguistics to describe simultaneous interpretation. Interpretation, she says (1976, p. 94), is so unconcerned with language (as a linguistic system) that it denies words or sentences any claim to translatability as long as they fail to merge into a meaningful whole: the discourse'. Compare this statement with the following one by a leading semiotician (Eco, 1976, p. 57): 'I am saying that usually a single sign-vehicle conveys many intertwined contents and therefore what is commonly called a "message" is in fact a *text* whose content is a multilevelled *discourse*.' Referring to the work of another semiotician (Metz, 1970) Eco (1976, p. 57) claims that 'in every case of communication (except maybe some rare cases of a very elementary and univocal type) we are not dealing with a message but with a text' and he defines a text as 'the result of the co-existence of many codes (or, at least, of many subcodes)'. Now, again, compare Seleskovitch (1976, p. 99):

"An interpreter receiving a speech never receives linguistic units entirely devoid of context (verbal and situational) but rather receives utterances spoken by a person whose position, nationality, and interests are known to him, speaking with a purpose in mind, trying to convince his listeners. Thus an utterance bearing a message differs absolutely from a sequence of words chosen at random, for the former evokes not only their intrinsic linguistic meaning but facts known to all those for whom the message is intended".

What Seleskovitch is saying, in essence, is that the interpreter must decode, transfer, and re-encode not single, linguistic messages and codes at a time but a multiplicity of messages in a multiplicity of interwoven codes with every single act of interpretation.

Treatments of interpretation in general tend to play down the significance of all codes except the linguistic ones, but interpreters of sign languages cannot afford this luxury. We have to interpret every act of communication – intentional or unintentional, human or non-human – that a receptor would normally perceive except for his hearing loss. For example, if a telephone rings during the course of an interview, that ringing must be interpreted. When static comes through the sound system in a conference room, interpreters of spoken language try to ignore the noise, but interpreters of sign languages have to interpret that noise. We interpret airplane noises, sneezes, falling chairs; anything and everything that the receptor would otherwise perceive if he were not deaf. The reverse principle applies as well. If the deaf person signs haltingly, our spoken rendition is halting. Paralinguistic manipulations of the hands, face, and body are interpreted as speech suprasegmentals. We do not filter out ambiguities, either in content or form. Rather, we try to match those ambiguities as best we can in the corresponding codes of the receptor. The primary codes with which we deal are linguistic codes, but we are also concerned to a considerable extent with non-linguistic codes, and, in this sense, sign language interpretation serves to remind us that only a semiotic view of interpretation can be sufficient to describe this complex process.

Possible contributions of linguistics

A major problem we face in sign language interpretation is the lack of data to describe the linguistic codes, i.e. the sign languages, we use. Of course, there have been linguistic studies of American Sign Language (ASL), much of which has been reviewed by Tweney in his paper, and there have also been studies of the sign languages of Denmark (Hansen, 1975; Lieth, 1976; Sorensen and Hansen, 1976), Sweden (Ahlgren, 1976; Bergman, 1976), Israel (Schlesinger, 1969), Japan (Tanokani et al., 1976), the South Sea island of Rennel (Kuschel, 1974), and elsewhere. Still, what we know of the linguistic structures of various sign languages, including ASL, is very meagre and very tentative.

A central issue in second language teaching concerns whether one should teach about the language or simply teach the language. With sign languages, unless we know about the language, we cannot at all be certain that we know the language. Sign languages have for so long been regarded as mere surrogates of speech, as noted by Murphy, that interpretations of sign languages all too often appear as transliterations rather than as interpretations. Not until we have adequate linguistic descriptions of sign languages will we be able to deal with this problem effectively. We need descriptions that will tell us not only how a given sign language differs from a given spoken language, e.g. how ASL differs from English, but also how various sign languages differ from one another. In recent years, we have seen a new kind of interpretation developing at international conferences – interpretation from one sign language to another, with or without the use of an intervening spoken language. Personally, I suspect that these sign-to-sign renderings are more like glossings than like interpretations, but we cannot be sure of this assumption, nor can we correct it if it proves to be true, so long as we lack accurate linguistic data.

There is another way that linguistics can help us, and that is in the development of approaches to the teaching of sign languages. In the United States alone, thousands of persons receive education in some form of American Sign Language every year. Yet, few, if any, of these courses are based on viable principles of linguistics or second-language learning (Ingram, 1977). It is possible to pursue a Bachelors degree with a major in sign language interpretation, but it is not possible to get a major in sign language per se. We pretend to offer training in the interpretation of sign languages, while at the same time we admit that we do not know enough about the sign languages involved and about methods of teaching those languages. 'The learning of a natural sign language ... requires not only the acquisition of new lexical items in new syntactic structures in a new frame of (semantic) reference but also the adjustment to perceiving language through the eyes rather than through the ears and to producing language through the manipulation of the hands, face, and upper body rather than through the vocal apparatus' (Ingram, 1977, p. 29). Exactly how this adjustment can best be effected is a task for psycholinguists and learning theorists. Brault (1963) has argued that the teaching of cultural gestures should be an integral part of second-language teaching, but by what methods should these gestures be taught? Perhaps studies of the leaching of sign languages can provide answers to this question. And what part do these gestures play in the interpretation of spoken languages? Here again, perhaps studies of sign language interpretation can provide the answers.

Deafness as a cultural distinction

In the study of sign language interpretation, we must combat the assumption that sign languages are not only grammatical surrogates of spoken languages, but also that they overlap spoken languages semantically. Eco (1976) defines meanings as 'cultural units', and a number of researchers (Boese, 1964; Lieth, 1977; Meadow, 1972; Padden and Markowicz, 1976; Reich and Reich, 1974; Schein, 1968; Schlesinger and Meadow, 1972; Vernon and Makowsky, 1969) have clearly established that deaf people constitute at least a subculture if not a separate culture. The emerging attitude among sign language interpreters, as discussed by Domingue and Ingram, is that sign languages are distinct forms of representing cultural experiences that are peculiar to deaf people. In other words, deafness is, for the interpreter at least, not a clinical condition but a cultural one. If, as Tweney says, meanings 'are mapped onto words in different languages in different configurations' and if there is no one-to-one correspondence of these mappings, then how do the cultural meanings of deaf persons (as reflected in their sign languages) differ from the cultural meanings of the hearing cultures around them? Here we have a challenge for ethnographic semanticists.

Sign language as a source language

Among interpreters of spoken languages it is considered axiomatic that one can interpret more easily into one's own native language than into a second or later-learned language. This axiom, however, does not hold true in the interpretation of sign languages. If it did, then we would expect to find that interpretation from a sign language into a spoken language would be easier for persons who have acquired a sign language as a second language, but what we find, in fact, is that almost all interpreters regard interpretation into the spoken language as more difficult than interpretation into the sign language. In a few rare cases, an interpreter will report that it is easier for him to interpret from the sign language into the spoken language, but these persons are invariably children of deaf parents who have acquired their sign language before they acquired a spoken language – a situation revealing the opposite of what we would normally expect in interpretation. Why should interpretation from a sign language to a spoken language be considered a more difficult process than interpretation from a spoken language to a sign language?

In the first place, that interpreters regard interpretation from a spoken language to a sign language as an easier task is no assurance that that process is more effective in terms of communication than the reverse process. A sign language output may seem easier to facilitate than a spoken language output simply because the former is easier to fake. The interpreter can always shift into a sign language form that is easier for him, but not necessarily more comprehensible to the deaf person receiving the message. Unfortunately, deaf persons receiving such interpretations frequently just shrug, 'Oh, well, he (the interpreter) signs like a hearing person', and let it go at that. A spoken language output, though, is not so easy to fake; its flaws become readily apparent to the hearing receptor, and the interpreter's only recourse is to complain that interpretation from a sign language to a spoken language is a more difficult task.

But suppose we give the interpreters the benefit of the doubt and assume that there is, in fact, a viable reason why interpretation should be more difficult when the source language is a sign language. What might this reason be? One possible reason might be the very high incidence in sign languages of what Eco (1976) calls *undercoding,* which he defines as 'the operation by means of which in the absence of reliable pre-established rules, certain macroscopic portions of certain texts are provisionally assumed to be pertinent units of a code in formation, even though the combinational rules governing the more basic compositional items of the expressions, along with the corresponding content-units, remain unknown' (pp. 135–36). In other words, 'undercoding is an assumption that signs are pertinent units of a code in absence of any pre-established rules, that is, it is an imprecise, and still rough coding' (Sherzer, 1977, p. 81). This is not to say that sign languages are, in general, imprecise and rough codes. Rather, what I am saying is that sign languages may frequently become imprecise in those moments when their users attempt to expand them beyond their current limits. Murphy has reported about the suppression of sign languages that has existed throughout the ages. But now deaf people are beginning to share in events and experiences that were once closed to them, and they are finding their sign languages much too inadequate to represent these new experiences. They are constantly borrowing new lexical items in the form of fingerspelled words and initialized signs, and they are developing their own new signs. When this linquistic creativity takes place across a single deaf culture, there is the opportunity for cultural criticism and standardization, but many signs developed at a given moment to express a given concept fall by the wayside as nonce signs, perhaps never to appear again. It is these signs which constitute the bulk of the undercoding in a sign language and which present perhaps the greatest difficulty in interpreting from a sign language to a spoken language. The problem of under-coding is particularly strong in sign languages, but it is not a problem that is restricted to sign languages. I suspect that the same phenomenon exists in the languages of all cultures that are undergoing technological development or languages that are struggling to break free of suppression. No, the problem is not unique to sign languages, but, here again, we see a problem that should be of concern to all of us most clearly represented in sign languages.

In sign languages, we also find a kind of *overcoding,* meaning that there 'is either an over-analysis from within the system, or a mis-analysis from outside the system' (Sherzer, 1977, p. 81). Sign languages code in ways quite different from spoken languages, as Tweney has demonstrated, not just in that they symbolize meanings through the manipulation of the hands but also in their extensive use of the face and upper body to signal grammatical functions. Fischer (1975) has shown that certain word orders can be deemed grammatical, ungrammatical, or anomalous by the raising of an eyebrow or the tilting of the head ever so slightly. Pro-nominalization takes place through the manipulation of space rather that through the ordering of lexical items (Friedman, 1975). These overcoded linguistic rules are known subconsciously to every native user of a sign language, but where many interpreters falter is in determining how a lift of an eyebrow or a twitch of a shoulder is to be expressed in a vocal interpretation.

Characteristics of sign language interpreters

As anyone who has ever attempted to work with interpreters (of spoken languages or sign languages) knows, we are a strange breed. Schein (1974) attempted to find out just how strange we really are. He administered the Edwards Personality Preference Schedule to 34 interpreters in three Northeastern United States cities. Analyzing the scores of the 20 interpreters who completed the tests, Schein concluded that the successful interpreter 'desires to be the center of attention and to be independent, is not overly anxious, does not seek sympathy for self, and is not rigid' (Schein, 1974, p. 42). Anderson (1976) discusses the interpreter and his role in terms of (1) the interpreter as bilingual, (2) ambiguities and conflicts, and (3) power. Each of these topics is applicable to the study of sign language interpreters.

Children of deaf parents usually learn their sign language before they acquire a spoken language (Cicourel, 1973; Cicourel and Boese, 1972; Klima and Bellugi, 1976; Mindel and Vernon, 1971; Schlesinger and Meadow, 1972). The sign language should, therefore, be the child's dominant language. But, societal pressures being what they are, it is likely that the spoken language eventually becomes established as the dominant language, at least most of the time. This reversal of dominant languages might help to explain why interpreters, even those for whom a sign language is their first language, consider interpretation from a sign language to be a more difficult task than interpretation into a sign language.

Anderson also observes that 'in general, it is expected that the greater the linguistic dominance the more likely an interpreter will identify with the speakers of the dominant language, rather than with clients speaking his "other" language' (1976, p. 213). Certainly, the problem of client identification is a major one for sign language interpreters, as we have heard from Domingue and Ingram. Some interpreters tend to identify with their signing clients in a paternalistic way; they feel they have to take a dominant role in 'straightening out' the deaf person. Some other interpreters tend to be maternalistic, to try to speak for the deaf person when he is perfectly capable of handling his own affairs. Clearly, the best interpreter and the one who is, in the long run, the most effective is the one who remains neutral in his role between two communicators.

The interpreter, whether of sign languages or spoken languages, is unquestionably a person in a position of power. Some children of deaf parents in particular, and some other people as well, become interpreters for this very reason. The child of deaf parents, says Lieth (1976, p. 318), 'is in an exceptional position; he will usually have sign language as his maternal language, but at the same time he will have to form a link to the hearing world; this gives him a special position within the family which may later cause him difficulties in adjusting himself to social situations where he has neither the responsibility nor the power he used to have in his home'. Rather than give up that power, many of these children of deaf parents assume the role of interpreter for other deaf people, a role which allows them to continue to exert power and influence.

Sociological and social psychological studies of interpreters and their roles are greatly needed to help us understand why people become interpreters and how they behave as interpreters. The added factor of deafness makes this line of inquiry all the more interesting, but the basic questions are essentially the same as those raised by the interpretation of spoken language.

Neurolinguistic and psycholinguistic studies

There are many more ways in which the relevance of sign language interpretation to the general areas of language, interpretation, and communication can be demonstrated. Not the least of these are the intriguing mechanisms by which the brain is able to process two languages simultaneously, particularly where one of those languages is perceived visually rather than auditorily. Kimura (1976) cites the five known cases of deaf aphasics, and other neurological evidence, to support her claim that 'the left parietal region is an important part of a system controlling certain motor sequences, both vocal and manual', and that 'the symbolic-language functions of the left hemisphere are assumed to be a secondary consequence of specialization for motor function' (1976, p. 154). The implications here for a theory of simultaneous interpretation are significant indeed, but just how that significance can be applied must await further evidence.

Conclusion

I believe I have made my point. Just as no theory of language is complete unless it accounts for the total linguistic competence of human beings, i.e. the ability of people to acquire and use language in *all* its forms, likewise no theory of interpretation is complete unless it accounts for interpretation of language in all forms. A theory of interpretation based solely on languages which are orally produced and aurally perceived is an incomplete theory. Research into interpretation of sign language serves two main purposes: (1) to develop models and explanations that will contribute to the practice of sign language interpretation, and (2) to develop models and explanations that will contribute to our general understanding of the nature of language and communication. Certainly, there is value in asking 'What can research contribute to the theory and practice of sign language interpretation?' but there is perhaps even greater value in asking 'What can research on sign language interpretation contribute to general theories of language, interpretation, and communication?' or, to put it another way, 'How can the general study of language, interpretation, and communication be advanced by the application of data from research on sign language interpretation?' I hope that some of the answers I have tried to provide to this question will stimulate collaborative research.

References

Ahlgren, I. *Rapport om planering och förarbete i projektet 'Tidig Sprdklig Kognitiv Utveckling Hos Döva och Gravt Hörselskadade' (Forsikning om Teckenspråk I).* Stockholm: Stockholms Universitet, 1976.

Anderson, R.B.W. Perspectives on the role of interpreter, in R. W. Brislin (Ed.). *Translation: Applications and Research,* New York: Gardner Press, 1976.

Bergman, B. *Teckenspråkets lingvistiska status: Rapport Nr. V (So-projekt LiS 237).* Stockholm: Stockholms Universitet, 1976.

Boese, R.J. *Differentiations in the deaf community.* Unpublished study submitted to the Department of Sociology, University of British Columbia, 1964.

Brault, G.J. Kinesics in the classroom: Some typical French gestures. *French Review,* 1963, 374–382.

Cicourel, A. *Cognitive Sociology.* Harmondsworth: Penguin Books, 1973.

Cicourel, A., and Boese, R. The acquisition of manual sign language and generative semantics. *Semiotica,* 1972, 3, 225–56.

Eco, U. *A Theory of Semiotics.* Bloomington: Indiana University Press, 1976.

Fischer, S. Influence on word order change in American Sign Language, in C. Li (Ed.). *Word Order and Word Order Change,* Austin: University of Texas Press, 1975.

Friedman, L.A. Space, time and person reference in American Sign Language. *Language,* 1975, *51:* 4, 940–61.

Hansen, B. Varieties in Danish Sign Language and grammatical features of the Original Sign Language. *Sign Language Studies,* 1975, 8, 249–56.

Hymes, D. On the origins and foundations of inequality among speakers. *Daedalus,* 1973, *102: 3,* 59–86.

Ingram, R.M. *Principles and Procedures of Teaching Sign Languages.* Carlisle: British Deaf Association, 1977.

Jakobson, R. On Linguistic aspects of translation, in R. A. Brower (Ed.). *On Translation,* Cambridge: Harvard University Press, 1959.

Jakobson, R. *Coup d'Oeil sur le Développement de la Sémiotique. (Studies in Semiotics, 3).* Bloomington: Indiana University Press, 1975.

Kimura, D. The neural basis of language qua gesture, in H. Whitaker and H. A. Whitaker, (Eds.). *Studies in Neurolinguistics, 2 (Perspectives in Neurolinguistics and Psycholinguistics),* New York: Academic Press, 1976.

Klima, E.S., and Bellugi, U. Poetry and song in a language without sound. *Cognition,* 1976, *4,* 45–97.

Kuschel, R. *Lexicon of Signs from a Polynesian Outlier Island (Psykologisk Skriftserie Nr. 8).* Kobenhavn: Kobenhavns Universitet, 1974.

Lieth, L. v. d. *Dansk Dove-tegnsprog.* Kobenhavn: Akademisk Forlag, 1976.

Lieth, L. v. d. The use of deaf sign language, in F. B. Crammatte and A. B. Crammatte (Eds). *Proceedings of the VIIth World Congress of the World Federation of the Deaf.* 1976.

Lieth, L. v.d. *Dov i Dag 3.* Kobenhavn: Danske Doves Landsforbund, 1977.

Meadow, K.P. Sociolinguistics, sign language and the deaf sub-culture, in T. J. O'Rourke (Ed.). *Psycholinguistics and Total Communication: The State of the Art.* Washington, D.C.: American Annals of the Deaf, 1972.

Metz, C. *Language et Cinéma,* Paris: Larousse, 1970.

Mindel, E., and Vernon, M. Psychological and psychiatric aspects of profound hearing loss, in D. E. Rose (Ed.). *Audiological Assessment,* Englewood Cliffs, N.J.: Prentice Hall, 1971.

Padden, C. and Markowicz, H. Cultural conflicts between hearing and deaf communities, in F. B. Crammatte and A. B. Crammatte (Eds.). *Proceedings of the VIIth World Congress of the World Federation of the Deaf.* 1976.

Reich, P.A., and Reich, C.M. *A follow-up study of the deaf.* Toronto: Research Service, Board of Education, No. 120, 1974.

Schein, J. *The Deaf Community: Studies in the Social Psychology of Deafness.* Washington, D.C.: Gallaudet College Press, 1968.

Schein, J. Personality characteristics associated with interpreter proficiency. *Journal of the Rehabilitation of the Deaf,* 1974, 7; *3,* 33–43.

Schlesinger, H.S., and Meadow, K.P. *Sound and Sign: Childhood Deafness and Mental Health,* Berkeley: University of California Press, 1972.

Schlesinger, I.M. *The grammar of sign language and the problem of language universals.* Hebrew University and Israel Institute of Applied Social Research (mimeo), 1969.

Seleskovitch, D. Interpretation, a psychological approach to translating, in R. W. Brislin (Ed.). *Translation: Applications and Research,* New York: Gardner Press, 1976.

Sherzer, D. Review of a Theory of Semiotics, by U. Eco, and Coup d'Oeil sur le Développement de la Sémiotique, by R. Jacobson. *Language in Society,* 1977, 6: *1,* 78–82.

Stokoe, W.C. *Semiotics and Human Sign Languages.* The Hague: Mouton, 1972.

Sorensen, R.K., and Hansen, B. *Tegnsprog: En Undersogelse af 44 Dove Borns Tegnsprogskommunikation.* Kobenhavn: Statens Skole for Dove, 1976.

Tanokami, T. *et. al. On the Nature of Sign Language.* Hiroshima: Bunka Hyoron Publishing Co., 1976.

Tweney, R., and Hoemann, H. Translation and sign languages, in R. W. Brislin (Ed.). *Translation: Applications and Research,* New York: Gardner Press, 1976.

Vernon, M., and Makowsky, B. Deafness and minority group dynamics. *The Deaf American,* 1969, *21,* 3–6.

2.4   Murphy, Harry. 1978. "Research in sign language interpreting at California State University Northridge." In *Language Interpretation and Communication,* ed. by David Gerver and H. Wallace Sinaiko, 87–97. New York: Plenum Press.

After becoming a teacher of the deaf, Murphy won a national scholarship to go to California State University at Northridge (CSUN) for a master's in administration and supervision, and later earned an Ed.D. as well. From 1972–1979, Murphy was assistant director for the National Center on Deafness, where he conducted research on topics associated with deaf students and their progress through a university education. He also wrote grants for student services, interpreting services, telecommunication training programs, and other services. In 1983 he moved to the CSUN office that handled all disabilities except deafness and began to get involved in technology. He remained at CSUN his entire career.

Research in sign language interpreting at California State University, Northridge

Harry J. Murphy

Introduction

The nature of communication through the use of sign language is of growing interest to educators, psychologists, and linguists. For example:

1. in California, Nevada, and Oklahoma, psychologists are exploring the ways and means by which primates communicate with each other, and with humans, after they have been taught sign language;
2. in Washington, D.C., and La Jolla, California, linguists are in the process of describing the grammar of a unique language, American Sign Language;
3. at California State University, Northridge (CSUN) the use of a sign language interpreter in regular classes offers an exciting alternative model of educating deaf college students.

Still, not much is known about sign language or a particular use of it which we call interpreting. One reason for the relative lack of knowledge is that the use of sign language has been discouraged in the education of deaf children. At the first International Congress of Educators of the Deaf, held in Milan, Italy, in 1880, a resolution was passed which declared the superiority of speech over signs and which stated that the preferred method of teaching deaf children was to be the oral method (Meadow, 1972). From 1880 until just the past ten years or so, most educators of the deaf assumed that the use of sign language by young deaf children would result in inhibited reading, writing, speaking, and speechreading skills. The Milan Conference held that sign language had the disadvantage of injuring the "precision of ideas". A small number of educators felt that the use of sign language would facilitate and accelerate the development of these same skills. Their model was a deaf child of deaf parents who learned sign language in the home, and who seemed to do as well, if not better, in language skills, academic achievement, and psychological growth.

The difference of opinion remained just that until some recent research brought some objectivity to what had previously been an emotional argument. Through the late 1960's and early 1970's, two developments paralleled each other. First, research was reported on the educational, psychological, and social gains of children who used, and did not use, sign language. Studies by Mindel and Vernon (1971), and Schlesinger and Meadow (1972) showed superiority of early users of sign language over non-users or late users of sign language. Deaf children of deaf parents – users of sign language from birth – achieved at greater academic levels and had fewer psychological or social problems than non-users, or late users. None of these studies showed negative effects in any phase of language development among the early users. Secondly, linguists (Stokoe, 1976; Bellugi, 1972) were coming to the conclusion that sign language, as used by most deaf adults and thought for so long to be "poor English" was not English at all, but a distinct language. The name, American Sign Language, was given to a symbol system which was ordered in a unique way; so unique, in fact, that it was concluded that it had the integrity of a distinct language, one that is not English. In other words, American Sign Language (sometimes called ASL or Ameslan), is *not* English.

Fant (1974) writes: "Ameslan is a legitimate language in and of itself. That is to say, it is not based on English, but stands by itself, on its own feet. If English did not exist, Ameslan could still exist, just as French or Spanish exist independently of English." The conclusion that American Sign Language is not English becomes more understandable when one realizes that the sign language used by most deaf people in the United States was imported from France in 1917. There appears to be a higher correlation between American Sign Language and French Sign Language than between American Sign Language and a system used in England. The system used in England has a different syntax and there is less mutual agreement upon the symbols used. While investigating the uniqueness of American Sign Language, it was found that not *all* manual expressions in that language are independent of English. In fact, it is possible to sign in one language (American Sign Language), or the other (English), or indeed, in a combination of both.

I feel the obligation to interject at this point that it is not the purpose of this paper to fully defend or explain these various systems. For those with a special interest in the distinct properties of the manual languages, let me refer them to the literature, and let me now say that the purpose of this paper is to describe how deaf students and sign language interpreters function at CSUN.

Deaf students at CSUN

During the Spring semester of 1977, 169 deaf students shared the college experience at CSUN with approximately 27,000 non-handicapped students. Deaf students attend regular classes. The faculty has no special knowledge or training to deal with the problems of deafness. A unit known as Campus Services for the Deaf provides "support services" to these deaf students to insure their academic success. The major support service is interpreting. Other services include note-taking, tutoring, and counselling. Approximately 80 part-time interpreters, most of whom are themselves students at CSUN, are available to serve these

169 deaf students. Deaf students registered in 485 classes, of which 268 classes, meeting on the average of three times per week, were served by interpreters. The typical classroom situation has these components: a regular professor, an interpreter, a deaf student or two, and 20–25 non-handicapped students. The interpreter hears the spoken remarks of the professor and translates the remarks into sign language for the benefit of the deaf student. When a deaf student wishes to ask a question or make a comment, he does so in sign language and the interpreter translates this into spoken language for the benefit of the professor and the other students.

This form of "integrated" education is an alternative model to the more traditional form of "segregated" education, where deaf students are educated only in the company of other deaf students and are taught by instructors who simultaneously transmit lectures in spoken language and sign language. The integrated model is thought to have these benefits (Jones & Murphy 1972, 1974; Carter, 1976):

1. There are considerably more curriculum offerings at CSUN from which deaf students may choose than at a smaller segregated institution.
2. Non-handicapped students come to understand the special talents of deaf people.
3. The normal working and social patterns of life bring handicapped and non-handicapped individuals together; therefore, it is felt that educational models should approximate the experience one will face upon leaving college.
4. Contact with deaf students influences the career choices of non-handicapped people. Hearing students who have had classes with deaf students are more likely to learn sign language and serve as interpreters while in college, and to consider careers in areas of service to deaf people.

Because the model of integrated education is relatively new and because our knowledge of sign language and sign language interpreting is relatively sparse, the Campus Services for the Deaf unit, in addition to delivering interpreting services, is also responsible for research and evaluation studies that deal with the effectiveness of the services.

Sign language and interpreting studies

The remainder of this paper is divided into two parts. The first part deals with brief reviews of studies of: the attending behavior of deaf people to the interpreter, the onset of fatigue on the part of the interpreter, and the ways in which deaf people respond to information transmitted in two different ways (American Sign Language, and Signed English). The second part of the paper deals with a series of current research studies designed to document the relative efficiency of sign language in the transmission and reception of messages.

PART I: Review of previous research

Attending cehavior

The deaf students at CSUN must *see* language. They must *actively* attend to the linguistic stimuli which they receive through an interpreter. The need to attend visually requires constant activation of the voluntary neuro-muscular mechanism and leads to fatigue. Information may be missed and misinterpreted if an attendee blinks or momentarily turns away. Imagine the ensuing confusion if one missed the word, NOT, in this sentence: There will not be a test tomorrow. Imagine also an environment in which there is dust, or smoke, or in which there is visual "noise" i.e. two or more people in the visual field, background movements, bright lights, clashing colors, etc. These things lead us to conclude that deaf people cannot attend, visually, 100% of the time to such things as a college lecture which could go on for an hour or more. This raises the question of interest: what is a reasonable estimate of attending behavior on the part of deaf college students at CSUN?

Rudy (1976) attempted to determine the rate of attending behavior of CSUN deaf students to their interpreters. The procedures were unsophisticated: he observed deaf graduate students and attempted to determine when they were, and when they were not, attending to an interpreter. He used a cumulative stopwatch as he observed 14 deaf students in 14 different graduate education-class situations. He observed attending behavior in five minute segments. He recorded attending behavior during the first, third, and fifth five minutes of each class period. In other words he recorded for five minutes, did *not* record for five minutes, recorded the next five minutes, did *not* record the next five minutes, recorded the next five minutes. Over a 25 minute period he recorded for 15 minutes of that time. Rudy found that the overall attending rate was 88%. In other words, these deaf students watched the interpreter 88% of the time and did not watch the interpreter 12% of the time. He also found attending behavior to be greater in the earlier periods of time. Attending rates tended then to drop as time went on. The attending rate of 88% is almost certainly an overestimate of attending behavior. This is so because Rudy used the *most* academically capable deaf students, i.e. graduate students at CSUN. Also, the subjects knew they were being observed and the measures were estimated only over the first 25 minutes of a class period whereas most class sessions go on for an hour or more. Nonetheless, Rudy's contribution is twofold: (1) documentation of the basic rate of attending behavior, and (2) documentation of the attrition of attending behavior over time. These two considerations are critical to the efficient use of interpreters and also suggest training strategies to increase attending behavior. Clearly the need for more research in this area, using more precise methodologies, is apparent.

Fatigue on the part of the interpreter

A deaf person may experience fatigue in attending to an interpreter. The interpreter may also experience fatigue in delivering sign language. Sign language is delivered with considerable physical effort. CSUN interpreters are asked to mouth what they hear as well as to deliver the message manually. The fingers and arms are mostly used in delivering signs and finger spelling, but the whole body comes into play as well. Consequently, fatigue on the part of the interpreter is a predictable factor. Brasel (1976) examined the error rate of information delivered by interpreters over time. It was found that interpreting skills remained at their highest levels during the first 30 minutes. After 30 minutes there was a slow but steady increase in errors, and after 60 minutes, the error rate became statistically significant. Brasel concluded that interpreting skills begin to deteriorate after 30 minutes of interpreting, and begin to deteriorate significantly after 60 minutes. Obviously, interpreters should be rotated or a single interpreter should have a rest period after about 30 minutes of interpreting, wherever possible.

American sign language and signed English

As noted earlier in this paper, it is possible to sign in American Sign Language, which is not English, or an English form of manual communication, Signed English, or a combination of both. College-level deaf students, who have mastered 12 years or more in a school system which emphasizes success in the use of English, obviously have high English skills, even though they may be most comfortable with American Sign Language. In a study by Murphy and Fleischer (1976), CSUN deaf students were asked to state their preference for either American Sign Language (ASL) or Signed English (Siglish). The ASL group was broken into two subgroups. Half received treatment in ASL; half received treatment in Siglish. The Siglish preference group was also divided into two subgroups, of whom half received treatment in Siglish whereas the other half received treatment in Ameslan. It was found that there were no statistically significant differences regardless of preference and no statistically significant difference regardless of treatment received. Those who preferred Ameslan and received Siglish did as well as those who preferred Ameslan and received Ameslan. Those who preferred Siglish and received Ameslan did as well as those who preferred Siglish and received Siglish. It is clear from this study that CSUN deaf students have bilingual skills as evidenced by equal facility in two languages, regardless of their stated preference for one language over the other. Since CSUN interpreters receive training in both languages, it would appear that they are appropriately prepared to deal with the CSUN population of deaf students.

PART II: Review of current research

Information processing models have been identified to test the efficiency of sign language in the transmission and reception of messages. These models approximate usual classroom practices in that they parallel (A) the transmitting mode of delivering sign language, and (B) the receiving mode of understanding sign language. In the first instance (see Figure 1) a spoken verbal message originates with a lecturer, is processed through an interpreter, and is received by a deaf person. The dependent measure is test scores of deaf subjects based on information processed.

The second processing model has two components (see Figures 2 and 3). In Processing Model B, a message has a manual origin, and is received by an interpreter. The dependent measure is test scores of material received by the interpreter. In Processing Model C, a message has a verbal origin and is received by an interpreter. The interpreter must now verbalize the message in spoken English to a third party. The dependent measure here is test scores of material received by a third person. With the above in mind, we may now talk about three behaviors of interpreters: transmitting (Model A), receiving (Model B), and reversing (Model C).

Verbal
Origin ─────────► Interpreter ─────────► Manual
Reception ─────────► Test

Figure 1. Processing model A transmitting behavior

Manual
Origin ─────────► Interpreter ─────────► Test

Figure 2. Processing model B receiving behavior

Manual
Origin ─────────► Interpreter ─────────► Verbal
Reception ─────────► Test

Figure 3. Processing model C reversing behavior

The following explanation for these terms seem to meet general agreement among interpreters:

1. To transmit: the interpreter listens to the spoken word and transforms the spoken message into sign language.
2. To receive: the interpreter attends to and understands the sign language of another person. He is not required to verbalize what he receives. This might also be thought of as "reading" the signs of another. One who is skilled at this is said to evidence "reading comprehension".
3. To reverse: in addition to being able to "read" the original signer, the interpreter must also vocalize the message. He follows the incoming signs and as he reads, he also verbalizes what he sees. Both are done at nearly the same time, with the verbalizing slightly behind the reading. This is considered the most difficult task for the interpreter because the initiator of the message may be transmitting in one language (American Sign Language) while the vocal translation may be in another language (English), and the reading and the translation must be done at almost the same time.

One of our research interests deals with the experience of the interpreter. CSUN is a major training center for interpreters and also the world's largest employer of sign language interpreters. We offer a certain sequence of training courses and assign and pay interpreters according to their experience. Hence, it would seem reasonable that we would explore this variable closely to see how efficient our training has been, and to suggest other ways to manipulate the quantity and/or quality of the experience in order to improve the entire interpreting situation.

In one study it was found that the transmitting skills of interpreters at different levels of experience were essentially equal. In other words, interpreters with Minimum experience transmitted about as well as interpreters with Maximum experience. This first study was limited to transmitting and did not deal at all with receptive (receiving) or reversing skills, which are generally considered by interpreters to be higher order functions of somewhat greater difficulty than simply transmitting. The practical application of the finding of this first study to postsecondary education is limited to specific situations where material needs only to be transmitted. This assumes a passive receiver. It is clear, however, that college students best acquire knowledge in an interactive environment, i.e. one in which information is received and where a student may question a lecturer and comment on the lecture material. It seems reasonable therefore, to examine the receptive skills of the interpreter, as well as the transmitting skills. Consequently, a second study was designed to gather evidence on the "receiving" or "reading comprehension" skills of interpreters at different levels of experience. Studies on the "reversing" skills of the interpreter are planned in the future.

Methodology

Reading comprehension of the interpreter was tested through a series of videotaped lectures. Typical college lectures originally devised by Jacobs (1976), were signed on camera and a master black and white tape, without sound, was made for research purposes. The material consisted of one practice lecture, and five research lectures. Each lecture averaged about five minutes in length. After each lecture, the interpreter-subject received a 10-item test. The on-camera signer held a Comprehensive Skills Certificate (CSC) from the Registry of Interpreters for the Deaf. He carefully rehearsed each lecture and played a verbatim audiotape in the studio to cue his signing. The audiotrack was erased in the master tape used in the study. The signer rarely used lip movements. He rendered the lectures in American Sign Language vocabulary, yet followed an English syntax.

Results

It was found that interpreters with a greater amount of experience outscored interpreters with less experience. More specifically, interpreters with 1,200+ hours of classroom interpreting experience at CSUN (N = 7) significantly outscored those who had less than 300 hours of classroom interpreting experience at CSUN (N = 24). Those with between 600–900 hours of classroom interpreting experience also significantly outscored the lesser experienced group, but were the approximate equals of the group with the most experience (N = 7). From these data it was concluded that reading comprehension appears to be a function of experience. It may also be concluded that interpreters of Moderate experience appear to "read" about as well as those with Maximum experience. One further conclusion is that interpreters with Moderate and Maximum experience appear to "read" somewhat better than interpreters with Minimum experience.

Data were analyzed in still another way. In the earlier cited Jacobs study, hearing students with no knowledge of sign language, and deaf students who normally use an interpreter in CSUN classes were subject to the same lecture. These were delivered orally in a live situation, and were interpreted at the same time in a single room in which there were hearing and deaf individuals. A comparison of their scores with the scores of interpreters with various levels of experience leads to some interesting conclusions:

Group I – Hearing subjects in Jacob's Study with no knowledge of sign language.
Group II – Deaf subjects in Jacob's study who depend on an interpreter at CSUN.
Group III – Minimal level interpreters.
Group IV – Moderate level interpreters.
Group V – Maximum level interpreters.

Post hoc comparisons showed no significant differences between scores of Minimum level interpreters and Deaf subjects on most tests. Therefore, it is concluded that Minimum level interpreters evidence reading comprehension skills at least equal to, and perhaps a little better than, CSUN deaf students. Further comparisons showed that Moderate level interpreters outscored the Deaf group, and that Maximum level interpreters outscored the Deaf group. It is concluded that the Moderate and Maximum level interpreters show greater reading comprehension skills than CSUN deaf students.

Additional comparisons were made between the three interpreting groups and the Hearing group from the Jacobs study. It was found that the Hearing group outscored the Minimum level interpreters. No significant differences were found between the Moderate and Maximum level interpreters and the Hearing group. It is concluded that scores obtained by Minimum level interpreters after reading sign language messages are inferior to scores of a Hearing group receiving information through audition. It is further concluded that Moderate and Maximum level interpreters "read" as much information through signs as CSUN hearing students do through normal audition. More will be said about this later in this paper.

Discussion

This research followed small group research models and the usual cautions govern interpretation of the following findings. It has been found that reading comprehension appears to be a function of the experience of the interpreter whereas transmitting skills apparently are not related to experience (as "experience" has been defined herein). It would seem that CSUN interpreters develop adequate transmitting skills after training and within the first 300 hours of paid experience whereas reading comprehension becomes most efficient after training and at least 600 hours of paid experience. This being the case, a clear recommendation to those who are responsible for the basic training of new interpreters, and in-service training of experienced interpreters, is to emphasize reading and reversing skills over transmitting skills. This assumes that transmitting skills are developing along predictable lines and meet minimum proficiency levels. The comparison of data between the Jacobs study and the present study leads to some interesting conclusions.

1. Jacobs found significant differences in favor of a hearing group receiving information through audition over a deaf group receiving information through an interpreter. The scores of deaf subjects averaged 16% below those obtained by hearing persons.
2. No significant differences were found on five of six measures between Minimum level interpreters in this study and deaf subjects in the Jacobs study.
3. Significant differences were found in favor of scores of Moderate and Maximum level interpreters in this study, over scores obtained by the deaf group in the Jacobs study.
4. No significant differences were found between Moderate and Maximum level interpreters in this study, and hearing subjects in the Jacobs study.

These data must be interpreted with care. The immediate temptation is to conclude that sign language is 16% less efficient than spoken language, that Minimum level interpreters "read" about as well as deaf subjects, and Moderate and Maximum level interpreter "readers" are superior to deaf "readers" of sign language. But the finding of no significant differences between Moderate and Maximum level interpreters and Jacobs' hearing subjects suggests a different explanation and this chain of thought: If Moderate and Maximum level interpreters acquire as much information through sign language as hearing counterparts do through normal auditory channels, then it must be concluded that sign language apparently equals spoken language, as an efficient channel for the communication of information. If sign language is the equal of spoken language, then the 16% gap in scores between deaf and hearing subjects, as found by Jacobs, is not attributable to deficiencies in sign language itself. If the 16% score gap between deaf and hearing subjects cannot be attributable to deficiencies in sign language, then the gap must be explained by other factors, most likely the basic language and educational deficit of deaf people. If deaf people score lower because of linguistic and educational deficits, then Minimum level interpreters may obtain equal "reading" scores, not necessarily because they read as well, but because they have superior language skills. Further support for this possibility comes from the fact that Minimum level interpreters have had only about three years experience with sign language whereas the deaf subjects have had considerably more years of experience, some from birth. If reading comprehension is a function of experience, as this study concludes, then we would expect the most experienced group of readers, i.e. deaf people, to score highest. They do not. This is probably so, not necessarily because they are poor at reading sign language, but because a basic language and educational deficit penalizes them as they process information through to the final measure of a formal paper and pencil test.

It appears, therefore, that the problem is neither with the ability of sign language to transmit information accurately, nor with the "reading" ability of the deaf person, but with unfamiliar words, or the multiple meaning of words, or other factors inherent in the basic problems associated with deafness. Some previous doubts about the efficiency of sign language in our field come from observations of deaf subjects. Research using hearing subjects with normal language skills *and* a knowledge of sign language is recommended in future studies of the efficiency of sign language, particularly in that it frees the researchers from the confounding variable of the language limitation of deaf subjects.

References

Bellugi, U., and Klima, E.S. The roots of language in the sign talk of the deaf. *Psychology Today,* June 1972, 76, 61–64.

Brasel, B.B. The effects of fatigue on the competence of interpreters for the deaf. In H. J. Murphy (Ed.), *Selected readings in the integration of deaf students at CSUN.* Center on Deafness Publication Series (No. 1). Northridge: California State University, Northridge, 1976.

Carter, S.H. Some effects of association with hearing-impaired students upon hearing students at CSUN. In H. J. Murphy (Ed.), *Selected readings in the integration of deaf students at CSUN.* Center on Deafness Publication Series (No. 1). Northridge: California State University, Northridge, 1976.

Fant, L.J. Jr., Ameslan. *Gallaudet Today,* 1974.–75, 5 (2), 1–3.

Jacobs, L.R. *The efficiency of sign language interpretation to convey lecture information to deaf students.* Unpublished doctoral dissertation, University of Arizona, 1976.

Jones, R.L. and Murphy, H.J. The Northridge plan for higher education of the deaf. *American Annals of the Deaf,* 1972, 11 7, 612–616.

Jones, R.L. and Murphy, H.J. Integrated education for deaf college students. *Phi Delta Kappan,* 1974, 55, 542.

Meadow, K.P. Sociolinguistics, sign language, and the deaf sub-culture. In T. E. O'Rourke (Ed.), *Psycholinguistics and total communication: The state of the art.* Washington, D.C.: American Annals of the Deaf, 1972.

Mindel, E.D. and Vernon, M. *They grow in silence.* Silver Spring, Md.: National Association for the Deaf, 1971.

Murphy, H.J. and Fleischer, L. The effects of Ameslan versus Siglish upon test scores. In H. J. Murphy (Ed.), *Selected readings in the integration of deaf students at CSUN.* Center on Deafness Publication Series (No. 1). Northridge: California State University, Northridge, 1976.

Rudy, L.H. A survey of attending behavior of deaf graduate students to interpreters. In H. J. Murphy (Ed.), *Selected readings in the integration of deaf students at CSUN.* Center on Deafness Publication Series (No. 1). Northridge: California State University, Northridge, 1976.

Schlesinger, H. and Meadow, K.P. *Sound and Sign. Deafness and Mental Health.* Berkeley, University of California Press, 1972.

Stokoe, W.C. The study and use of sign language. *Sign Language Studies,* 1976. *10,* 1–36.

2.5   **Hurwitz, Alan. 1980. "Interpreters' effectiveness in reverse interpreting: Pidgin Sign English and American Sign Language." In** *A Century of Deaf Awareness in a decade of interpreting awareness: Proceedings of the 6th National Conference of the Registry of Interpreters for the Deaf*, **ed. by Frank Caccamise, James Stangarone, Marilyn Mitchell-Caccamise, and E. Banner, 157–187. Silver Spring, MD: Registry of Interpreters for the Deaf.**

T. Alan Hurwitz became the tenth president of Gallaudet University on January 1, 2010. Before arriving at Gallaudet, Hurwitz was president of the National Technical Institute for the Deaf (NTID); one of eight colleges within the Rochester Institute of Technology (RIT) in Rochester, N.Y. Hurwitz earned a BS in electrical engineering from Washington University at St. Louis, Missouri, and an MS in electrical engineering from St. Louis University in Missouri. His doctorate (Ed.D.) is in education from the University of Rochester.

Hurwitz's career at RIT/NTID began in 1970 when he was hired as an educational specialist in RIT's College of Engineering after working five years for McDonnell Douglas Corporation as an associate electronics engineer and senior numerical control programmer. He served as dean of NTID from 1998 to 2009, and as vice president and dean of RIT from 2003 to 2009. During his career, Hurwitz served on the boards of the Rochester (N.Y.) School for the Deaf, of which he was also president, the National Captioning Institute, and is a past president of the National Association of the Deaf as well as a past president of the World Organization of Jewish Deaf.

Interpreters' effectiveness in reverse interpreting pidgin signed English and American sign language

T. Alan Hurwitz*

Deaf people often need help in making themselves understood by hearing people for two reasons. First, hearing people sometimes have difficulty understanding "deaf speech" because it is not intelligible to them. Second, many hearing people do not understand the manual communication used by some deaf people. Therefore, deaf people rely on interpreters to provide voice (reverse) interpretation or transliteration to hearing individuals. This study examined the relationship between the types of sign language used by deaf people and the effectiveness (accuracy and quality) of reverse interpreting.

Past research has not provided information on factors which relate to effective voice (reverse) interpreting for deaf people. This research, however, suggests that the effectiveness of reverse interpreting is dependent on the type of sign language used by deaf people; i.e. Pidgin Signed English (PSE) or American Sign Language (ASL).

In this study the subjects (Ss) were 32 interpreters employed at the National Technical Institute for the Deaf (NTID), divided into two groups based on their interpreting experience and certification from the Registry of Interpreters for the Deaf (RID). Four treatment/story conditions were developed by a deaf storyteller who presented two different stories, each in two different sign languages (PSE and ASL). Each S was measured on four criteria including accuracy and quality of reverse interpreting under each of two different treatment conditions. The percentage of correct propositions successfully reverse interpreted into spoken English and simultaneously recorded onto audiotape by Ss was used as the measure of accuracy. The quality of the interpreted message (i.e. comprehension, transmission, language use, moods, and feelings) was judged by a panel of three comprehensively certified (CSC) interpreters.

The results of this study showed that experience with interpreting does play a significant role in the effectiveness of reverse interpreting both PSE and ASL. Generally, interpreters can reverse interpret PSE better than ASL. This evidences the importance of improving voice (reverse) interpretation of ASL messages into spoken English for deaf individuals. The implications of these statements for the use of reverse interpreting in classrooms as well as in other situations and in research activities are discussed.

---

* T. Alan Hurtwitz is an Associate Dean for Educational Support Service Programs, National Technical Institute for the Deaf (NTID), Rochester Institute of Technology (RIT), Rochester, New York, 14623.

Introduction

Statement of the problem

Large numbers of deaf people need help in making themselves understood by hearing people. This occurs because hearing people often have difficulty understanding "deaf" speech." Also, many hearing people do not understand the manual communication used by some deaf people. Therefore, deaf people often rely on interpreters to interpret or transliterate their signed and/or spoken communication into spoken English. This practice is commonly known as voice or reverse interpreting. In situations where deaf people use manual communication (sign language), the interpreter must understand the signs being presented in order to comprehend the message (Hoemann, 1975) and reverse interpret the message adequately into spoken English. The effectiveness of reverse interpreting is presumably related to the interpreter's ability to understand manual communication.

Fant (1972), Hoemann (1975), Fischer (1975), Siple (1978), and Ingram (1974) have provided support for American Sign Language (ASL) as a language distinct from English, although English does impact on ASL given the proximity of the two languages (Battison, 1978). Hence, people (including interpreters) have suggested that it is helpful if a deaf person uses Signed English rather than ASL, presumably because it is easier to transliterate a signed communication approximating the interpreter's own native language into spoken English than to interpret into spoken English the less familiar language of deaf native signers of ASL. In brief, one would expect that persons who do not use sign language fluently or naturally, would require less knowledge, skills and experience for learning to transliterate from signed English into spoken English than to interpret from a non-familiar language (e.g. American Sign Language) into spoken English. Hence, the purpose of this study is to investigate the effect of the types of sign language used by deaf people on the performance of reverse interpreters.

Statement of the hypotheses

The following research hypotheses (H_1, H_2) were formulated:

H_1 – Interpreters with a high (extensive) or low (limited) level of interpreting experience will be equally effective in reverse interpreting information presented in Pidgin Signed English (PSE).

H_2 – Interpreters with a high (extensive) level of interpreting experience will reverse interpret information presented in ASL more effectively than interpreters with low (limited) interpreting experience.

Operational definitions

For the purposes of clarifying the research design and aiding in the interpretation of the findings and conclusions, the following terms require definition:

1. <u>American Sign Language treatment</u> – a story presented on a videotape generated by a deaf person using American Sign Language (ASL). Facial expression and body language are often strong characteristics that accompany ASL. In a sense, such characteristics are analogous to voice tone, inflection and emphasis in spoken English. It should be added that an interpreter should be aware of and able to convey these sometimes subtle nuances into her/his spoken interpretation. Mouthing (with or without voice) of English words associated with an ASL message may accompany the ASL rendition. However, since the word order is not according to standard English syntax, the Ss would have to be prepared to understand ASL well enough to be able to comprehend the cues, synthesize the information, and interpret it into spoken English. In this study the Ss' reverse interpreting performance was recorded onto an audiotape. Many experts claim that it is virtually impossible to interpret an ASL message concurrently with its reception. They believe a more effective way would be for interpreters to acquire as much information as possible beforehand regarding the content of forthcoming manual communication before attempting to interpret it. In this study audible components of the ASL presentation by the deaf person were eliminated, even though it is generally assumed that intelligible speech of a deaf person would enhance the reverse interpreting process. However, unintelligible speech of a deaf person may inhibit the interpreter's ability to reverse interpret effectively. Hence, the elimination of the audible components was a control factor that held constant the influence of speech intelligibility over the interpreter's effectiveness.

2. <u>Pidgin Signed English treatment</u> – a story presented on a videotape generated by a deaf person using Pidgin Signed English (PSE) with silent mouthing of words. This mode enables Ss to acquire as many cues as possible from a variety of components in the system (e.g. signed/fingerspelled words in English syntax, mouthing the words through lip movements, and facial and body expressions) and transliterate the message onto an audiotape.

3. <u>High Interpreting Experience (HI)</u> – interpreters (Ss) who hold a Comprehensive Skills Certificate (CSC) from the Registry of Interpreters for the Deaf (RID) and have a minimum of 1800 hours of classroom interpreting experience. Eighteen hundred hours was selected as the minimum to ensure that the Ss have at least three years experience interpreting in an educational setting.

4. <u>Low Interpreting Experience (LO)</u> – interpreters (Ss) who hold no more than one form of RID certification – Expressive Interpreting Certificate (now Interpretation Certificate; IC) or Expressive Translating Certificate (now Transliteration Certificate; TC) and have had no more than 600 hours of classroom interpreting experience. The 600-hour figure indicates less than one year's experience interpreting in an educational setting.

Significance of the study

This study was designed to begin to answer questions that interpreters, deaf people and others have raised concerning the relationship between the type of sign language used by deaf people and the interpreter's effectiveness in reverse interpreting. Support for the hypotheses would suggest that an interpreter's fluency in ASL is one relevant component in being able to reverse interpret effectively for many deaf people. However, if the second hypothesis failed to be rejected (i.e. that skilled interpreters are more effective in reverse interpreting the ASL treatment than the interpreters with lesser experience), then the reverse interpreting component in interpreter training programs or the equivalent type of experiential functions will require additional attention or different intervention to allow further development of this skill.

Since the voice of the deaf person is eliminated from presentations in this study, no conclusions regarding the contribution of voice to the effectivenss of a reverse interpretation are made. However, use of voice may enhance or hinder the reverse interpreting process; for instance, unintelligible speech of a deaf person may be distracting for the interpreter. Also, voices from the deaf person and interpreter at the same time may be distracting to the audience. A separate study in the future should focus on these situations.

Little is known regarding the elements that constitute skilled and effective reverse interpreting. The broad categories of the independent variables employed in this study are not defined to take into account the specific effects of either ASL or PSE influencing decoding and encoding by the interpreter. Neither does this study explore the standard English skills of interpreters and how they contribute to the overall success of reverse interpreting, although it is anticipated that standard English and sign language skills interact to produce competence (i.e. skills in reversing both sign language versions). It is hoped that this study will encourage researchers to explore the effects of specific elements in different manual communication systems that may contribute to the performance of skilled and effective reverse interpreters.

Methodology

Subjects

Of the 69 interpreters at NTID in this study, 26 held Comprehensive Skills Certificates (CSC) from the RID, 13 held Expressive Translating Certificates (ETC), Expressive Interpreting Certificates (EIC), or both ETC/EIC from the RID; and 30 held no certification. Two groups of 16 subjects (Ss) were selected, considering RID certification and length of experience with classroom interpreting at NTID: (1) a low experience (LO) group – Ss with less than 600 hours of classroom interpreting and who hold no more than one RID certification (ETC or EIC); and (2) a high experience (HI) group -Ss with a minimum of 1800 hours of classroom interpreting experience (or its equivalent in community interpreting experience) who have Comprehensive Skills Certification (CSC) from the RID.

Two pools of 17 interpreters each (LO and HI) were identified, and then 16 people were randomly selected from each pool as Ss for the experiment to equalize the number of subjects in each cell of the experimental design. The remaining 35 interpreters at NTID did not satisfy the criteria established for high and low levels of experience.

Materials

Four different stories related to personal experiences were created by a deaf storyteller. The storyteller was selected on the basis of his reputation for anecdotal story-telling ability in both sign language systems (i.e. PSE and ASL). The storyteller holds the Reverse Skills Certificate (RSC) from the RID.

The storyteller prepared an outline for each of the pre-selected four stories that were based on stories commonly used for sign language instructional purposes (Hoemann, 1975). Each outline was divided into approximately 14 events and written on a chalkboard. The events were used as cues for the storyteller during the videotape production. In the presentation of each story the storyteller expressed the propositions within each narrative event in a manner that maintained content consistency between alternate versions (i.e. PSE and ASL) of each story. A proposition is defined as a clause or sentence containing an active or stative verb. Relationship between modifiers and their modified terms are not considered separate propositions unless they appear as relative clauses (Thorndyke, 1977).

The first story was presented in PSE and followed by the ASL version. The initial presentation of the second story was in its ASL version, followed by the PSE version. For the presentations of the third and fourth stories, language was alternated in the same manner.

During the videotape production the storyteller's signed messages were voiced onto an audiotape. The audiotapes were transcribed and edited as necessary to coincide with the story events. These materials were reviewed and critiqued by an evaluation team to evaluate and select the most appropriate pair of stories as stimuli materials.

The evaluators included the storyteller, the assistant to the principal investigator and two deaf NTID faculty members who are proficient in PSE and ASL. Both faculty members hold RSC from the RID and have served on the RID evaluation team for a number of years. The assistant to the principal investigator has RID's Comprehensive Skills Certification (CSC) as well as the Legal Skills Certification (LSC).

The criteria used in the evaluation were set up to judge consistency and equivalency in the level of difficulty, related especially to vocabulary usage and degree of abstraction, among different stories presented in the same sign language version. Additional criteria included were equivalency in the duration and number of propositions in each presentation. It was noted that the first and third stories were ordered chronologically and narrated sequences of events that spanned the entire period from childhood to adulthood. The second and fourth stories narrated events of brief duration. All four stories involved expression of a high level of affect, a property helpful in facilitating qualitative evaluation of audiotaped reverse interpretations. Further, it was judged by the evaluation team that stories 2 and 3 were continuous in sequence of events and included a variety of concepts (e.g. numbers and time transitions). The levels of difficulty in these two stories were judged consistent. The team felt that the syntactic and grammatical features of standard English (e.g. word order) in the PSE presentations was appropriate in both stories and that the essential principles and features of effective communication in ASL (e.g. directionality, use of space, and time order) were properly utilized in both stories. The ASL versions of both stories were judged to convey a sense of naturalness and to include appropriate and similar levels of emotion. It was also agreed that presentation of stories 2 and 3 were presented at a normal conversational pace.

Stories 1 and 4 lacked consistency within stories in the English versions and lacked equivalence of propositions expressed in the corresponding PSE and ASL versions. Story 1 included signs inappropriate to ASL. Also, story 4 did not represent a commonly encountered situation and was judged inappropriate for that reason. It was decided that the storyteller should not repeat story presentations since Hatfield and Caccamise (1980) have cautioned that if the test run is repeated even twice in the preparation of such stimulus materials, the presentation may lose naturalness in its style.

The panel concluded that stories 2 and 3 (hereafter designated as stories X and Y, respectively) would be used in this study and that parts of stories 1 and 4 would be used for purposes of exemplification during the pre-experimental instruction sessions for subjects. The duration of each story-version selected is shown in Table 1. The mean length of presentation for all versions was 162.5 seconds with a standard deviation of 12.3 seconds. [. . . .]

Research design

A factorial, posttest-only experimental design with repeated measures on the treatment factor was employed in this study to permit comparison of the performances among groups on two post-treatment criterion measures. The posttest-only design was selected because it was possible to effect complete stratified randomization in assigning treatment combinations to Ss, making the assumption of pre-experimental equivalence among groups on the criterion measures reasonable. Randomization of treatment conditions is considered to afford the most adequate assurance of minimizing effects of sampling bias (Stanley & Campbell, 1963). Basically, a $2 \times 2 \times 2$ factorial design brought each S group (HI and LO) into contact with each of the two manual communication treatments, PSE and ASL, under two different story content conditions, counterbalanced with respect to the order (XY and YX) of story-treatment combinations. Ss received and reverse interpreted different story content under each treatment condition. Figure 1 reports the sample sizes (N_1) of groups (i = 1 to 4) assigned to the various combinations of treatment (PSE, ASL), level of interpreting experience (HI, LO), and order of story presentations (XY, YX).

		PSE	ASL
HI	Story Order XY	N_1 (8)	N_1 (8)
	Story Order YX	N_2 (8)	N_2 (8)
LO	Story Order XY	N_3 (8)	N_3 (8)
	Story Order YX	N_4 (8)	N_4 (8)

Figure 1. Sample Size (N_1) of experimental groups, by treatment, experience level, and treatment order

Individuals with different levels of interpreting experience were assigned to treatments and orders of treatment presentation in the following manner:

1. N_1 consisted of a group of 8 Ss with a high level of interpreting experience. All members of this group received the same story order (XY); and within this group half the Ss got one treatment order (PSE, ASL) and the other half got the other treatment order (ASL, PSE).
2. N_2 consisted of a second group of 8 Ss with a high level of interpreting experience. All members of this group received the same story order (YX); and within this group half the Ss got one treatment order (P5E, ASL) and the other half got the other treatment order (ASL, PSE).
3. N_3 consisted of a group of 8 Ss with a low level of interpreting experience. They were exposed to the same treatment/story combinations as group N_1.
4. N_4 consisted of a second group of 8 Ss with a low level of interpreting experience. They were exposed to the same treatment/story combinations as group N_2.

Dependent variables

The dependent variables were the accuracy and quality of the reverse interpreted messages. Accuracy was measured by the percentage of correct reverse interpreted propositions (Thorndyke, 1977). A mean score on the accuracy measure for each S was computed from scores based on the independent judgements of two raters. The quality of the reverse interpreted messages was measured in a composite mean score, taking into consideration four factors believed to affect the effectiveness with which the actual intent of the original message is communicated by the interpreter's rendition of the message. Quality was judged on a five-point rating scale using an instrument which is a condensed version of the RID interpreter evaluation instrument (Pimentel, 1972). The highest possible score for each qualitative factor in the condensed instrument was 5.

The following factors were examined in this evaluation of the performance quality of reverse interpreted messages: (a) understanding the message, (b) transmission of the message, (c) language used to transmit the message, and (d) conveying the storyteller's attitudes and feelings adequately.

1. Understanding the message: This factor is the basic component of reverse interpreting skill. It includes the ability to follow and comprehend a deaf person's thoughts to the extent that these thoughts are actually expressed through manual communication forms, ranging from ASL to Signed English.
2. Transmission of the message. This factor evaluates how the reverse interpreter re-expresses what he/she has received from "reading" the deaf person. Some individuals, for instance, may understand a deaf person's signs well enough, but may have difficulty re-expressing the deaf person's thoughts in standard English due to inadequate ability to paraphrase their meaning into speech.
3. Language used to transmit the message: This refers to how completely the message is conveyed. Often interpreters re-express only partially or generally the message that the deaf person wishes to communicate.
4. Conveying the storyteller's attitude and feeling adequately: This factor is largely self-explanatory. Difficulties may arise in conveying both the nature of the emotional content of the message and the full extent of the deaf person's expression of affect.

A panel of three NTID staff members who hold CSC, but are not employed as interpreters, judged the quality of the reverse interpreted messages. Each judge rated all subjects in random order on all four factors. The judges listened to the audiotapes made of the reverse interpreting and recorded their ratings on a modified version of the RID interpreter evaluation instrument.

[. . . .]

Statistical summary of criterion performance

For purposes of statistical analysis, a single interaction hypothesis, regarding the joint effects of treatment (ASL and PSE) and level of interpreting experience of the Ss was tested. Performance measures included an accuracy measure (the percentage of the propositions in each story correctly interpreted on an audiotape recording) and the quality of standard English renditions of the reverse interpreted messages.

The inter-rater reliability between the two raters who independently judged the accuracy measure was found to be .9758. The pairwise inter-rater reliabilities among the three raters who recorded their ratings of the quality of S's reverse interpreting performances were found to be .4853, .5905 and .7229.

The intercorrelations of the four part-scores of the quality measure, which were scored separately, were examined and found to range between .8003 and .9383. Although inter-judge consistency varied considerably between judges, the judges were internally quite consistent in their individual assessments of performance quality across the four part-scores. Since part-scores were highly intercorrelated, it was decided to combine these four quality part-scores which were based on an average of the three judges' scores into a unit-weighted composite mean of the scores for each subject. The correlations between the composite mean score and the four part-scores were found to range between .9131 and .9677. The correlation between the accuracy measures and the composite mean scores of the quality measures was found to be .8288.

Group means and standard deviations on both criteria were calculated for each level of the independent variables (treatment, experience level, and story orders) and were based on the combined performances on both stories under the same treatment conditions. These findings are reported for the accuracy measure in Table 9 and for the quality measure in Table 10. The .05 level of significance was selected as the criterion for rejection of the null hypothesis in the analysis of variance.

Table 9. Means and standard deviations of accuracy scores (%) obtained by high experience (HI) and low experience (LO) interpreters on stories presented under different sign language conditions*

		PSE	ASL	Total
HI	Story Order XY	85.08 (5.52)	74.90 (6.90)	79.99 (6.21)
	Story Order YX	91.13 (3.82)	61.27 (9.06)	76.20 (6.44)
	Subtotal	88.10 (4.67)	68.08 (7.98)	78.09 (6.33)
LO	Story Order XY	78.94 (11.31)	59.48 (14.43)	69.21 (12.87)
	Story Order YX	79.43 (9.28)	37.19 (12.17)	58.31 (10.73)
	Subtotal	79.18 (10.30)	48.34 (13.30)	63.76 (11.80)
	Total	83.64 (7.49)	58.21 (10.64)	70.92 (9.07)

*Standard deviations are reported in parenthesis

The mean score of the accuracy measure for a story is expressed as a percentage of the total propositions contained in the story (cf. Table 3). In all cases the HI group of subjects received higher mean scores than the LO group of subjects and mean scores of translations from PSE narratives were higher than for ASL narratives.

[. . . .]

The mean scores on the quality measures are expressed as raw score means on a scale ranging from 1 (least favorable) to 5 (most favorable). The highest possible number on the rating scale is 5. The HI group of subjects obtained higher mean scores than the LO group of subjects and mean scores of quality performance in translating from PSE narratives were higher than for ASL narratives.

Statistical analysis

Performance measures of the accuracy and quality of the reverse interpreting efforts of Ss were subjected to a univariate three-way factorial analysis of variance with repeated measures on the treatment factor. The results of the ANOVA tests for both accuracy and quality measures are reported in Tables 11 and 12, respectively. The between-subjects main effect of levels of experience (HI vs LO) on the performance of the subjects was found to be statistically significant at the .05 level for both dependent measures. Therefore, the groups of Ss with HI experience level performed significantly better on the accuracy and quality measures than the groups with low amounts of experience. The other main between-subjects effect of story order (XY vs YX) on the performance of the subjects was found to be non-significant for both dependent measures (accuracy and quality measures). The first order interaction effect between levels of experience and story order on the performance of the subjects was also found to be statistically non-significant for both the accuracy and quality measures.

The <u>Within Subjects</u> portion of the analysis reported in Tables 11 and 12 indicates that the main effect of treatment conditions (PSE vs ASL) on the performance of subjects was found to be statistically significant (at the .05 level) for both dependent measures. Therefore, Ss reverse interpreted the PSE story significantly better than the ASL story as determined by measures of accuracy and quality. Both first-order interaction effects (treatment condition × level of experience and treatment condition × story order) on the performance of the subjects were also found to be statistically significant for both dependent measures. The second order interaction effect (treatment condition × level of experience × story order) on the performance of the subjects was not statistically significant for either dependent measure.

Of primary relevance in this study was the interaction effect between treatment condition and level of experience. Post hoc statistical comparisions of pairwise means with respect to the research hypotheses (H_1 and H_2) using Tukey's statistic (Q) test, a variation of the Newman-Keuls method, at 4 and 28 degrees of freedom showed that the critical value for the accuracy and quality measures were $Q = 8.47$, p .05 and $Q = .12$, p .05, respectively. It has been observed in Figures 2 and 3 that the differences between means of the HI and LO groups of the PSE and ASL treatments in the accuracy and quality measures exceeded the respective critical values. Hence, the observed differences among the means in Figures 2 and 3 are statistically significant.

[. . . .]

For higher levels of interpreting experience the difference in performance between the ASL and PSE treatment conditions, though large (20.02), and statistically significant is substantially smaller than the difference in performance between the treatment conditions for lower levels of experience (30.84) which is statistically significant. In other words, experience level differentially affects response to treatment. The more interpreting experience one has, the less a person is likely to differ in the accuracy or quality of interpretation of PSE and ASL stories. Viewed from a different perspective, the difference in performance under the PSE treatment condition between the HI and LO subjects is smaller (8.92) than the difference in the performance under the ASL treatment condition between these groups (19.74). These differences were shown earlier to be statistically significant. This means that interpreters with different experience levels exhibit more similar levels of interpreting accuracy under the PSE condition than interpreters with different experience levels exhibit under the ASL condition.

Figure 3 shows a similar pattern of results for measures of quality. At the higher experience level, interpreting is of better quality, and the difference in quality between ASL and PSE performance is less extreme than the difference observed among Ss with low interpreting experience. One notable difference in the manner in which the treatment by experience- level interactions are manifested is that for the measure of interpreting quality both HI group performances exceeded LO group performances (Figure 3). This was not true of the accuracy. On the other hand, PSE performance at both experience levels exceeded ASL performance at either level of experience (Figure 2). In any case, it may be noted that on the quality measures the discrepancy between treatment effects for the LO group is greater than for the HI group.

Other relevant information

Table 13 summarizes the 32 Ss' responses to the question regarding their opinion about their response to treatment. Ten HI Ss felt that they did better in the PSE treatments; 2 in the ASL treatments; and 4 felt they did equally well in both treatments. Fifteen LO Ss felt that they did better in the PSE treatments, and one felt she performed poorly under both treatment conditions. The non-parametric statistical analysis using the Chi-Square test rejects a null hypothesis of equal numbers of Ss in each cell of Table 13 ($X^2 = 54.5$) at the .05 significance level. The majority of Ss in both groups felt that they did better under the PSE treatments than under the ASL treatments. This observation is consistent with the statistical findings in this study which determined that the PSE performances were significantly higher than the ASL performances. Ss were clearly conscious of and accurate in the assessment of their reverse interpreting effectiveness in these two manual languages.

Table 13. Summary of opinions of Ss on their performances

Group	N	PSE treatments	ASL treatments	Both PSE and ASL treatments	Neither PSE nor ASL treatments
HI	16	10	2	4	0
LO	16	15	0	0	1

Discussion of the results

The following research hypotheses were generated regarding the performance of interpreters receiving and reverse interpreting information under the two presentation conditions:

H$_1$ –   Interpreters with a high (extensive) or low (limited) level of interpreting experience are equally effective in reverse interpreting information presented in Pidgin Signed English

H$_2$ –   Interpreters with a high (extensive) level of interpreting experience reverse interpret information presented in American Sign Language more effectively than interpreters with low (limited) interpreting experience.

For purposes of statistical analysis, the hypothesis stated that there would be no difference attributed to level of experience in the accuracy or quality of performance by interpreters who received signed information under two randomly assigned treatment/story order conditions. The accuracy criterion was measured as the number of propositions contained in a story that were reverse interpreted in a manner identical or equivalent in meaning to the original signed version of the story. The quality criterion was measured in the form of ratings, using standards of quality employed in the certification of interpreters. Data on each of the criteria were analyzed by univariate three-way analysis of variance utilizing a $2 \times 2 \times 2$ (sign language type × story order effect × level of interpreting experience) factorial design with repeated measures on the sign language factor. Tests of all hypotheses were conducted at the .05 level of significance.

On the between-subjects factor of experience-level, significant differences between groups were found for both criteria. The second between-subjects main effect of treatment/story order combinations was statistically non-significant in both cases. Additionally, on both the accuracy and quality criteria the effect of interaction between experience level and treatment/story order combinations was non-significant. The within-subjects effect of exposure to different sign language systems was significant on both criterion measures, as were the treatment × experience level interaction and the interaction between treatment × treatment/story order combinations. The second order interaction effect (treatment × experience level × treatment/story order combinations) was found to be statistically non-significant.

Comparisons of cell means (Tables 9 and 10; Figures 2 & 3) showed for both accuracy and quality measures that at higher levels of experience the difference in performance between the ASL and PSE treatments,though substantial, were smaller than the performance difference between the treatment conditions at lower levels of experience.

The subjects in the study were asked to evaluate their own performance. Their belief in the superiority of their performance in the PSE treatment situation was supported by results observed on both criteria. For the accuracy measures within the PSE treatment, the HI subjects received mean scores of 88.10%, compared to the LO subjects' mean scores of 79.18%. In the ASL treatment the observed mean for HI subjects was 68.08% compared to a mean of 48.34% for LO subjects. Comparable results were noted on the measure of quality of reverse interpreting performance. Under the PSE treatment condition, HI subjects obtained a mean of 4.46, whereas the LO subjects' mean was 3.82. ASL treatments produced means for HI and LO subjects of 4.26 and 3.00 respectively.

Although the principle hypothesis of an interaction between treatment conditions and experience levels was confirmed, several questions regarding the differential effects of story difficulty, order effects, and their relationship to both interpreting experience and the comparative interpretability of ASL and PSE, remain unanswered. The factorial design of this study was based upon the assumption that the stories used would be equivalent in difficulty within treatment condition and experience level of interpreters. Had this assumption been met, the generality of the treatment by experience- level interaction across story content (controlling experimentally for story order by stratification and for treatment order by randomization) would have been enhanced. Although precautions were taken to equate the difficulty level of stories, these efforts were not completely successful. It is apparent that for one treatment condition (ASL) story order differences within HI and LO experience groups differ substantially from story order differences within experience groups under the other treatment condition (PSE). The consequence of this is that story difficulty was inextricably confounded with story order. The result is that the interaction between story order and treatment and the interaction between story order and experience level suffer from the operation of the confound. Reasons for the failure of efforts to equalize the difficulty of stories in this study cannot, of course, be definitively determined. It is possible, however, that one factor contributing to the difference in difficulty is the differential duration of story-telling time observed (Table 1) under different treatment conditions. This suggests the possibility that something about the structure or content of the stories makes them differentially susceptible to narration in PSE and ASL. A similar kind of difference between stories was observed for the two treatments in the number of propositions required to express their essential content. It is particularly noteworthy that on Story X substantially less time was required to narrate the story in ASL than in PSE, while the number of propositions required to narrate the story in either language was quite similar. On the other hand, the time required to narrate story Y in either language was virtually identical, while the number of propositions required for presentation of the story differed.

The results of the study indicated considerable within-group variability in the accuracy measures as shown in Table 9. The high within-group variability for the HI subjects compared to the LO subjects on both measures may be partially accounted for by the screening criteria for subject selection. The screening criteria may not have discriminated as sharply among subjects on background characteristics related to the effectiveness of reverse interpreting as they might have. Initially, the experience level of prospective subjects was identified on the basis of personnel records. A questionnaire was used to collect additional information about each subject after he/she completed the experiment. HI subjects (see Table 6) exhibited high within-group variability in their sign language experience in spite of the fact that they shared comprehensive certification from the RID. They also showed higher within-group variability in interpreting experience (see Table 7) than the LO group, the experience that included both classroom and community interpreting. Fifty percent of the HI subjects have deaf members in their families and 75% of these individuals always use sign language to communicate with deaf family members. None of the LO subjects have deaf members in their families. Four HI subjects possessed less than 1500 hours of classroom interpreting experience (see Table 8), but were included because they had at least 4 years of comparable interpreting experience in a wide variety of settings similar to classroom interpreting responsibilities at NTID (e.g. in a community college, vocational education, and counseling).

A more precise description of the background characteristics of the HI group (Table 14 suggests that interactions involving experience levels, treatments, and story order effects might be attributable to a specific subgroup of the high experience sample. LO subjects, in contrast to the diversity of HI subjects, were evenly distributed on the background characteristics. [. . . .]

The results of this investigation indicate that experience level is a factor in the relative effectiveness of reverse interpreting under either treatment. It is possible that having more experience with sign language and interpreting, as well as having deaf members in their families, have helped the N_1 subjects to perform better in both PSE and ASL treatments than the N_1 subjects. Additionally, the results suggest that the PSE condition is easier to reverse interpret than the ASL condition for both HI and LO groups.

Further study seems warranted on reverse interpreting for deaf persons and the usefulness of skilled reverse interpreters. More knowledge is needed about the effects not only of experience, but of specific elements of different manual communication systems that may contribute to the performance of reverse interpreters. Questions related to reverse interpreting should be investigated in many different settings, especially in relation to differences in communication skills possessed by deaf persons for whom such services are provided.

Conclusions

Research hypothesis H_1, stated that both HI.and LO groups would do equally well in the PSE treatments. The results of the investigation (see Figures 2 and 3) showed, however, that in this respect the HI groups outperformed the LO groups. Hence, the research hypothesis H_1 is not consistent with the statistical findings.

Research hypothesis H_2 had suggested that the HI group would do significantly better than the LO group in the ASL treatments. The results of the investigation showed that, as predicted, the HI groups performed better on these treatments than the LO groups.

The following conclusions, therefore, can be drawn from the findings in this study:

1. Interpreting experience does play a significant role in the effectiveness of reverse interpreting under both PSE and ASL conditions.
2. Independent of experience, interpreters receive and reverse interpret information better under PSE conditions than under ASL conditions.

[. . . .]

Implications

The implications of the findings for the effect of the type of sign language on the performance of reverse interpreting in various settings (e.g. academic classrooms, doctor's office, courtroom and employment/unemployment office) are discussed here. Briefly, the implication of story order and story effect on this type of research is discussed. Some insights about the Registry of Interpreters for the Deaf (RID) evaluation system are also discussed here.

Since the sample in this study is not representative of the total population, it cannot be generalized from this study that most interpreters for deaf people need more experience with understanding ASL and with effective reverse interpreting of the signed message in ASL into spoken English. However, it can be assumed that interpreters with strong skills for understanding ASL and effective reverse interpreting from the signed message in ASL into spoken English would be in a better position to assist classroom teachers in regular schools because they would facilitate a better appreciation of the meaning of deaf students' efforts to express themselves. This approach can be viewed as an educational tool for helping deaf students to improve their English skills since it provides a feedback mechanism for interpreters and teachers to better understand deaf students who express themselves in a language (e.g. ASL) that is not understood by the general population. Hence, school administrators should consider providing highly experienced interpreters, taking into account the importance of reverse interpreting roles in regular classes where deaf students are enrolled as well as the need for direct interpreting services.

This implication, moreover, should not be confined to an educational setting alone. This consideration can be extended to other situations (e.g. legal and medical/clinical). Usually a deaf client experiences a negative encounter if he/she is not adequately able to use speech or written methods in standard English to convey his/her special needs or problems to a doctor or a lawyer. The impact is obviously profound for those individuals who lack adequate standard English language skills. Because interpreters performed differently under PSE and ASL conditions, it appears likely that an interpreter who lacks appropriate skills for understanding ASL will be less useful in such situations. It may, in fact, be crucial that an interpreter with strong ASL skills be assigned to a situation involving a deaf person who uses ASL or a similar type of sign language as his/her primary mode of communication. In certain situations where it is not possible to find an interpreter with strong ASL skills, it is sometimes possible to assign another deaf person who has the ability to understand both ASL and standard English as an intermediary between the deaf speaker and the interpreter. It might in this way be possible to circumvent the ASL deficiencies of reverse interpreters with limited training and experience.

We need to focus on what might be causing difficulties and creating differences between two stories presented to the subjects in this study. The story difficulty and order difference for both HI and LO groups were not very large in the PSE conditions, but in both groups there were large story-order differences in the ASL conditions. It is possible that the PSE stories may be easy enough to learn, due to a low-difficulty level of the stories themselves, and that the performance of the interpreters was affected by the differences in their ability to reverse interpret the material. Part of the problem with a greater story order difference in the ASL conditions may be that the story difficulty of both ASL conditions was not adequately controlled. It is possible that difficulty in one language under different story conditions is not directly comparable to differences between story order effects in another language. It can, however, be presumed that if interpreters have basic training in interpreting and possess skills adequate to the work of professional interpreters at NTID, their interpreting skills are good enough to satisfy the demands of both PSE stories equally well. However, when they attempted to interpret those stories in the ASL conditions, where their interpreting skills were weaker and more variable, it is possible that other factors (e.g. differential difficulty of story content, or story-order effects) became operative and influenced interpreter performance.

The implication of the method of data analysis used in this study (proposition analysis versus qualitative analysis) should be mentioned. The qualitative analysis is similar to the portion of the evaluation on reverse interpreting in the RID evaluation instrument except that the method for computing performance scores is different. The RID system uses a weighted score for each factor measured, whereas the method used in this study gives equal weight to each factor in the modified instrument. This is not the major issue here; the issue is to determine the difference between the proposition analysis and the qualitative analysis. We need to realize the implication of the evaluation part for reverse interpreting skills in the RID evaluation instrument which is principally subjective in nature and somewhat similar to that of the qualitative analysis used in this study. Although the correlation between the accuracy measures (proposition analysis) and the quality measures (qualitative analysis) was found to be .8288, we should look more closely at the reliability of the quality measures. The correlation between the composite mean scores of the four quality measures and the four individual quality measures were found to range between .9131 and .9677. These measures are highly intercorrelated. However, when we further scrutinize the ratings we will see that the major concern is with the pairwise inter-rater reliabilities among the three raters which were found to be .4853, .5905 and .7229. These figures are relatively low and mean that there is a great deal of inconsistency among the rating performances of these three raters, all of whom are certified to perform RID evaluations. The question here is whether the high variability noted in this study is recognized as a problem in the RID evaluation program. If this is a concern of the RID, then I would strongly recommend that the RID consider using the proposition analysis method which was found in this study to have a higher level of consistency (inter-rater reliability for accuracy scores was found to be .9758) than the qualitative method. Nevertheless, the subjective component should not be disregarded as it can be useful for the purpose of sharing qualitative information with the individual being evaluated. This has not been done in this study, but I believe that if this approach were to be used more intensively in the RID evaluation program it might have positive effects on the professional development of interpeters.

Recommendations for further research

The topic of reverse interpreting and providing interpreting services to deaf students who are heavily dependent on the services of reverse interpreting should be explored in greater depth. A need remains to address many of the questions raised in this study. Some suggestions for further research are as follows:

1. The value of reverse interpreting should be further studied by conducting research in settings that are similar to typical classroom situations. Situations where discussion occurs within the classroom, and where significant factors inhibit understanding the sign language and/or speech used by deaf student(s) are examples of such research settings that might be investigated.

2. The effects of using reverse interpreters with a variety of different populations in various educational settings should be investigated. Elementary-aged deaf children, secondary-aged deaf children, deaf persons with minimal or no sign language skills, and deaf persons with minimal standard English language skills are examples of populations that might be considered for further research investigation.

3. Similar research efforts should also be concentrated in other community settings (e.g. counseling and testing, job interviews, legal hearings, and medical inquiries).

4. Research on reverse interpreting should be conducted using stimulus materials that differ from the types employed in this study. Variance in the content/subject matter or the degree of difficulty of the material presented are variables that should be considered. Difficult material would perhaps require the presenter to rephrase and detail a great deal more of the material than was done in this study. A more sophisticated linguistic assessment measurement technique may be necessary to assure validity in story equivalency under different treatment conditions.

5. The characteristics of good reverse interpreting should be defined, including a careful analysis of the specific, idiosyncratic effects of either ASL or PSE that influence decoding and encoding by the interpreter as a way of defining this.

6. The interaction between standard English skills and sign language skills should be explored to determine effects on the encoding and decoding process of reverse interpreting.

7. A separate study should focus on the impact of deaf persons' using their voices during the reverse interpreting process. The use of voice by a deaf person may enhance or hinder the reverse interpreting process; for instance, unintelligible speech of a deaf person

may distract the interpreter's concentration from the signed presentation. It is also possible that getting two voice signals at the same time may be distracting to the audience.

8. Another study should focus on the impact of speechreading a deaf person regardless of the speech intelligibility on the reverse interpreting process. Siple (1977) has found that the visual center of the signing space is the nose-mouth area. Many signs are made in close proximity to this visual center, but seldom are signs made within this center. Caccamise, Ayers, Finch, and Mitchell (1978) state that when reading signs people tend to watch the face area of the signer, rather than the signer's hands. This observation is consistent with the contention that facial expressions and lip movement (whether or not words are mouthed or spoken) are important parts of manual communication. Frishberg (1975) found that signs made in the mouth area tended to move away from the mouth toward the sides of the mouth or the chin area. For example, the sign RED used to be made on the lips (and is still depicted that way in many sign books); however, many signers now make the signs lower, on the chin. Therefore, an emphasis is made not to obstruct the mouth area when signing.

9. As more data are gathered on reverse interpreting, information on training reverse interpreters can be obtained. Models for providing that training should be investigated.

10. A validation study of the RID Evaluation Instrument should take place at the earliest convenience, including inquiry into its correlation with the results of proposition analysis used in this study.

Acknowledgement

This paper was produced in the course of an agreement with the Department of Health, Education, and Welfare.

Much appreciation goes to many people, too numerous to mention, who made significant contribution to this research study. A special appreciation goes to my dissertation committee for their diligent guidance and direction: Dr. Jack Miller, Dr. Larry Dolan, and Dr. Michael Smith. Finally, but not the least, to the Word Processing Center at NTID for typing this manuscript, and to my secretary, Nancy Demarest for editing and typing the revision for publication.

References

Battison, R. *Lexical borrowing in ASL*. Silver Spring, Maryland: Linstok Press, 1978. Caccamise, F., Ayers, R., Finch, K., & Mitchell, M. Signs and manual communication systems: Selection, standardization, and development. *American Annals of the Deaf*, 1978, *123* (7), 877–902.

Fant, L. *Ameslan: An introduction to American Sign Language.* Silver Spring, Maryland: National Association of the Deaf, 1972.

Fischer, S. Influences on word order changes in American Sign Language. In Li, C. (ED.), *Word order and word order change,* Austin, Texas: University of Texas Press, 1975, 1–26.

Frischberg, N. Arbitrariness and inconicity: Historical change in American Sign Language, *Language,* 1975, 51, 696–719.

Hatfield, N., & Caccamise, F. Assessment of sign language and simultaneous communication. In D. Johnson, G. Walter, K. Crandall, D. McPherson, 3. Subtelny, H. Levitt, F. Caccamise, & M. Schwab (Eds.), *Communication performance evaluation with deaf students: A Review.* Springfield, Virginia: National Technical Information Service, 1980.

Hoemann, H. *The American Sign Language: Lexical and grammatical notes with translation exercises.* Silver Spring, Maryland: National Association of the Deaf, 1975.

Ingram, R. A communication model of the interpreting process. *Journal of rehabilitation of the Deaf,* 1974, 7, 3–8.

Peterson, P. *The influence of horizontal camera angle on deaf viewers' understanding of and preference for a televised presentation using simultaneous sign language and speech.* Unpublished doctoral dissertation. Syracuse Unviersity, 1976.

Pimental, A. *National Certification of Interpreters: A Manual for Evaluators.* Silver Spring, Maryland: Registry of Interpreters for the Deaf, 1972.

Siple, P. Visual constraints for sign language communication. In E. S. Klima and U. Bellugi (Eds.), *The signs of language.* Cambridge, Massachusetts: Harvard University Press, 1977.

Siple, P. *Understanding language through sign language research.* New York: Academic Press, 1978.

Titus, J. The comparative effectiveness of presenting spoken information to post-secondary oral deaf students through a live speaker, an oral interpreter, and an interpreter using signed English. Unpublished Doctoral Dissertation, University of Pittsburgh, Pittsburgh, Pennsylvania, 1978.

Thorndyke, P. Cognitive structures in comprehensions and memory of narrative discourse. *Cognitive Psychology,* 1977, 9, 77–100.

CHAPTER 3

Practitioners become Researchers (1980s)

Introduction

By the 1980s the scientific study of SLI began to undergo a shift from the psychological and psycholinguistic experiments about cognitive processing models, to descriptions and analyses that relied on filming interpreters and interpreted events. As the growing acceptance of sign languages began to impact perceptions of interpreting, practitioners increasingly applied the frameworks of linguistics and its sub-fields, such as sociolinguistics and applied linguistics. Accordingly, interpreting between two languages and cultures becomes comparable to the practice of spoken language interpreters, thus their training exercises and courses of study can be applied or adapted to SLI. As SLI practitioners became educators, the desire to understand the segments of the interpreting process sent them towards research. As practitioners became researchers, they scoured not only previous SLI research, but also spoken language interpreting research, discovering scholars like Gerver and Brislin, who recognized that the process of interpreting is not tied to any particular language combination, but is rather a cognitive, linguistic, and social process of its own.

Throughout this decade, SLI researchers and educators turned to spoken language colleagues for perspectives on both research and education. In 1983, Robert Ingram urged the program committee of the Conference of Interpreter Trainers (CIT) to invite Etilvia Arjona, Barbara Moser-Mercer, and Sylvie Lambert, all of whom were faculty members and researchers at the Monterrey Institute of International Studies (MIIS) where spoken language conference interpreters were trained, to present at the conference. The MIIS faculty discussed the existing research on conference interpreting at that time, and for many SLI educators and other SLI international visitors it was their first exposure to such studies and the resulting pedagogical techniques of spoken language training.

The American engagement with spoken language interpreter educators was also seen in the enormous popularity of Danica Seleskovitch's 1968 book, *Interpreting for International Conferences*, which did not appear in English until 1978, but rapidly became a required textbook in most U.S. SLI interpreter education programs. Seleskovitch, a member of the International Association of Conference Interpreters (AIIC) and its Executive Secretary (1959–1963), a professor at the School of Interpreters and Translators at the University of Sorbonne/Paris and who established the first Ph.D. program in interpreting, was known for her theoretical stance that ignored linguistics (referring to the older structural frameworks which were applied to translations at the lexical or phrasal level) and argued for visualizing meaning and creating a target message that made 'sense' in the target language. SLI educators found this helpful in designing exercises, such as visualization, and then sequencing exercises so as to acquire simultaneous interpreting skills slowly and over time, many of which are still in use.

Along with the growing appeal of spoken language interpreting models, SLI in the U.S. began moving into university-level bachelor programs by the mid to late 1980s and with that transition came a demand for academic and research publications. The Registry of Interpreters for the Deaf (RID) began its *Journal of Interpretation* in 1985, and recruited Nancy Frishberg, a Ph.D. in linguistics and a sign language interpreter, to begin a major revision of the introductory text on SLI. In 1986, *Sign Language Studies* (SLS), a journal that published papers about sign languages, devoted a special issue to SLI.

Other countries also began to establish university level programs that pushed for studies of SLI. For example, in Hamburg, Germany, a Deafness-related publication began in 1987, and published Masters SLI papers by students from German-speaking countries. Like the *SLS, Das Zeichen* continues to publish SLI papers.

In the U.K., Bristol University established the Centre for Deaf Studies (CDS) in 1978 and began to conduct research into the acquisition and usage of BSL. By 1987, CDS began to offer a part-time course in sign language interpretation, which became a full-time course of study in 1990. Gallaudet University in Washington, D.C., launched a Masters degree in Linguistics in 1981 and most of the early applicants were interpreters, many of whom focused on SLI (Roy 1987; Davis 1989; Winston 1989). By 1988, Gallaudet opened the first Masters degree in SLI with a curriculum based on the scaffolding sequence found in spoken language programs – a skill-based sequence of translation, consecutive interpreting, and then simultaneous interpreting which began with an introductory course in linguistics and communication.

Searching for doctoral-level disciplinary frameworks, many practitioners and educators turned to linguistics departments in universities that did not necessarily specialize in deafness, sign language, or interpretation. Cokely and Roy, for example, turned to sociolinguistics, a convergence of anthropology, sociology, and linguistics, for its varied methodologies for investigating SLI, while Winston turned to applied linguistics for its recognition that teaching about language was a crucial aspect of teaching interpreting and its practical perspectives on language use in action.

All the authors in this section are practitioners who became researchers, sought degrees in higher education, and were also educators, looking for better explanations of the interpreting process to inform their teaching practice. While this section is still heavily American, the articles included here represent data-based research, drawing from both experimental methodologies and qualitative methodologies found in the approaches of linguistics, along with insights from their own experience as interpreters. Moreover, studies in SLI began to turn their attention to the interactive, face-to-face nature of the work that most sign language interpreters were doing.

Peter Llewellyn-Jones, an interpreter and interpreter educator in the U.K., presented his research on psycholinguistic processes in 1980. He conducted empirical studies of interpreting, proposing both a model of the working memory in interpreters, and a model for simultaneous interpreting. Both Cokely and Llewellyn-Jones, influenced by the information processing models of Gerver (1976) and Moser (1978), focused on the psychological and psycholinguistic aspects of interpreting and the mental models of the interpreting process. In the first part of the paper, Llewellyn-Jones recounts previous studies that demonstrate a repertoire of styles in British Sign Language (BSL). The second part of the paper demonstrates, via quizzing Deaf participants about their understanding of the information, that interpreters who coded the message into signs poorly did so for a number of reasons that can be demonstrated within the initial part of a cognitive processing model. Although this paper covers a number of studies, its major point is that an interpreter must have an understanding of the different language varieties with which she works, which warrants more research on the varieties of signing and the nature of interpretation as well as the preparation of those who work as professional interpreters.

Dennis Cokely worked in a variety of positions at Gallaudet University before becoming a research associate in William Stokoe's Linguistics Research Laboratory at Gallaudet University, where Stokoe encouraged him to do research on interpreting. By 1981, Cokely created *The Reflector, A Journal for Sign Language Teachers and Interpreters,* as a venue for sign language teachers and interpreters to publish essays and research studies. One of the first studies Cokely conducted was to investigate why Deaf students at Gallaudet University were complaining about the interpreting at the student health center on campus where the doctors required the services of interpreters. Cokely created two mock medical interviews, each with a Deaf patient, a nurse, and an interpreter. Analyzing the video recordings of these interviews, he found that the interpreters made psycholinguistic errors of perception, memory, semantics and performance. Studying the psycholinguistic process of interpreting proved fascinating and Cokely went on to expand this type of study with his dissertation research.

Among the last few studies done from a psychological framework were studies done by **Steven Fritsch-Rudser** and **Michael Strong** at the Center on Deafness at the University of California San Francisco. Like many such centers, research focused on deafness and related issues which included interpreting. In this paper, Fritsch-Rudser and Strong test the merits of subjective assessments of interpreters hoping to demonstrate that such assessments are unreliable, and are often influenced by personal characteristics unrelated to competence. This study occurred during a time with the RID certification exam depended heavily on the subjective judgment of its raters, and suffered from complaints of bias. One of the most interesting aspects of this paper is that they used interpretations filmed in 1973 for a Quigley et al. (1973) study. They presented twenty-five interpretations into ASL to a group of Deaf raters and twenty-five interpretations into English to a group of people who could hear. Both of these groups filled out forms asking questions like, "was the interpreter easy to watch," or "was the interpreter easy to listen to." Interestingly, there was a high correlation between both groups and within groups. But when compared with an objective instrument that measured accuracy, the correlations were not high enough compared to correlations expected for other types of professional exams. By 1988 RID significantly changed the evaluation and certification process.

Transliteration, the term SLI used for literal interpretations of an English source message, was the type of interpreting promoted by many public schools in the U.S., under the assumption that Deaf students would learn English and learn other content through this literal presentation of English. **Elizabeth Winston,** while a graduate student in the Linguistics program at Gallaudet University, decided to take a more objective look at what interpreters were actually signing when transliterating. At the time, Deaf people and interpreters assumed that signs could represent the structure of English visually and literally. In this case study, Winston looked at four strategies and features: additions, omissions, vocabulary choice and movements of the mouth. She found that the interpreter used a number of features that were grammatical for ASL, but not English. These ASL-like features included the use of space, classifiers, and sections in which English syntax was rearranged into a more "ASL-like" English. Her comparison of the source language, English, with the target language, demonstrates the types of contact features that appear in the interpreted message. Her study has become a seminal work for two reasons: First, this is the first study to examine the discourse features of a literal interpretation, and therefore, to identify linguistic evidence of language contact within the target text. Second, the Registry of Interpreters for the Deaf (RID) selected this study as the sample representing the standard for professional certification, when being tested for literal interpretation, or transliteration. Thus, this study is often cited with regard to literal interpretation.

Language contact phenomena are a sociolinguistic aspect of SLI first explored by **Jeffrey Davis,** influenced by the work of Lucas and Valli (1992). In a body of work based on his doctoral research, Davis (1990, 2003, 2005) discusses ASL/English interpreters' translation style (or code choices) when interpreting in a language contact environment, by analyzing the linguistic interference and transference that took place when a lecture was interpreted from English into ASL and a more literal rendition. Davis focuses on the occurrence of code-switching, code-mixing (switching within a sentence or clause) and lexical borrowing within the interpretations of the lectures, and found that linguistic interference happened far less than linguistic transference.

Davis' work appeared around the same time that other papers appeared about literal renderings, or transliteration (e.g. Winston 1989; Siple 1996), all of which recognized that an effective literal rendering involved more than just producing one sign for every word. This body of work began to change the thinking regarding transliteration, with discussions of a continuum of translation styles, whereby interpreters employ a more 'literal' or 'free' approach (e.g. Metzger 1999; Napier 2002). The Deaf consumer comprehension of literal as compared to more free interpretation approaches also became a topic of research interest, as seen in a paper featured in Chapter 4 by Rachel Locker.

All these research studies cited here we consider to be seminal in the SLI Studies field, as not only were they conducted by 'practisearchers' (Gile 1994) with an intuitive understanding of the interpreting 'problems' to be examined, but also because they shifted our understanding of interpreting practice by drawing on evidence-based, or data-driven, analysis, which subsequently led to the groundswell of SLI Studies research in the 1990s.

3.1 Llewellyn Jones, Peter. 1981. "Target language styles and source language processing in conference sign language interpreting." Paper presented at the *3rd International Symposium on Sign Language Interpreting*, Bristol, UK.

Peter Llewellyn-Jones learned sign language as a trainee Welfare Officer for Deaf people and after he qualified in 1972, immediately specialized in interpreting. In the mid-1970s he coordinated the British Deaf Association's Standing Conference on Interpreter Training and, in 1979, co-founded the University of Bristol sign language and interpreting research team with Jim Kyle. Llewellyn-Jones was a founding member of the U.K.'s Register of interpreters and, in 1987, the first Chair of the U.K.'s Association of Sign Language Interpreters (ASLI).

He wrote the U.K.'s first undergraduate degree course in Sign Language Interpreting for Wolverhampton University in 1991 (which he taught for two years) and, in 1997, wrote the Postgraduate Diploma in Interpreting for the University of Central Lancashire, spending the next fifteen years there as Joint Course Leader. In 2003 he was commissioned to write the MA in Interpreting: BSL-English for the University of Leeds Centre for Translation Studies, where he was Program Director until 2012. Now a Visiting Research Fellow at Leeds, he still supervises Ph.D. students for the university. In July 2010 Llewellyn-Jones was awarded an Honorary Fellowship by the University of Central Lancashire for his outstanding achievements in the field of interpreter training.

Target language styles and source language processing in conference sign language interpreting

Peter Llewellyn-Jones

Conference interpreting for deaf people in Great Britain has traditionally been considered the province of the Welfare Officers or Social Workers for the Deaf. Indeed, as part of the training and qualification for this profession the act of interpreting from speech to sign and from sign into speech was practised and examined. With changing approaches to social work practice and training the traditional qualification for work with the adult deaf, the Deaf Welfare Examination Board Diploma or Certificate, was phased out, to be replaced in the mid 1970s by one-year post-qualifying specialist courses for generic social workers. Due in part to this change in training and in part to the swing from voluntary society based services to direct Local Authority based services for deaf people, fears regarding the supply and quality of interpreters for the deaf have grown. It is neither possible nor particularly profitable to try to compare the interpreting services of today with those of 15 or 20 years ago, but it is true to say that as the deaf community becomes more aware of the opportunities open to it, both educational and social, the demands upon interpreters are increasing. The interpreters themselves have long recognised the need for, but total lack of formalised training.

The shortage of suitably trained and qualified interpreters is not questioned and official recognition of this shortage was given in 1977 in the form of funding, by the DHSS, of the British Deaf Association 'Communication Skills Project'. Approximately one half of this grant was earmarked for the establishing of a Registry of Interpreters for the Deaf. The call for a registry, welcomed both by the professionals and the deaf community, has brought with it demands for the setting of a minimum acceptable standard and a standardised assessment end training procedure.

The attempts over the past two years to draw up suitable training and assessment procedures have highlighted the need for a clear definition of the role of the interpreter and of the component skills and processes needed for the interpreter to be effective.

Llewellyn-Jones (1981) in looking at Sign Language Interpreter effectiveness, discussed information processing models proposed for foreign language interpreting. Drawing on the work of Moser (1977), and Baddeley (1979) the paper concluded that there were indeed many parallels that could be drawn between sign language and foreign language interpreting. Before examining these similarities further, however, there are two central questions that must be asked:

1.   Can British Sign Language be regarded as a foreign language?
2.   If so, is BSL an appropriate Target Language for conference settings?

BSL as an autonomous language

Hearing sign users have tended to regard communicating with and interpreting for deaf adults as unique. The deaf community has been viewed predominantly as a handicap group, and sign language, not as a language, but as a range of communication techniques, the particular form selected being dependent on the educational achievement and linguistic competence (i.e. literacy) of the deaf person being communicated with. These traditional attitudes towards Sign Language are now, however, being challenged. Linguists maintain that sign languages in fact meet all the requirements necessary for them to be regarded as real languages (Klima & Bellugi 1979; Wilbur 1979) and the evidence available so far suggests that BSL is no exception (Kyle, Woll & Llewellyn-Jones 1981). Moreover, parallels have been drawn between the deaf community and minority language groups (Markowicz & Woodward 1975). Full membership of this community is not dictated by the notion of handicap but by the sharing of a common first language. Markowicz and Woodward have taken this parallel so far as to suggest that Pidgin Sign English i.e. a point somewhere between ASL and Signed English, marks the 'ethnic' boundary between the deaf and hearing communities.

Is BSL appropriate for the conference setting?

Deuchar (1979) argues that a diglossic situation exists in sign use in Britain. She proposes that within the deaf community Signed English is regarded as the prestigious form of signed communication (High) and BSL as the less prestigious (Low). If this were indeed the case then it would be a powerful argument in favour of using Signed English in formal settings e.g. conferences, with BSL being seen as appropriate only for informal settings. This view is discussed at length in Llewellyn-Jones, Kyle & Woll (1979). Doubt is cast on whether the High form (Signed English) is actually used *within* the deaf community or whether it is simply accepted as appropriate for formal settings because these settings have traditionally been controlled by hearing people.

   Clearly the appropriateness or otherwise of BSL for formal settings must be decided by deaf people themselves. The eliciting of this information, however, is not easy. People's expressed attitudes towards language use may not necessarily coincide with their 'covert' feelings. Trudgill (1972) has argued that 'non-standard' speech may be highly valued in a manner not usually expressed and "Statements about 'bad-speech' are for public consumption only". Consequently deaf people may produce judgements 'for public consumption' that they do not hold for sign language use in practice.

As a test of 'covert' feelings towards BSL and Signed English, Llewellyn-Jones, Kyle and Woll produced a sign language version of the 'Matched Guise test' (Lambert et al. 1960; Giles 1971). The original procedure for spoken languages is as follows: subjects are told that they will hear two different speakers and following presentation are asked to rate them on attitude scales. The two speakers are, in fact, one speaker using different accents or different languages. The full procedure followed by Llewellyn-Jones et al. and a statistical analysis of the results will be published in the final report of the DHSS-funded 'Sign Language Learning and Use' project (Kyle, et al., in preparation). The results should be treated with caution as this was only a preliminary study of a very complex and important area, however they do point to a clear mismatch between expressed opinions and indirect judgements. In summary, when two matched groups of deaf people were presented with the same signer, one group seeing him produce a BSL version and the other seeing him produce a Signed English version of the same message there was a significantly more positive reaction to him from the group watching BSL. He was, for example, rated as being more friendly, more helpful, more likeable and even better looking. Importantly, for our purposes, it should be noted that both versions scored equally on ratings of competence, i.e. intelligence, professionalism, adequacy of signing, etc. These were not the judgements one would expect from a community that rates Signed English as having high prestige and BSL as low.

Perhaps a more obvious way of getting deaf people's attitudes towards appropriateness of sign language styles for different settings is by examining the varieties they use themselves. Pitt Corder (1973) in discussing language functions in spoken languages expresses the importance, for the native speaker, of his 'repertoire' or 'sheaf of grammars' from which he selects the appropriate language forms according to the situation. Pitt Corder goes on to discuss the learner of a language and the importance of teaching him the repertoire he will need to participate in a variety of settings. An inadequate repertoire will result in the language speaking community not accepting him as fluent and always regarding him as a 'foreigner'.

If BSL is not merely a variety of sign use but is in itself an autonomous language, in common with other languages one would expect to find contained within it a range of styles to meet the many and various needs of the sign language community.

Style or varietal differences within BSL

Margaret Deuchar's notion of diglossia was based on data collected in two very different settings, a deaf club (BSL) and a church service (Signed English). There are many factors that influence style, but perhaps one of the most important from the sign language interpreter's point of view is the degree of formality of the setting. Her data is of limited value in trying to identify style shifts influenced by degree of formality, as it allows for too many other variables that are likely to affect style change.

These are:

i.   Physical surroundings: Giles & Powesland (1975) discuss how a religious setting is likely to affect style change in speech, simply because of the 'atmosphere' inside a church or cathedral, regardless of the topic of conversation.
ii. Topic: Lawton (1965) found that levels of abstraction influenced complexity of grammatical structures as does humorousness (Giles & Powesland, 1975)
iii. Deaf signers versus hearing signers: a major limitation in Deuchar's study, for our purposes, is that for informal data she used deaf signers and for the formal style a hearing social worker (albeit a native signer). Llewellyn-Jones, Kyle and Woll (1979) underline the differences in sign use between hearing and deaf signers.

To isolate and identify those features of BSL that are influenced by the informality/formality of the setting, and not by the other factors listed above, it is useful to identify the types of language change that occur in spoken languages. There are, broadly speaking, three categories of style change that can be readily observed:

i.   Grammatical shifts: e.g.   "The person about whom I was talking" (formal)
                                 "The person I was speaking about (informal)
ii. Lexical shifts: e.g.   "Colleagues" – "Workmates"
                                 "Refurbish" – "Paint"
iii. Phonological shifts: e.g.   "Is not" – "isn't"
                                 "Yes" – "Yeah"

If Sign Language functions in the same way as a spoken language, one would expect similar shifts to occur. Some of the features of BSL (grammatical, lexical and phonological) that are capable of such change are listed below:

1. Fingerspelling
2. Modulation
3. Lip movements
4. Two handed (as opposed to one handed) signs
5. Simultaneity
6. Facial expression
7. Placement
8. Eye Gaze

By mapping these features on to the original three categories of change that occur in spoken language, it is now possible to predict style shifts that might occur. It can, for example, be hypothesised that an informal setting when compared to a formal setting will result in:

1. Grammatical Shifts
    i.   more modulation of signs
    ii. more simultaneity
    iii. a difference in the use of placement
2. Lexical Shifts
    i.   less fingerspelling (or more use of reduced sign-like forms)
3. Phonological Shifts
    i.   less English-like lip movements
    ii. less use of two-handed signs (as opposed to one-handed variants of the same sign)

It is probable that changes in the use of facial expression and eye gaze in Sign Language are features of discourse behaviour rather than signals of style shift.

The above hypothesis was tested by observing deaf sign users in a range of settings.

Method

It can be clearly demonstrated that, in the presence of hearing people, deaf people tend to alter their signing style to accommodate the hearing person's assumed or actual linguistic limitations – in much the same way, for example, as an English speaker would talk to a foreigner. It was necessary, therefore, to collect data in an 'all-deaf' setting, with the hearing researcher being as inconspicuous as possible. To satisfy this condition and avoid the other possible variables discussed earlier, a meeting was chosen of the Western Deaf Sports Council, an organisation made up of representatives of each deaf club in the South West of England. For the morning meeting, the 20-strong council was seated in a semi-circle facing the officers' table and, to minimise the effect of filming, the researcher was seated in the semi-circle with the portable video equipment concealed under a table and only the small camera with zoom lens in view. No artificial lighting was necessary as the camera is equipped with a Nuvicon tube designed for low lighting levels.

The meeting consisted of two parts – a closed full council meeting in the morning, with an open Annual General Meeting in the afternoon. It was possible then to identify three different settings:

a. The formal Annual General Meeting where the officers presented reports to a large audience
b. A semi-formal council meeting mainly consisting of discussions
c. An informal lunch break where the members, most of whom have known each other for many years, 'chatted' and joked over a snack meal

The camera was left on during the lunch break.

Data

The tapes of four officers of the council were chosen for detailed analysis and one edited tape made, to include samples of their signing in the three settings.

Analysis and results

As a preliminary analysis, one component from each of the categories in the hypothesis were studied by carrying out a simple frequency count, and the number of times each feature occurred per minute of actual signing time, excluding prolonged pauses etc., was recorded (Table 1). The figures set out in Table 1 clearly support the hypothesis for these three features. The decrease in number of fingerspelled items used by all four signers when comparing the formal setting 'a' with the informal 'c' is quite marked. The slight increase in the fingerspelling of Signer 3 in the semi-formal setting is probably as a result of contextual influences rather than style, as neither he nor Signer 4 used any fingerspelling at all in the informal setting. The fingerspelled items counted did not include proper or place names, as it is accepted that fingerspelling of one form or another must be used to convey this type of information. It is noticeable however that in the informal setting greater use is made of abbreviated or reduced forms, e.g. BATH (the city) becomes BH with an accompanying "th" lip pattern, and often, as in this case, the fluency and speed of the reduced form are such that it becomes a sign rather than a fingerspelled item.

Table 1. Features occurring per minute of signing time

	Setting	F:S	Modulation	Signs without English lip patterns
Signer (1)	A	4	5	5
	B	2.83	5.16	5.33
	C	1.4	7.71	2(?)
Signer (2)	A	10.2	2.2	2.2
	B	6.85	4.28	7.71
	C	2.35	14.11	11.76
Signer (3)	A	3.84	2.16	2.4
	B	4.66	3.33	7.33
	C	0	12	21
Signer (4)	A	12.85	3.85	3.42
	B	5.03	2.5	6.78
	C	0	11.42	39.99
Settings	A	Formal (AGM)		
	B	Semi-formal (Council Meeting)		
	C	Informal (Lunch break)		

At the grammatical level, there is a very significant increase in the frequency of use of modulated signs by all subjects when in the informal setting. This would suggest that syntactic structures in the informal setting were quite different to those used in the formal setting, with more information being given simultaneously rather than sequentially.

Frequency in itself does not describe *how* the signs are used differently, only that they are and, clearly, to extract more information from this data, a much finer linguistic analysis is needed.

It is clear, though, from a simple two line transcription of sign glosses and lip patterns that the style chosen by the subjects for the formal setting (A) is not 'Signed English'. It is, though, certainly more English-like at a superficial level, e.g. greater use of English word lip-patterns, more finger-spelling, and less simultaneity in the form of modulation. The grammatical structure would not, however, be regarded as 'good' English, yet the intellectual and linguistic ability of the four subjects, all well respected leaders within the deaf community, is not questioned.

The evidence suggests, then, that there is a 'repertoire' of styles *within* BSL and that there are agreed ways of signalling style shifts. A much more detailed study of style and style appropriateness is now underway, but the above results do serve to imply that for the interpreter, decisions regarding choice of Target Language are far more complex than simply Signed English versus BSL. Whether Signed English is understood effortlessly enough for it to be a suitable Target Language for the majority of the deaf community is discussed later.

The effect of target language styles on source language processing

In a study measuring the overall effectiveness of two small groups of sign language interpreters (Llewellyn-Jones 1981), one of native sign users (N = 6) and the other of experienced signers with at least seven years interpreting experience (N = 7), it was found during comprehension tests completed by the prelingually deaf viewing panels that a substantial proportion of the original information was being lost (Table 2).

By examining the individual performance of the interpreters in the light of an existing model of the simultaneous interpreting process (Moser 1977) Llewellyn-Jones proposed that the least effective fell into 4 broad categories.

1. Those with insufficient knowledge of the Target Language (Interpreters B5, B6, B7)
2. Those with good Target Language knowledge but insufficient processing of the Source Language (Interpreter A5)
3. Those with adequate processing skills and knowledge of Target Language, but who chose an inappropriate form of Target Language for the viewers (Interpreters A3, A4, B2, B3)
4. Those with good Target Language knowledge but who chose a Target Language form that interfered with internal processing (Interpreters A6, B4)

Table 2. comprehension of interpreted passages by deaf panels 100% = Comprehension of same passages by hearing control group (N = 15)

Group A – Native sign users		Group B – Non-native sign users	
Interpreter	Comprehension score	Interpreter	Comprehension score
1	95%	1	83%
2	83%	2	71%
3	59%	3	65%
4	53%	4	48%
5	48%	5	41%
6	40%	6	35%
		7	35%
Average	63%	Average	54%

One of the models of language processing discussed in Llewellyn-.Jones is based on the work of Baddeley (1979) and others on 'Working Memory' (Figure 1) and deals only with the understanding of the original source language.

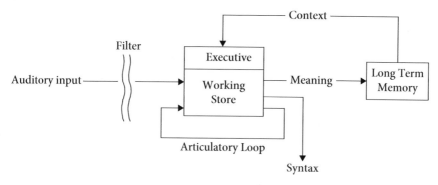

Figure 1. A processing model of "working memory"

After cursory acoustic filtering, to discard non-meaningful auditory signals (noise, etc.) the incoming information is passed into the working store. The executive scans the information and passes the meaning on to the long term store. Contextual information from the long-term store programmes the Executive, telling it what to look for and what to reject. It is here that syntax is discarded; in other words, the exact wording of the source language is forgotten, and only the meaning retained. If, however, the executive fails to extract the meaning on its first attempt, the information can be recycled through the Articulatory Loop and scanned again. A similar process can be observed in children reading. When a sentence is not understood, a child will read it again out loud. Adults will do the same, but much more infrequently and usually silently, or sub-vocally. Heard information can be 'rehearsed' in the same way, thus giving the Executive a second chance to scan for meaning. The capacity of the Articulatory Loop is, according to Baddeley, time based rather than limited by the number of items that can be held. His evidence suggests that the maximum capacity, without missing or 'forgetting' information is approximately 4½ seconds.

The above model is, however, too simple to allow sufficient description of the effects on processing of different target language forms and it is necessary to separate the actual language processing or 'parsing' from the function of the executive. A modified model which might describe processing of the source language *and* generation of the target language is shown in Figure 2. This model assumes that the interpreter is equally fluent in both source and target language and ideally, as in the case of some spoken language interpreting, there should be no interference between the two. With the less effective interpreters described above, however, variations of this model can be used to describe the processing problems.

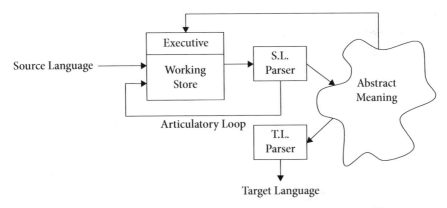

Figure 2. A processing model of simultaneous language interpreting

Let us first consider those native signers who, although possessing adequate knowledge of both English and Native Sign Language, chose Signed English as the target language form, i.e. categories 3 and 4.

Figure 3 describes the processes involved in interpreting from speech into Signed English, and as can be seen, strictly speaking, language interpretation is not taking place, i.e. the original message is simply being repeated in the same language, albeit in a different modality. It is interesting though to compare this model with what appears to be happening to the interpreters in category 4.

Although they seemed to choose the same target language form, there was a considerable difference in performance (Figure 4)

The interpreters in Category 3 (Figure 3) were obviously fully understanding the original message and, as an indication of this, it was noted that the final signed version, although still in English, was often produced in a slightly re-worded or paraphrased

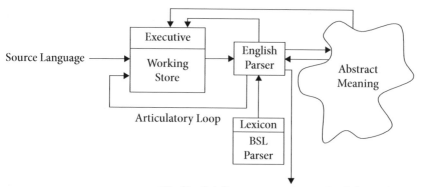

Figure 3. A processing model of spoken english to signed english "interpreting"

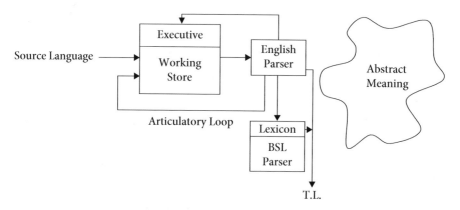

Figure 4. A processing model of word-sign matching

form. The interpreters in Category 4 (Figure 4) however, attempted merely to repeat the original message in a lip-spoken form whilst matching and relating signs on a sign for word basis. In effect they were attempting to 'shadow'. An indication of the lack of depth of processing, i.e. not basing the signed version on any understanding of the original message, was shown quite clearly by one interpreter in particular (A4). Having difficulty in keeping up with the speaker, on two occasions the interpreter attempted to re-start the Signed English production mid-sentence and was obviously only processing at word or lexical level.

The effect on the functioning of the executive of repeating the original message 'verbatim' is discussed in Llewellyn-Jones (1981). The silent exact repetition of the source message, it is argued, could have the effect of bringing into service the articulatory loop, the interpreter then consciously trying to remember what is being said. The more conscious the effort the more the processing capacity is used up. The interpreter then is concentrating on remembering the original message rather than effortlessly processing it and concentrating on production into the target language. This might have two effects*

i.   Mistakes in production (choice of inappropriate signs, etc.)
ii.   Overload of the articulatory loop, resulting in losing or forgetting chunks of information.

The experience of the interpreters in Category 4 would seem to support (ii) above in that they appeared to find the spoken passages (Source Language) too fast and 'broke down' either by missing chunks of information in order to catch up or by, in some instances, stopping altogether. The Category 3 interpreters, by concentrating on meaning rather than words were able to avoid this effect. The target version, although still in English, was nevertheless different enough not to trigger the rehearsal loop.[1]

With the interpreters who chose BSL as the target language, one would expect the model shown in Figure 2 to apply, with little or no interference between the two separate language parsers.

When working from English into BSL one would expect the interpreter with native fluency in both languages to function as in Figure 2. The majority of sign language interpreters are not, however, native sign users, and their interpreting performance and effectiveness reflects their inadequate knowledge of an appropriate BSL repertoire. The reasons for this are fairly clear when one looks at the opportunity afforded to the interpreter to learn this repertoire.

A recent survey carried out by the Bristol University Sign Language Research Project (Kyle, Woll & Llewellyn-Jones 1981) has shown that Sign Language is rarely taught by deaf people themselves and, as is noted earlier in this paper, the variety of sign language used by hearing professionals (the majority of the sign language teachers) is very different to varieties used by the deaf community. The result is that although non-native interpreters may have a good knowledge of 'standard sign language' ('standard' that is in the eyes of hearing users), they are likely to have a limited style repertoire. This limitation probably accounts for one of the most striking differences between Sign Language Interpreters and Foreign Language Interpreters. Spoken language interpreters at least in Europe and America nearly always, for reasons of preference and effectiveness, interpret from their "B" language into their "A" language, i.e. into their native language. The overwhelming majority of non-native sign interpreters, however, prefer to interpret from English (their A language) into Sign

---

1.   It should perhaps be remembered that the target audience is also having to process the target language produced by the interpreter. If that target language is in a form not normally used by the target audience, i.e. Signed English, it is possible that much of the processing capacity is used up trying to understand the message, leaving less capacity for concentrating on the meaning (implications, etc.) of the content.

(their B language). As deaf people do not conveniently use the hearing 'standard' style form, limitations in the interpreter's BSL repertoire may lead to comprehension problems. It is easier, then, for the interpreter to work from English into his hearing-standard form of sign language, and leave the comprehension problems for the deaf consumer to work out. The processing problems encountered by the non-native interpreter working from BSL into English could be described as in Figure 5.

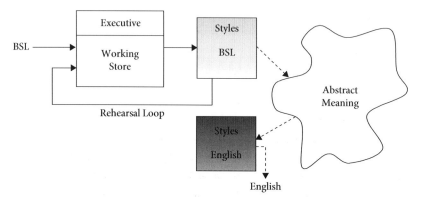

Figure 5. A processing model of interpreting from BSL into English with an inadequate BSL repertoire

The scanning of the original message (source language) by the Executive is normally triggered by the section of the parser that deals with repertoire. For example, a southern English person listening to English produced in a heavily accented northern dialect will readily identify the dialect and accent, and providing his repertoire includes sufficient knowledge of that variety, he is able to cope with and process the information content quite effortlessly. If that dialect however falls outside the listener's repertoire, problems of scanning will occur and processing will no longer be effortless. As was shown in the earlier models, one effect of inefficient scanning is the triggering of the rehearsal loop. The source message is then consciously rehearsed and analysed before comprehension takes place. Taking this argument further, if the rehearsal or articulatory loop represents the subvocalising of the original message, this rehearsal will become more difficult the more the original message is outside the available repertoire. A non-Russian speaker, for example, would experience great difficulty in trying to repeat either vocally or sub-vocally a Russian sentence made up of sounds he could not recognise, let alone pronounce. Similarly then an interpreter with a limited BSL repertoire, watching a source message consisting of sign forms and modulations he would not normally have access to, is unlikely to be able to rehearse effectively. Consequently, if the message is not completely understood at the first scanning of the Executive, he is unlikely to be able to rehearse accurately enough to allow the Executive a second chance. When, as in Figure 5, the source language parser is unable to cope with the message and hence unable to extract the abstract meaning, the interpreter has a choice of either stopping altogether, or trying to make sense of the message by 'translating' the individual signs he does recognise, and passing them on to his more complete native language parser for processing. Much information is likely to be lost during this circuitous route through the processing system, and an interpreter intent on making sense of the original message may resort to filling in the gaps by guessing what is being missed. If the interpreter knows the deaf person and the topic well enough, his guesswork might be quite inspired and reasonably accurate, but the chances are slim.

More often, the interpreter will give up trying to determine the meaning and produce instead a word for sign rendering of the incomplete message, so leaving the target audience to sort out the meaning for themselves. The result is an incomplete spoken gloss of the source message.

Interestingly this same result is often observed with native sign interpreters who are fluent in BSL, but in this instance the reasons are attitudinal and not attributable to an insufficient repertoire. Once again this reflects the traditional views held by many interpreters towards the linguistic status of BSL and the attitude that for an 'accurate' interpretation the target language must reflect the form of the original or source language as well as its content. If we accept BSL as an autonomous language then this view is patently absurd. No English target audience would accept a German-English interpretation that still retained the original German syntax. The audience would immediately accuse the interpreters of incompetence, yet many sign language interpreters consistently perform in this way with seeming impunity. It is perhaps easy to understand the hearing community's acceptance of this type of interpreting when one considers that the deaf community and hence individual deaf 'speakers' are likely to be viewed as 'handicapped' rather than as simply using a different language. The audience is more likely to think that the original 'speaker's' language skills are deficient, rather than the interpreter's.

This attitudinal block on the part of interpreters is apparent in data collected during tests designed to measure the sign – English interpreting effectiveness of a group of very experienced native sign interpreters.

As part of the many tests administered, the interpreters were asked to take down in note form a message from a deaf person and relay this message some time later to a hearing person (in this case on to a cassette tape recorder). A few moments later they were asked to simultaneously interpret, again on to a cassette recorder, a story signed by the same deaf person. The first task was not seen as an interpretation, but simply as a relaying of a message. The second task was obviously regarded as a formal interpretation. The resultant differences in target language form between the two tasks are quite striking as the following extracts show:

Message 1

"The message reads "Please will I telephone Allans coaches to confirm that a bus has been booked for a deaf club outing. The bus is to leave Bath Deaf Club at 8 a.m. – will stop outside Bath Deaf Club at 8.a.m. picking up 20 people, and will arrive outside Bristol Deaf Club at 8.30 a.m. picking up 25 people. The coach will be going to…"

Message 2

"On Saturday I arrived – you were waiting for your friend – yes – waiting, waiting – friend came – you walked to deaf club – sitting in deaf club – waiting … Manchester? Waited and waited – the bus came – quickly got into bus – quickly – the bus went quickly and they arrived in Manchester …"

These examples of target language were produced by the same person – a native sign user – interpreting for the same deaf person. The style of source language did not change, but the first task was regarded as a 'relaying of information' and the second as an 'interpretation'.

The target language form used for the 'interpretation' implies a lack of linguistic ability on the part of the 'speaker'. As we base many of our judgements of people (including their intellectual ability) on their linguistic competence, this style of 'interpreting' is nothing short of a misrepresentation of the deaf person's real ability.

Conclusion

If we accept the ever-growing body of knowledge regarding the linguistic status of Sign Language (and surely we cannot ignore it) and the resultant changes in attitude towards the nature and needs of the deaf community, then the implications for the sign language interpreter are enormous. It is not enough to merely *call* sign language a language, we must begin to *treat* it as one. If deaf people are to gain access to, and full participation in, conferences and meetings then clearly the target language form used by the interpreters must be that which is most easily understood and the most meaningful to the majority of the deaf community.

In Britain we now have a 'chicken and egg' situation. The relatively few deaf people who regularly attend national conferences often state their preference for 'Signed English', so it can be argued that we do, in fact, meet the needs of the typical Target Audience. However, until we provide interpretation into the language used *within* the deaf community, and hence a language form more easily understood by a greater number of prelinguilly deaf people, we are not fully providing opportunities of participation to the deaf community as a whole. It must be noted that some deaf people who do now regularly attend conferences have objected to the few attempts that have been made to interpret into BSL. Typical of the comments received is "We want the message in full – not a simplified version". One reason for this attitude is, of course, the expectations of the conference goers. Traditionally the message has always been given in 'full' i.e. Signed English and the receiver has been given the task of making sense of it as best he can. It also, perhaps, suggests an element of distrust in the ability of the interpreter to 'interpret' i.e. his ability to clarify and explain without 'missing things out'. Is it, though, the job of the interpreter to clarify and explain?

Accurate interpretation has traditionally been seen by conference sign language interpreters in Britain (and also possibly by their typical target audiences) to mean adherence, not only to the meaning, but also to the form of the original message. The attitude of foreign language interpreters is, however, less rigid and, surely, more constructive.

> "An accurate interpreter preserves meaning, not words".

and

> "It is not enough for the interpreter to merely understand the message and translate it in its entirety: he must also formulate it in such a way that it reaches his target … he explains the message to them more than he translates it".   (Seleskovitch 1978)

The models proposed in this paper underline the complexity of the psychological processes involved in simultaneous interpretation. They also perhaps hint at the nature and amount of training needed for an interpreter to function effectively and so gain the trust of the target audience. A thorough knowledge of both the source and target languages is a pre-requisite, but by no means the whole story. (It is interesting to note that Interpreter A5 (Table 1) was judged by our deaf informants as the 'best' interpreter and interpreter Bl (Table 1) as the 'worst' and most difficult to understand). By examining the component skills in the light of the most recent work on information processing, by drawing on research into foreign language interpreting and examining training methods employed by foreign language interpreter trainers to develop those same skills that are central to the interpreting process, whether it be into spoken or signed languages, we can begin to offer a training for sign language interpreters that really does treat and respect sign language as a "language".

References

Baddeley, A.D. (1979) 'Working Memory and Reading', in P.A. Kolers, M. Wrolstad and H. Baima (eds) *The Processing of Visible Language*, New York: Plenum Press.

Deuchar, M. (1979) 'Diglossia in British Sign Language', unpublished Ph.D. dissertation, Stanford University.

Giles, H. (1971) 'Ethnocentrism and the Evaluation of Accented Speech', *British Journal of Social and Clinical Psychology*, 10, 187–8.

Giles, H. and Powesland, P.H. (1975) *Speech Style and Social Evaluation*, London: Academic Press.

Klima, E. and Bellugi, U. (1979) *The Signs of Language*, Cambridge, Mass.: Harvard University Press.

Kyle, J., Woll, B. & Llewellyn-Jones, P. (1981) 'Learning and Using BSL', *Sign Language Studies*, 31.

Lambert, W., Hodgeson, R., Gardner, R.C. & Fillenbaum, S. (1960) 'Evaluational Reactions to Spoken Languages', *Journal of Abnormal and Social Psychology*, 60, 44–51.

Lawton, D. (1965) 'Social Class Language Differences in Individual Interviews', Mimeo, Institute of Education, University of London.

Llewellyn-Jones, P. (1981) Simultaneous Interpreting, in B. Woll, J. Kyle and M. Deuchar (eds) *Perspectives on British Sign Language and Deafness*, London: Croom Helm.

Llewellyn-Jones, P. (1981b) 'Sign Language Interpreting', Unpublished paper, School of Education, University of Bristol.

Llewellyn-Jones, P., Kyle, J. & Woll, B. (1979) 'Sign Language Communication', Paper presented at International Conference on Social Psychology and Language, Bristol.

Markowicz, H. & Woodward, J. (1975) 'Language and the Maintenance of Ethnic Boundaries in the Deaf Community', paper presented at the Conference on Culture and Communication, Philadelphia.

Moser, B. (1978) 'Simultaneous Interpretation: A Hypothetical Model', in D. Gerver and H.W. Sinaiko (eds), *Language Interpretation and Communication*, New York: Plenum Press.

Pitt Corder, S. (1973) *Introducing Applied Linguistics*, Harmondsworth: Penguin Books.

3.2   Cokely, Dennis. 1982. "The interpreted medical interview: It loses something in the translation." *The Reflector* 3: 5–10.

Dennis Cokely is the Director of the ASL Program, Professor, and the Chair of the Modern Languages Department at Northeastern University in Boston, Massachusetts. He received his doctorate in Sociolinguistics from Georgetown University and has a Master's degree in Applied Linguistics. For 15 years Cokely worked in various positions at Gallaudet University (as a teacher of elementary and high school students, an administrator, an Assistant Professor in the Graduate School, and as a Research Associate in the Linguistics Research Lab where he worked with William Stokoe. A long time member of the Registry of Interpreters for the Deaf, he served as president from 1983 through 1987 and was instrumental in revising the RID's certification and testing program.

His publications include numerous articles, a series of five textbooks on American Sign Language (generally known as "The Green Books"), which he co-authored with Charlotte Baker-Shenk. His book *Interpretation: A Sociolinguistic Model* (1992), based on his doctoral research, has been translated into German and excerpted into Swedish and Japanese. Through the company he co-founded, Sign Media, Inc., Cokely has produced and/or directed over 250 videotape programs focusing on America n Sign Language, Deaf Culture, and Interpreter Education.

The interpreted medical interview

It loses something in the translation

Dennis Cokely

Introduction

Linguistic investigations of the medical interview have shed light on a number of actual and potential factors that may interfere with effective doctor-patient communication. However, most of these investigations have focused upon situations in which the doctor and patient use the same language (or a variety of that language) and, in general, share similar cultural values. If problems arise between doctor and patient under these conditions one might ask whether these problems are heightened or whether new problems arise when the doctor and patient do not share the same language and, hence, must rely upon a interpreter to facilitate communication. This paper offers a preliminary analysis of the interpreted medical interview in which three people are involved: a registered nurse (hearing), a patient (Deaf), and a certified Sign Language interpreter.

The sign language interpreter

Unlike other ethnic and minority groups in the United States, there are almost no professional services offered directly to members of the Deaf Community by individuals who are themselves members of the Community.[2] That is, while it is possible to find Hispanic doctors, lawyers, law enforcement personnel, etc. who are fluent (or native) users of Spanish, it is extremely difficult (and perhaps impossible) to find members of these professionals who are members of the Deaf Community and/or fluent users of ASL. Thus, very often communication between Deaf people and hearing professionals takes place via the services of an interpreter.

In any situation, the interpreter is expected to convey a message originally encoded in language X (the source language) into language Y (the target language)

---

2.   The term Deaf Community is used in this article to refer to those deaf individuals who consider themselves members of the Community and who have the linguistic, social, and political attitudes that are appropriate to be accepted as members of the Community. For a further discussion, see Baker and Cokely, 1980.

(Seleskovitch, 1978) while maintaining the meaning, intent, mood and style of the original speaker. In order to accomplish this feat, there is a complex set of psycholinguistic factors which must operate in the interpreter's mind (Cokely, 1980). Although there are a number of other factors that exert varying degrees of influence on the interpreter and the interpreting process (e.g. "audience" feedback and the environment), the present discussion will focus only on this set of psycholinguistic factors.

The Sign Language interpreter receives messages either auditorily (i.e. English) or visually (i.e. ASL). The interpreter must then perform the following mental operations:

1. the message must be received in the auditory (English) or visual (ASL) register of the interpreter, i.e. the auditory or optic nerves are stimulated. At this point the interpreter may begin to draw upon long term memory to prepare for and to aid in the next step of the process.

2. upon receiving the message in the appropriate sensory register, active attention is drawn to the message. The interpreter begins the process of syntactic and semantic decoding by attempting to search for recognizable patterns in the incoming message. At this point, the interpreter draws upon long term memory to assist in pattern recognition and to aid in future steps of the process.

3. the message, composed of recognizable syntactic and semantic patterns, now enters the interpreter's short term memory. It is here that the elaborative processes of message analysis occur. The interpreter thoroughly analyzes the syntactic and semantic structure of the message. During this phase it is necessary to draw upon long term memory and to retain (via rehearsal) portions of the message already analyzed while other portions are being analyzed. Of course, decay (i.e. forgetting) can occur before and after elaborative operations have been conducted on the message.

4. the interpreter must now determine the semantic intent that the message is intended to convey. In other words, the interpreter must understand the message. Knowledge of the general content area of the message would seem to be a prerequisite to this step in the process. Certainly the interpreter will rely upon long term memory to aid in this step.

5. having determined the semantic intent of the message, the interpreter must then search his/her long term memory store to arrive at a semantic equivalent in the target language. At this point, the interpreter must rely upon long term memory for concepts, knowledge, cultural differences, etc. in the target language. This means that, at this step the interpreter must match the semantic intent of the source message with its closest possible equivalent in the target language. Presumably, of course, the interpreter possess adequate skill in and experience with the target language to be able to match the range of semantic intents s/he is likely to encounter in any given situation.

6. next the interpreter must begin to (re)structure the semantic intent in the target language according to the syntactic and semantic constraints and requirements of the

target language. While the previous step depends perhaps more on the interpreter's overall knowledge and understanding of the target culture, this step focuses primarily upon the interpreter's knowledge of the target language itself.

7. the next step, drawing upon the syntactic and semantic (re)structuring, involves the selection of appropriate lexical items in the target language. It is at this point where nuances and subtle meaning differences are handled if they are not or cannot be conveyed by syntactic means.

8. at this point, the interpreter has (re)structured the semantic intent of the original message and formulated an appropriate equivalent in the target language. For the Sign Language interpreter, unlike spoken language interpreters, it is necessary to convey the interpreted message in a modality that is different from the modality in which the original message was received. This means that an oral message received auditorily must be conveyed gesturally and a gestural message received visually must be conveyed orally. Thus, the Sign Language interpreter must activate the necessary neuro-mechanisms required to make this modality switch.

9. finally, the (re)structured message is transmitted. Needless to say, the message must be transmitted in such a way that it is intelligible to those receiving the interpreted message. Of course, while the interpreter is interpreting message A, s/he is processing message B and message C is being received by the sensory registers.

Listing the steps involved in the interpreting process in this way may convey the impression that they occur in a sequential manner. However, it is probably more accurate to say that they occur in a semi-sequential manner. That is, obviously some of the steps must occur before others but at some point several of them probably occur simultaneously.

It is highly likely that the first four steps are quite similar or even identical to the process involved for message comprehension in a monolinqual user of any language. This is to be expected since, on one level, the interpreter must decode the source language message and reach the same level of understanding that a monolingual native user of that language would reach. It is true, however, that in anticipation of future steps in the process of interpretation, the interpreter must analyze the syntactic structures and semantic intent of the message at a more active, conscious level (and hence more thoroughly) than a native user. It is precisely the steps that occur after reaching this level of native-like comprehension that makes interpreting the exacting task that it is.

Through step seven, the psycholinguistic process is probably identical for all interpreters – whether of spoken or signed languages. What sets the Sign Language interpreter apart from spoken language interpreters are steps eight and nine. These steps arise because of the modality differences between spoken languages (aural/oral) and signed languages (visual/gestural).

Further elaboration of each of the steps outlined above is necessary to understand fully and to appreciate the complexity of the interpreting process. However, this brief discussion is sufficient to demonstrate that, in any situation, the possibility of errors or misunderstandings is greatly increased when the two principals in a communication situation must rely on the services of an interpreter.

The interpreted medical interview

A number of articles have addressed some of the major barriers to effective doctor-patient communication during the medical interview (Shuy, 1976, 1979; Coulthard and Ashby, 1975). Among the potential problems discussed are the issues of "doctor talk" (i.e. the use of technical jargon on the part of the doctor) and cultural differences between patient and doctor. Given that these factors are potentially problematic when both patient and doctor are able to communicate directly, does the use of an interpreter as a communication intermediary add any additional potential problems to the medical interview?

In order to address this question, a small pilot study was designed in which color videotapes were made of two interpreters during a medical interview. To control as many content and personal variables as possible, the same setting, nurse, and Deaf patient were used for both interpreters. Thus, close comparison of the interpreter's performance is possible. The following information is available on the parties involved in this study:

Deaf Patient (DP): native user of ASL; age: approximately 30; female; graduate of Gallaudet College.

Nurse (RN): registered nurse; female; age: approximately 30; displayed no knowledge of Sign during either interview.

Interpreter 1 (INT 1): holds the Comprehensive Skills Certificate from the Registry of Interpreters for the Deaf; female; age: approximately 27.

Interpreter 2 (INT 2): holds the Comprehensive Skills Certificate from the Registry of Interpreters for the Deaf; male; age: approximately 39.

Both interviews took place at a college infirmary. The purpose of each interview was a case history in which the nurse was seeking a general medical history of the patient. Approximately half an hour after the first interview (using INT 1), the nurse (RN) and the Deaf Patient (DP) were asked to hold a second interview using a second interpreter (INT 2). Both consented and were instructed to repeat the same interview as closely as possible. Since RN used a medical case history form, this added structure and order to the interview and made replication much easier.

An analysis of the tapes of these two interviews reveals a number of factors that interfered with effective communication that could be directly attributed to the interpreters. These interference factors can be categorized into four main types of errors or miscues: perception miscues, memory miscues, semantic miscues, and performance miscues. These miscues or errors generally do not occur within normal doctor-patient communication. Hence, they can be attributed directly to the interpreters and the interpreting process.

(A) Perception Errors

Errors in this category occur either because the interpreter did not register/recognize a particular message or message component or because the interpreter misregistered/misrecognized a particular message or message component. Examples of this type are found in both interviews:[3]

> (1) RN: what is your name?
> DP: M-A-R-Y-A-N-N W-A-L-T-E-R-S
> INT 1: marion waters

In this case, INT 1 apparently failed to register/recognize the full or correct spelling of DP's name. (For purposes of this article, DP's name has been changed but the error-type is the same). RN, assuming that she could spell the name based on INT 1's pronunciation, did not ask for clarification and none was offered by either DP or INT 1. DP could not offer any clarification since she thought that INT 1 was interpreting accurately and she could not hear INT 1's pronunciation. INT 1 did not offer or ask for any clarification since she thought that she perceived the spelling accurately. A similar error was avoided by INT 2 who asked for clarification of misregistered/misrecognized information:

(2)   RN: do you have any idea if your mother took a medication which was known as diethilstibesterol?

INT 2: D–O YOU HAVE ANY IDEA IF YOUR MOTHER TAKE-PILL MEDICINE THAT NAME can you spell that please?

> RN: uh-uh it's diethilstibesterol
> INT 2: D-I-E-T-H-I-L-S-T-I-pes?
> RN: s t i b e s t e r o l
> INT 2: B-E-S-T-E-R-O-L

In this case, the interpreter checks with the nurse to see if his initial perceptions (… pes?) are correct and learns that they were not correct.

Another example of a perception error occurs when RN asks about the occupations of DP's parents. INT 1 does not register/recognize DP7s response:

> (3) RN: and your mother's occupation?
> INT 1: YOUR MOTHER WORK WHAT
> DP: B-I-N-D-E-R
> INT 1: baker

---

3.   The transcription conventions used in this article are as follows: words written in capital letters are English words used to gloss the meaning of a sign (e.g. MOTHER) a string of letters separated by hyphens are fingerspelled words (e.g. U-L-C-E-R) sentences written in lower case letters represent spoken English words (e.g. do you have).

Obviously the implications and consequences of such perception errors can be catastrophic. Generally, such perception errors will remain undetected and uncorrected since the interpreter thinks s/he saw or heard correctly and since neither the Deaf patient nor the nurse can monitor the interpreter's performance. Thus, both DP and RN trust that the interpreter has seen/heard correctly and is faithfully rendering the signed/spoken message. Ironically, the interpreter may also think that s/he has accurately seen/heard the message and has accurately registered the message. Thus the interpreter may be completely confident in interpreting what s/he thinks the original message was. However, what the interpreter thinks was the original message and what the original message actually was may be quite different.

(B) Memory Errors

Errors in this category occur because the interpreter's short term memory does not have sufficient ceiling to permit retention of portions of the original message. The result is a type of unconscious editing of the original message. In general, this "editing" consists of omitting certain portions in the middle or at the end of the original message.

(4) RN: do you nave any idea if your mother used the medication known as diethilstibesterol? that's abbreviated d e s sometimes people refer to it as d e s when she was pregnant with you?

> INT 1: YOU KNOW IF MOTHER USE
> MEDICINE NAME E-D-E-T-H-O-S-D-E-S-D-E-T-H-O-S-T-A-B-E-T-H-A-L

In this instance, INT 1 omitted that portion of the original message that gave some clue as to when DP's mother might have taken the medication ("… when she was pregnant with you"). Presumably this omission is unintentional on the part of INT 1 and can be attributed to short term memory limitations. An alternate explanation is that the mental attention required for INT 1 to process the initial portion of the message was so intense that she did not perceive, i.e. did not hear, the latter portion of the message.

The use of convoluted questioning style by RN only makes the interpreter's task more difficult. Notice that parenthetical information is embedded into the actual question:

Question: Do you have any idea if your mother used the medication known as diethilstibesterol when she was pregnant with you?

Parenthetical information: That medication is abbreviated d e s. Sometimes people refer to it as d e s.

Short term memory limitations force INT 1 to start interpreting before the entire message (i.e. the question) has been processed. Having begun to interpret the initial portion of the message, INT 1's attention is then focused upon trying to fingerspell the name of the medication (see performance errors). The final portion of the message apparently decays in short term memory and thus is not interpreted. Memory limitations are also one of the factors contributing to semantic errors.

(C) Semantic Errors

Errors of this type occur for three main reasons:

the interpreter does not understand the original message and thus cannot accurately interpret it;

memory limitations cause the interpreter to omit portions of the original message and thus a different intent is expressed than that of the original message; the interpreter's knowledge of the target language and/or culture is not fully developed. Thus the interpreter may misuse lexical items and/or syntactic structures of the target language and may convey a message that is different than the original.

> (5) RN: have you ever been treated for an ulcer?
> INT 1: YOU HAVE U-L-C-E-R QUESTION
> DP: N–O N-O

In this instance RN wishes to know if the patient is presently being treated for or has ever been treated for an ulcer. INT 1, however, interprets the message so that the intent expressed is "do you presently have an ulcer?". One possible, but unlikely, explanation for this misinterpretation is that INT I's sign vocabulary does not include signs like the completive FINISH or the temporal PAST. Since INT 1 is a fluent speaker of English, it is highly unlikely that she does not understand the intent of the English message – "have you ever been …"

The result of this misinterpretation is that DP's negative response may, in fact, be an incorrect answer to RN's question. That is, DP may actually have had an ulcer at one time, but DP assumes that RN wants to know if she has an ulcer now. Since DP's negative response is appropriate for both RN's original question and INT's interpretation of that question, no further clarification is sought.

Semantic errors may also occur because the interpreter misunderstands the original message:

> (6) RN: … it's a medication that was used by women who were threatening to abort several years ago
> INT 1: THAT MEDICINE, WOMAN INDEX-rt USE INDEX-rt WOMAN WANT A-B-O-R-T …

In this case, INT 2 does not use contextual knowledge and information to correctly determine the meaning of the phrase "… threatening to abort …". While it is true that in some contexts, threatening to do something implies a voluntary, self-controlled, conscious act, it is highly unlikely that that meaning is applicable in this medical context. INT 2 by misunderstanding this portion of the original message, misinterprets the message and conveys misinformation to DP (i.e. that the medication was used by women who wanted an abortion). In fact, the information conveyed by INT 2 is the exact opposite of the information RN wished to convey (i.e. women took the medication to prevent involuntary or accidental abortions).

INT 2's difficulty may have stemmed from the fact that RN used the word 'abort'. Since, in recent years, the words 'abort' and 'abortion' have gained popular meanings that do imply willful, conscious decisions, INT 2 may have been influenced by these popular meanings. It is probable that INT 2 would not have misinterpreted this segment of the message if RN had used a more 'medical-sounding' word such as 'miscarriage'.

Another source of semantic errors occurs when the interpreter uses a target language lexical item that has a more restricted (i.e. limited) range of meanings than the meaning intended by the original message.

(7) RN: do you have any idea if your mother took a medication …
INT 2: YOUR MOTHER BEFORE MEDICINE TAKE-PILL …

In this instance, RN did not specify the form of the medication (e.g. pills, liquid, shots) but used the somewhat ambiguous and general phrase "took a medication". INT 2, however, uses a sign that does specify the form of the medication – pills or capsules. DP's negative response may have been based on the false assumption that the nurse was only asking about the pills/capsules that her mother took. INT 2, by using the sign TAKE-PILL, has restricted the semantic intent of the original message and has evoked a response from DP that may be accurate for the interpreted question but may be inaccurate for the original question.

(8) RN: what I want to know is if at any time you have dizzy spells?
INT 1: WANT KNOW IF ANY YOU FEEL DIZZY
DP: TEND NOT N–O
INT 1; no uh-uh

In this case, DP intends a tenuous and ambiguous response to RN's question – "I generally don't get dizzy" or "I don't have a tendency to get dizzy". This response does not rule out the occurrence of dizzy spells, but rather indicates that, in general, DP does not become dizzy. However, INT 1 apparently did not understand the initial portion of DP's response (or perhaps did not register/recognize it) and the interpreted reply is a much more definite negative response than DP intended. Theoretically, a more tentative response might have resulted in follow-up questions from RN.

(9) DP: MY MOTHER other-TELL-TO-me AIN'T-GOT-NONE
     PROBLEM PREGNANT WITH ME AIN'T-GOT-NONE
INT 2: my mother never told me about any problem that she had during pregnancy

In this instance, DP's intent is to tell RN that her mother told her that she had no problems when she was pregnant with DP. However, the intent conveyed by INT 2 is quite different. While DP's statement is quite definitive ("My mother told me that she didn't have any problems …"), INT 2's interpretation is much less definitive ("My mother never told me about any problems …"). One possible meaning of INT 2' interpretation is that DP's mother did have problems but never told DP about those problems. Thus, DP's original intent was altered by INT 2 in a such a way that RN might wonder whether DP's mother did have any problems during pregnancy.

A final, and perhaps less significant, type of semantic error occurs when the interpreter's knowledge of the target language and culture does not include an understanding of style level differences. Thus, although the information conveyed by the interpreter may be accurate, the style level used may be more formal or less formal than the style of the original message.

(10) RN: do you have any allergies that you know of?
INT 1: YOU HAVE A-L-L-E-R-G-I-E-S QUESTION
DP: AIN'T-GOT-NONE
INT 1: none

In this instance, DP has responded negatively to RN's question and INT 1 has provided an interpretation of DP's response that is also negative. However, DP used a sign (AIN'T-GOT-NONE) that is generally used in informal or casual situations. This level of informality or casualness is not conveyed by INT 1's interpretation. A more stylistically appropriate interpretation might have been "Ain't got a one" or "Nope, don't have no allergies".

While this level of semantic error may not result in any factual misinformation, it may cause the principals in any interpreted situation to form erroneous impressions of each other. Thus, RN may have little or no idea of how comfortable DP actually is nor any indication of the level of informality with which DP has approached the interview.

(D) Performance Errors
Errors of this type occur when, while producing the target language equivalent of the original message, the interpreter either makes certain production errors or adds extraneous behaviors to the interpreted message.

(11) RN: do you have any idea if your mother used the medication known as diethilstibesterol? that's abbreviated d e s sometimes people refer to it as des when she was pregnant with you?
INT 1: YOU KNOW IF MOTHER USE MEDICINE NAME
E-D-E-T-H-O-S-D-E-S-D-E-T-H-S-T-A-B-E-T-H-A-L

This is an illustration of one type of performance error. First, INT 1 apparently makes two attempts to fingerspell the name of the medication, neither of which is accurate. The first attempt (E-D-E-T-H-O-S) is stopped because INT 1 has heard that this medical term can be abbreviated and so proceeds to fingerspell the abbreviation (… D-E-S …). Notice that there is no pause or other indication that D-E-S is an abbreviation. Then INT 1 begins the second attempt to spell the name of the medication (… D-E-T-H-O-S-T-A-B-E-T-H-A-L). Again there is no pause or other indication that she is beginning to a second attempt. The result of this performance error is that DP can only assume that RN is asking about a medication that is called 'edethosdesdethostabethal'. Of course no such medication exists. Unlike INT 2 (see example #2), INT 1 does not ask RN to spell the name of the medication.

A second type of performance error occurs only with INT 2. It appears that INT 2 has a habit (unconscious?) of vocalizing what he is interpreting after RN has finished speaking.

(12) RN: you ever been treated for an ulcer?
INT 2: HAVE FINISH MEDICINE FOR/for U-L-C-E-R/ulcer U-L-C-R/ulcer

Aside from the fact that INT 2's interpretation may not convey the meaning of the original message, it is interesting to note his behavior after RN is done asking the question. Immediately after RN is finished speaking, INT 2 begins to speak while he is signing (… FOR/for U-L-C-E-R/ulcer U-L-C-R/ulcer), the effect of this simltaneous gestural/oral message presentation is twofold. First, it may give RN the impression that while DP cannot hear RN's voice, DP can hear INT 2's voice. Second, and more importantly, at those times when INT 2 simultaneously produces a gestural/oral message, he is producing a message that is syntactically closer to English than it is to ASL. That is, he uses ASL signs but orders them according to the syntax of the English sentence he is producing. In those cases INT 2's performance can no longer be called interpreting. Rather he is transliterating – an exercise in lexical substitution.

It may be that INT 2 vocalizes for the benefit of RN so that she can monitor what he is signing. However, what cumulative effect such echoic behavior has on RN is unknown. It may be that this behavior so distracts RN that she is unable to process DP's responses accurately.

Summary

The purpose of this study was to determine whether or not there are any specific factors which potentially interfere with effective communication in the medical interview setting when an interpreter is used. The preliminary analysis offered suggests that there are interpreter-specific interference factors that are in addition to doctor-specific and patient-specific factors. It is suggested that the complexity of the interpreting task itself is such that the presence of these factors may be unavoidable and that the possibility of miscommunication may be greater than direct doctor-patient interaction.

Those interpreter-specific factors that may lead to a greater level of miscommunication are: perception, memory, semantics and performance. Any error or miscue attributed to one or more of these factors can be significant enough to result in distortion or omission of the original message. In fact, these factors and the potential for misinterpretation are present in any interpreted situation. In the medical setting, however, there are serious consequences for not obtaining accurate case histories or arriving at appropriate diagnosis and treatment of Deaf patients.

Certain steps can be taken to reduce the occurrence of interpreter miscue or error in the medical setting (although it is unlikely that the possibility of error can ever be completely eliminated.) Among these steps are the following:

An increased level of awareness on the part of medical personnel and Deaf patients toward the interpreting task and process could reduce the severity of any errors/miscues. The practical implications of such heightened awareness might be a decrease in the use of "doctor talk", re-phrasing and re-stating complex questions, the use of more regular follow-up questions, and re-checking information by medical personnel and by patients. Interpreters who work in medical settings should familiarize themselves with medical terminology. There are several concise dictionaries of medical terminology available that would be extremely helpful to interpreters. Additionally, if the interpreter does not understand a particular message or is not sure of the meaning and intent of a particular message, s/he should not hesitate to ask for clarification.

Since the majority of doctor-patient encounters are planned (i.e. are scheduled in advance), a brief meeting between the doctor/nurse and interpreter could be scheduled to discuss certain terminology that may arise during the doctor-patient encounter. This step may be highly impractical and unlikely given time constraints on medical personnel. However, it is an option that should be pursued by interpreters.

Perhaps the wisest course of action for doctor/nurse, Deaf patient and interpreter to take is to remember that, no matter how skilled the interpreter is, the possibility is always there that interpreted message may "lose something in the translation".

References

Baker, C. and D. Cokely. *American Sign Language: a teacher's resource text on grammar and culture,* T.J. Publishers, Silver Spring, Md.: 1980.

Cokely, Dennis. Psychological Processes of Interpreting. Working paper, Linguistics Research Lab, Gallaudet College, Washington, D.C., 1980.

Coulthard, M. and M. Ashby. Talking with the Doctor, 1, *Journal of Communication,* Summer, 1975.

Seleskovitch, D. *Interpreting for International Conferences.* Pen and Booth, Washington, D.C.: 1978.

Shuy, R. The Medical Interview: Problems in Communication. *Primary Care,* Vol. 3, No. 3, 365–386, 1976.

Shuy, R. Three Types of Interference to an Effective Exchange of Information in the Medical Interview. Paper presented to the Society for Computer Medicine, Atlanta, Georgia, November, 1979.

3.3   **Strong, Michael and Steven Fritsch Rudser. 1986. "The subjective assessment of sign language interpreters."** *Sign Language Studies* **15(53): 299–314.**

Michael Strong is lead researcher for the National Laboratory for Educational Transformation, a new non-profit research organization, and is the former Director of Research at the University of California Santa Cruz (UCSC) New Teacher Center. He is responsible for designing and conducting studies that investigate the nature and effectiveness of teacher preparation and support. Dr. Strong has a Masters degree in Applied Linguistics from the University of London and a doctorate in Language and Reading Development from the School of Education, University of California at Berkeley. He has taught students of all ages from elementary through adult. Before coming to the UCSC New Teacher Center, he was an Associate Adjunct Professor of Psychiatry at the Center on Deafness at UC San Francisco; as Director of Research, he led a program of studies on various aspects of the language development, education, and mental health of deaf children. He has published two books and more than 30 academic papers in the last 20 years.

Steven Fritsch Rudser has been an interpreter, interpreter educator, and researcher for many years. He has a bachelor's degree in liberal studies with an emphasis on American Sign Language and interpreting from Antioch University, and he taught American Sign Language and interpreting at University of California, San Francisco (UCSF); Vista Community College; and Ohlone College. A freelance interpreter since 1975, he has a special interest in performing arts interpreting. He was also active in the Registry of Interpreters for the Deaf at the local, state and national levels. Fritsch-Rudser was a researcher and interpreter at the Center on Deafness at UCSF where he was co-principal investigator on several projects with Michael Strong that resulted in numerous publications as well as twelve articles of his own on interpreter competence and interpreting. His other research interests included sign language and interpreter training, mental health interpreting, supervision of interpreters, and general issues around interpreter assessment.

In 1989 he switched careers and began working in human resources. Since then he has had progressively increasing responsibility including serving as vice president of a major nation-wide bank.

The subjective assessment of sign language interpreters

Michael Strong & Steven Fritsch Rudser

A group of hearing raters were asked to make a subjective evaluation of the signed and spoken output of 25 sign language interpreters, using taped samples recorded under test conditions. Three hypotheses were examined: (1) that raters would agree with one another, (2) that subjective evaluations would correlate positively with interpreter accuracy ratings, and (3) that subjective raters would be able to determine whether the interpreters had deaf or hearing parents. Results showed that rater agreement was high (0.52–0.86) but much lower than would be required between raters on an objective measure. Correlation between subjective and objective assessment was also high (0.59–0.79). Subjects were not successful at identifying which interpreters had deaf parents. Implications are drawn for interpreter assessment in general, particularly that employed by the Registry of Interpreters for the Deaf.

Introduction

Training methods and assessment techniques are still at relatively early stages of development. Strong and Rudser (1985) have developed an instrument for the assessment of sign language interpreting skills that attempts to eliminate, as far as possible, the need for subjective decisions by the rater. It does so by focusing solely on the accuracy with which individual propositions are represented by the interpreter, thus reducing the number of value judgments a rater is required to make. Other existing techniques (e.g. that used by the Registry of Interpreters for the Deaf) involve considerable subjective evaluation and thus are more open to the possibility of rater bias. While it may be desirable to have a measure of objective evaluation, subjective evaluations are being made all the time by teachers, trainers, students, and the deaf and hearing interlocutors for whom the interpreters work. It is therefore of some importance to examine the process of subjective evaluation, particularly by consumers (as they will have considerable influence on which interpreters are requested for particular tasks), in order to learn which aspects of an interpreter's performance might be most salient in determining the rater's evaluations, and whether subjective evaluations are likely to be at variance with more objective assessments of the same people.

For many years social psychologists have been interested in the processes by which impressions, opinions, or feelings about other persons are formed. Frequently judgments are made about an individual based on minimal information, such as the sound of a voice, physical appearance, or a self-written resume. In such cases, the perceiver is frequently influenced by existing stereotypes that may be attached to certain accents, physical features, or places of residence or education. Lambert et al. (1960) examined this phenomenon specifically as it applied to language stereotypes. Using a "matched guise" technique (bilingual speakers reading the same message in two languages, subjects questioned on their impressions of the speakers without knowing that the same individuals appeared in two guises), the authors found that evaluations of personality characteristics of the speakers reflected the prevailing majority/minority group stereotypes. Thus both English speaking and French speaking Canadians evaluated the English guises more favorably than the French guises, and the French speaking subjects evaluated the French guises significantly less favorably than did the English speakers. This was interpreted as evidence for a minority group reaction on the part of the French sample.

Although related, the questions we raise in this study do not focus on the effects of language use on personality perception, but rather on the relationship between perceived language skill (specifically interpreting) and perceived cultural background, and the relationship between subjective and objective assessments. It is of interest whether raters' perceptions of the interpreters appear to be influenced by personal characteristics unrelated to competence, and whether different raters tend to like the same interpreters. Also there is a persistent informal claim among fluent signers (both deaf and hearing) that they can identify the hearing status of other signers, and of their parents, by the way they sign. It is not clear exactly what signals are supposed to reveal this information to the observer, but part of the claim is subject to scrutiny from the data reported in this study – at least with regard to the hearing status of the interpreters' parents.

Three formal hypotheses are specifically addressed:

1.   Raters will agree with one another in their subjective evaluations of sign language interpreters.
2.   Subjective ratings will be positively correlated with objective assessments of accuracy.
3.   Subjective raters will be able to determine whether interpreters had deaf or hearing parents.

The experiment

The testing materials consisted of four passages, each approximately two and one-half minutes long and excerpted from the tape-recorded tests of 25 sign language interpreters originally taken in 1973 for a study on interpreter competence (Quigley et al. 1973, Rudser & Strong 1985). Two of the passages were samples of the subjects signing. In one they had been instructed to transliterate (i.e. "sign in English"); in the other they were required to interpret (i.e. use American Sign Language, ASL). The signed passages were copied on half-inch VHS videotapes in four different random orders. The spoken passages were recorded on audio cassettes, also in four different random orders.

A note on terminology

Significant changes have occurred in sign language interpreting in the twelve years since these data were collected, particularly in the vocabulary used to describe the various interpreting processes. These changes underlie major differences in the understanding of the processes themselves. Traditionally the terms "interpret" and "translate" were often used synonymously; when a distinction was made, "interpret" referred to speech, and "translate" referred to writing. In the early years of the sign language interpreting discipline, publications reflected very different use of the terms. Youngs, in the first handbook for interpreters, defined "interpreting" as "an explanation of another person's remarks through the language of signs, informal gesture, or pantomime" (1965:6); and "translating" as a "verbatim presentation of another person's remarks through the language of signs and fingerspelling (1965:7). Working from sign language to English was referred to as "reverse translating" and "reverse interpreting." Rudser (1978) discussed the difficulties with these early terms and definitions, and more recently, new terminology has come into general use. In the current RID Handbook (Caccamise 1980), for example, "interpreting" is described as operating (in either direction) between American Sign Language and spoken English, and "transliterating" (replacing the term "translating") as operating between Manually Coded English and spoken English.

Procedures

Twelve subjects took part in this study; six of them were deaf and six hearing. The deaf subjects rated the signed passages, and the hearing subjects rated the spoken passages. The deaf raters watched the interpreted excerpts on a 25-inch television monitor (fed by a JVC portable VHS playback deck), seeing the interpreters in one of the four different random orders. The study was introduced to them as an experiment to find out the opinions of subjective judges concerning the performances of a group of sign language interpreters. Subjects were told they would see each interpreter performing two short parts of two interpreting tasks, in one of which the interpreter would be likely to use ASL. They were asked to watch the excerpts and fill out a short evaluation form (See Appendix 1), indicating whether they liked the interpreter, the level of signing ability, the degree to which he or she was easy to follow and pleasurable to watch, whether his or her parents may have been deaf, and whether more English-like or ASL-like signing was used. Additional comments were invited at the bottom of the form. Raters were not given the original texts of the passages and were asked not to take into account how accurate they imagined the interpreter to be. They could fill out the rating sheet as they watched, or after pausing the tape. The task reguired about 90 minutes to complete and the subjects were each paid twenty dollars.

The hearing raters were given a small portable audiotape recorder (Panasonic RQ337) with a set of lightweight headphones and a tape with the spoken excerpts in one of four random orders. The study was introduced to them as an experiment to find out the opinions of subjective judges in evaluating the spoken output of sign language interpreters. They were told that they would hear two short voicing episodes for each interpreter, but were not told that in one case the signer had used ASL and in the other, English. They were asked to listen to the excerpts and fill out the relevant forced-choice evaluation form (appendix 2) indicating whether they found the interpreter jerky or fluent, unpleasant or pleasant to listen to, difficult or easy to understand, and an overall like or dislike. In addition they were asked to indicate whether the interpreter did better on the first or second passage and may have had deaf parents. Additional remarks were invited. As with the deaf raters, the hearing subjects had no access to the original texts and were asked to ignore the level of accuracy they imagined the interpreter to attain. This task also required about 90 minutes and the subjects were paid twenty dollars each.

Scoring

Each evaluation sheet was checked for completeness and the rater asked to fill in any missing items. A total score of 21 points was possible, 15 for the three multiple choice scales (scored 1–5), and 6 on the overall rating (e.g. 6 for "like," 0 for "dislike"). The minimum possible score was three.

Subjects

The deaf subjects were all adults, three male and three female, and all prelingually deaf. All had some college education and while better qualified educationally than most deaf individuals were suited to the subject matter of the interpreted extracts. All six were fluent signers. Three (of hearing parents) had been educated primarily in oral programs; the other three (two of deaf parents) had attended residential schools that were not considered oral. The study was described to them in sign by a sign language interpreter with excellent skills in both ASL and English.

The six hearing subjects, five females and one male, were also college educated. Three had had regular experience communicating with deaf people and were skilled signers, while the others had had no previous contact with deaf people. They were given directions by the same interpreter, using normal spoken English. None of the hearing subjects had deaf parents. The 12 subjects were between 22 and 39 years old.

Interpreters

Recorded excerpts from 25 interpreters, 12 male and 13 female, were used in this study. Ten of them had hearing parents and the other 15 (5 male, 10 female) had deaf parents. Their range in age was from 25 to 56. They had originally been chosen to represent a range of abilities; a subsequent analysis of their test performances confirmed this. The interpreters in the deaf-parent group obtained the ten highest scores and also the two lowest. Those in the hearing-parent group ranked in the lower middle part of the distribution.

Agreement of subjective raters

The relationships among the ratings by the deaf subjects were found to correlate well for each pair (Table 1), with Pearson r coefficients from 0.54 to 0.86. High correlations were also found for the hearing raters' (Table 2), with a range from 0.52 to 0.86. Furthermore, a comparison between the deaf and hearing raters shows quite high levels of agreement (Table 3),

Table 1. Pearson r correlation coefficients: deaf raters' judgments of interpreters' signing

	R2	R3	R4	R5	R6
R1	.86	.75	.71	.70	.62
R2		.66	.70	.73	.70
R3			.66	.61	.56
R4				.73	.63
R5					.54

Table 2. Correlation coefficients: hearing raters' judgments of interpreters' spoken performance

	R8	R9	R10	R11	R12
R7	.54	.64	.68	.82	.83
R8		.69	.52	.61	.58
R9			.70	.66	.78
R10				.69	.70
R11					.86

although one would not expect subjective ratings of signing and voicing by different judges to be comparable. These high correlations are almost certainly partly due to the wide spread of abilities among the interpreters, a spread plainly evident in the samples used for rating. Although raters were instructed not to take perceived accuracy into account, the interpreters' varied abilities apparently influenced their interpreting styles and thus probably the ratings.

Table 3. Correlation coefficients: hearing & deaf raters' judgment of interpreters' voicing and signing

	R1	R2	R3	R4	R5	R6
R7	.46	.54	.53	.57	.52	.51
R8	.49	.45	.58	.53	.44	.50
R9	.33	.31	.46	.63	.30	.33
R10	.59	.54	.67	.69	.57	.40
R11	.47	.49	.61	.57	.51	.55
R12	.38	.40	.42	.60	.42	.49

Subjective versus objective ratings

To test whether subjective ratings related to objective measures, the raters' scores were compared with accuracy scores by using the Strong and Rudser (1985) instrument for the assessment of sign language interpreters. Two scores were used for this purpose, a combined score on signing tasks and a combined score on the voicing tasks. Correlations between the subjective ratings of the deaf judges and signing accuracy of the interpreters ranged from 0.63 to 0.70 (Table 4). Between scores of the hearing judges and voicing accuracy scores the correlations ranged from 0.59 to 0.79 (Table 5). These consistently high correlations further indicate potentially strong effects of the interpreters' basic abilities on how positively they are perceived by judges who have no objective data on the strict accuracy of the interpretations they are witnessing.

Table 4. Correlation coefficients: deaf raters' judgments with signing accuracy scares (All values significant at $p \leq 0.001$, 1-tailed)

Rater judgment:	R1	R2	R3	R4	R5	R6
Accuracy score:	.64	.70	.68	.63	.64	.64

These findings might be taken as evidence supporting the use of more subjective methods of assessing sign language interpreters. However, such conclusions would be shortsighted for two reasons. First, although the correlations are high enough to reach statistical significance at the one-one thousandth level of probability, no coefficient was

Table 5. Correlation coefficients for hearing raters' judgments of interpreters' vocing with voicing accuracy scores (All values significant at $p \leq 0.001$, 1-tailed)

Rater judgment:	R7	R8	R9	R10	R11	R12
Accuracy score:	.79	.63	.72	.59	.78	.76

higher than 0.79, which implies rank orders considerably at variance from those arising from the objective evaluations. Furthermore, although inter-rater reliability was high, the average quotient (0.52 to 0.86) was far lower than that achieved among the objective raters (0.93 to 0.99; Strong & Rudser 1985) – lower indeed than would be required of any instrument used for rating job applicants or examinees for a professional license. Thus a measure relying on subjective ratings alone, even with good reliability, would almost certainly misclassify quite a large percentage of whatever sample was being rated.

Deaf or hearing parents?

Ten of the 25 interpreters were from hearing families, while 15 had deaf parents. In most cases, the number of judges' correct guesses was no greater than one would expect from chance. Among the deaf raters, of the 90 guesses (number of judges times number of interpreters), 55 were incorrect. The same interpreters were consistently mis-identified (4 from the deaf-parent group were wrongly assigned to the other group by all 6 judges), although all but two obtained at least one false nomination. However, the deaf judges were more successful at identifying members of the hearing-parent group, making only 7 errors out of 60 (see Table 6). The guesses of the hearing judges approximated chance for both hearing-parent (27 out of 60) and deaf-parent groups (42 out of 90), with at least one wrong identification going to all but one of the interpreters.

Table 6. Number of incorrect guesses as to parental hearing status of sign language interpreters (HP, hearing parents; DP, deaf parents)

Judges	Interpreters	
	HP	DP
Deaf	7/60	55/90
Hearing	27/60	42/90

It would appear from these data that the hearing status of a signer's parents is only likely to be identifiable with any consistency if the parents were hearing. It is apparently impossible to make such an identification from samples of spoken interpreting. One may make some speculations as to the kind of information the raters used in arriving at their decisions on parents' hearing status by looking at which interpreters they assigned to which group, and at their comments. By far the most common strategy among the deaf raters seemed to be to assign the interpreter to the deaf-parent group if they liked him or her (and they tended to like them the more accurate they were), and to the hearing-parent group if they did not. This explains some of the mis-identifications among the deaf-parent group (i.e. some of the poorest performers had deaf parents); also the successful identifications among the hearing-parent group, most of whom were in the moderate to low end of the rankings. One rater, however, from an oral background and with hearing parents, went against the trend by identifying the most liked interpreters as having hearing parents, thus contributing to the number of erroneous guesses, because the most skilled interpreters in this sample indeed had deaf parents. A second discernible strategy involved the judgment of use of ASL or English. Five of the six deaf raters tended to assign interpreters to the deaf-parent group if they also rated them as using more ASL than English, particularly if they liked them overall. They correspondingly identified the interpreters they liked least as using mostly English. There were more exceptions to this rule than for that linking liking and deaf parents.

One of the deaf raters seemed to associate degree of expressiveness with having deaf parents. In many cases this rater added comments such as "very expressive," "signing lacked expression," or "no facial expression, body too stiff." Without exception this rater identified the more expressive signers as having deaf parents. Among the hearing raters perceived quality also appeared to be the main deciding factor. For four of the hearing raters the most liked interpreters were assigned deaf parentage, but for the other two the high scoring interpreters were assigned hearing parentage. One hearing rater (who had worked in the field of deafness for several years) frequently used age as a criterion, feeling (often correctly) that the older sounding speakers probably had deaf parents. However, overall skill seemed to be the most crucial factor for this rater, whose top selections were all assigned deaf parents and whose least favored were assumed to have hearing parents. It should be noted that the best interpreters today are less likely all to be from deaf families than they were when the data used in this study were originally collected. The strategy that was apparently successful in identifying interpreters from hearing families is unlikely to work as well under current conditions.

Conclusions

From this study of a small sample of hearing and deaf raters of sign language interpreters some tentative conclusions can be drawn and implications considered for future research. First, judges tend to like and dislike the same interpreters, regardless of their own background (but given a higher than average education and a somewhat narrow age range). This may be partly attributable to the wide range of abilities among the sample of interpreters observed and needs to be further examined with interpreters of more comparable skills.

Second, subjective judgments tend to correlate with objective measures of accuracy in interpreting, again with the proviso that wide-ranging abilities might have been partly responsible for this finding. Nonetheless, these correlations were not perfect, and inter-judge agreement was not nearly as high as that found among raters using an objective instrument. This suggests that while subjective ratings provide an interesting and useful dimension of interpreter assessment, they should not replace a sound objective measure. This finding has implications for the evaluation procedure of the Registry of Interpreters for the Deaf, which is essentially subjective, although the questions are phrased in the form "Did the interpreter do …?" or "Did the interpreter use …?" rather than "Did you like the interpreter?" The RID uses three raters to evaluate each interpreter and averages their scores. No inter-rater reliability figures are published, but if they are not consistently above the 0.90 mark, this could lead to vulnerability in issues of discrimination under Title VII of the 1964 Civil Rights Act. Such problems might be avoided if a demonstrably objective dimension were added to the evaluation procedure, such as that proposed by Strong and Rudser (1985).

Third, deaf raters were not successful in identifying which interpreters had deaf parents by the way they signed, although they correctly identified those with hearing parents 88 percent of the time. This would suggest that the primary criterion for identifying a signer with deaf parents is the quality of the signing. A study using signers of equivalent ability might reveal secondary criteria that are obscured when the range of skill is great as in the sample described here.

Note

This study was made possible partly through Grant G 008 300 146 from the National Institute for Handicapped Research to the University of California, San Francisco, RT 23 Center on Deafness. Some of the original data were collected by Stephen Quigley, Barbara Brasel, and Dale Montanelli under the support of Grant SRS 14P 55400/5 from the Division of Research and Demonstration Grants, Social and Rehabilitation Service, Department of Health, Education, and Welfare, Washington, DC 20201. The authors thank these original investigators for making their data available for our analysis. Thanks also to the 25 interpreters who allowed us to question them all these years later and who provided us with valuable information about their backgrounds.

References

Caccamise, F. 1980. Introduction to Interpreting. Silver Spring, MD: Registry of Interpreters for the Deaf.

Lambert, W., R. Hodgson, R. Gardner & S. Fillenbaum 1960. Evaluational reactions to spoken language. *Journal of Abnormal & Social Psychology* 10, 44–51

Quigley, S., B. Brasel & D. Montanelli 1973. Interpreters for Deaf People: selection, evaluation, and classification. Final Report HEW SRS 14-P-55400/5.

Rudser, S. 1978. Interpreting: Difficulties in present terminology, Interpreter News.

Rudser, S. & M. Strong 1985. An examination of some personal characteristics & abilities of sign language interpreters. Unpublished manuscript, Center on Deafness, University of California, San Francisco.

Strong, M. & S. Rudser 1985. An assessment instrument for sign language interpreters. *Sign Language Studies* 49, 344–362.

Youngs, J. 1965. Introduction: Interpreting for deaf peersons. In *Interpreting for Deaf People*. Washington, DC: U.S.Department of Health, Education & Welfare.

APPENDIX 1
INTERPRETER RATING FORM
Sign Language

Name _____   Subject #_____

Circle one choice on each line

(Low sign language ability)	1	2	3	4	5	(High sign language ability)
(Hard to follow)	1	2	3	4	5	(Easy to follow)
(unpleasant to watch)	1	2	3	4	5	(Pleasant to watch)

Overall evaluation

Dislike   O.K.   Like

This interpreter uses more

English   ASL

This interpreter's parents were

Hearing   Deaf

Comments:

APPENDIX 2
INTERPRETER RATING FORM
Spoken Language

Rater _____   Subject #_____

Circle one choice on each line

(Jerky)	1	2	3	4	5	(Fluent)
(Unpleasant to listen to)	1	2	3	4	5	(Pleasant to listen to)
(Difficult to understand)	1	2	3	4	5	(Easy to understand)

Overall rating

Dislike   O.K.   Like

The interpreter did a better job on

Passage 1   Passage 2

The interpreter's parents were

Hearing   Deaf

Comments:

3.4 Winston, Elizabeth A. 1989. "Transliteration: What's the Message?" In *Sociolinguistics of the Deaf Community*, ed. by Ceil Lucas, 147–164. New York: Academic Press.

Elizabeth A. Winston is a nationally and internationally recognized educator and consultant in educational linguistics, discourse analysis, and interpreting. She holds a Ph.D. in Applied Linguistics from Georgetown University and a Masters in Linguistics with a focus on American Sign Language from Gallaudet University, and a M.Ed. in Technology & Education from Western Governors University. Her special areas of interest include ASL discourse analysis, interpreting skills, development, second language acquisition, educational interpreting, and multimedia applications in ASL research and teaching at a distance. Winston has taught at many universities and colleges in the US, including Gallaudet University in Washington, DC.

Winston was the Director of the National Interpreter Education Center at Northeastern University, (2005–2010) a grant-funded project (RSA #H160B0002) to increase the number of qualified interpreters in the US. She has also been the Coordinator for the ASL Graduate Program at Northeastern University, including the M.Ed. in Interpreting Pedagogy and the Master Mentor Certificate Program. She is the Director of the Teaching Interpreting Educators and Mentors (TIEM) Center; a Center focused on excellence and integrity in interpreter and mentor education and research, and an adjunct professor at Gallaudet University and Cincinnati University. Winston is a prolific researcher, author and editor, and among her publications are: *Educational Interpreting: How it can succeed* (2004) and *Storytelling and Conversation: Discourse in Deaf Communities* (1999).

Transliteration

What's the Message?

Elizabeth A. Winston

Introduction

Transliteration is a specific form of sign language interpreting. It is the process of changing one form of an English message, either spoken English or signed English, into the other form. Interpreting, in contrast, refers either to the general process of changing the form of a message to another form, or to the specific process of changing an English message to American Sign Language (ASL), or vice versa. The assumption in transliteration is that both the spoken and the signed forms correspond to English, the spoken form following the rules of standard English and the signed form being a simple recoding of the spoken form into a manual mode of expression. The guidelines for the spoken form are relatively clear. It is the signed form that lacks any sort of standardization at the level of systematic recoding of spoken utterances. Indeed, the signed forms themselves are variously referred to as Pidgin Signed English, Manually Coded English, and even foreigner talk.[4]

It is not the aim of this chapter to discuss the labels used for the forms of the signed message. Rather, the goal is to describe some of the features of the signed forms in relation to the strategies used to produce a message match in the target language. The focus in this study is on the form of the signed message when it is the target form because it is the form often requested by those using a transliterator. The question of the form of the signed message when it is the source language is equally significant, and a similar study

---

4.   These terms represent a few of the terms used to describe the contact varieties of signing and speaking (or mouthing without voice) that are used when deaf people who rely on signing and hearing people who rely on speaking wish to communicate. Pidgin Signed English (PSE) is discussed by many authors, including Marmor and Pettito (1979). Manually Coded English (MCE) refers to forms of signing that encode various formal features of spoken English in manual signs. These features are generally morphemic: copula, tense agreement, inflectional and derivational morphemes, as well as root morphemes of English. They are intended to be literally represented on the hands through the use of signs, many of which are borrowed from the lexicon of American Sign Language (ASL). Further description of these forms is in S. Supalla (1986). Cokely (1983) describes the contact varieties as forms of foreigner talk. For a broader understanding of the complex nature of the manually signed versions of English, the reader is referred to the literature already cited as well as to various items listed in the reference section.

centered on this aspect will be invaluable to our understanding of the English forms of signing and transliterating.[5] The present study proposes that the signed form is more than a simple recoding of spoken English into signed English. It is a complex combination of features from ASL and from English and is accomplished by conscious strategies employed by the transliterator. The form of the target message is analyzed here in terms of these conscious strategies, conscious in that they are planned by the transliterator as opposed to being either randomly or erroneously produced.

Definitions of transliteration

The form of signed transliteration is vaguely defined in a few texts. In fact, it is not actually the form of the message that is described but the process of transliteration that produces the form. Frishberg's (1986, p. 19) text, which is used for teaching sign language interpretation, defines transliteration as "the process of changing an English text into Manually Coded English (or vice versa)." This definition is only marginally helpful in understanding transliteration and the forms of the signed message since there are several signed codes for English, each with its own distinct principles for encoding English. (See S. Supalla, 1986, for a discussion of these forms.)

In the process of transliteration, any of these codes, or any combination of these codes, might be used. The effectiveness of these codes for transliteration has not been studied. However, their effectiveness for everyday communication has been seriously questioned. Marmor and Petitto (1979) found that even skilled users of these codes did not accurately represent the spoken message on their hands in one-to-one communication. If this is a problem for speakers who control both the speed and the content of the communication, it is logical to assume that an even greater problem in message match develops for the transliterator. In a transliterated setting, it is the speaker who has control of the speed and content of the source message, not the transliterator. Since the transliterator does not have control of either speed or content, the use of such coding systems for transliterating must also be seriously questioned. Thus, this first definition of transliterating as a simple encoding process inadequately describes both the form of the message and the production process.

The instructional text of Caccamise et al. (1980, p. 3), describes transliteration as changing "'only' the *mode* of the sender's communication or message ... e.g. English speech to a signed or manual code for English." This definition allows for more flexibility in the form

---

5. A study of this kind is now in progress at Gallaudet University, under the direction of Ceil Lucas and Clayton Valli. The data collected and the results of this study will provide much-needed information in the area of transliteration.

of the message since it allows for more of the contact varieties of signing. This increased flexibility, however, leads to the question of which variety or varieties can be used or expected by any given consumer and transliterator. There are no comprehensive descriptions of any of the contact varieties that are in use among English speakers and ASL signers. The variety of forms is multiplied when deaf consumers whose native language is some type of signed English, rather than ASL, are included in the group of target consumers. This definition, while allowing for more flexibility, thus does not provide a clear description of the signed output.

One approach to the description of transliteration entails analysis both of the problems faced during the transliteration process and of the strategies used by transliterators to deal with these problems or constraints [Conference of Interpreter Trainers (CIT), 1984]. This perspective describes transliterating as English-like signing, which by its very nature does not have a standardized form. This lack of standardization of sign forms results in "intermediate varieties" of signing that are "incapable of fully conveying the grammatical/syntactic information" (CIT, 1984, p. 95) of the source language. This perspective views the target form as a less than complete message, more in the form of a pidgin that can provide a means of communication but cannot provide all the subtleties of either language. The CIT discussion of transliteration centers on strategies used by transliterators to add clarity and meaning to the inadequate form of signed English, these strategies being various borrowings from ASL. Their discussion also provides many insights into the problems of making an inadequate form (signed English) more meaningful and clear. It stresses the need for borrowing features from ASL in order to produce this clarity.

S. Supalla (1986) approaches the question of signed forms of English from a slightly different perspective. His discussion centers on the occurrence of features of visual languages in signed forms of English, not because of the inadequacy of English but because of the adequacy of signed languages in dealing with visual needs. This is a different but important perspective in an analysis of transliteration. Since the goal is to provide a visual target form that not only resembles to some extent spoken English structures but at the same time is also comprehensible, it is appropriate to use forms that are specific to visual languages such as ASL in order to achieve clarity and meaning. It is also appropriate to include features of English that are visual, such as mouthing. The present study is conducted from the perspective that visual features from ASL, borrowed to clarify an English message, can be expected in the target form; their occurrence is a logical result of trying to use a visual mode for a spoken language. Any definition that precludes or ignores the features of visual communication in favor of English structure cannot adequately describe transliteration.

It was helpful during the course of this project to consider perspectives on interpretation that are not specific to sign language per se but make pertinent reference to the principles and practices of interpreting between various spoken and written languages. Many of these descriptions and discussions can be extended to include sign language interpreting, and specifically, transliterating. Nida (1976) discusses the question of translatability, in general, and whether any sort of information transfer by means of interpreting is even feasible. He concludes that, while exact equivalence of meaning, including all the linguistic and cultural nuances of one language transferred completely to another, is not possible, functional equivalence is possible. By functional equivalence, he means the production of a message that is pragmatically similar. He (Nida, 1976, p. 63) includes the following reminder about the general nature of communication, a factor often forgotten by those who discuss the "correctness" of an interpreted message:

> Even among experts discussing a subject within their own fields of specialization, it is unlikely that comprehension rises above the 80 percent level. Loss of information is a part of any communication process, and hence the fact that some loss occurs in translation should not be surprising, nor should it constitute a basis for questioning the legitimacy of translating.

This statement does not excuse inadequate transliteration but simply reminds us that there are many aspects of the process that need further study and improvement. Interpreting and, more specifically, transliterating, can still be successful. The point is that we must analyze successful transliterated messages and describe how and why they are successful. Nida's comment serves as a reminder that there are limitations on even the most effective forms of communication. The legitimacy of transliterating is often questioned on the basis of its inadequacy. But perhaps the rather limiting definitions of transliteration make the process appear inadequate; perhaps, also, expectations about the capabilities of any sort of information transfer are higher than normally expected of even direct communication processes.

Another valuable discussion of interpreting, specifically, translation from one written form to another, is provided by Casagrande (1954). He describes four possible goals of the translator when producing a text, each of which can affect the final form of the message. These goals are the following:

1. Pragmatic: the goal is to translate a source message as efficiently and as accurately as possible, with a focus on the meaning rather than on the form of the message.
2. Linguistic: the goal is to "identify and assign equivalent meanings" (Casagrande, 1954, p. 337) between the source and target languages; the form of the target is directed by grammatical concerns rather than by meaning.
3. Aesthetic-Poetic: the goal is to produce the message in a form that is aesthetically similar in both languages.
4. Ethnographic: the goal is to include cultural background and explanations of text from one language to another.

These goals are not mutually exclusive; each translator works to achieve a final text that reflects the original message by balancing the requirements of each goal. Transliterators likewise work to achieve a final message that is a balance of these goals. Transliterators are more constrained by the linguistic goal than are other kinds of interpreters because they are expected to produce a form that resembles the source English message. They also deal with the pragmatic goal of producing a message simultaneously with the speaker, as well as with the final two goals.[6] The balancing of these goals results in a form that resembles English in some of its features, ASL in other of its features, and a blend of both that may be specific to the contact varieties and the effects found whenever a spoken message is recoded in a visual-manual mode.

The present study

The output, or target form, of any interpreted message is always determined by those consumers directly involved in the communication. Even interpreters working between languages with very standardized forms can produce different interpretations of the same message. When dealing with forms that are not standardized, the variety of interpretations can be even greater. The present study describes the form of a transliterated message that occurred in one setting with one transliterator and one consumer. The objective is not to assess this form in terms of the appropriateness of its use in transliteration. Rather, the objective is to analyze the form in terms of the strategies used by transliterators. These strategies are reflected by the features of the transliterated target form. Transliterators use these strategies to produce a target form that conveys most of the information of the source language message. A basic assumption of this study is that a transliterated message is not simply a codified, inadequate version of a spoken English message. On the contrary, it is proposed that transliteration is a process that includes a combination of English and ASL features capable of conveying the source message as clearly and unambiguously as any other form of interpreting. It is necessary to reiterate that this is true when the client is to some extent bilingual in ASL and English. The features from English include word order and mouthed English words.[7] ASL features include lexical choice, head and body shifting for marking phrases and clauses, and use of location.

---

6.   Another interesting assumption made about transliteration is that this English also reflects the form of the speaker's message It is assumed that, even though many of the spoken English morphemes such as tense marking and plurals are omitted from the signed version, the structure and order of the signs produced follow the structure and order of the speaker. The data of the present project indicate that this is not necessarily the case. Although the form produced can reflect an English order, it is not necessarily the order of the speaker. This difference is described in this chapter under the section about restructuring.

7.   It may be that the word order is not English word order per se but an order that is shared by both English and ASL.

The hypothesis of the present study is that transliterators produce signed target language messages that contain a mixture of English and ASL features. This mixture of features, rather than causing confusion to the watcher, provides enough detail to produce a message that is clear and unconfusing to the watcher.

In addition, it is proposed that these features reflect conscious strategies used by transliterators during analysis and production of the target form, rather than random productions or errors. This is evidenced by the transliterator's feedback and comments about the target forms during an interview conducted after the data were analyzed. The strategies discussed here and the features that they reflect are (1) conceptual sign choice, (2) addition, (3) omission, (4) restructuring, and (5) mouthing. Additional features of the data corpus are not analyzed in comparable detail. The target form features are categorized in terms of differences from the source form of spoken English. In the evaluation of the data, the features that added to the clarity of the message are analyzed; those portions of the form that contained mistakes or errors are not analyzed or described. This determination is subjective in the same way that any discussion of "correct" interpretation is subjective. In addition to the researcher's judgment, the transliterator was consulted in many of the cases about her reasons, or strategies, in using specific features. There are other measures that can and should be used to further determine the adequacy of any transliterated message, for example, the consumer's comprehension, the comprehension of other consumers, other interpreters' agreement with the form choice. For the preliminary description presented here, the researcher's judgment, the interpreter's judgment, and the apparent satisfaction of the consumer with the transliteration are relied upon in assessing the adequacy of the message form.[8]

Data collection and transcription

The data for this study were collected from a university-level course that was regularly transliterated by the same person. The transliterator and the deaf consumer had, at the time of the videotaping, worked together in this course once a week over a span of eleven weeks, as well as in another course during the same semester and over the same amount of time. The topic of the course was familiar to both the transliterator and the consumer; they were accustomed to working with each other and with the instructor, as well as experienced with the procedures for the class and the vocabulary and content. The purpose in choosing these particular data was to exclude, as much as possible, the type of transliteration that occurs when the transliterator is unfamiliar with the topic, the consumer, and the vocabulary. In the present case, the goal is a processed, analyzed form of the target message, as opposed to a more mechanical reproduction of the English sounds. This, of course, reflects

---

8.   Consumer satisfaction, apparent or real, is an issue that is often only superficially discussed at best. It is an area of extreme importance that warrants serious attention.

the assumption that this type of transliteration is appropriate and does provide an accurate portrayal of the source message. In addition, the consumer is not a native ASL signer but an English signer in the process of learning ASL. The consumer expected the transliteration to be patterned on English but also "conceptually accurate," that is, effective in conveying the meaning of the speaker as well as the form. This represents a balancing of two of the goals outlined earlier: pragmatic and linguistic transliteration. It is assumed, for this particular situation, that the need for efficiency and clarity motivates use of ASL features, and the need for English structures motivates use of English features.

The transliterator in this study is a nationally certified transliterator. In addition to her qualifications as a transliterator, she has a Master's degree in die academic specialty in which she transliterated for the data corpus of this study. Information about the strategies used in the transliteration process was gathered in an interview with the transliterator after the data were analyzed. The researcher's experience as a transliterator, as well as discussions with other transliterators, provided additional insights about features found in the data and their relation to the strategies employed.

A transcription of approximately twenty-five minutes of the classroom lecture was analyzed. Segments of the text from two different time periods were selected for the analysis. Constraints on the choice of text segments included high audibility of the source message, for purposes of comparison, and high visibility of the transliterator. One important area excluded from this study is teacher-student interaction. The description of features used by transliterators both to indicate the speakers and to include as much information as possible is essential to understanding transliteration. Unfortunately, most of the student participation is unintelligible on the videotape. The present analysis is thus limited to the transliteration of the instructor's lecture.

The transcription of the data consists of three parts: transcription of the source message; transcription of the manual signs by means of a gloss and any additional description needed to identify the form of the sign produced; and a transcription of the mouthing that accompanies the signs. Only the mouthed words and parts of words that are clearly recognizable on the videotape are included in the transcription. This leaves many gaps in the mouthed transcription since many parts of the words are not visible, especially with a two-dimensional videotape picture. Mouthing, however, is an important part of transliteration and is included in the analysis whenever possible. In discussing data from the tapes, and in presenting examples, the following conventions are used: first, the original spoken message is orthographically represented, in italics; next, ASL signs are represented with an English gloss-label, in uppercase (any further description needed to clearly identify an ASL sign is added parenthetically after the ASL sign citation); finally, the mouthed form that accompanies the manual signs is framed with double quotation marks, all within square brackets. An example of this transcription technique is the following:

Go to the store → GO (to the right) STORE ["go to the store"]

The analysis focuses on the five categories, or strategies, earlier described as sign choice, addition, omission, restructuring, and mouthing. Although several additional features were identified in the target form that added clarity to the message, these are not discussed in detail here. They appear to be very important, but there is not enough information about these features, as they are used in ASL, to be able to analyze their uses when borrowed for transliterating. A more detailed description of these features and many others is needed.

Analysis of strategies

Sign choice

The first strategy, sign choice, was originally defined in this study as the use of a conceptually accurate sign in place of a literal translation of the English word. Although the idea of conceptual accuracy is somewhat elusive, the reference is to the appropriate portrayal of meaning in each language involved in the transliteration process. To claim that a manual sign is more or less conceptually accurate depends entirely on one's understanding of the meaning of the sign and of the intended word. In sign language interpreting, however, the term "conceptual accuracy" is used most often to refer to the use of a sign that portrays the meaning of the word rather than the form of the word. An example of this is the English word *get*. A literal linguistic transliteration of this word would use the sign GET, which in ASL means to actually take something into one's possession. In English, the word *get* is used with many different meanings, only one of which corresponds to the ASL sign GET, as in the sentence, "I got the book." A literal transliteration would use the same sign in sentences such as the following:

1. "I got sick."
2. "She got hit."
3. "They got there."
4. "I got it," meaning 'I understand'.

None of the verbs in these four sentences uses *get* to mean to take into one's possession. A conceptually accurate transliteration would entail representation of the word *get* with a manual sign that has the meaning of the sentence rather than the form of GET. The verbs in the listed sentences might be conceptually transliterated with the following signs:

1. BECOME
2. something HIT her
3. ARRIVE
4. UNDERSTAND

An example of this strategy in the data is found in relation to the spoken utterance: *the person might <u>wonder</u> if they should happen to turn around and see you checking things off.* Here, the transliterator uses the sign PUZZLE 'to be puzzled' instead of the sign WONDER, which corresponds to the actual English word *wonder*. The transliterator's comment about this choice is that the sign PUZZLE reflects the meaning of the speaker better than the sign WONDER. This is clearly a conscious decision of the transliterator to use a lexical item from ASL that matches the meaning of the speaker rather than the English lexical item of the speaker.

Another example is the spoken utterance:*I want you to take a few minutes now,* where the transliterator uses the sign USE instead of the sign TAKE, which would have matched the English word. In English, the word *take* is similar to the word *get* in the earlier examples. It has many different meanings, only one of which corresponds to the ASL sign TAKE. The transliterator again chooses an ASL sign that matches the meaning of the speaker rather than the words of the speaker. The following spoken word-manual sign pairs from the data also demonstrate this sign choice strategy. In each case, it is the underlined portion of the spoken English message that is recoded to achieve a meaning-match, as opposed to a lexical correspondence:

> *for speech varieties which correspond to solidarity*
> Signed: WITH
>
> *it looks like everyone*
> Signed: *YOU-plural* A-L-L
>
> *because it doesn't work as well as*
> Signed: SUCCEED
>
> *could you make it up*
> Signed: INVENT
>
> *and turn it in so you can get credit for it*
> Signed: GIVE-TO-ME

Another example of this strategy is the use of reduplication for pluralization, which is a feature of ASL, rather than the use of a plural -s marker added to a manual sign, which is a feature of signed English. This use of reduplication was classified as a sign choice rather than an omission from the English message because the latter label would make the actual signed form seem less than adequate. The ASL feature, as part of the form of the transliterated message, shows the richness of the actual form. One example from the data is the following:

> *many societies* → MANY SOCIETY-*plural*

As discussed in the next section, reduplication can also be aptly described as an addition of an ASL feature to the English message. The categories of omission and addition are not discrete; they overlap, and several features can be found in any given sentence. They are divided here into separate categories for discussion, but they are not so easily divided in a message.

The definition of conceptual sign choice, then, is the use of a conceptually accurate sign instead of a sign that portrays the English word form. This definition is extended to include not only words for which both a literal and a conceptual sign could be used, but also those English words that have no exactly comparable form in ASL. These words are occasionally represented by fingerspelling of the exact word and, more frequently, by the use of a manual sign with a similar meaning together with simultaneous English mouthing of the word. An interesting aspect of this is the choice of the word that is mouthed. It is sometimes the speaker's original word and, at other times, the word that is often used to gloss the sign itself. An example of this is the word *versus*. The sign that is generally gloss-labeled OPPOSITE is used for this word in the data. In this instance, the transliterator signs OPPOSITE and simultaneously mouths "versus" to match the speaker's choice of words. Other examples are the following:

Source word		Sign	Mouthing
assignment	→	HOMEWORK	["assignment"]
wonder	→	PUZZLE	["wonder"]
brillian	→	SMART	["brilliant"]

In these instances, the transliterator chooses a conceptually appropriate sign while mouthing the exact form of the source English word to achieve clarity in the target form.

This strategy of conceptual signs plus mouthing is used in a second way by the transliterator. Rather than mouth the word choice of the speaker, a word that is usually associated with the sign is mouthed:

Source word	→	Sign	Mouthing
appear	→	SHOW-UP	["show up"]
data sheet	→	DATA PAPER	["data paper"]
normally	→	MOST TIME	["most time"]
stuff	→	EVERYTHING	["everything"]

No particular pattern is discernible in the data in terms of mouthing of the speaker's word versus the transliterator's own word. It is noteworthy that both are used and that the speaker's word choice does not completely dictate the mouthed form, as is widely assumed. The transliterator suggested a possible explanation for her choice of mouthed form. She feels that it is more natural for her to mouth the word that she associates with a sign. But her training, which defines transliteration as a sign-to-word correspondence, leads her to use the speaker's words. She also stated that choice of mouthing is partly determined by the amount of processing that a Message requires. In a difficult passage that requires a great deal of analysis, her mouthing is much more likely to be her own. When a passage requires less analysis to provide a clear target form, she can give greater attention to reproducing the original words on her mouth. This insight supports the suggestion that both pragmatic and linguistic goals determine the form of the transliteration.

Sign choice, as a feature of transliteration, reflects a strategy used by transliterators to achieve the pragmatic goal of the task, the efficient production of a functionally equivalent message. At the same time, the addition of mouthing seems to be an attempt to more closely approximate the English form of the message.

Addition

The second strategy, addition, refers to the use of a conceptually accurate sign either before or after a more literal equivalent. An example of this is the use of the more literal sign equivalents for the phrase "don't want," where a transliterator signs DON'T, follows it with WANT, and then signs the ASL form typically used, DON'T-WANT. This configuration expresses both the form and the meaning of the source message, thereby achieving both pragmatic and linguistic representation. Included in this category of addition are a number of ASL features that are added to signs in the target message. These features include the use of space to establish a referent (a feature used in ASL but not in English) and the addition of a negative headshake to negative signs, a nonmanual form that is used syntactically in ASL to mark negative clauses. The transliterator in the present study adds head shaking to negative signs. The addition of ASL adverbial markers with verbs occurs in one case as well.[9]

Examples of additions of signs are found in the following discourse fragments from the data corpus. In each case, the transliterator produces the addition after signing the source message fragment:

> *that place has to be within sight*
> Addition: an index 'in this area'
>
> *that doesn't happen one right after the other*
> Addition: NO plus a negative marker
>
> *a week from today*
> Addition: MONDAY

These additions occur after a restructuring of the spoken phrase. Because these data do not provide a sufficient base for generalizing about processes of transliteration, it is important to continue the search for patterns of addition in the data bases of other, similarly designed studies.

An example of the addition of a negative headshake with negative signs occurs in the sequence I–F NOT. A negative headshake is added to the sign NOT. This is not a grammatical feature of English. It is used in ASL to mark clauses rather than single signs, but it appears to have been added here for clarity in the message.

The use of space in ASL is a feature that adds clarity to information by locating objects and entities in the signing space. For example, the speaker talks about a person who, after walking away, might turn around and look back. The transliterator, when signing this stretch of the discourse, adds a classifier predicate indicating that the person walked away to the right. When the speaker talks about the person turning back around, the transliterator signs LOOK-AT-the signer 'looking back at me' and places the sign in the same

---

9.   A discussion of ASL adverbial markers can be found in Liddell (1980).

location on the right where the person had already been established as walking toward. This use of space is a feature that is not available in English but that seems to add clarity to the signed version of the source message. This entire sequence appears to combine the substitution of ASL classifier signs for the more literal signs that could have been used and the addition of signing space used as an established location for a referent.

A second example of use of signing space in the data is the establishment of a person referent to the right of the signing space. Each time the speaker refers to this person, the transliterator points to the previously established location, thereby clearly referring to the person.

Only one example of the addition of ASL adverbials was found in the data corpus. ASL uses specific nonmanual behaviors for expressing an adverb. For example, "to walk carelessly" is expressed by the sign WALK plus the simultaneous addition of the -th adverbial produced by the mouth, meaning 'careless'. Specifically, with this adverbial, the mouth is slightly open and the lips and the tongue protrude slightly. The example found in the present data is the -mm adverbial, meaning 'casually, in an off-hand way'. In this adverbial, the lips are together and protruding. The nonmanual sign -mm is added to the verb WRITE when the speaker discusses the possibility of recording data on a sheet without really doing any of the research. The actual spoken English words are *to mark down at random*. There are no literal equivalents of these words in ASL that express the same meaning that -mm expresses so clearly. With the addition of -mm, the goal of efficient, pragmatic transliteration is achieved.

Another feature added to transliteration is facial expression. ASL, as a visual language, relies much more than spoken English on facial expression. The kind of facial expression referred to here is in addition to the facial expression that accompanies nonmanual adverbs in ASL. A frequent complaint of consumers is that transliterators are monotone, that is, they lack any sort of facial expression. This aspect of a visual language, although not always a grammatical feature of ASL, adds clarity to the visual message and is often missing in a transliterated message. This use of facial expression appears to be one way of representing stress and intonation. It is usually assumed that these spoken language features cannot be adequately transferred to a signed language. This is another area requiring much more investigation. The first of this type of addition in the present data is the use of an exaggerated facial expression with the sign BIG to portray the meaning 'very big'; the second example is the facial and body expression added to the signs SELF RESPECT. An expression of pride on the face and an expanded chest accompanies this sign sequence.

It can be argued that some of the features classified as additions are not additions at all but are required elements in an appropriate and accurate transliteration. The elements add clarity to the message and portray meaning in ways that are not necessarily represented by literal recoding of English words into manual signs. They are classified here as additions only because they are not generally discussed as part of the output of signed transliteration. The use of addition as a strategy is perceived as necessary for clarity in the visual message, both by the transliterator in this study and by other transliterators who served as consultants.

Omission

The third strategy consists of the omission of portions of the source language in the target form. This strategy is used to achieve the goal of efficiency: pragmatic transliteration. Many parts of English words and phrases are not necessary to the overall meaning in context; they are redundant. For example, across a stretch of discourse in English, the use of the past tense marker on each verb is unnecessary from the standpoint of context-bound, referential-and-predicational effectiveness. ASL users mark tense at the beginning of a topic and then do not mark it again until the tense needs to be changed. The transliterator in the present data deletes tense markers in recoding the English message even though there exists a set of literal sign equivalents. Likewise, English plural markings are deleted, as are affixes, such as *-ful* in the word *powerful*. The copula is also almost entirely missing from these data. Although there is a full set of literal sign equivalents for the forms of the English copula, mere is only one instance of use.[10] When the speaker emphasizes the phrase *should be,* the transliterator includes the copula, not by using the sign for 'be' but by spelling B–E and emphatically mouthing it at the same time.

Another omission that occurs less consistently than those already noted is the omission of prepositions not necessary to the message. The phrase *groups of people* is signed GROUP PEOPLE. It is significant that even though the sign is omitted, the word itself is often mouthed by the interpreter. This provides a more linguistic, literal representation on one set of articulators (oral) while providing a more efficient message with the other set of articulators (manual). Mouthing seems to provide a much more consistent reflection than the hands of the literal English message.

Omission of previously established subject pronouns also occurs. The English sequence *I'm not* is transliterated as WILL NOT. This type of structure, with the pronoun omitted, is not a feature of formal English. It is a feature of ASL that is borrowed by this transliterator as a strategy to achieve the goal of efficiency in the transliteration.

Restructuring

The fourth strategy, restructuring, refers to the replacement of one grammatical structure with another. This is different from the sign choice category because sign choice mainly involves one or two-word sequences; restructuring involves changes in longer utterances. Restructuring can occur in combination with any and all of the earlier-mentioned

---

10.   Copula is not used in ASL; the sign equivalents are based on a single sign meaning 'true' or 'real'. This basic form is assigned specific modifications in order to provide sign equivalents.

strategies. Examples of restructuring occur within the following discourse fragments. In each case, it is the underlined portion of the spoken English message that is restructured:[11]

> *Which is <u>voiced 'th'</u>*
> Restructured to: T–H WITH VOICE ('"th" with voice')
>
> *I'm giving you a <u>week from today</u> off*
> Restructured to: NEXT-WEEK MONDAY
>
> *more friendly and more <u>trustworthy.</u>*
> Restructured to: CAN TRUST MORE
>
> *it has to be a <u>location which is within sight</u>*
> Restructured to: PLACE YOU CAN SEE
>
> *All you're after is one word.*
> Restructured to: ONLY WANT ONE WORD
>
> *<u>if it's within sight</u> then people will*
> Restructured to: I–F CAN SEE THAT PLACE

These restructured discourse fragments are accompanied by mouthing of English words that correspond to the restructured form and not to the source message. This is another indication that transliteration involves more than a literal representation or recoding of spoken English.

It is noteworthy that three of the source forms are structures involving the copula, a feature not used in ASL. It may be that one cause of restructuring is forms or configurations in the source message that cannot be comparably recoded in ASL. The present transliterator, although aware that she uses this strategy, could not identify any particular feature of the message that caused restructuring. Her explanation was limited to an express awareness that some of the English utterances, as structured, would not provide a clear visual message when recoded into the target form, and, therefore, she restructured them.

Mouthing

The fifth strategy, mouthing, is described earlier in relation to sign choice. There are instances in the data when the mouthing matches the source form, and other instances when it matches the transliterated form. A match with the transliterated form is also seen in the mouthing that accompanies restructuring in the transliteration. In addition to these uses of mouthing, there is another use that occurs in the data when a specific sign that occurs can serve to recode more than one English word. On these occasions of potential ambiguity in the manual mode, mouthing is used to indicate which English word is

---

11.   Note that the second example of restructuring here is also cited earlier, in the section on the strategy of addition. The sign MONDAY is an addition embedded within a restructuring.

being transliterated. The following examples show the many-to-one relationship between mouthed English words and, in each case, the co-occurring manual sign:

Sign	Mouthing
RELATE-TO	["correspond"] ["associated"]
SITUATION	["situation"] ["domains"]
MUST	["will"] ["should"] ["have to"]
SMART	["smart"] ["intelligent"] ["brilliant"]
VARIOUS	["variety"] ["variable"]

Not all of these mouthed English words have literal sign equivalents. The transliterator, rather than using a different sign for each meaning, uses the same sign and simultaneously mouths the English form. In each instance, the mouthing serves to distinguish the intended meaning of the manual sign. This use of mouthing, which presupposes consumer reliance on speech-reading, is an important strategy in transliterating. The effectiveness of this strategy, like the effectiveness of all the other strategies, is dependent on the consumer's skills and knowledge of the target form. It is one more strategy for producing both a conceptual and a literal message at the same time.

The transliterator agreed that the mouthing strategy was important for the particular consumer in the present study. Although some of the strategies, such as restructuring, are chosen because of structural incongruities between languages, the use of mouthing is determined by the consumer's needs. For different consumers, the transliterator can employ different techniques, such as fingerspelling, to provide the English equivalent.

An additional aspect of transliterating that is not described here is the phenomenon of pacing or phrasing. This includes the features used by transliterators to mark the separation of clauses in the target form. This type of marking is achieved through stress and intonation in English and through various features in ASL, some of which are described in this chapter. These features include body shifts, head nodding, signing space, and facial expressions. These features appear in the transliterated data of this study, although not necessarily in combination with ASL sentence structures. These features, in ASL, are used with entire phrases or clauses. In the transliterated message, nonmanual features similar in form to those of ASL appear to mark the beginning and ending points of the English structures. This combination of ASL and English features is a transliteration strategy that adds clarity to the message.

Summary and conclusions

Although the analysis and description of the target message examined in this study are preliminary, the findings indicate that the form of transliteration is different from what is assumed by both transliterators and consumers. On the whole, it is apparent that at least some forms of transliteration include not only English-like signing of the source message but also many features of ASL. This type of transliteration requires skills in both ASL and English in order to achieve and blend pragmatic and linguistic goals in the production of a target message. Analyzing the source message and producing a target form that is both functionally equivalent and structurally similar to the source is a complex process and requires more than the simple recoding of English words.

This study, in the tradition of preliminary investigations, raises more Questions about transliteration than are answered. It is hoped that as we understand more about the structure of ASL and the process of interpreting in general, the process of transliterating will also be better understood. Areas of research suggested by this study include a description of the source message when it is a signed form of English and a description of different varieties of transliteration, including the varieties requested by bilingual ASL and English users as well as the varieties primarily understood by English signers. It will also be important to study the effects of a variety of speakers on the form of the signed output produced by one transliterator for one consumer.

Acknowledgments

Funding for this research was provided through the Small Grants Fund, Gallaudet University, Washington, D.C. I thank all of those who participated in the data collection for this study: the deaf and hearing students, the instructors, and, most especially, the transliterators.

3.5   Davis, Jeffrey. 1990. "Linguistic transference and interference: Interpreting between English and ASL." In *Sign language research: Theoretical Issues*, ed. by Ceil Lucas, 308–321. Washington, DC: Gallaudet University Press.

Jeffrey Davis has worked as an interpreter, educator, and researcher in the field of SLI for the past four decades. He began his work as a sign language interpreter in the community in Austin, Texas, and completed a Masters degree in Linguistics at Gallaudet University and then a doctorate in educational linguistics at the University of New Mexico.

He began his university teaching career in 1983 at Gallaudet University in Washington, DC. There, he taught in the Master's Degree in Interpretation program in the Department of Linguistics and Interpreting until 1990. He served on the faculties of the Sign Language/Deaf Studies program in the College of Education at the University of Arizona (1990–1994) and the Sign Language Interpretation Program at Miami-Dade College (1994–2000). In addition to extensive field practice and research, he has developed and taught undergraduate and graduate coursework in Education of the Deaf, Sign Language/Deaf Studies, Linguistics, and Interpreting. He joined the University of Tennessee faculty in 2000 where he is now a professor of ASL, Linguistics, and Interpreting in the Educational Interpreting Program.

Since his earlier work on language contact and interpreting, Davis has been involved in many innovative SLI projects, including the development of a multicultural curriculum model in the USA, and SLI training in Trinidad and Tobago. He has received accolades for his seminal study on native Indian sign language in North America, based on the analysis of authentic data filmed in the 1930s (Davis 2010).

Linguistic Transference and Interference

Interpreting Between English and ASL

Jeffrey Davis

Research suggests that interlingual transference – for example, code-switching, code-mixing, and lexical borrowing – typically characterize conversational style in bilingual communities (Gumperz and Hernandez-Chavez, 1971; Gumperz, 1976; DiPietro, 1978; Poplack, 1980; Poplack, Wheeler, and Westwood, 1987). The fact that there has been prolonged and intensive contact between ASL and English has resulted in linguistic outcomes similar to those found in other bilingual communities. These outcomes are shaped by factors unique to the ASL-English contact situation (for example, linguistic channel availability and manner of language acquisition).[12]

The complexity of the ASL-English contact situation in terms of participant characteristics and varieties of language used by these participants has only begun to be systematically described (Lucas, 1989; Lucas and Valli, 1989; Davis, 1987, and 1989). Interpreting between ASL and English has significant implications for signed language interpreters, who function at the point of interface of both languages and cultures. The interpreting field is an excellent arena for the study of language contact phenomena, but has heretofore been neglected by researchers.

Code-switching and code-mixing, for example, have been identified as devices for elucidation and interpretation (Kachru, 1978; Davis, 1989). Code-switching and code-mixing may be viewed as a liability or an asset in interpretation – the former being the case when the switch or mix is sporadic and unsignaled (interference), the latter as a linguistic strategy used to avoid vagueness and ambiguity (transference).

The questions to be addressed in this paper are these: How do interpreters visually or manually represent source language forms (English) in the target language output (ASL)? What is the nature and the structure of the interpreters' representations of English forms in the visual-manual modality of ASL? When can interlingual transfer between ASL and English be considered code-switching, code-mixing, or lexical borrowing? I analyze English to ASL interpreting data for examples of interlingual transference and interference in the target language (ASL) output. I make a distinction between interlingual transference and

---

12.   Linguistic channel availability means that the oral channel, more specifically the mouth, when not otherwise being used for ASL grammatical purposes (for example, adverbials), may be available to encode English. Manner of language acquisition refers to the fact that for the majority of deaf individuals, ASL is acquired from deaf peers and/or in the residential school setting, as opposed to from parents.

interference. Transference happens when interpreters encode English forms in the ASL output, as opposed to interpreting them. When interpreters encode English forms visually, they mark them in very systematic ways. This is a strategy that disambiguates and elucidates discontinuities between ASL and English. Interference, on the other hand, occurs when the encoding of English forms in the ASL output interferes with the propositional content of the message. Encoded English forms that are sporadic and unsignaled appear to be a form of interference.

English-to-ASL interpreting[13]

In the case of English-to-ASL interpreting, English is the source language and ASL is the target language. Interpretation is a process whereby the source language message is immediately changed into the target language. Interpretation requires comprehension of the source-language input, immediate discarding of words from the source language, analysis of the source message for meaning, and restructuring the source message into the target language output (Seleskovitch, 1978). This endeavor is more difficult when the two languages involved are structurally divergent, as would be the case, for example, with English and Russian, Finnish and Spanish, and English and ASL. English-to-ASL interpretation involves not only two structurally different languages, but different linguistic modalities as well (aural/oral versus visual/gestural). If the situation weren't complex enough, it is exacerbated by the fact that one language has traditionally enjoyed greater status and wider use than the other. That is, English (the majority language) has heretofore been the primary language used in deaf education and is held to be the language needed for purposes of upward mobility. ASL (the minority language) has traditionally been relegated to use in informal settings and used primarily for intragroup activities.

ASL and English bilingualism

The ASL-English contact situation is parallel to cases of societal bilingualism – that is, one language enjoys greater prestige and wider use than the other. In language contact situations where there is uneven situational and functional allocation of the languages, the

---

13.   ASL interpreting is to be distinguished from signed language transliterating – that is, changing an English message from one form of English to another. The goal of transliteration is to produce a morpheme to morpheme correspondence between spoken English and sign language. In a broad sense, this is a visual representation of English. The transliterator attempts to render spoken English in a visually accessible form. Depending on the topic and context, and if no qualified ASL interpreter is otherwise available, a deaf individual fluent in English may sometimes request transliteration.

result is typically different configurations of bilingualism – that is, dominance in the majority language, balanced bilingualism, or dominance in the minority language (Mougeon, Beniak, and Valois, 1985). Grosjean points out that "most bilinguals use their languages for different purposes and in different situations, and hence 'balanced' bilinguals, those who are equally fluent in both languages, are probably the exception and not the norm" (1982, 235). At the societal level, then, the U.S. deaf community can be best described as multilingual, since ASL, English, English-based signing, and contact signing[14] are used to varying degrees. Individual deaf Americans are also likely to be bilingual – that is, most members of the community use signed, written, or even spoken English in addition to ASL.[15]

A unique characteristic of interpreting in an ASL-English contact situation, then, is that the deaf audience who are the consumers of English to ASL interpretation usually exhibit some degree of bilingual proficiency. In other words, while interpreting into the target language (ASL), the interpreter may assume that the deaf audience has some written or even spoken proficiency in the source language (English). The audience, of course, may not always be bilingual. There are situations where the deaf consumer(s) may be ASL monolingual and expect a different interpreting output (that is, ASL with minimal transference from English). When the deaf audience is bilingual, however, the interpreter may sometimes encode spoken English words or phrases in the visual mode, as opposed to interpreting them. That is, in some instances, English words or phrases can be fingerspelled; a visual representation of English syntax can be given in the sign modality; or ASL signs can be accompanied by the mouthing of English words. In the present study, I am interested in describing when interlingual transference from English to ASL is patterned and rule governed, as opposed to random and sporadic (that is, interference).

Definitions

Linguistic transference results from prolonged language contact. Code-switching, code-mixing, and lexical borrowing are the most common forms of transfer found among bilingual communities of the world (Poplack, 1980; Sankoff and Poplack, 1981; Mougen, Beniak, and Valois, 1985). Code-switching is the broader term used to refer to any stretch or portion of discourse where there is alternation between two languages. In other words,

---

14.   Lucas & Valli (this volume) describe contact signing which results from the contact between ASL and English, and which exhibits features of both languages.

15.   In the case of the deaf community, the lack of bilingual proficiency for some deaf individuals seems exacerbated by the lack of bilingual education for deaf children, the inability of most families to use ASL with their deaf children, and the barrier deafness imposes to spoken English input via the auditory channel.

in code-switching there is a complete switch to the other language, including switching the phonology and morphology. According to this definition, "code-switching" can be used to refer only to cases where someone signing ASL stops and starts speaking English, or vice versa.

Code-switching, however, is usually extended to include switches from ASL signing to English-based signing – that is, switching within modality (Lee, 1983). Switches that are motivated by a change in the speech event or situation have been referred to as "situational code-switching" (Gumperz, 1976). When bilinguals switch for stylistic or rhetorical purposes, this is referred to as "conversational code-switching" (Gumperz and Hernandez-Chavez, 1971). Lee (1983) finds that, depending on the topic, situation, and participants, a signer may switch from ASL signing to signing that is more like English (that is, situational code-switching). At other times, usually for stylistic purposes or as a rhetorical device, an ASL signer may manually encode an English word or phrase in the visual mode (that is, conversational code-switching). The research done by Lee (1983) supports the notion that the types of code-switching found in bilingual and multilingual hearing communities are also evident in the signing of bilinguals in the multilingual deaf community.

Code-mixing, on the other hand, is much more difficult to distinguish. In code-mixing, "pieces" of one language are used while a speaker is basically using another language. The language used predominantly is the base or primary language, and the language from which the pieces originate is the source language. There is debate in the literature about the appropriate use of the code-mixing and code-switching labels. The debate arises out of how to differentiate switches within sentences (intrasentential) from switches at or between sentence boundaries (intersentential). Some researchers argue that the term "code-mixing" rather than "code-switching" should be used to refer to intrasentential phenomena – for example, switches occurring within a sentence, clause, or constituent (Kachru, 1978; Sridhar and Sridhar, 1980; Bokamba, 1985).

Lucas and Valli (in press) discuss how code-mixing is used by deaf individuals in the ASL-English contact situation and distinguish it from cases of code-mixing described for spoken language situations:

> Mixing within components, while possible, is necessarily sequential – that is, it seems impossible to produce two phonological events from two different spoken languages simultaneously. However, in the contact signing described here, in which a signer produces ASL lexical items on the hands, and simultaneous mouthing of the corresponding English lexical items, the result seems to be simultaneous production of two separate codes.

"Code-mixing" is used in this paper to describe the interpreters' simultaneous mouthing of English words while signing ASL.

Lexical borrowing is different from code-switching and code-mixing (Poplack, Sankoff, and Miller, 1987). In the case of lexical borrowing, words from one language are used repeatedly in another language until they eventually become indistinguishable from the native vocabulary. That is, the borrowed lexical item becomes assimilated into the borrowing language. The borrowed form gets used longitudinally across speakers until it takes on the phonological and morphological characteristics of the borrowing language. In contrast to established loan words, "nonce borrowings" are words that do not have frequent or widespread use in the borrowing language (Weinreich, 1953; Sankoff, Poplack, and Vanniarajan, 1986). They may be used only in one context by one speaker. Similar to established loan words, however, nonce borrowings share the phonological and morphological characteristics of the borrowing language.

"Linguistic interference" is the transfer of rules from one language to another. This is in contrast to the interlingual transfer of material from the source language while the rules of the base language are maintained – that is, "transference" (Mougeon, Beniak, and Valois, 1985). In spoken-language interpreting, for example, if a monolingual English audience were depending on an interpreter to understand the lecture of a visiting Russian scholar and the interpreter used an occasional Russian word or sentence construction, this use might be considered a form of interference. In the case of signed-language interpreting, the inappropriate use of English mouthing during ASL interpretation could be considered a form of interference. For example, the interpreter might use English mouthing where ASL nonmanual markers are needed (for example, adverbials). Glossing of ASL signs during ASL to English interpretation would also be a form of interference. If the ASL verb GO-TO is reduplicated, for example, an interpreter might incorrectly interpret "go, go, go," rather than the appropriate English translation – "to frequent."

Since sign language interpreters are usually required to interpret simultaneously between spoken English and ASL – two structurally different languages – some interference between the languages can be expected. Unfortunately, it is notoriously difficult to ferret out factors that contribute to interference – for example, difficulty of the topic, lack of linguistic proficiency in one of the languages by the interpreter, simultaneously versus consecutively interpreting the message, etc.

It is conceivable that the interpreter's lack of ASL proficiency can significantly contribute to linguistic interference. For example, an interpreter who learned ASL as a second language might be more likely to use idiosyncratic grammatical constructions. In order to separate outcomes of language contact that may be the result of second-language acquisition (that is, if the interpreter learned ASL as a second language and uses idiosyncratic grammatical constructions – interference) from outcomes of language contact (that is, regular and rule-governed linguistic behavior like code-switching and lexical borrowing), the data used in this study are from interpreters whose native language is ASL. Since the interpreters are interpreting into their native language (ASL), I assume that interference from English is minimal. I will systematically describe how interpreters "flag" a switch from ASL to English-based signing, or simultaneously mark an ASL sign with English mouthing.

The database[16]

Sign Media, Inc. (1985) has produced and marketed a videotape entitled *Interpreter Models: English to ASL (lectures)*. I examined the interpreting performance of the two ASL interpreting models presented in this tape because it is specifically designed to present models of English-to-ASL interpretation.[17] For the purposes of this study, I transcribed the first spoken English lecture and simultaneous ASL interpretations. The topic of this lecture was radio and television measurement services – for example, Arbitron and Neilson. These measurement services determine which radio and television programs consumers are listening to or watching.

I transcribed the spoken English using conventional orthography, and transcribed the interpreted ASL into gloss form including information about the use of ASL grammatical features – nonmanual behaviors, use of space, indexing, and mouthing. This resulted in three sets of transcriptions: the spoken English and both ASL interpretations. Two hearing graduate assistants verified the English transcriptions, and two deaf native ASL consultants and one interpreter consultant verified the transcriptions of the ASL interpreting. All transcriptions, verifications, and analyses were done using videoequipment that allows forward and backward slow-motion viewing and full stop with minimal distortion. Following verification of the transcripts, the spoken English text was matched with the interpreted ASL.

I then analyzed the data to determine if and when the interpreters were using code-mixing, code-switching, or lexical borrowing. There are at least three major ways in which English words or phrases are represented in the visual modality during ASL interpreting: (1) pronounced mouthing of English words (without voicing) while simultaneously signing ASL, (2) prefacing or following an ASL sign with a finger-spelled word; (3) marking or flagging a fingerspelled word or the signed representation of an English word or phrase with certain ASL lexical items – for example, the index marker, the demonstrative, quotation markers, etc. Each of these categories will be discussed along with examples from the

---

16.   Davis (in process) has collected interpreting data in a controlled study of signed language interpreters, and is in the process of analyzing these data for examples of code-switching, code-mixing, and lexical borrowing. In that study, four interpreters (two native and two non-native ASL signers) were filmed simultaneously interpreting a spoken English lecture. Comparing the ASL interpreting of native and non-native ASL interpreters can perhaps further our understanding of linguistic transference as a strategy among bilinguals and interpreters, and linguistic interference as faulty second language learning or as instances of processing errors.

17.   There are two interpreted lectures on the tape produced by Sign Media, Inc. (1985). The tape first shows one of the spoken English lectures, followed by the two ASL interpretations of that lecture, then both interpreters and lecturer are shown simultaneously. This is the format for both lectures. The source language was English and the target language ASL (see, for example, Interpreter Models: English to ASL [lectures], Sign Media, Inc. 1985).

data. I will also discuss how the visual representation and flagging of English may or may not be code-switching, code-mixing, and/or lexical borrowing.

Mouthing English words while simultaneously signing ASL

Because of the differences in linguistic modality (visual-gestural versus aural-oral), interlingual transference between spoken English and ASL is of a different nature than between two spoken languages. Because of the constraints to the auditory channel imposed by deafness, vocalization is not used to convey linguistic meaning in ASL. The mouth, on the other hand, because it is highly visible, is sometimes used to convey linguistic meaning (for example, adverbials). Because the mouth is sometimes available, one salient characteristic of intensive language contact between ASL and English is that the mouth is sometimes used to visually represent certain English words. This appears to be a type of simultaneous code-mixing that occurs rather than sequential switching from one language to another. In this system, the features of both languages are produced simultaneously. Over time, many of the mouthed English words are no longer recognizable as English, and in many cases, native ASL users may not even recognize the mouthing as a phonological remnant from English. The interpreters' mouthing is included in the present data corpus through the use of forward and backward slow-motion and full-stop videoequipment, and through verification by the deaf consultants.

In the following examples, the spoken English input is given first, followed by the ASL interpretation. The level of transcription shown above the glosses of the ASL signs is the interpreters' use of mouthing. The following diacritics are used: *ENG* ↑ indicates the clear use of English mouthing; *ENG* ↓ means that there was reduced English mouthing; *ASL MOUTH* refers to the use of adverbials (for example, MM, TH, PAH, CHA, etc.) A switch from English mouthing to ASL mouthing, or vice versa, is indicated with //. In the case of reduced English mouthing, the part of the gloss that gets mouthed is marked with double underlines. Finally, the symbol # preceding the example indicates fingerspelling, the + symbol indicates sign reduplication, and *means that the sign is articulated emphatically.

The following examples show how the interpreters simultaneously use English mouthing, reduced English mouthing, and ASL mouthing across the interpreted ASL text:

(1a)   Spoken English input: … lots of people have heard about Neilson television rating services which is on the television side of the fence and we are a, ah, kind of share that market in terms of providing measurement data for the television services. But in radio, Arbitron is the "major book."

                         ENG ↓   //ENG ↑   //ASL MOUTH//

(1b)   Interpreter 1: MANY PEOPLE KNOW NAME#NEILSON, FOCUS

       ENG ↑ //   //ASL MOUTH   //ENG ↑ ENG ↑

       #T.V.+ +, (left space) POSS-PL, (shift to right space) THAT#ARBITRON,

<u>   </u>   ENG↑   // //ASL MOUTH   //

#NEILSON (shifts back to left space)#TV ++, HAVE SHARE PL-POSS

       //ENG↓   //   //ENG ↑ //

(hesitates) <u>BUSI</u>NESS (shift back to right space)#RADIO (left indexic marker),

//ASL MOUTH// ENG↑ //ASL MOUTH

REALLY#ARBITRON TOP

<u>   ASL MOUTH   //ENG ↓   //ASL MOUTH// ENG ↓</u>

(1c) Interpreter 3: UNDERSTAND, <u>PEOP</u>LE-INDEXIC-PL, FAMOUS <u>KNOW</u>

<u>   //ENG↑   //ASL MOUTH//   </u>

<u>NA</u>ME <u>WHICH</u>, #ANIELSON (interpreter self corrects) THAT (right indexic

<u>   ENG ↑   //ASL MOUTH   //ENG ↑ // ENG ↓   </u>

marker)#NEILSON, STRONG CONNECTION#TV + +, FAMOUS <u>SAME</u>-AS

<u>//ENG ↑   //ENG ↓   //ASL MOUTH//ENG ↑ //ENG ↓   </u>

#ARBITRON <u>SAME</u>-AS FOCUS#TV+ + + + <u>MEA</u>SURE <u>PEOPLE</u> <u>WATCH</u>,

<u>   //ASL MOUTH   //ENG ↑   </u>

<u>HOW-MA</u>NY SO-FORTH, UNDERSTAND + + FOCUS RADIO (left indexic

<u>   //ENG ↓   </u>

marker), #<u>ARBI</u>TRON *<u>STRONG</u>

(2a) Spoken English input: So you listen to it in the morning as you're getting up, then you go out in your car and the drive times as they refer to them, are the major times that people listen in the United States to the radio, is when they're driving to work, and when they're coming home.

<u>   ASL MOUTH//ENG ↓   //ASL MOUTH   //ENG ↓   </u>

(2b) Interpreter 1: WELL, <u>MOR</u>NING GET-<u>UP</u> LISTEN-TO +, <u>OUT</u> <u>CAR</u>,

<u>//ASL MOUTH //ENG ↑ //ENG ↓   //ASL MOUTH   </u>

DRIVE-TO   CALL   DRIVE-TO (hesitates) <u>TIME</u>, THAT, DRIVE-TO,

<u>//ENG ↓   //ASL MOUTH   //ENG ↓   //ASL MOUTH   </u>

MOST-<u>TIME</u> TEND-TO DRIVE-TO <u>WORK</u>, #<u>BACK</u> <u>HOME</u> DRIVE-TO

<u>   //ENG ↑   </u>

LISTEN-TO RADIO

<u>   ENG ↓   //ASL MOUTH   //ENG ↓ //ASL MOUTH</u>

(2c) Interpreter 2: <u>GET-UP</u>   <u>MOR</u>NING   LISTEN,   GET-IN   <u>CAR</u>   DRIVE

//ENG↑ "called"   ENG ↑   //ASL MOUTH   //

QUOTATION MARKERS D-R-I-V-E T-I-M-E QUOTATION MARKERS

ENG ↑   //ASL MOUTH //ENG ↑ //ASL MOUTH //ENG ↓   //ASL MOUTH //ENG ↓

THAT, DURING TIME DRIVE THAT WHEW <u>IMPOR</u>TANT FOR <u>RADIO</u>

<u>//ASL MOUTH</u> //ENG ↑//

<u>BECAU</u>SE <u>PEOP</u>LE TEND-TO DRIVE-FROM-HERE-TO-THERE + + WORK

<u>ASL MOUTH</u>

COMMUTE LISTEN-TO

From analysis of these data, there appears to be a range of mouthing in the ASL interpreting data. In what is perhaps best described as code-mixing, English words are sometimes clearly visible on the mouth – for example, nouns, question words, numbers, lists, and fingerspelled words. At the other extreme, most mouthing in ASL is no longer seen as representing ENGLISH (for example, the mouthing that accompanies the ASL signs LATE, HAVE, and FINISH). In the latter examples, English words appear to have been borrowed into ASL by way of mouthing and subsequently lexicalized into ASL. Further research is needed in order to elucidate these processes. There are cases where the use of mouthing can be accurately described in terms of code-mixing. In other instances, the use of reduced English mouthing may be best described as a form of lexical borrowing; other times, mouthing appears strictly a feature of ASL – as is the case with adverbial markers that bear no synchronic or diachronic relation to English.

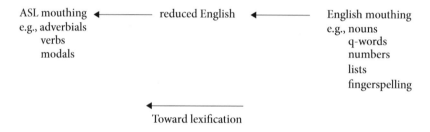

Figure 1. A range of mouthing during ASL interpretation

ASL signs prefaced or followed by a fingerspelled word

Fingerspelling is a system for representing the English alphabet manually by varying handshapes. It is used primarily to represent proper nouns and English terms that do not have ASL lexical equivalents. Fingerspelling is usually articulated in the space between the face and dominant shoulder and the palm orientation is toward the addressee. Clearly, fingerspelling forms an integral part of ASL (as opposed to being a part of English). In contrast to single ASL signs, which usually involve one or two handshapes, fingerspelling a word often involves many different handshapes.

Battison suggests that borrowing lexical items from English via fingerspelling and restructuring them phonologically and sometimes morphologically is an active process in ASL. Fingerspelled words, which are structurally different from ASL signs, are restructured systematically to fit the formational patterns of ASL. Some of the systematic changes a fingerspelled word undergoes in this process are deletion of handshape letters, dissimilation of handshapes and assimilation of the number of fingers involved, location changes, movement additions and orientation changes, and semantic restructuring of the signs. The lexical items that result from this process have been referred to as "fingerspelled loan signs" (Battison, 1978, 218–19).

It can be argued, however, that the fingerspelling of English words is not lexical borrowing in the literal sense (Liddell and Lucas, personal communication). That is, in the lexical borrowing that takes place between spoken languages, a lexical item, a form-meaning pairing in one language, is borrowed into another language. When this happens, there are typically phonological and/or semantic adjustments that make the form-meaning relationship in the borrowing language different from the source language. For example, the French lexical item *croissant* ([kwasõ]) was borrowed into English and is now pronounced [krowsant].

This process is not exactly what takes place in the ASL–English situation. For example, the orthographic representation of the English word "date" occurs as a fingerspelled lexical item in ASL, consisting of a sequence of four ASL morphemes, D-A-T-E. In spoken-language borrowing situations, a relationship exists between the phonologies of two languages, but the relationship here is between the orthographic system used for representing one language (English), and the phonological system of another, ASL. Furthermore, the relationship between the phonologies of the spoken languages is one of "borrowing" – one language borrows the sounds of another – and the result is a loan. At no point, however, can the relationship between English orthography and ASL phonology be characterized as borrowing. ASL morphemes are never borrowed from the orthographic English event; they are simply used to represent the orthographic event.

A fingerspelled word, then, can never technically be described as English. Fingerspelling, by its very nature, is an ASL phonological event. In a pattern similar to lexical borrowing, however, a fingerspelled word may get used repeatedly and eventually become lexicalized into ASL. In other words, a fingerspelled word begins to undergo systematic phonological, morphological, and semantic changes like those described by Battison (1978). Fingerspelled words that undergo the process of lexicalization may eventually become an integral part of the ASL lexicon. This usually happens when the fingerspelled word gets used longitudinally across speakers, but lexicalization is also evident when words get fingerspelled repeatedly in a single context.

The interpreters in this study use fingerspelling in the following ways: lexicalized fingerspelled signs, which have been lexicalized into ASL through the processes described earlier; nonce fingerspelling, which are context and topic specific, but follow the pattern of lexicalization already described; and full fingerspelling, wherein each letter of the word is clearly represented. Some examples from the data are:

Lexicalized fingerspelled signs used by Interpreter 1:

#WHAT	#DATE
#TV	#CAR
#SPORTS	#IF
#CARTOONS	#BACK
#DO-DO	#NEWS
#HOBBY	#CO
#US	

Lexicalized fingerspelled loan signs used by Interpreter 2:

#BOYS (2-handed)	#SHOW
#OR	#BUSY (2-handed)
#CO	#WHAT
#SPORTS	#NEWS
#TV	#ALL

Some fingerspelled signs are used like nonce events. In these data, these nonce events typically start out as examples of full fingerspelling (that is, produced in the area typically used for fingerspelling, with all handshapes represented, and with palm orientation away from the signer). Examples include: #RADIO, #ARBITRON, and #NEILSON. These words are context and topic specific. Both interpreters, following repeated use by the speaker, start treating these words like ASL lexical items as opposed to fingerspelled representations of English orthographic events. For example, there is deletion and/or assimilation of the number of handshape letters involved during the production of these repeated fingerspelled words.

Sometimes the interpreters preface or follow an ASL sign with a fingerspelled word. For example:

(3)   Spoken English input: public affairs Interpreter 1: <u>DISCUSS #PUBLIC AFFAIRS</u>

(4)   Spoken English input: cartoons Interpreter 1: <u>FUNNY #CARTOONS</u>

(5)   Spoken English input: billboards Interpreter 2: <u>#BILLBOARDS OPEN C-CL</u>

(6)   Spoken English input: drive times Interpreter 2: <u>QUOTATION MARKERS,</u>
       <u>#DRIVE TIMES, QUOTATION MARKERS, THAT DRIVE-TO THAT</u>

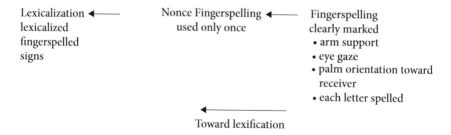

Lexicalization ◄——— Nonce Fingerspelling ◄——— Fingerspelling

lexicalized   used only once   clearly marked

fingerspelled   • arm support

signs   • eye gaze

                                            • palm orientation toward
                                               receiver

                                            • each letter spelled

Toward lexification ◄———

Figure 2. A range of fingerspelling in ASL interpreting

In these cases it appears that an English word gets fingerspelled because there is no lexical counterpart for that word in ASL. The fingerspelled word often gets flagged with an ASL lexical marker (for example, a classifier predicate, demonstrative pronoun, or quotation mark). Other times, the interpreter chooses to tag an ASL sign with the fingerspelled representation of the English word used by the speaker (Examples 3 and 4). From the preliminary analysis of these data, there appears to be a range of fingerspelling being used.

Fingerspelling, then, gets marked in very patterned ways by the interpreters. For example, mouthing of the English gloss accompanies all fingerspelled words – even lexicalized fingerspelled signs. Indexing, eye gaze, and support of the active arm with the passive hand also marks the fingerspelling used. In their use of fingerspelling, the interpreters appear to follow a pattern of movement toward lexification of fingerspelled signs into the structure of ASL.

In sum, it appears that fingerspelling serves a variety of purposes in ASL. Personal communication with deaf consultants indicates that ASL signers sometimes use fingerspelling for stylistic purposes. For example, an ASL signer may opt to fingerspell a word rather than sign the ASL equivalent. An ASL sign may be prefaced or followed with a fingerspelled representation of that sign. What is also evident in these examples is the simultaneous use of two phonologies – an ASL representation of an English orthographic event that is accompanied by English mouthing. The processes involved in fingerspelling need further elucidation before accurate labels can be attached, although it is suggested that "fingerspelled representation" may characterize the phenomenon more accurately than "fingerspelled loan sign" or "lexical borrowing."

Marking or flagging a fingerspelled or signed English form with ASL lexical items

In this category, we find English forms that are visually represented and flagged in very specific ways. Consider the following:

(7a) Spoken English input: A lot of parents, young parents, use television as a babysitter.

ENG↓	//ENG↑

(7b) Interpreter I: MANY MOTHER-FATHER YOUNG, FINE #TV++,

//ASL MOUTH	//ENG↑ //	ASL MOUTH

TAKE-ADVANTAGE-OF, BABY TAKE-CARE-OF, SO-TO-SPEAK

In Example 7, the interpreter marks the speaker's metaphoric use of the television as a babysitter with the ASL sign SO-TO-SPEAK. This sign is similar to the one for QUOTATION MARKERS, except that the former is done lower and more rapidly in sign space. In the following example, the QUOTATION MARKERS sign and the demonstrative THAT is used:

(8a) Spoken English input: Then you go out in your car and the drive times as they refer to them …

(8b)   Interpreter 2: GET-IN CAR, DRIVE-TO, <u>QUOTATION MARKERS</u>, #DRIVE-TIMES, <u>QUOTATION MARKERS</u>, <u>THAT</u> DRIVE-TO <u>THAT</u>

(8c)   Interpreter 1: OUT CAR, DRIVE-TO, <u>CALL</u> DRIVE (hesitates) TIME, <u>THAT</u> DRIVE-TO

Interpreter 2 fingerspells 'drive times' and marks it before and after it is spelled with QUO-TATIONS. It is as though the interpreter is setting this form off as a lexical item that is not ASL. Interpreter 1 prefaces DRIVE TIME with the labeling sign CALL, hesitates, then marks it with the demonstrative followed by what 'drive times' means – that is, DRIVE-TO. Interpreter 2 also incorporates the use of the demonstrative.

Summary and conclusions

In this paper I describe how interpreters sometimes encode spoken English words or phrases visually. For example, an interpreter can fingerspell the orthographic representation of an English word or can give a visual representation of English syntax in the sign modality. Other times, an interpreter accompanies ASL signs by the simultaneous mouthing of English words. I have discussed the possibility that these visual representations of English qualify as code-switching, code-mixing, and lexical borrowing.

The results of intensive contact between two structurally different languages like ASL and English is extremely complex and points to a need for modification of the terms traditionally used to characterize language contact phenomena. For example, according to the literal definition of "code-switching," there needs to be a complete switch to another language, including a switch to the phonology. According to this definition, a "true" switch could only occur if an ASL signer stopped signing and began speaking English (or any other language for that matter). In order to understand the underlying linguistic and socio-linguistic processes involved in code-switching, the literal definition must be extended to include a switch from ASL to English-based signing, that is, switching within modality.

The term "code-mixing" should not be loosely applied either. It does not imply that the two contact languages are thrown together in a random and ungoverned fashion. In the form of the simultaneous use of English mouthing and ASL, code-mixing appears to be highly rule-governed. This is demonstrated by the fact that both native ASL interpreters use it in very similar ways. Code-switching and code-mixing must also be distinguished from interference (which is often a result of inadequate second language acquisition) and lexical borrowings (which are commonly used even among monolinguals).

These data exhibit the movement toward lexification within the target language (ASL). The manual representation of English forms visually is primarily an intra-sentential phenomenon. That is, the interpreters' representation of English in the visual-gestural modality is restricted to single or double lexical items within what otherwise is an ASL text.

That English mouthing sometimes marks the ASL interpreting output has to do with the cross-modality nature of the ASL–English contact situation – that is, visual-gestural and oral-aural. Because deafness closes the auditory channel to linguistic input, vocalization is not used for linguistic encoding purposes in ASL. But because the mouth is highly visible, it is used to convey linguistic meaning (for example, adverbials). One of the characteristics of intensive contact between ASL and English, then, is that the mouth may sometimes be used to represent certain English words visually. In the vast majority of cases, the interpreters do not mouth what they hear. Rather, they gloss by way of mouthing, what is on their hands. This appears to be a type of simultaneous code-mixing, rather than a sequential switch from one language to another.

Since both native ASL interpreters in this study produce mouthing in similar ways, the use of mouthing seems patterned. English mouthing marks fingerspelled words and most lexicalized fingerspelling; is used for emphasis; and marks lists, numbers, and question words. The deaf consultants agreed that both interpreters used mouthing appropriate to ASL. In fact, it was only through slow-motion viewing that the native ASL signers recognized some of the mouthing as being pronounced English. Both consultants felt that deaf signers use mouthing in much the same way as did the interpreters. This paper proposes that there exists a range of mouthing in ASL. At one extreme, English words are clearly mouthed; at the other, mouthing is no longer seen as representing English. It appears that some English words are borrowed by way of mouthing and subsequently lexicalized into ASL (that is, native ASL signers see the use of mouthing as a part of ASL).

The use of fingerspelling also appears to follow a pattern toward lexification into ASL. The interpreters in this study sometimes represent an English word or phrase through fingerspelling because there is no translation equivalent for that word in ASL. Other times, a multimeaning ASL sign is tagged or prefaced with a finger-spelled English word. In such cases, the fingerspelled word is flagged in very specific ways – for example, mouthing, eye gaze, indexing, labeling, quotation markers, palm orientation, and so forth. When a fingerspelled word gets used repeatedly in a single context, it begins to be lexicalized in ASL according to patterns similar to those found with lexicalized fingerspelled signs.

The degree to which there is interlingual transference during English to ASL interpretation appears to be determined by the participants, topic, and setting. In many interpreting situations, the deaf audience has some degree of written or spoken proficiency in the source language (English). In a sense, the interpretation is needed not because the deaf audience members don't understand English, but because they cannot hear it. Based on the assumption that the audience may be bilingual, the interpreter has the option of encoding some spoken English words in the visual mode. The mouthing and fingerspelling of English words by the interpreters in this study appears to be not sporadic or unsignaled, but rather patterned and rule governed. It serves to disambiguate and elucidate the interpreted message.

References

Battison, R. (1978). *Lexical borrowing in American Sign Language.* Silver Spring, MD: Linstock Press.

Bokamba, E.G. (1985). Code-mixing, language variation and linguistic theory: Evidence from Bantu languages. Paper presented at the Sixteenth Conference on African Linguistics, Yale University.

Bokamba, E.G. (1987). The nature and structure of sign language variation in the United States deaf community. Doctoral comprehensive paper, University of New Mexico, Albuquerque.

Davis, J.E. (1989). Distinguishing language contact phenomena in ASL interpretation. In *The sociolinguistics of the deaf community,* edited by C. Lucas, San Diego, CA: Academic Press.

Davis, J.E. (in process). Interpreting in a language contact situation: The case of English to ASL interpretation. Ph.D. diss., University of New Mexico, Albuquerque.

DiPietro, R.J. (1978). Code-switching as a verbal strategy among bilinguals. In *Aspects of bilingualism,* edited by M. Paradis, 275–82. Columbia, SC: Hornbean Press.

Grosjean, Francois. (1982). *Life with two languages.* Cambridge, MA: Harvard University Press.

Gumperz, J.J. (1976). The sociolinguistic significance of conversational code-switching. In *Papers on language and context.* Working Papers of the Language Behavior Research Laboratory, no. 46. Berkeley, CA: University of California.

Gumperz, J.J., and Hernandez-Chavez, E. (1971). Bilingualism, bidialectalism, and classroom interaction. In *Language in social groups: Essays by John J. Gumperz,* edited by A. S. Anwar, 311–39. Stanford, CA: Stanford University Press.

Kachru, B.B. (1978). Code-mixing as a communicative strategy in India. In *International dimensions of bilingual education,* edited by J. Alatis, 107–24. Washington, DC: Georgetown University Press.

Lee, D.M. 1983. Sources and aspects of code-switching in the signing of a deaf adult and her interlocutors. Ph.D. diss., University of Texas, Austin.

Lucas, C. (1989). "Introduction." In *The sociolinguistics of the deaf community,* edited by C. Lucas. San Diego, CA: Academic Press.

Lucas, C., and Valli, C. (1989). Language contact in the American deaf community. In *The sociolinguistics of the deaf community,* edited by C. Lucas. San Diego, CA: Academic Press.

Mougeon, R., Beniak, E., and Valois, D. (1985). *Issues in the study of language contact: Evidence from Ontarian French.* Toronto: Centre for Franco-Ontarian Studies.

Poplack, S. (1980). "Sometimes I'll start a sentence in Spanish y termino en espanol": Toward a typology of code-switching. *Linguistics* 18:581–618.

Poplack, S., Sankoff, D., and Miller, C. (1987). *The social correlates and linguistic consequences of lexical borrowing and assimilation.* Social Sciences and Humanities Research Council of Canada, March 1987 Report.

Poplack, S., Wheeler, S., and Westwood, A. (1987). Distinguishing language contact phenomena: Evidence from Finnish-English bilingualism. In *Proceedings of the VI International Conference on Nordic and General Linguistics,* edited by P. Lilius et al., 33–56. Helsinki: University of Helsinki Press.

Sankoff, D., and Poplack, S. (1981). A formal grammar for code-switching. *Papers in Linguistics* 14:3–46.

Sankoff, D., Poplack, S., and Vanniarajan, S. (1986). The case of the nonce loan in Tamil. Centre de recherches mathématiques. Technical report 1348. University of Montreal.

Seleskovitch, D. (1978). *Interpreting for international conferences.* Washington, DC: Penn and Booth.

Sign Media Inc. (1985). *Interpreting models of English to ASL (Lectures)*. Commercial videotape produced by Sign Media, Inc., 817 Silver Spring Ave., Suite 206, Silver Spring, MD.

Sridhar, S., and Sridhar, K. (1980). The syntax and psycholinguistics of bilingual code-mixing. *Canadian Journal of Psychology* 34:407–16.

Thelander, S. (1976). Code-switching or code-mixing? *Linguistics* 183:103–23.

Weinreich, U. (1953). *Languages in contact*. The Hague: Mouton.

CHAPTER 4

Insights into practice (1990s)

Introduction

In addition to a wider array of publications from different countries (see Chapters 5 and 6), it was during the decade of the 1990s that empirical research on SLI began to flourish, rather than publications of personal observations and anecdotal examinations. This shift was much the same as the change observed in spoken language interpreting research (Gile 1998), but the key difference is that spoken language interpreting research was still dominated by experimental, quantitative research of conference interpreting; whereas SLI research began to adopt more qualitative research methodologies to explore issues in depth, rather than to compare phenomena across many incidences of practice.

Often this research investigated the actual practice of interpreting in a variety of settings. In this chapter, the researchers examine university classrooms, conferences and meetings, the courtroom, and examine errors, naturalness, the facilitation of effort, and interaction management.

The decade of the 1990s saw a huge amount of global activity in SLI research and knowledge exchange, and increasing interaction across spoken and sign language interpreting studies scholars. For example, in 1991 Danica Seleskovitch was the keynote speaker at the conference of the Registry of Interpreters for the Deaf in the USA; Susan Berk-Seligson (1990) published a landmark study of Spanish-English interpreters in courtrooms; and Cecilia Wadensjö (1992) published her groundbreaking study of Swedish-Russian interpreters in community settings, particularly medical and immigration hearings. In the U.K. the journal 'Deafness' published by the Alliance of Deaf Service Users, Providers and Purchasers (ADSUP) was re-launched in collaboration with the Forest Bookshop in 1996 as 'Deaf Worlds'. The Deaf Worlds journal went on to publish 12 articles on SLI during its lifetime (its last volume was in 2007), one of which is featured in this reader (Chapter 5).

One of the most exciting developments of the 1990s was the inaugural conference of practitioners, service providers, scholars, researchers and educators focused on interpreting in settings other than conference or lectures: The First International Conference on Interpreting in Legal, Health, and Social Service Settings ("The Critical Link: Interpreters in the Community") in Canada in 1995 (Carr et al. 1997) bringing together sign and spoken language interpreters to discuss issues concerned with interpreting in small, face-to-face settings. As Pöchhacker (2004, 8) notes, this conference "enabled colleagues in different regions and countries to share hitherto isolated findings and experiences, and served as a catalyst to networking and even to collaborative research." This network would bring together sign and spoken language colleagues and convene a conference every three years. This was a significant step in the wider context of interpretation in that SLI people participated as equal colleagues, rather than being set aside as different from spoken language interpreting. It also brought attention to the work of 'community' interpreters, a term that would come into common usage, and that such work had been and continues to be 'dialogic', a term Wadensjö's work (1992, 1998) has brought into wide usage, meaning the back-and-forth, interactive nature of interpreting between two primary speakers and an interpreter.

Up until the mid-1990s, the academic study of interpreting had been largely subsumed under the more established umbrella of Translation Studies (Venuti 2000) in spoken languages and, in SLI, under the disciplinary areas of psychology and linguistics, primarily. As community interpreting gained wider recognition and acceptance, it was also clear that interpreting with all its possible settings, domains, modes, and such was a large puzzle that could be solved only by including the perspectives of many disciplines. Eventually the term 'Interpreting Studies' would be used as the disciplinary label for studies of interpreting, endorsed most visibly by the appearance of two publications: *The Interpreting Studies Reader,* edited by Franz Pöchhacker & Miriam Shlesinger (2002), and *Introducing Interpreting Studies by* Franz Pöchhacker (2004).

While English was still the language of the majority of texts on SLI produced during this decade, there was a rise of texts written in languages other than English, and reports from countries outside of the U.S. and U.K. began to emerge. Other journals widely known and read in translation and interpreting studies of spoken languages began publishing articles and special issues on sign language interpreting, for example, a special 1997 issue of a leading journal in interpreting studies, *Meta*, featured articles on sign language interpreting in various countries. Two of these articles are included in this Reader in Chapter 6. Furthermore, the first issue of the international journal *Interpreting* in 1996, features an article by Cynthia Roy on interaction management and turn-taking in a sign language interpreted event.

Therefore the articles in this section continue our theme of research development in SLI, using Cokely's (1985) model to explore transliterating, adapting Gile's (1991) effort model for a sign language interpretation, considering naturalness and interactions within a specific setting. In this chapter, we present a paper originally written in French, published in a journal that is no longer in print, which became a classic in French and German SLI communities. The other articles are found in publications that are fairly easy to locate, but are not often read in SLI education programs. Thus, they are but a sample of the explosion of research that would continue throughout the 1990s and on into the 2000s.

As did Elizabeth Winston (see Chapter 3), **Rachel Locker** (now Rachel Locker McKee), capitalized on her background and training in applied linguistics, to report on a study of lexical equivalence in literal interpretations (transliterations), with a focus on university settings in the U.S. Locker's study was particularly significant as it built on earlier work by key SLI researchers: Fleischer's (1975) research with 40 Deaf students determined the amount of lecture information they received from watching interpreters with or without subject-specific knowledge, and who interpreted into ASL or a more literal rendering; and Cokely's miscue analysis technique (originally from his 1985 dissertation, and later published in his 1992 book), to analyze interpreting output. She videotaped six interpreters working in half an hour segments with three different Deaf students, two studying graduate courses, and one studying an undergraduate course. The videotapes were then analyzed for lexical errors. Locker conducted follow-up interviews where the participants were shown their original and second translations, and asked to comment on their reasons for making the original choices, which enabled Locker to categorize the error types. Finally, Locker interviewed three Deaf university students to elicit their feelings about the effectiveness of literal interpretation generally, and how they coped with errors made by interpreters. This study could be categorized as one of the earliest 'mixed-methods' studies in SLI research, an approach that is now becoming more popular in interpreting studies generally (Hale & Napier, 2013; Pöchhacker, 2011). Locker's study influenced the later work of Napier, in her mixed-methods study of university interpreting in Australia (Napier, 2002).

June Zimmer addresses the issue of naturalness when interpreters work in the direction from a sign language into a spoken language – often referred to as 'voice-over,' that is, when the interpreter is 'giving voice' to the Deaf person's message presented in a sign language. Complementing an earlier article by Roy (1987), that identified how an interpreter had used a childlike register when interpreting into English for a formal lecture presented in ASL, Zimmer discusses how educators must attend to student practice working into a spoken language, and not focus solely on work into a sign language (which tends to be more common). In earlier literature, authors would often refer to the modality 'sign-to-voice,' and in some countries it was called 'reverse interpreting' (see Hurwitz 1980 paper in Chapter 2 of this Reader, and Napier, McKee & Goswell 2010, 38). Gradually, educators and practitioners are becoming more aware of referring to the languages, rather than modalities such as ASL to English, (e.g. Finton & Smith 2005).

In the 1990 paper included here, Zimmer concentrates on the fact that when interpreters work from a sign language into a spoken language, their voice should not only express meaning but also needs to represent the Deaf consumer's communication style and impact of their message. That is, the interpreter needs to match the discourse features appropriately, and not just "say what you see" (Owens 2012), but also say what it means with equivalent contextual (illocutionary) force. A central theme of this paper is the focus on matching Deaf consumer needs, that is, the importance of interpreters adapting their language output to meet the demands of the situation and the sign language user.

Danielle-Claude Bélanger's essay in French appeared in two parts. The first part examines Gile's (1991) Effort Model in terms of interpreting from LSQ (the sign language of French Canada) to French. She begins by describing Gile's Effort Model: listening/understanding (L), memory (M), and production (P), how it works and examples, and then presents a chart of these three parameters noting the challenges of unfamiliar contexts, syntactical differences, technical lexicon, and sociocultural differences. From this assessment, she proposes two groups of techniques: first, 'prevention' which suggests being fluent in both languages, being prepared, knowing jargon and using a team, and the second technique, 'preservation', which involves a number of cognitive, communicative and linguistic resources. She concludes that the Effort Model provides a vocabulary for interpreting challenges that would benefit sign language interpreters as well as spoken language interpreters.

In the second part of Bélanger's essay, she describes in more depth the resources interpreters have to facilitate their efforts and to preserve balance while interpreting. She returns to the techniques of 'prevention' and 'preservation' as a way of maintaining balance. Prevention includes achieving fluency such that expressions in either language are automatic and a variety of kinds of preparation an interpreter can do. She describes in detail what cognitive, communicative, and linguistic resources are at an interpreter's disposal, including a discussion of Cokely's (1985) study of lag time and errors.. Bélanger's paper is one of the first to adapt a model created by a spoken language interpreting scholar (Gile) and apply it to SLI.

The final paper we have chosen for this section comes from another applied linguist, **Graham H. Turner**, who wrote this paper based on his experience as a Research Associate on a larger study about access to justice for Deaf people throughout the UK (Brennan & Brown 1997, 2004). In the broader study, Mary Brennan, Richard Brown, Graham H. Turner and other members of the research team surveyed and interviewed interpreters and Deaf prisoners, observed British Sign Language (BSL) interpreters working in court in England, and videotaped and analyzed BSL interpreters working in Scottish courts. Spin-off articles were also produced from the same project (Brennan, 1999; Turner & Brown 2001).

In this article, Turner discusses features of courtroom talk and also issues that specifically arise in 'deaf' courts, and goes on to make recommendations for the provision, recording and monitoring of SLI in courts, training of interpreters and research. We have selected this article, as it is the first paper that we know of that specifically used the term 'co-construction' in relation to sign language interpreter-mediated interaction. In this paper, Turner describes specific instances of co-construction that he has observed in interpreted court cases, whereby interpreters directly address participants, anticipate (and therefore mediate) interjections, interrupt for clarification requests, provide explanation for approval, produce signed asides to Deaf participants, and indicate direct address to participants: all instances of interpreter (non) renditions as would be classified by Wadensjö (1998). The term co-construction is now heavily referred to in interpreting studies literature that discusses interpreter participation in interaction from a discourse perspective, among both spoken language (Angelelli, 2003; Wadensjö, 2008; Pasquandrea, 2012; Li, 2013) and sign language (Napier, 2004; Janzen & Shaffer, 2008) researchers, so it was telling that Turner used this term in his early discussions of courtroom interactions. Since this early research work on legal interpreting, there has been a growing body of work in this area (e.g. Napier & Spencer 2008; Napier 2011; Russell 2002; Miller 2001, 2003, Roberson, Russell & Shaw 2011) that is attempting to lay foundations for access to justice for Deaf people.

4.1   Locker, Rachel. 1990. "Lexical Equivalence in Transliterating for Deaf Students in the University Classroom: Two Perspectives." *Issues in Applied Linguistics* 1(2): 167–195.

Rachel Locker McKee began her career as a New Zealand Sign Language (NZSL) interpreter, and was a member of the first cohort to be trained in New Zealand through an intensive 4-month course in NZSL and interpreting in 1985. In search of more rigorous training, McKee migrated to the U.S. and enrolled in a SLI education program where she learned ASL and became certified as an ASL/English interpreter. She then pursued Masters and Doctoral Studies in Applied Linguistics. In 1992 she returned to New Zealand to establish the Diploma in NZSL/English Interpreter at Auckland University of Technology (which is now an undergraduate degree). In 1995 she moved to the School of Linguistics and Applied Language Studies at Victoria University of Wellington to participate in the establishment of the Deaf Studies Research Unit, where she is now Program Director of Deaf Studies and created a training program for Deaf teachers of NZSL.

She has worked extensively as a sign language interpreter in both New Zealand and the U.S., and still practices in court and other contexts. Her publications have focused on analysis of sign language interpreting, linguistic description of NZSL, and the New Zealand Deaf community. With Jeffrey Davis, she co-edited the volume *Interpreting in Multilingual, Multicultural Contexts* for Gallaudet University Press. She is also co-editor of *Sign Language Interpreting: Theory and Practice in Australia and New Zealand*.

Lexical equivalence in transliterating for deaf students in the university classroom

Two perspectives

Rachel Locker

This study examines the accuracy of transliterated messages produced by sign language interpreters in university classrooms. Causes of interpreter errors fell into three main categories: misperception of the source message, lack of recognition of source forms, and failure to identify a target language equivalent. Most errors were found to be in the third category, a finding which raises questions not only about the preparation these interpreters received for tertiary settings, but more generally about their knowledge of semantic aspects of the American Sign Language (ASL) lexicon. Deaf consumers' perceptions of problems with transliteration in the classroom and their strategies for accommodating various kinds of interpreter error were also elicited and are discussed. In support of earlier research, this study's finding that transliteration may not be the most effective means of conveying equivalent information to deaf students in the university classroom raises questions about the adequacy of interpreters' preparation for this task.

Introduction

Since the passage of federal legislation – the Rehabilitation Act of 1973, Section 504 – mandating accessibility to federally funded facilities, an increasing number of deaf students have entered programs of study in tertiary institutions. Sign language interpreters have been the primary resource for making university classrooms accessible to them by providing simultaneous signed interpretation. This service usually takes the form of "transliteration," a part-English, part-ASL form of translation (see detailed definition below). But while a great deal of interpreter training and service provision has taken place over the last fifteen years, relatively little empirical research into the results and ramifications of what happens in the classroom with interpreters has been undertaken. This study is a small-scale descriptive investigation of the effectiveness of sign language interpreting as found in the university classroom, examined from two perspectives.

The first section of the study entails a pilot analysis of lexical choices made by sign language interpreters transliterating from spoken English to a signed form. Given that ASL and English are two distinct languages, the semantic range of an English word and ASL sign holding the same dictionary gloss is often different, (Colonomos, 1984). Lexical choice can therefore be problematic for an interpreter attempting to achieve message equivalence in a "word-for-word" transliterated form. The second, complementary section of this study is a survey of three deaf university students' perceptions and responses to interpreting error. The information gleaned from both these sources may be useful for emphasizing the need for study of semantic equivalence between languages in the professional preparation of sign language interpreters, and for raising questions about the viability of "transliteration" as a means of conveying equivalent information to deaf consumers.

Definition of terms

The following definitions of basic terms are presented to orient the reader to the field of sign language interpreting:

American Sign Language (ASL) is a complete and independent language, with complex systems of phonology, syntax, and semantics (Bellugi & Klima, 1980). Furthermore, ASL expresses/creates a specific system of cultural meanings shared by the American deaf community, in the same way that Russian or Japanese embodies the conceptual universe of these cultures. It is important to stress, therefore, that any discussion of interpreting or transliteration must assume the interaction of two languages, not simply a coding operation from one modality to another.

Transliteration is broadly defined for this study as changing a spoken English message into a manual form (using the vocabulary of ASL) in order to represent the lexicon and word order of English (but not necessarily the grammatical affixes of English, e.g. suffixes for verb agreement, tense, plurals). In fact, there is no well defined or standardized description of transliteration (even though the term is used as if there were), since this target form attempts to accommodate both the syntactic order of spoken English and a range of ASL features (including principally the lexicon) in order to convey the message in a signed modality. Transliteration thus results in a variety of interlanguage signing that is "less than a complete message ... something approximating the source message but not expressing the same subtleties of either source or target language" (Winston, 1989, p. 149). Winston notes that transliterators are more constrained in their task than translators or interpreters, because they are expected to produce a form that resembles the source message in English and yet is comprehensible in a visual-manual mode, while drawing on ASL features as part of the target form. Despite the lack of clear definition, however, transliteration appears to be the predominant style of "interpreting" found in higher educational settings in the United States.[1]

---

1. The dynamics of how, where, and why code-switching occurs spontaneously between ASL and English-like forms of signing by deaf and hearing signers is treated at length in Lucas (1989, Chapter 1).

Interpreting, within the field of sign language interpreting, is a term often used generically to include both transliterating (as discussed above) and the more generally understood "interpreting," meaning to translate in real-time between two distinct languages (which in this case would be English and ASL). While in this study the focus is on transliteration, the people doing the transliterating are referred to as "interpreters," even though there is a move now in the field to call them "transliterators." This debate over terms hinges on whether transliterating is viewed as a process distinct from what an interpreter does when decoding and reconstructing meaning between English and ASL, or whether the only significant difference between interpreting and transliterating is the surface form in which the target message is represented. Lacking evidence that there exists any difference in the basic *process* involved in reconstructing an ASL or signed English (i.e. transliterated) message from a source message, participants in this study will be referred to as "interpreters" rather than "transliterators," but my choice of terms should not be read as definitive.

Review of studies on sign language interpreting effectiveness

The literature in this area follow one or the other of two main approaches: (i) measuring interpreting effectiveness according to the overall comprehension of consumers (although no satisfactory definition of "effective interpreting/transliterating" has yet emerged), and (ii) analyzing interpreter errors in relation to a theoretical model of interpretation.

In a comparison of deaf and hearing students' ability to receive and recall information from an interpreted/heard lecture, Jacobs (1981) found that hearing students received higher combined scores on tests of lecture material than deaf students. Deaf students scored correctly on only 84% as many items as did the hearing students, and test scores averaged 83% for hearing, 69% for deaf. Since Jacobs also notes, however, that other studies have found no significant difference in grade point average between deaf and hearing college students, it is still unclear as to how (or if) the remaining information gap is closed by deaf students. Apparently, deaf students rely on other, as yet unknown, strategies for acquiring and assimilating the information necessary for success in college.

Rather than contrasting the efficiency of signed interpretation with audition, however, Fleischer (1975) compares the effectiveness, for deaf consumers, of four different types of classroom interpreting conditions. According to his results, conditions were ranked in the following descending order of effectiveness: ASL with background knowledge, ASL without background knowledge, signed English (transliteration) with background knowledge, and, lastly, signed English without background knowledge, the least effective interpreting condition. While Fleischer's study does not define "signed English," the term is widely understood in the field to mean some combination of ASL vocabulary produced in predominantly English word order, with fingerspelling of terms and some use of ASL parameters, such as the use of placing and indexing locatives in the signing space. This type of signing is distinct from a contrived signing system which represents the derivational affixes on English words, such as "Signing Exact English." Fleischer also notes that "[t]he higher the level of complete bilingualism the deaf student has, the higher the amount of information he receives from the interpreter" (pp. 74–75). His study concludes that it is the dominant or preferred communication mode of a deaf consumer which is crucial and which needs to be included as a factor in assessing interpreter effectiveness in any given situation.

Neither of the above studies explores the possibility that recall from a lecture situation may not be an accurate measure of interpreting effectiveness in other types of educational setting, e.g. the seminar format, in which the communication process is complicated by interactional dynamics, and hence the amount of information and participation lost is potentially greater. These issues have been addressed by Johnson (1989), however, in an examination of conflicting communication strategies used by deaf and hearing participants in a the university classroom situation. Johnson found that miscommunication was sometimes due to the conflict of aural/oral and visual/manual norms for conveying information. For instance, when visual aids were used in class, deaf students were forced to choose where to direct their attention, thereby losing out on some of the information being responded to in class. Differences in conversation regulators (e.g. turn-taking signals) in auditory as opposed to visual modes also created problems for deaf students in the interpreted situation, particularly in the discussion situations typical of graduate classes.

Johnson also found that transliteration was problematic and confusing when the source message involved spatial descriptions or references to real-world images for which the interpreter had no available referent for visualization purposes (e.g. the appearance of a biological structure or a building layout). In such instances, interpreters tended to resort either to fingerspelling or to using citation forms of signs whose glosses matched individual English words but not necessarily the overall structure or sense of the utterance. This strategy, which did little to give the deaf student a visual equivalent to the spoken description, resulted in loss of information because the deaf students were unable to recover the intended source language (SL) meaning.

An interpreter's degree of familiarity with the subject matter at hand is also an important factor in achieving an understandable and functionally equivalent translation of the source message in a signed form. Wilcox & Wilcox (1985) explored the applicability of schema theory to interpreter accuracy by correlating interpreting proficiency with the ability to make "probability predictions" from an incoming message through use of an auditory cloze. The idea behind the study was that as the message unfolds, a probability prediction field is built up, the closure for which an interpreter may draw on the situational context and his or her own world knowledge. This process enhances comprehension and allows the interpreter to plan ahead based on a sense of what to expect next in the incoming message. Wilcox & Wilcox suggest that an interpreter's ability to make use of the clues in a message and predict accurately may be a major determiner of sign language interpreter proficiency.

Representing the second approach taken in the literature, Cokely (1985) analyzed the frequency and distribution of several types of interpreter target language (TL) errors in relation to a seven stage model of the process of interpreting between spoken English and ASL. While Cokely notes that syntactically related errors are overall the most severe obstacles for a consumer's recovery of the SL message, he found that lexically related errors were also problematic. The skilled interpreters he studied were found to produce an average of 1.21 lexical errors and unwarranted substitutions per syntactically acceptable TL sentence. Of these errors, about half were categorized as seriously deviating from the intended meaning of the source message. Using Cokely's theoretical model, analysis of the source of these types of error should be helpful in that it would isolate the different points at which an interpreter might strike trouble in the process of transferring an equivalent message, although as Cokely states, in reality there is more likely to be "a multiple nesting of stages" (p. 173) as the process takes place. In relation to the present study's focus on lexical errors due to mishearing, misunderstanding, or mistranslation, Cokely's model of the stages in the interpreting process (pp. 169–174) are informative, but four are particularly relevant to this study:

i.   *Message reception:* At the initial point of "message reception," if the SL message is auditorally perceived incorrectly by the interpreter, an error will result even if subsequent stages are executed accurately. Sometimes the interpreter self-corrects after recognizing errors, but usually he or she interprets the error confidently, assuming the message perceived was the same as the one spoken.

ii. *Preliminary processing:* In this primary recognition process, lexical and other units are identified and "accessed" (or not, as the case may be) in the listener's – in this case the interpreter's – lexicon. Errors often arise at this point due to a lack of prior understanding of semantic and syntactic context. When interpreter "lag time," to allow for contextual processing, is insufficient, adverse effects on the processing of meaning result.

iii. *Realization of semantic intent:* At this stage, the interpreter arrives at some level of comprehension of at least a portion of the SL message. Ideally this comprehension coincides with the speaker's intent, but it is dependent upon the level (lexical, sentential, phrasal) at which the particular portion of the SL message was analyzed.

iv. *Determination of semantic equivalence:* After the interpreter has attributed meaning to the chunk, he or she now has to determine which linguistic/cultural factors are relevant to conveying that meaning in the TL. Proficiency in this task, according to Cokely, is dependent on the interpreter's linguistic and cultural competence in the TL. It is also important to note that at this stage if the interpreter has not extracted meaning from the SL message and is simply processing the form of the message at word level (as frequently happens in transliteration), errors will arise because a one-to-one relationship between SL and TL lexical forms does not exist.

There are cases, though, in which the interpreter has understood the SL message but failed to accurately determine a semantic equivalent in the TL. Understanding the SL message does not, therefore, guarantee that a TL equivalent will be identified and produced by the interpreter. Cokely explains this by contending that these two processes are separate. This observation was also borne out in the present study by the results of questioning and retesting interpreters' lexical choices for incorrect interpretations, as will be discussed below. Of overall importance, however, is that according to Cokely's model of the cognitive steps involved in interpretation from one language/mode to another, deviations occurring at any stage of the interpretation process will affect subsequent stages. His analysis of the cognitive tasks involved at each stage of the interpreting process provides a useful theoretical model of the interpreting task, in that it may increase the chances not only of identifying and strengthening an interpreter's areas of weakness, but also of devising strategies for self-monitoring and repair of "faults in the circuit," as it were.

In practical terms, findings from all these studies suggest that deaf students need to be made aware that the sense of confusion they often experience in a classroom situation probably does not originate in their own inability to comprehend the class material. Rather, their confusion may derive from the distortion of a message as it is rendered from one form to another or from the different rules for organizing discourse (e.g. turn-taking) which obtain in aural/spoken vs. visual/manual interaction.

Methodology

Setting

The present study was carried out in a university setting, in the classes of three deaf students-two graduate students and one undergraduate. Six interpreters were videotaped in half-hour segments as they interpreted for graduate classes in anthropology and TESL, and for undergraduate classes in chemistry and physics. The six interpreters were selected on the basis of availability and willingness to participate, but also because the classes in which they worked represented a range of subject matter. All interpreters used a predominantly English-like style of signing which would fit the definition of transliteration given above. In addition, the two graduate classes were seminar classes, involving student participation, while the undergraduate science classes were lecture classes.

Interpreter error analysis

Videotapes of the six interpreters were initially analyzed for nonequivalent meanings resulting from lexical choices in the target form of the message. Of the six interpreter data samples, only three were found to contain lexical errors relevant to this study (see definition of semantic sign choice errors below). It is interesting to note that the three interpreters who did *not* produce any lexical errors had higher levels of education than the other three (i.e. they all had at least a bachelor's degree, whereas the three who produced lexical errors had been through some kind of interpreter training program but did not hold a university degree). In addition, two of the more highly educated interpreters also had professional interpreter certification, whereas the other four were not certified. Thus, the three interpreters who did produce errors were all interpreting at an educational level above their own and in subject areas with which they were not personally familiar, a situation which probably affected their ability to make lexical choices that would achieve semantic equivalence.

Once the data samples had been narrowed to three, interpreter's errors on the videotapes were first transcribed and sorted into two categories: misperception errors and semantic sign-choice errors (see Appendix A for the complete list). Next, the three interpreters who produced lexical errors were "retested" on their interpreting errors. For this procedure, each interpreter was presented with a sample of his or her original errors two weeks after the class had been videotaped. From the English source message only, each interpreter was then asked to reinterpret these chunks for the researcher. The original incorrect interpretation was not shown or described to the interpreter during this part of the task. Although the chunks were presented out of context, each chunk was introduced with an explanation of the context by the researcher. In most cases the interpreters had some recall of the general topic of the class from which the example was drawn, although none recognized the specific items presented to them as instances in which they had interpreted incorrectly the first time. Interpreters' second translations from the interview were then compared with the original inaccurate transliteration, and interpreter ability to self-correct was calculated, based on a comparison of the accuracy of first and second interpretations.

In a follow-up discussion with each of the three interpreters (after they had completed the retranslation), interpreters were shown their original and second transliterations and questioned about their reasons for making the original translation they had made on the videotape. Through this discussion, and by asking the interpreters to come up with explanations and definitions of the original English source messages which they had incorrectly interpreted, the researcher attempted to determine whether the error was due to a failure to understand the SL message, an inability to determine a conceptually accurate lexical equivalent, or a decision to simply relay the SL form rather than to determine meaning.

Definition of semantic sign-choice errors analyzed in the study

As has been mentioned, even though transliteration cannot usually represent the exact grammatical inflections of either spoken English or ASL, a minimal expectation is that an interpreter will use a conceptually equivalent sign rather than a literal representation of the English word. For example, the word *take* may be used in phrases with diverse meanings, such as "take some notes," "take a few minutes," "I'm going to take this beaker and pour it …" In these contexts, *take* means 'write,' 'use,' and 'pick-up,' respectively. When interpreters failed to convey the context-specific meaning in their choice of sign and instead produced a sign that matched the phonological form but not the meaning of the source message, this was considered a lexical (or sign-choice) error.

Another area of potential nonequivalence is when English words are used metaphorically or in a way which conjures up an image different from the literal sense of the word itself. For instance, "a tree diagram" usually refers to a downward branching information structure, for which the ASL sign "TREE," representing a standing tree with branches pointing upwards, is conceptually wrong, and thus a different sign should be used which visually matches the concept of a "tree diagram."

Deaf student interviews

In the second part of this study, the perspective of deaf students regarding interpreting error was sought. Three deaf students were selected by virtue of their being in the classes of the three interpreters who produced lexical errors. These deaf students were interviewed about their general perceptions of interpreter accuracy and specifically about which kinds of errors they notice the most. In addition, they were asked to describe how they deal with ambiguity or distortions in the signed messages produced by interpreters (see interview questions in Appendix B). It should be noted that the interviews with the deaf students did not involve showing them the videotaped error samples, since the aim was to elicit general observations about interpreter error rather than responses to specific errors or specific interpreters.

Results and discussion: Interpreter error analysis

Misperception errors

A small proportion (17%) of all errors were due to the interpreter's misperception of the source message because of the inability to hear the speaker clearly or to recognize what was actually said. These errors resulted in TL messages which were clearly nonsensical or unrelated to the context (also referred to as *anomalies*). Examination of the videotaped situations in which the following examples occurred indicated that some were due to difficulty in hearing the utterance fully (especially in discussion settings), but many of the errors derived from constraints on the interpreter's ability to accurately predict in order to extract a meaningful message when an utterance may have been less than 100% clearly perceived. Yet, whether these constraints lie in the individual's "probability prediction" skill (Wilcox & Wilcox, 1985), in auditory distraction or interference is impossible to discern from this data. Examples of errors in perception of the SL message include the following:

Spoken English	Signed transliteration (# indicates a fingerspelled word)
it says "**title**" – " give title"	NOT STEAL IT–TITLE
describe the **hypothesis, subjects,** method	DESCRIBE FIVE OFFICES, TITLE (subject heading), METHOD
I talked to a **lady** she said	ME TALK–TO **BOY**–BOY SAY
share-ware computer programs	CHAIR #W-A-R-E PROGRAM (looks puzzled)
These (*computer programs*) are written for a college audience	THIS WRITE FOR COLLEGE **FOOTBALL**

Based on the interpreters' confused facial expressions (furrowed brow, squinting) and apparent straining to hear (head tilting, looking at the speaker) which were evident on the videotape, it appears that the trouble which produced these kinds of errors arose at the initial stages of "message reception" and "preliminary processing" (Cokely, 1985), when the unsuccessful recognition of auditory signals subsequently results in deviations from the SL message in later stages of interpretation.

Sign-choice errors

A much larger proportion (83%) of the semantic mismatches occurring in the data were categorized as sign-choice errors. Examples of this sort include:

Spoken English	Signed transliteration (# indicates fingerspelled word)
The phones were down (*because of the earthquake*)	PHONE **BANKRUPT/FOLD**
So – **how are you doing** with this?	#S–O–WHAT'S UP? (*informal ASL greeting = how are you?*)
In the **meantime**	LATER
had certain symbolic **advantages**	HAVE SYMBOL TAKEADVANTAGE-OF (*rip-off*)
since this is (*because*)	SINCE (*time passing*)
argumentative type of writing	ARGUE (*two persons*) KIND WRITE

Sign-choice errors could have been due to time constraints in the transliterating situation (insufficient lag time to understand the surrounding context or speaker's rate of speech), ignorance of the exact meaning of a SL word as used, or unfamiliarity with the conceptually equivalent ASL sign. Since it would be difficult to isolate and control for these potential sources of error in specifying a cause, interpreters were subsequently retested on interpreting some of the same phrases they had made errors on in the data. The assumption was that making the same error on the retest would indicate either that an interpreter lacked a correct translation in his or her TL lexicon or that he or she could not match the SL word with a definition in their personal English lexicon.

Retest of interpreters on sign choice errors

The results of the three interpreters' second attempt at interpreting semantic sign-choice errors were as follows:

	Errors corrected on retest %	Errors *not* corrected on retest %
Interpreter 1	40	60
Interpreter 2	57	43
Interpreter 3	50	50
(Average)	(49)	(51)

Given that 49% of the errors were corrected on the retest (i.e. the second translation offered was more semantically equivalent), it seems most likely that constraints of the transliterating situation itself (e.g. time, ability to hear the speaker clearly, fatigue) were probably influencing the interpreters' preliminary processing and leading to inaccurate lexical choice, rather than the interpreters' knowledge of the meaning of SL or TL forms.

In order to determine the source of error for those items which were not corrected on the retest, each interpreter was subsequently asked to explain the meaning of the problematic SL word or phrase. The discussion with the interpreters revealed that of the repeated incorrect translations, the error source could be identified (using Cokely's model) as follows:

	Failure to realize semantic intent (not understanding SL message) %	Failure to determine semantic equivalence (incorrect lexical choice in TL) %
Interpreter 1	50	50
Interpreter 2	21	79
Interpreter 3	60	40
(Average)	(44)	(66)

In the case of the third interpreter, the abstract and philosophical nature of the subject matter and vocabulary might account for failing to understand 60% of the retested SL errors; however, the unknown words in question were not terms specific to the field and are found in general academic English usage. These include: *disenfranchise, articulated* set of goals, *English-dominated, reformulate* culture.

Overall, slightly less than half of the retested errors were due to a lack of understanding of the SL message, suggesting that first language (English) proficiency and background knowledge plays an extremely important role in interpreter effectiveness. As for failure to determine semantic equivalence in choosing signs, this type of problem accounted for more than half of the retested persistent errors and may be attributable either to a limited range of lexical choices available to the interpreters as second language users or to an incomplete understanding of the semantic properties of certain ASL vocabulary items.

The extent in this small study to which English words were outside the interpreters' receptive vocabulary and the frequency of cases in which lexical equivalents were genuinely not known give pause for thought. The results point to possible weaknesses in the interpreters' training in the semantics of both English and ASL. Since in both lexicons words and signs have various meanings in various contexts, subtleties of semantic equivalence and contrast may need to be studied more thoroughly. Moreover, fluency in source language (English, in this case) and target language (ASL) may need to be treated with more equal emphasis than is done in interpreter training programs, which often tend to take first-language (L1) proficiency for granted.

As for specific problems with English vocabulary in a university setting, this study suggests that the rate of error may be linked to an interpreter's level of formal education, since the three university-educated interpreters, of the original six participants, did not produce lexical errors of this type and were thus excluded from the error analysis. One obvious implication is that interpreters working in higher education need to avail themselves of the content matter of various fields before expecting to be competent interpreters of these subjects, even if this extra training only extends to the level of conceptual familiarity with the language and typical phrases commonly encountered in that field. An alternative implication is that recruits for interpreter education programs need to have at least a bachelor's level of education, in addition to bilingual proficiency as a prerequisite to entry (as is the case with spoken language interpreters), so as to be equipped for all the contexts in which they might work.

Results and discussion: Deaf students' perceptions of interpreter errors

The deaf students interviewed for this study differed from each other in terms of experience with interpreters, bilingual proficiency, and language preference. Student 1, a native ASL signer from a deaf family, describes himself as bilingual (in ASL and English) but ASL-dominant in terms of his everyday, preferred mode of communication; although Student 2 was deafened at age 5, entered a residential school for the deaf at that time, and has used ASL ever since as her primary mode of communication, she is a fluent bilingual and has taught English; Student 3 was born deaf but educated orally. She is fluent in spoken English (her primary mode of communication) but learned sign language as an adult and now signs fluently with English-like syntax, relying on lip-reading with signing for receptive communication. In terms of bilingual fluency and language preference, these three students represent the sort of range of deaf language backgrounds that is found in higher

educational settings. Their responses to the interview questions (see Appendix B) are discussed below.

Proportion of information received through an interpreter

In answer to the first question, all three students said that the percentage of information in
class they understood through an interpreter depends on the individual interpreter. Students 1 and 2 felt that if the interpreter is highly skilled, they can receive 90–100% of the
information, but if the interpreter is "not good" this percentage would drop to somewhere
below 40 or 50%. In Student 3's answer to this question, she drew a distinction between her
level of comprehension in a lecture as opposed to a seminar class, saying that her estima-
tion for a seminar class would be around 50% while for a lecture closer to about 80%. The
explanation she offered for this discrepancy was that seminar/discussion classes are complicated by interactional dynamics as well as by the physical constraints on an interpreter's
ability to interpret more than one voice at any one time or to hear all participants clearly.
This is certainly a valid distinction not only in terms of the potential for interpreter accuracy, but also in terms of the student's capacity to follow the flow of a discussion when it is
received through a single channel, sometimes without identification of different speakers.

The students' higher estimates for "good interpreter" conditions (80–100% recovery
of class content) more or less concur, though perhaps rather on the generous side, with
Jacobs' (1976) finding of an 84% comprehension level for deaf students. Since students in
this interview were only estimating and not actually being tested on how much information
they successfully received, it is not surprising that their estimations are somewhat higher
than one might expect, given the interpreters' error data and Cokely's analysis of error
frequency. In light of Nida's (1976) assertion that comprehension even between speakers of
the same language might not typically rise much above 80%, these deaf students' estimates
seem optimistically high. For now there seems no direct way of measuring understanding
other than by taking the word of consumers. The *perceived* experience of learning through
an interpreter, however, is what is of interest in this study.

Effect of subject matter

When asked if the accuracy of an interpreter is affected by the specific subject matter,
Students 1 and 2 replied that the interpreter's general level of skill was a far more important determinant of the interpreter's ability to convey information clearly and accurately
than the subject matter. However, Student 1 also observed that an interpreter could be an
effective interpreter in the arts and humanities yet have a hard time interpreting science
classes to the same standard – in other words, that the subject matter can affect performance but not to the same extent as the general proficiency and flexibility of the individual
interpreter. Student 3 responded that although proficiency level was generally a better predictor of accuracy in any given subject, some subjects in her experience, such as English

literature, had presented serious hurdles even to very skilled interpreters because of the unusual nature of the language involved. She felt that social science subjects were generally easier to interpret because content consisted of more generalizations and everyday language than special terminology. Two of the respondents also commented that interpreters coming into a new field understandably make more errors in fingerspelling words and names related to the specific subject.

Awareness of interpreter errors: Sign choice

The students were also asked what kinds of errors were noticeable and bothersome in their perception of the message. All the students noted that the major source of conceptual errors, and the most distracting to watch, were either inappropriate lexical choices (e.g. "the phones were down"/"PHONE BANKRUPT/FOLD") or transposing the auditory form of the English word to a sign form which didn't match the meaning (e.g. "he paid *interest* on his **mortgage**"/"HE PAY *INTEREST* (*ASL verb: to be interested in*) ON HIS #M-O-R-T-G-A-G-E."

When students were asked how these types of inaccuracy affected their understanding of the message, they described different strategies for coping. Student 1 said that the first time the incorrect sign choice appears, he immediately analyzes where the confusion is (relying on context and his knowledge of English homynyms) and translates the form to the appropriate meaning in his head. If the error recurs, he makes a mental note of the deviation, puts it into a kind of short-term reference lexicon for that interpreter for the duration of that class, and refers to this lexicon for clarification each time the error appears in the interpreter's message. His strategy is thus one of accommodation to the interpreter's level of conceptual accuracy, meaning that he takes responsibility for doing the extra work required to recover the intended meaning of the SL message. Student 2 also goes through the process of mentally translating the lexical item once she has recognized a discrepancy between meaning and form, but when the error recurs a second time, she corrects the interpreter by modelling the correct sign. This approach returns the responsibility for conveying meaning appropriately to the interpreter, hopefully reducing the student's distraction from the content caused by incorrect forms and encouraging the interpreter to be more aware of accuracy. Student 3 was not conscious of how she coped with sign-choice errors, although she reported them to be highly distracting to her comprehension of the content of the message.

Redundant/confusing grammar forms

Students were asked to comment on their reactions when interpreters attempt to sign exact representations of English grammatical function words and structures which do not exist in natural ASL forms (e.g. articles, -ing, -ed, copula forms). All three students said that this bothered them because it looked "unnatural" and unnecessary, though they could usually still manage to extrapolate the meaning. Of course, if this very literal type of transliteration is used for a specific purpose, such as demonstrating an English sentence structure or for a quotation, then it was regarded as perfectly appropriate. In other cases, while the students didn't exactly consider this phenomenon to be "error," they did regard it as unhelpful and even a hindrance for effectively conveying the concept of the SL message. However, Student 3 commented that one area of confusion she had experienced repeatedly is when important grammatical information about passive structures is *omitted* from or not conveyed equivalently in the signed form (because inflections, such as copula and -ed affixes, are not usually conveyed in transliteration). Student 3 said she was frequently confused about who was the agent and who was the object of an action in passive constructions for which the interpreter might transliterate a sentence **such as *"I feel I'm not being understood"* to "ME FEEL ME NOT** UNDERSTAND."** In such a transliteration, the opposite meaning is conveyed, since the subject and object of the sentence are represented in the passive order but without any indication in the sign gloss of an agent (or the lack of one). As Levitt (1984) notes, the best alternative in these situations is to completely reorder the sentence into an active form (i.e. to reorder or insert the subject and object of the sentence) or to make use of the directional properties which many transitive verbs in ASL possess (in other words, to interpret into ASL rather than transliterate word glosses). Given the frequency of passive constructions in academic discourse, it is not surprising that at least one of the deaf students interviewed in this study cited this as a source of frequent confusion. She also commented that it had taken her a long time to understand why she was experiencing this sense of confusion and of never being sure what the intended SL message could have been.

Misuse of classifiers

Classifiers, a highly productive system of predicate morphology in ASL (Schick, 1987), are handshapes used to represent objects, people, locatives, and actions. ASL classifiers use three dimensional space to incorporate pronouns, verbs, adverbial aspect, and adjectives, often simultaneously. The classifier system is often quite difficult for second language speakers of ASL (most interpreters) to acquire. When asked if they noticed errors in interpreters' use of classifiers, all three students reported that the inaccurate use of classifiers (to describe spatial relationships or movement between objects or people) was especially frequent and problematic when the teacher was verbally describing a scene or picture without the aid of a diagram or model in the classroom to refer to. The students agreed that if there were a visual aid of some sort to refer to or if the relationships had previously been made clear, they could accommodate deviations in the interpreter's representation without major disruption of the message (although use of visual aids does require deaf students to make a momentary choice as to where to direct their attention). When visual aids are lacking, however, the interpreter's accuracy in the use of classifiers to specify spatial relationships becomes crucial to understanding the message, and all students reported that this type of information is frequently lost or confused through the translation process (see also Johnson, 1989). For conveying information in a visual modality such as sign language, classifiers are uniquely efficient in making use of three-dimensional space to indicate spatial relationships, quality and type of movement, or subject/object marking in a sentence. Yet the achievement of message equivalence for the accuracy and specificity of meaning conveyable in a signed form by classifiers is often impossible or cumbersome in signed English transliteration. Thus, even interpreters who work principally in a transliterated mode (as opposed to ASL) can greatly enhance the range of communicative tools at their disposal by becoming skilled in the use of ASL classifier systems.

Misperceived "anomalies"

The three students were also asked about "anomalies" in interpreted information (i.e. instances when the message seemed to be nonsensical or wildly divergent in context), such as those caused by the interpreter mishearing or somehow completely misunderstanding the SL utterance. All the students reported that this kind of error is difficult to identify. Student 1 said that he often sees something that looks like a deviation from the context but is never absolutely sure whether the source of the anomaly is the speaker, the interpreter, or his own comprehension. Students 2 and 3 made similar comments, emphasizing that confusion often occurs in such instances without any conscious explanation or resolution. Student 3 said that she can sometimes "hold onto" these puzzling fragments for a short time and "figure it out" in light of subsequent context in the incoming message. Both students 2 and 3 mentioned relying on their notes (taken by a hearing notetaker) to clarify or discount any anomalous deviations noticed during class. From these reports it is clear that deaf students are doing extra cognitive "work" in their processing and review of incoming information as they analyze and filter possible sources of misunderstanding coming through the interpreter.

Omission

When asked to comment on interpreter omission of information, the students made the general observation that it is difficult for deaf consumers to know for sure if something has been omitted unless they are in a position to clearly see if speech or conversation is taking place which is not being transmitted by the interpreter. Student 2, however, noted that she is sensitive to whether the interpreter has lost or is omitting information either by his/her facial expression and body cues or (sometimes) the interpreter's aside that he or she has missed something. This student also commented that she appreciates it when an interpreter takes the initiative to ask the speaker for clarification if something is not heard clearly or is an unfamiliar term, instead of simply continuing and hoping to pick up the information from context later on, as is commonly done by interpreters in those situations. Student 1 noticed that he is most aware of information omission when the speaker is following a predictable course (e.g. explaining a diagram to which she is pointing systematically, following an outline previously specified), or when other class members react visibly to something to which he was not privy, such as an aside comment or a joke that the interpreter felt unable to translate effectively and so chose to ignore.

Student 3 cited instances of interpreters beginning a sentence, then breaking off abruptly in the middle and going on to something else with no explanation or apparent cause for the lack of completion. She found this partial conveyance of information very irritating and puzzling, for she was left trying to guess what interference might have affected the reception of the source message or the interpreter's translation. Sometimes, of course, interpreters are capturing a speaker actually breaking off in mid-sentence, a not uncommon occurrence in extemporaneous speech, especially when a teacher might be performing two tasks at once (for example, writing on the board and talking). Similarly, a speaker may begin a sentence and then decide to retract or rephrase the statement part way through without signifying this in any way except with the briefest pause. At other times, particularly in discussions, it appears that an interpreter has to make choices between competing voices. An interpreter thus might begin interpreting one speaker, then suddenly become aware of an interjection and begin to interpret that voice instead, leaving the deaf consumer hanging as to what happened to the first half-utterance. When faced with competing, overlapping voices, an interpreter is also frequently unable to hear any one speaker clearly enough to continue interpreting and may therefore choose to sign fragments. These are clearly unavoidable contingencies in the interpreting process, but the implication of these students' comments is that it would be informative if interpreters would at least briefly indicate the loss of information to the deaf consumer, rather than just obscuring or ignoring it.

Interpreter's representation of new terms

When asked about the issue of interpreting new terminology or words for which no commonly used sign exists, students varied somewhat as to how they thought the information should be conveyed. All the students agreed that a new term must be clearly fingerspelled initially, but for repeated translation of the word they expressed different preferences. Students 1 and 3 had no objection to an interpreter inventing a sign on the spot to be used for the duration of that class if it facilitated the smooth flow of information. However, Student 1 said that repeated fingerspelling presented no comprehension problems for him (unless the interpreter is not a proficient fingerspeller), whereas Student 3 felt that repeated fingerspelling definitely required extra decoding concentration on her part and was disruptive to the flow of the message. Student 2 felt strongly that invention of signs by interpreters exceeds the interpreter's role (and their limitations as second-language acquirers of sign language in most cases). She reported that she prefers to provide the interpreter with a sign or to quickly negotiate a translation form which is mutually acceptable to both of them to be used from then on. Some tension in attitudes and responses was evident here, between pragmatic concerns for getting the information, on the one hand, and concerns as to whether the role of an interpreter warrants creation of new lexical sign forms, on the other.

Strategies for coping with ambiguity

As a native ASL signer (i.e. born to deaf parents and raised with ASL as a first language), Student l's comments reveal a willingness to tolerate and accommodate interpreter distortions to a much greater degree than Student 2 whose comments show her to be more interested in being actively involved in attaining accuracy in the interpreting process. This tendency on her part might come from her being experienced in teaching sign language to hearing people, in that she has a teacher's instructive instinct when faced with language errors. Student 3, the more English-oriented signer, also expressed a tolerance for interpreters' conceptual inaccuracy in the classroom, though it was she who reported the greatest degree of confusion and ambiguity in the messages she perceived in class, a response which was consistent with the low estimates for overall comprehension she gave in Question 1. Of course, since tolerance levels for ambiguity vary from individual to individual, this might also be a factor in coping with interpreter distortion, aside from language preference or degree of bilingualism.

The experiences of these deaf students correspond with Cokely's (1985) assertion that transliteration is only viable for bilingual consumers because "transliterations … require that TL consumers understand the SL form in order to understand the intended SL meaning … the strategy merely places the burden of coping with SL message form on the TL consumers" (pp. 220–221). This burdening effect is even more apparent when the transliteration or interpretation is conceptually inaccurate at the lexical level. The ability to decode transliteration is thus clearly contingent upon familiarity with the forms and structures of the two languages involved (in this case, English and ASL), but consumers also apparently need to be able to extrapolate meaning from partial, incomplete, or distorted forms of both languages, which comprise a substantial portion of the TL message in signed transliteration.

Overall interpreting preference

Finally, when asked to make an overall choice between an interpreter who is a proficient transliterator, conveying every word uttered in class but in a less fluent signing style, and an interpreter who translates concepts and structures into more ASL-like forms, but is fluent and comfortable to watch, all three students unhesitatingly said they would pick the latter. Student 1 remarked that no matter how accurate a transliterator may be, if the transliterated message produced is visually boring to watch, the deaf consumer will be unable to focus attention and will lose the information in the long run, despite the interpreter's diligence in conveying every word. Such comments support the view that "where conceptual exchange between teacher and student is far more crucial than proper language exposure, the interpreter should be sensitive to and in tune with Deaf students' maximum comfort in regard to communication mode" (Fleischer, 1975, p. 75).

Conclusion

Given that Fleischer's suggestion appeared in 1975, it might seem redundant to be citing new data that supports the same conclusion. Yet, the results of this small study reveal an anachronistic reality in which at least a proportion of interpreters are still making the same kinds of mistakes fifteen years later. One major difference between now and then, however, is that an increasing number of deaf students are entering mainstream universities for study at all levels. The issue of an interpreter's ability to convey accurate and equivalent information to deaf students has thus become even more crucial than in the mid-1970s, when studies on interpreter effectiveness in the classroom were just emerging. Another difference is that today there exists a larger body of research, information, and expertise in the field of sign language linguistics and interpreting, all of which could be more effectively applied to improving interpreters' understanding and performance of their important task.

This study has reiterated the observation that the most conspicuous problem arising in transliteration is the transfer of source language forms rather than meanings into the signed modality. This problem involves three main challenges for the interpreter: (1) complete comprehension of the meaning of the source language message; (2) accurate selection of equivalent lexical forms for expressing that meaning in the target language; and (3) whether the task is approached as simply coding or as one which requires mental processing identical to interpreting, i.e. analysis of meaning at the phrasal and textual level. If this third question of interpreters' perception and practice of their task would be more thoroughly grounded in research, the answer could be applied to interpreter preparation, and specifications for the requisite skills of a "qualified" interpreter might be better defined. Once accomplished, this definition of the interpreter's task and reorientation of training goals might then lead to eventually redressing the first two problems.

It should be noted that when the interpreters in this study were interviewed, they seemed to find the analysis of their errors to be enlightening and even surprising in many cases. The interpreters were challenged to question what interpreting decisions they had been making and why, and they found this interaction with a critical observer to be productive. Their reactions suggest that regular external feedback could significantly enhance interpreters' awareness and monitoring of meaning equivalence. Many interpreters no doubt know this, but they can't, don't, or won't put this knowledge into practice, to the probable ongoing detriment of deaf consumers. Unfortunately, the kinds of errors considered here to be avoidable by improved training are those which result from the lack of intuitive judgments about semantic equivalence, which accompanies a lack of second language proficiency/experience. This is a familiar problem to teachers of foreign languages, but it is even more crucial for professionals working between two languages, for the success or outcomes of communication rest partly on their lexical decisions (among other factors, of course).

In addition, this study shows that the perspectives on sign language interpreting/transliterating gained from interviews with deaf students are informative, both in terms of their common observations and of the individual variation in responses that they reflect. Indeed, research that elicits this sort of consumer feedback can be of benefit both to deaf consumers and to interpreters working in educational settings. The combination of presenting interpreters with the type of errors analyzed in this study and of eliciting feedback from deaf students about distortions they perceive in transliterated information may be just the kind of stimulus required to jolt interpreters and interpreter educators into addressing more analytically the problem of semantic equivalence in interpreter education.

References

Bellugi, U. & Klima, E. (1980). *The signs of language.* Cambridge, MA: Harvard University Press.

Cokely, D.R. (1985). *Towards a sociolinguistic model of the interpreting process: Focus on ASL and English.* Unpublished doctoral dissertation, Georgetown University, Washington, D.C.

Colonomos, B. (1984). A semantic look at sign glosses. *The Reflector, 9,* 5–11.

Fleischer, L. (1975). *Sign language interpretation under four conditions.* Unpublished doctoral dissertation, Brigham Young University, Provo, UT.

Jacobs, L.R. (1976). *The efficiency of sign language interpreting to convey lecture information to deaf students.* Unpublished doctoral dissertation, University of Arizona, Tucson.

Johnson, K. (1989). *Miscommunication between hearing and deaf participants via the interpreter in a university classroom setting.* Unpublished M.A. thesis, UCLA.

Levitt, D. (1984). *Dealing with passives.* Unpublished manuscript.

Lucas, C. (Ed.). (1989). *The sociolinguistics of the deaf community.* San Diego: Academic Press.

Nida, E.A. (1976). A framework for the analysis and evaluation of theories of translation and response. In R.W. Brislin (Ed.), *Translation applications and research* (pp. 47–91). New York: Gardner Press.

Schick, B.S. (1987). *The acquisition of classifier predicates in American Sign Language.* Unpublished doctoral dissertation, Purdue University, Lafayette, IN.

Wilcox, S. & Wilcox, P. (1985). Schema theory and language interpretation: A study of sign language interpreters. *Journal of Interpretation, 2,* 84–93.

Winston, E. (1989). Transliteration: What's the message? In C. Lucas (Ed.), *The sociolinguistics of the deaf community* (pp. 147–164). San Diego: Academic Press.

Appendix A: Error data

Key:
# indicates a fingerspelled word
parenthetical remarks provide contextual and semantic explanations
++ indicates repetition of a sign to show continued progressive aspect

Misperceived Errors	
it says "tide" – "give title"	NOT STEAL IT-TITLE
describe the hypothesis, subjects, method	DESCRIBE FIVE OFFICES, TITLE (*subject heading*), METHOD
I talked to a lady – she said	ME TALK TO BOY BOY SAY
I'm not saying this is pedagogically defensible – vocabulary in context and so on – obviously you don't have to draw pictures on the screen	ME NOT-KNOW HOW PUT IN ALL WORDS BUT OBVIOUS NEED USE WORDS BUT NOT HAVE-TO DRAW
share-ware (*computer*) programs	CHAIR #W-A-R-E PROGRAM
These (*computer programs*) are written for a college audience	THIS WRITE FOR COLLEGE FOOTBALL
then it's very difficult for me to give you anything but zero for that problem	THEN VERY HARD FOR ME GIVE ZERO POINTS THAT PROBLEM
but he did it, he came up with – any questions about retrograde motion – just the idea?	BUT HE #D-I-D #I-T-KNOW ANY IDEA ITSELF CONNECT (*about*) #R–M (*affirmative head nod*)
The reason this trick works for drawing ellipses	#S-T-O-R-Y WORK – BECAUSE
sociolinguistics – the study of national identity and what language you do your paper-work in – it's very interesting. It's a whole kettle of worms	SOCIOLINGUISTICS – CONNECT SOCIETY LANGUAGE – WHICH PAPER WITH – WHOLE QUOTE #K-E-T-T-L-E #O–F WORMS
in more traditional societies it works better than ones that show obvious variation on the surface	NOT ALWAYS SHOW VARIATION SURFACE
several disparate groups	SEVERAL DESPERATE GROUPS
Semantic Sign-Choice Errors	
have a certain predisposition	HAVE SPECIFIC POSITION
that implies	THAT IDEA
an abiding personality type	OBEDIENT PERSONALITY
I wasn't having much luck with it	ME NOT LUCKY
My hobby is amateur radio	#A-M-A-T-E-U-R-E – BEGINNER RADIO
the phones were down (*because of the earthquake*)	PHONE BANKRUPT/FOLD

The hospital was a mess	HOSPITAL TERRIBLE
Dennis has given us a little cognate	#D-E-N-N-I-S GIVE LITTLE-BIT HELP
I called at 8pm, at that time they didn't know	ME CALL TIME 8 – BEFORE (*long time ago*) THEY NOT-KNOW
(*pointing to sentence on blackboard*) If you have two spaces here	IF TWO (*hits thumb as on typewriter spacebar*)
It's something like a tree – a branching out kind of program, with options – you can see how it has a tree pattern, where if you pick one thing you get something else down below	SAME TREE (*upright tree sign*) – OPTIONS – TREE (*makes action of selecting from tree fingers, in upward direction*)
translate to Spanish	BECOME SPANISH
So – how are you doing with this?	#S-O – WHAT'S UP? (*informal ASL greeting = how are you?*)
a "how to" kind of outline	HOW TO (*directional*) KIND OUTLINE
argumentative type of writing	ARGUE (*two persons*) KIND WRITE
Most molecules can be made into a solid	MOST MOLECULES CAN SHAPE SOLID
If I'm going to handle it I need to wear a mitt	IF GOING CONTROL NEED GLOVE
we'll see if we can get it (*the experiment*) to behave	SEE IF CAN CONTROL #I-T
in the meantime	LATER
We can guess the amount of oxygen	CAN GUESS HOW-MANY (*question form*) #O-X
in small amounts	IN SMALL COUNTS
We get a chemical reaction	GET CHEMICAL RESPONSE (*reply*)
carbon compounds	#C-A-R-B-O-N PARTS – #C-O-M-P-O-U-N-D-S
has the same properties	HAVE SAME PARTS
This process absorbs heat	THIS PLAN ABSORB HEAT
on a similar vein to these questions	ON SAME WAY THIS QUESTIONS
Let's hope he comes through on that (*marking the homework*)	HOPE HE SHOW-UP
There have been – historically – two major advances in theories of gravity	#H-A-V-E #B-E-E-N 2 THEORY RAISE-LEVEL IN GRAVITY
So – if you're not careful you'll conclude that Mars is moving from left to right, which is actually <u>backwards</u> to the direction Mars is going	NOT CAREFUL YOU THINK #M-A-R-S ITSELF MAYBE LEFT (*sign moves left-to-right across sign space*) NOT (*negative headshake*) BACK (*over shoulder*) FROM MARS #I-S- GO
their profit orientations	THEIR PROFIT KNOWLEDGE-EXPERIENCE
had certain symbolic advantages	HAVE SYMBOL TAKE-ADVANTAGE-OF (*rip-off*)
Most churches are English-dominated	MOST CHURCH ENGLISH CONTINUE
allows them to reformulate (*culture*)	ALLOW AGAIN – FORMULA (*math*)

you disenfranchise many people	DISCONNECT MANY PEOPLE
it relieves the burden of having to know	OFFER – TAKE RESPONSIBILITY PEOPLE MUST KNOW
shared, articulated set of goals	SHARE. SPEECH SET-UP GOALS
substantial sharing of cultural knowledge in general	#S-U-B-S-T-A-N – ENOUGH SHARE INFORMATION GENERAL
general cognitive sharing and non-sharing about cultural knowledge	GENERAL understand++share AND NOW SHARE ABOUT KNOWLEDGE
takes a point of view	SET-UP POINT LOOK-AT-PERSON
He was combatting a dominant view at the time	HIMSELF AGAINST TIME (*period*)
this idea that there's an ideal personality	IDEA THAT HAVE SPECIFIC TASTE – ALL MATCH ONE
we can assume that	WE CAN TAKE-UP/ADOPT THAT
Around the 9th century	AROUND (*encircling*) 9TH #C-E-N-T-U-R-Y
a major battle	MOST BATTLE
since this is (*because*)	SINCE (*time passing*)
What does that remind you of?	WHAT THAT REMIND (*tap shoulder/get attention*) YOU #O–F?
Someone's hoarding them!	SOME ONE COLLECT++HOLD
they managed to destroy	THEY MANAGE (*control*) DESTROY
it was largely in the process of	LARGE PROCESS #O-F
that very behavior is	THAT VERY (*intensifier*) BEHAVIOR
this cylinder will turn it upside down on top of the candle burning here	(*CLASSIFIER hold tubular shape and upturn*) TOP #O–F #C-A-N-D-L-E
The test will be 8 to 10 questions	TEST WILL #B-E- 8 TO (*directional*) 10 QUESTION
an expository, narrative outline	CONVERSATION OUTLINE
Have you tried to write?	HAVE (*possessive*) YOU (*plural*) TRY WRITE?
Have you looked at that program?	HAVE (*possessive*) YOU (*plural*) FINISH READ?
and so will the midterm	#S–O WILL MIDTERM
This was made into a solid	THIS MAKE IN SOLID
now I'm going to take a liquid	NOW ME GO TO (*directional*) TAKE #L-I-Q-U-I-D
it will change into a gas	WILL CHANGE IN GAS
how complicated it must have been for Kepler	HOW COMPLEX MUST (*modal*) HAVE (*possessive*) #B–E FOR #K-E-P-L-E-R
You might have noticed	YOU MAYBE HAVE (*possessive*) NOTICE

Appendix B: Interview questions for deaf students

1. Approximately what percentage of a lecture do you feel you understand through an interpreter?
2. Does the type of subject (e.g. a more technical subject) make a difference as to how well the interpreter can get the information across?
3. Do you ever notice that interpreters make errors?
4. Do any *kinds* of interpreter errors bother you in particular?

For example:

    (i) Interpreter uses wrong sign, e.g. EVERYDAY instead of SAME to mean something *in common.*

    (ii) Interpreter signs English grammatical words that have no meaning in ASL, e.g. MUST HAVE (*possessive*) BEEN VERY DIFFICULT.

    (iii) Interpreter wrongly uses ASL classifiers to indicate visual elements such as diagrams (e.g. wrong direction or placement).

    (iv) Interpreter mishears/misunderstands then signs something anomalously out of context.

    (v) Interpreter omits information, comments, etc.

5. If an unfamiliar word comes up in the lecture, do you prefer the interpreter to finger-spell or make up/approximate a sign for it, or do you tell the interpreter what to sign?
6. What do you do when you think the interpreter has made an error? Can you make sense of the message?
7. Which is more important to you: (i) that the interpreter accurately signs absolutely everything said in class in the same order it was said, or (ii) that the interpreter translates the ideas and language in a way that is more ASL-like, but is fluent and comfortable to read?

Rachel Locker, a native of New Zealand, is a doctoral student in applied linguistics at UCLA, from where she also holds an M.A. in TESL. As a professional sign language interpreter, she has practiced in New Zealand as well as in the United States. Her research interests include second language acquisition of signed languages by hearing people, acquisition of English by deaf people, New Zealand sign language (NZSL) research, and analysis of the interpreting process.

4.2   **Zimmer, June. 1992. "Appropriateness and naturalness in ASL-English interpreting." In** *Expanding Horizons: Proceedings of the Twelfth National Conference of Interpreter Trainers,* **ed. by J. Plant-Moeller, 81–92. Silver Spring, MD: Registry of Interpreters for the Deaf.**

An experienced ASL interpreter and interpreter educator, June Zimmer completed her Masters in Linguistics at Gallaudet University, and enrolled in a Ph.D. from Georgetown University but never completed the degree as she passed away in the mid 1990s. She was a faculty member and the program director of the Sign Language Interpreting program at the University of New Hampshire at Manchester from 1990–1993. Zimmer was known for her particular interest in discourse analysis and how to bridge our understanding of discourse, interaction and interpreting. With her earlier work, she began to blaze a trail in the application of discourse analysis to interpreting, and many agree that she would have continued to be a major contributor to the field had she still been alive.

Appropriateness and naturalness in ASL/English interpreting

June Zimmer

Introduction

It is the goal of any interpretation to produce an equivalent message in a target language for that which was originally produced in the source language. This is far from a simple task, as any professional interpreter knows. It is not enough to merely encode the lexical items and grammatical structures of the source language into the correct lexical items and grammatical structures of the target language.

Clearly an interpreter needs to possess native or native-like competence in both languages and some familiarity with the subject matter in question. However, these are only preliminary skills. In order to do an adequate job of interpreting a particular text, an interpreter also needs native-like competence in the linguistically and non-linguistically realized cultural conventions that are relevant in any given situation. Competence in this area is essential in order to successfully translate the "speaker's meaning" into the target language.

The question of meaning

Obviously the phenomenon of meaning is of utmost importance to interpreters. We must grasp the meaning of the source language text and reproduce it in the target language. To a lay person this may seem like a straightforward task. Many times I have asked a speaker for clarification of some discourse only to be told, "Just tell her what I said." The assumption is that interpretation involves nothing more than the coding of lexical items produced in the source language into the correct lexical items of the target language. In this view, the coding should be almost automatic. Any interpreter realizes, however, that this is an extremely naive view of what actually takes place. Cross-linguistic meanings are anything but straightforward. There is rarely a direct one-to-one correspondence between a lexical item in the source language and a lexical item in the target language. When we move to the level of a whole utterance, the situation is even more complex.

The term "meaning" actually encompasses several different notions as indicated by the following sentences:

"Banana" means the fruit of a tree-like tropical plant.

Did he mean that we should do this now or later?

Clouds mean rain.

"Means" in the first sentence refers to the dictionary definition for the lexical item "banana." "Mean" in the second sentence refer to what Seleskovitch (this volume) calls the "speaker's meaning." In the third sentence "mean" has to do with the sign for a natural phenomenon. The first two types of meaning involve language and how it is used.

The type of meaning referred to in the first sentence is called "semantic" meaning. Semantic meaning is carried by linguistic forms (i.e. words/signs, sentences, etc.) devoid of any context in which they may be spoken or signed. The semantic meaning of a word or sign may be extremely complex, broad, and hard to pin down. Take, for example, the English word "game." It is extremely difficult to find a core meaning for this word which can apply to all the instances in which the word is used. Most games are for fun, but others are deadly serious. Most games involve more than one participant, but others can be played alone. Many games involve the use of objects, but others don't. In fact, it seems to be impossible to find any one characteristic which all games have in common.

The more semantically complex a lexical item is, the less likely it is that there will be a direct word-to-word correspondence for it in another language. Becker (1982) says that a language will always have both "exuberancies" and "deficiencies" in regards to any other language. Languages develop in ways that make them particularly suited to the cultures which use them. Thus Eskimo languages have many different words for "snow," while English has only one. English has many different words for sounds, while ASL has many different signs for ways of seeing or looking at things. In other words, English is exuberant in relationship to ASL in terms referring to sound but deficient in terms referring to sight.

Thus, even the interpretation of semantic meaning is anything but straightforward. When we consider pragmatic meaning, the situation becomes even more complex. Whereas one can decipher the semantic meaning of a sentence out of context, pragmatic meaning is totally dependent on context. Pragmatic meaning occurs when the language is used by a particular person in a particular situation. Pragmatic meaning is roughly equivalent to what Seleskovitch (this volume) calls "speaker's meaning."

The English utterance "Gee, it's hot in here" can be used to distinguish semantic meaning from pragmatic meaning. Semantically this utterance means that the air temperature of the room is above that which is comfortable for the speaker. Pragmatically, however, this statement may be functioning as a request to turn down the heat, turn up the air conditioner, or open a window. Without access to the context, we can't know which of these actions is being requested, or even whether the utterance is functioning as a request or merely a complaint. This depends on whether the person to whom it is addressed has the power to do something about the temperature in the room.

Pragmatic meaning is determined by two factors: cultural convention and personal choice. Cultural convention helps to determine a range of behaviors that are acceptable in a particular situation. Most individuals will choose a behavior that is somewhere in this range. The relative use and acceptance of indirectness is one of the culturally determined dimensions of linguistic behavior. The speaker in the example above could have made the request directly by saying "Please turn down the heat." Cultural norms, however, may encourage the use of an indirect form which is seen as more "polite."

In another culture, however, such an indirect request may not be interpreted as a request, but merely as a statement. For example, I have asked many Deaf people whether they would interpret a statement like "Gee, it's hot in here" as a request. All of the Deaf people I asked told me that that they would not interpret such a statement as a request, Interpretation of pragmatic meaning, then, is entirely dependent on knowledge of the cultural conventions of the groups one is interpreting for. In order to produce a natural and appropriate interpretation, we must produce a target language utterance that is equivalent to the source language utterance at both the semantic and the pragmatic levels.

Register and genre

One of the pragmatically determined dimensions of language is that of register. Halliday (1968) describes register variation as "variation according to use" and he distinguishes it from dialect variation or variation according to user. Register is a function of what a speaker is doing in terms of social activity. The activity or genre helps to determine the linguistic style or level of formality one will use.

Several models for register variation have been put forth. The model most often cited in the field of sign language interpreting is one proposed by Joos (1968). He says that there are a finite number of linguistic styles and distinguishes five in particular. These are (in order of formality): intimate, casual, consultative, formal, and frozen. The intimate and casual styles, he says, are quite informal and are characterized by a heavy use of ellipsis (especially of phonological segments and certain lexical items such as articles, subject pronouns, etc.). Interlocutors use intimate style only with people they know well, and it is marked by a great deal of "private language." Casual style is much like intimate style but doesn't include private language. Consultative style is the one used in everyday conversation among speakers who do not know each other well and who are conducting some kind of business. Colloquial speech will be used but there is an emphasis on making the speech as clear and unambiguous as possible. At the formal level, according to Joos, the most important function of speech is to impart information and the talk does not have a great deal of "social importance." Frozen style is characterized by language that is formulaic and is usually found in situations such as religious services and the courtroom.

Other writers avoid talking about registers as discrete varieties. Instead they describe the contextual factors that will help to determine a range of language use that is acceptable in a given situation. The most sophisticated model for a description of register variation is proposed by Halliday (1968, 1978) and expanded upon by Gregory and Carroll (1978).

These authors describe register variation according to three categories of features: the field, the mode, and the tenor of discourse. The field involves the physical setting and the physical activity surrounding and defining a speech event. The mode includes the channel used (i.e. written, spoken, or signed) and involves factors such as whether the speech is memorized or spontaneous and whether it is monologic or dialogic. The tenor concerns the participants and the interpersonal dynamics involved in their relationship. According to this model, features that are usually associated with a particular register can also be found in other registers of speech. It often happens that a more "informal" feature will be used in a context where more "formal" features are usually found and vice versa. In a formal lecture in an academic setting, for example, the speaker may switch to a casual register while telling a joke or reporting a conversation with a colleague.

Register is an abstract notion that is not easily defined. However as Enkvist (1987) has noted, we spend a great deal of time observing speech of different styles and comparing these texts with each other. In this way we gain insight into the "subvarieties" of language that we can expect in any speech situation. Even though a particular text can be difficult to categorize, the notion of register does have psychological reality for native users of any language. Individuals have the ability to recognize a significant speech style out of context. For example, it would probably be quite easy for a native American English speaker to label audiotapes of a radio announcer, a lawyer in court, and a sermon.

Joos' model would categorize each of these texts as formal and/or frozen, and gives us no way to distinguish between them. Halliday's model, on the other hand, allows us to talk about specific features that distinguish these three types of discourse. Vocal intonation, for example, may vary greatly. Lexical and syntactic choices would undoubtedly be extremely different. The level of emotion and rapport with the audience may be quite high in the sermon and the lawyer's presentation, but would probably be low in the radio broadcast, etc.

There is also a problem with Joos' description of "frozen" style as the highest or most formal level, since formulaic elements can occur in even the most casual speech. Greeting behavior, for example, is extremely formulaic even though it would fall at the casual end of a continuum between formal and informal language use. The other models are more helpful because they allow us to talk about particular features we may expect to find in any particular situation of language use.

Closely allied with the notion of register is that of "genre." Bakhtin ([1952–53] 1S86, p. 60) describes this phenomenon. He says:

> Genres correspond to typical situations of speech communication, typical themes, and consequently, also to particular contacts between the meanings of words and actual concrete reality under certain typical circumstances.

Every genre has a repertoire of features which characterize it. These features may be aspects of either the text or the context. Textual features include lexical choices, syntactic structures, and meter. Contextual features include the speaker's goals, the subject matter, tone, the attitude of the speaker, and the speaker's relationship with the audience. Bakhtin ([1952–53] 1986) notes that genres can be more or less conducive to the creation of an individual style (e.g. poetry vs. business documents).

Genres can also be distinguished according to whether they are primarily monologic or primarily dialogic. In monologic communication, speaker and audience roles are clearly delineated. The speaker will usually be physically separated from the audience in some way, i.e. the speaker will be on a stage or behind a table or podium, etc. Monologic events include performances such as theater, poetry, and story telling and presentations such as a lecture at a conference or in a classroom. In a dialogic event there is more than one active participant. These include conversations, interviews, and meetings.

For each genre, there is a range of linguistic register that is typically used. A lecturer at an academic conference generally uses quite formal register, whereas a storyteller often uses a very casual one. The range of register variation that is appropriate in any given situation is culturally determined. An event that may be seen as quite formal in one culture may be much less so in another culture. Individual speakers usually choose the features they are comfortable with from within the range of register variation that is acceptable in a given situation. However, they are not precluded from choosing a register that is not typically used. This "flaunting" of the norms is often used for effect. Thus a speaker at an academic conference may choose to deliver her speech in an informal register. Depending on the preferences of audience members, they may find this to be either refreshing or scandalous.

Before an interpreter arrives at the work site, she usually knows a great deal about the situation. She is told what type of linguistic event will be taking place, e.g. an academic lecture, a job interview, etc. In other words, she knows the genre of the event. From this she also knows something about the register that is typically used at this type of event. These situational cues can make our job much easier, but can also, at times, throw us off balance. As stated above, cultural convention only helps us to determine a range of features that are appropriate. The features actually used by speakers or signers are entirely up to them. Also, an individual may decide to flaunt convention and use a register that is atypical.

The importance of coherence

Any time a speaker formulates a chunk of discourse, the issue of coherence comes into play. Coherence is of two basic types:

1. external coherence which involves ties between the text and the present or imagined speech situation, and
2. internal coherence which involves ties within the text itself.

External coherence involves factors like register which are determined by the context. In other words, when a speaker adheres to cultural norms, the discourse is coherent in a particular situation. The very same discourse occurring in another situation, however, may be extremely incoherent.

Understanding another's discourse is largely a process of making sense of the utterances that person produces. Utterances only "make sense" if a listener can find the fit between the speaker's utterances and the present situational and linguistic content. Interlocutors, however, usually go to great lengths to interpret a speaker's utterances as coherent.

External coherence is also a function of the interpersonal dynamics that are operative between interlocutors. Coherence in dialogic discourse is largely a matter of alignment towards one's interlocutors. In order to correctly understand another's utterances one must be aware of the role the speaker is taking in relationship to oneself. According to Ragan (1983), alignment has the function of managing coherence. One would expect that in interactions in which there is a power differential between the participants, interlocutors would use different types of alignment strategies. This is, in fact, what Ragan found in the interview data she examined.

Bakhtin ([1952–53] 1986) says that even speech that appears to be monologic, will be full of "dialogic overtones." On some level, a speaker is always responding to things other people have said and anticipating responses from others. Words and even phrases and clauses from the speech of others can find their way into one's own speech. In this way, we are always building our speech from the entire kaleidoscope of speech we have used before and heard others use. Bahktin says:

> In each epoch, in each social circle, in each small world of family, friends, acquaintances, and comrades in which a human being grows and lives, there are always authoritative utterances that set the tone… which are cited, imitated, and followed… (So) the unique speech of each individual is shaped and developed in continuous and constant interaction with others' individual utterances…. Our speech, that is, all our utterances (including creative works), is filled with others' words, varying degrees of otherness or varying degrees of "our-own-ness. …These words of others carry with them their own expression, their own evaluative tone, which we assimilate, rework, and re-accentuate.
> (p. 88–89)

In other words, a speaker's words/signs must be coherent with culturally relevant discourse that has come before. Certain generic types of utterances, such as interrogative, exclamatory and imperative sequences, may even be, and often are, imported whole from prior discourse.

Whereas external coherence depends on ties between a text, the present situation and other culturally relevant situations, internal coherence depends on ties within a text. It is internal coherence which relates a group of utterances to each other. Without such coherence, we would have a series of unrelated utterances, rather than a cohesive text. There are many different linguistic devices involved in internal coherence.

On a textual level, rhythm and repetition are often used to create coherence. Tannen (1989) notes that rhythm and repetition are important in many speech genres, including such different types as everyday conversation and literary discourse. Her work shows that repetition is pervasive in both planned and unplanned spoken discourse. Because it serves to create coherence, repetition aids both production and comprehension of speech.

Johnstone (1985) observes that even though repetition is pervasive in the speech of Americans and plays an extremely important role in communication, Americans claim to disfavor its use. We also claim not to like or use formulaic language. One indication of this is the negative connotation attached to the word "cliche." Unfortunately this speech taboo has found its way into the philosophies of interpreter trainers. Interpreting students are often urged to find new and different ways to interpret a sign or phrase that recurs too often in a discourse. However, rather than making interpretations more "interesting," this technique may actually make them dull, difficult to understand, and less aesthetically pleasing.

Another textual level device is thematic coherence. Thematic coherence comes about when a particular theme is operative throughout an entire text. Sub-themes will continue throughout portions of a text, and help to tie individual utterances together. According to Goldberg (1983), thematic coherence can be of three different types. In the first type, which she calls "simple linear," the new information in one utterance becomes the given information in the next utterance. In the second type, called "constant theme," the given information remains consistent through a series of utterances. The third type, called "derived theme" occurs when each utterance references a general theme which may be only implicitly stated. In ASL, thematic coherence is often signaled by topicalization. Episodes will often begin with a topicalized element from prior discourse or a reference to a general theme.

Goldberg's model for conversational coherence is based on different types of "moves" an interlocutor may make. The moves are of four different types:

1. introducing,
2. reintroducing,
3. progressive-holding, and
4. holding.

Certain discourse particles are typically associated with particular types of moves (e.g. "you know" tends to begin an introducing or re-introducing move, whereas "well" is usually associated with progressive-holding moves, etc.).

Lexical substitution is a particular device which is used to link utterances together. The use of pronouns is the most common type of lexical substitution. Note the following examples:

This woman came up to me yesterday. She tried to sell me a book. Well, I told her I wasn't interested in it.

The use of pronouns to refer back to nouns lends coherence to these sentences. Compare the example above with the one below:

A woman came up to me yesterday. The woman tried to sell me a book. I told the woman I wasn't interested in the book.

Without the pronouns, the sentences sound choppy and unnatural. However, they still can be seen as a coherent text of three related sentences. The following sentences, on the other hand, appear to be about unrelated events:

A woman came up to me yesterday. A woman tried to sell me a book. I told a woman I wasn't interested in a book.

In the first and second examples, the indefinite determiner "a" has been, replaced by the definite determiner "the." Like pronouns, the use of definite rather than indefinite determiners indicates that one is referring back to prior discourse and creates coherence. Continuing to use the indefinite determiner "a" makes these three sentences appear to be unrelated to each other.

Another type of lexical substitution occurs when a more general noun is substituted for a more specific noun or vice versa, as in the following examples:

> My friend's dog is so cute. Guess what Fido did yesterday. Fido is so cute. Do you know what that dog did the other day?

In the case of dialogic discourse, interlocutors repeat and respond to each other's utterances. Jacobs and Johnson (1983) see conversation as a series of language games. Interlocutors are seen as players in an ever unfolding and changing game. There are two basic levels of knowledge necessary in order to play the game. First there is the system of basic rules. The second level involves knowledge of what constitutes "rational play." Play is cooperative and consists of a series of moves by which the players attempt to achieve their goals while maintaining a certain alignment to other players. Goals can be limited or broad, focused or diffuse, intrinsic or extrinsic to the conversation. Play is "rational" in that players only begin moves which they believe other players will go along with.

Coherence is of utmost importance to interpreters. In order to sound natural and appropriate, our target language texts must be coherent within themselves and with the situation. Hopper (1983) says that interpreting another's utterances always involves the "manufacture of coherence." In his view, an understanding of coherence must take account of the "twoness" inherent in it; "to cohere" means to bring together two disparate elements. An interpreter must find the unity within and between the two elements, the text and the context.

Conclusions

In this paper, I have discussed several phenomena which help to determine the naturalness and appropriateness of the language used in any given situation. These are some of the things interpreters need to keep in mind in order to produce target language texts which sound or look natural and appropriate. An in-depth discussion of the individual phenomena with examples from naturally occurring and interpreted discourse is beyond the scope of this paper. It is my hope, however, that these topics have created food for thought and that you will pursue these studies. This can be done by reading some of the cited material.

I especially want to encourage all of you to become observers of the language that is around you – both ASL and English. Much can be learned in this way. Notice how language seems to differ in different social situations. Notice how people use language differently depending on the social status of their interlocutors and the relationships they have with them. When a text seems coherent, notice what it is that makes it seem to flow. When a text is incoherent, notice why this is so. Becoming astute observers of the language around you will have a positive effect on your interpreting. Over time many of the things you have observed will become internalized and you will produce them automatically The first step is to notice and recognize the phenomena you see and hear.

Notes

1. For a more extensive discussion of register variation with specific examples from ASL and interpreted discourse, see Zimmer, 1989 and **1990**.

2. For a more extensive discussion of cohesion, see Halliday and Hassan, 1976.

3. For a general discussion of many features found in naturally occurring discourse see Tannen, 1984 and 1989.

References

Bakhtin, M.M. *Speech genres and other late essays,* ed. C. Emerson and M. Holquist, trans. V. W. McGee. Austin: The University of Texas Press, (1952–53) 1986.

Becker, A.L. Beyond translation: Esthetics and language. In *Contemporary perceptions of language: Interdisciplinary dimensions,* ed. H. Byrnes. Georgetown University Round Table on Languages and Linguistics. Washington, DC: Georgetown University Press, 1982.

Enkvist, N.E. What has discourse linguistics done to stylistics? In *Developments in linguistics and semiotics: Language teaching and learning communication across culture,* ed. S.P.X. Battestini. Georgetown University Round Table on Languages and Linguistics. Washington, D.C: Georgetown University Press, 1987.

Goldberg, J. A move toward describing conversational coherence. In *Conversational coherence,* ed. R. Craig and K. Tracy. Beverly Hills: Sage Publications, 1983.

Gregory, M. and R. Carroll. *Language and situation: Language varieties and their social contexts.* London: Routledge and Kegan Paul, 1978.

Hopper, R. Interpretation as coherence production. In *Conversational coherence,* ed. R. Craig and K. Tracy. Beverly Hills: Sage Publications, 1983.

Halliday, M.A.K. The users and uses of language. In *Readings in the sociology of language,* ed. J. Fishman. The Hague: Mouton, 1968.

Halliday, M.A.K. and R. Hassan. *Cohesion in English.* London: Longman, 1976.

Language as a social semiotic. Baltimore: University Park Press, 1978.

Johnstone, B. An introduction. In *Perspectives on repetition,* ed. B. Johnstone, (special issue of text, 7.3: 205–14).

Joos, M. The isolation of styles. In *Readings in the sociology of language,* ed. J. Fishman. The Hague: Mouton, 1968.

Ragan, R. Alignment and conversational coherence. In *Conversational coherence,* ed. R. Craig and K. Tracy. Beverly Hills: Sage Publications, 1983.

Tannen, D. *Conversational style: Analyzing talk among friends.* Norwood, NJ: Ablex, 1984.

Talking voices: Repetition, dialogue, and imagery in conversational discourse. Cambridge: Cambridge University Press, 1989.

Zimmer, J. Toward a description of register variation in American Sign Language. In *The sociolinguistics of the Deaf Community,* ed. Ceil Lucas. New York: Academic, 1989.

Zimmer, J. From ASL to English in two versions: An analysis of differences in register. *Word.* vol. 41, no. 1 (1990).

4.3 Bélanger, Danielle-Claude. 1995. "The specificities of Quebec Sign Language Interpreting. First part: Analysis using the Effort Model of Interpreting." *Le Lien* 9(1): 11–16; "How to maintain the balance in Interpreting." *Le Lien* 9(2): 6–13. [Translated by Lee Williamson]

Danielle-Claude Bélanger worked as a sign language interpreter between French and Langue des Signes Québécoise (LSQ – the sign language used in the Québéc region of Canada) for 20 years, often working in conference and legal contexts. She earned a BA in social science, and then two MA degrees, one in Communication Studies at the University of Montreal, and one in French literature from McGill University, and began a Ph.D. in education. Her Master's thesis analyzed a dialogic, interpreted event, the first analysis of its kind in Canada. She has taught interpreting for ten years at the university level, has worked on various teaching projects for interpreting, and been active in professional associations, both locally in Quebec and in the Association of Visual Language Interpreters of Canada (AVLIC) for 15 years. She has published many papers in French and her best-known paper in English, "Interactional Patterns in Dialogic Interpreting" was published in the RID *Journal of Interpretation.*

After working as an educational consultant and researcher for a few years, Bélanger then focused her work specifically with the police as a teaching and research consultant in both linguistics and interpreting. She is now Director of the Department of Educational Development and Research at the National School of Police for Québec.

The specificities of Quebec Sign Language interpreting

First part: Analysis using the effort model of interpreting

Danielle-Claude Bélanger

This is the first of two articles in which I discuss Daniel Gile's Effort Model of Interpreting.* It is a very simple model that puts the simultaneity of the interpreting process into perspective whilst explaining the conditions under which the interpreting performance is carried out. In addition, it identifies the risk of failures and explains certain interpreting errors. Following a description of the model, we will discuss the specificities of interpreting in Quebec Sign Language (*langue des signes québécoise, LSQ*) and try to identify the predictable difficulties that a French-Quebec Sign Language interpreter must overcome. In the second article, which will appear in the next issue, we will examine the resources the interpreter has at his or her disposal to reduce the difficulties during the interpreting performance using the model presented here.

Introduction

Interpreting is a complex act which can be understood using different complementary models. The best known is certainly the model that describes the mental process of the interpreting performance. With this approach we are answering the question: "What do we do while we interpret?" However, it is not enough to understand this process in order to verify that we know what the interpreter means. We must also answer this second question: "How can we succeed in doing all these tasks simultaneously?"

We have a relatively thorough knowledge of the mental processes that French Sign Language interpreters go though during the interpreting performance. In addition to the seminal work of Danica Seleskovitch, who developed the Interpretive Theory, most of us can cite the fundamental principles of Betty Colomonos' model without

---

* Daniel Gile (A), "Le modèle d'efforts et de l'équilibre d'interprétation en interprétation simultanée", *Méta*, vol. XXX, no. 1, 1985, pp. 44–48.

any problem: Concentrating, Representing, Planning.[2] Presented very briefly, the mental process of the interpreting performance involves receiving a message in the source language L1 (Concentrating), representing this message and mobilising the stock of knowledge stored in our short- and long-term memory (Representing) and reconstructing and transmitting this same message in the target language L2 (Planning).[3] So far, we have dissected the process in order to align each of the components on the operating table through this rational approach. However, it will suffice to bring it back to life in order to understand how we are able to carry out this process which has multiple simultaneous phases.

Presentation of the model

Daniel Gile explains that a search takes place during the interpreting act to achieve a state of equilibrium between three efforts required to carry out the interpreting process. These are the Listening and Analysis Effort (Listening Effort for short); the Memory Effort and the Production Effort. The Listening Effort corresponds to the first phase, *Concentrating*, the Memory Effort relates to the *Representing* phase, and the Production Effort to the *Representing* phase.

The interpreter must keep these three efforts in balance in order to avoid errors and loss of information. Each task requires a minimum level of energy, which may vary depending on the interpreter's skills and preparation. An additional effort in one of these spheres unavoidably takes place at the expense of another effort.

The interpreter has a maximum level of energy available for the interpreting process. This capacity is shared between the three efforts. The maximum capacity varies according to the physical state of the interpreter.

---

2. Betty Colomonos does not refer to Danica Seleskovitch in her model (Working Model, Betty Colomonos, 1984). However, this forms the basis of it. This was confirmed to me by a friend from Ottawa with whom I raised the similarity in the identification of the interpreting process. I observed that all of the elements in the Colomonos model were already present in various texts by Seleskovitch, especially the *Interpreter in International Conferences* (1968), and *Langages, langue et mémoire* (1975) and the different authors of the *École supérieure d'interprétation et de traduction de Paris*, Marianne Lederer, Karia Déjean-Le Féal et Mariano Garcia Landa amongst others.

If the intellectual integrity demanded that Colomonos cite her sources of inspiration, it remains that this model is interesting and, above all, that it has the intelligence to integrate feedback into the interpreting process.

3. See that article by Sylvie Lemay, "Le processus mental de l'interprétation: Concentration, Visualisation, Reproduction", *Le Lien*, vol. 4, no. 2, June 1990, p. 8.

These three types of efforts have a cumulative effort that we call the Total Effort, which cannot exceed the maximum capacity of the interpreter at that moment.

Daniel Gile's Effort Model of
Interpreting

The diagram above shows a short interpreting period. It is a representation of the message to be interpreted (informational delivery of the speaker) and the simultaneous distribution of efforts during the interpreting performance (E, Listening and Analysis; P, Production; M, Memory), divided into six different time periods. Imagine the following situation: the speaker begins his or her presentation (T0), the interpreter immediately produces a Listening and Analysis Effort while the Memory and Production Efforts are maintained at the minimum threshold. "Ladies and gentlemen, we are very happy to see you in such great numbers so late in the afternoon…" At the end of this sentence, the interpreter produces a Production Effort which is added to the Listening Effort. As the first part of the sentence is a formula for a standard greeting, the interpreter does not have to make a particularly great Memory Effort and he or she will manage to work from the minimum threshold. "To follow on from the Marie-France Daniel conference (T3), still in keeping with John Dewey's pragmatism, (T4) we welcome Michel Sasseville from the *Université Laval* (T5)…"[4] In the third time period of the presentation (T3) the interpreter accumulates a time lag

---

4. The model reproduced in this text is taken from the article by Daniel Gile (A), p. 47. The French statement in this example is my own. In the original text, this passage is: Gentlemen. The Pacific Islands Development Fund and other organizations have committed large funds…".

and increases his or her listening effort because a proper noun has just been uttered so the Listening Effort remains high while in T4, the Memory Effort increases. It is only in T5 that the interpreter begins to transmit the message. Therefore, depending on the context, the informational output of the speakers, the type of information, etc., the different efforts fluctuate and combine in different ways during each period of the interpreting performance.

1. The balance of efforts

The interpreter must control the distribution of efforts in order to avoid errors. For example, too great of a time lag would require a Memory Effort so great that it could prevent the interpreter from hearing part of the message, resulting in a loss of information. The balance is fragile: a sudden noise and the balance is threatened because the interpreter only devotes part of his or her attention to listening. Interpreting imbalances occur when an effort falls below the minimum threshold. In the case of a noise that would prevent the recognition of a word, a far greater Listening and Analysis Effort is required to recover the missing information from the context. From then on the interpreter is in a state of imbalance as he or she no longer has enough Memory Effort at his or her disposal and can forget a part of the message already stored in the short-term memory. Additionally, the job of analysing and reconstructing the original message causes a subsequent increase in the time lag and intensifies the Memory and Production Efforts, which will impact on the quality of the interpreter's hearing. To give another example, let us imagine that we cannot find the equivalent of a word in the L2 and the Production Effort takes up all of the space as a paraphrase is delivered to make sense of a concept at the expense of the other efforts.

The interpreter's task is thankless and difficult. Some information can unconsciously escape the interpreter when it is shared between different efforts, even during a simple speech. Yet we know that certain bilingual audience members (on occasion sometimes other interpreters) are quick to judge and denounce the interpreter when they are only concentrating on the reception of the message. Moreover, the success of one interpreting performance seems clear when the participants themselves have understood the message in which they detected no difficulty.

Yet it is possible to identify the factors that pose a specific difficulty for each of these efforts and consequently, greater mobilisation of energy on the part of the interpreter.

1.1 The listening and analysis effort

Daniel Gile explains[5] that the listening and analysis effort is inevitably more intense depending on: the delivery, the speaker's pronunciation, the technicality of the message,

---

5. The points presented in Sections 1.1, 1.2 and 1.3 have been assembled from the three texts by Daniel Gile cited in the references.

the acoustic environment, the use of lists, figures and proper nouns. Added to this are foreign words and impromptu interventions of interlocutors.

1.2   The memory effort

The Memory Effort is more intense depending on: the time lag, the lack of knowledge of the working languages (L1-L2), the gap between the syntactical structures between L1 and L2 and the active knowledge of the interpreter.

1.3   The production effort

The Production Effort is more intense depending on: the time lag, the density of the message and the technicality of the message (in particular passages that are far removed from verbal automatisms). Added to this are readjustments during production (slips, feedback, etc.).

2.   The specificities of sign language interpreting

The difficulties listed above are only part of the obstacles that arise during sign language interpreting. This language and the cultural situation of the Deaf community contain many specificities that directly influence the split of efforts during the interpreting performance. These factors concern syntactical order, lexical and sociocultural features.

2.1   The syntactical structure

Daniel Gile demonstrates that working languages that differ in in the linear distribution of the information demand an increased Memory Effort: the interpreter must maintain a larger time lag before processing and transmitting the information. This is a syntactical problem. In this respect, the sign language interpreter is in a difficult position from the outset because the syntactical structure of the target language, LSQ, is radically different from the source language, French.[6] For example, in French, indications of time can be found at the end of the sentence while time is usually at the start of the sentence in LSQ. In the sentence: *it is important to remember the speeches of Plato, delivered many centuries ago*, must be transmitted in LSQ in an order comparable to the following: *Many centuries ago, Plato, what he had said, it is important to remember it*. In this example, the interpreter must keep a sizeable time lag, make a significant Memory Effort and, unavoidably, wait until the end to be able to reproduce the message.

---

6.   On this topic, see Colette Dubuisson and Marie Nadeau, eds., *Études sur la langue des signes québécoise*, Montréal-Presses de l'Université de Montréai, 226 p.

2.2 Technical terms

All natural languages have, on occasion, a delay before new words related to theoretical fields and specialised languages are naming. For example, French is enriched annually with around 10,000 new terms in the scientific and technical domains alone.[7] This is a lexical problem. This phenomenon occurs in LSQ. However, it is greater depending on the domains concerned; indeed, it seems to me that terminology in Quebec Sign Language specific to accounting, administration and information technology is better established than that relating to aeronautics or international law. In the absence of specific words in sign language, the interpreter can resort to different strategies to transmit different concepts. He or she can spell out the term in French, come to an agreement about a particular sign or use a paraphrase. However, these strategies involve greater or lesser Production Efforts and later on, a change in the balance of efforts. In having to make a greater effort to transmit the message, the sign language interpreter can lose pieces of information that are stored in the memory or not hear the words uttered at the same moment.

2.2.1 Spelling

When faced with a word that has no recognised equivalent in sign language, the interpreter can choose to spell it out. This choice is made depending on the context and the importance of the concept in the message as a whole. For example, during a sociology class, the term *anomie* should be spelled out because it is one of the fundamental concepts of this discipline, while *tribulations* will probably not be. Spelling involves a longer production time than a sign. Yet resorting to spelling is frequent in Quebec Sign Language interpreting and is almost systematic in the case of proper nouns. We saw earlier that proper nouns already command a particular Listening Effort. For the sign language interpreter, this not only involves a Listening Effort and a Production Effort, but also an additional Memory Effort because the interpreter must also cross over into the written code in order to reproduce the orthography of the words spelled out in its place, which is a specificity of sign language interpreting. On the subject of linguistic competences Daniel Gile notes "the mastery commanded [of interpreters of oral languages] focuses on the spoken word and not on the written, on the auditory reception capacity and not the visual."[8] In our profession, Wittgenstein or even Watzlawick are are some of the cursed authors for sign language interpreters: Listening and Analysis Effort, memorisation work (the interpreter must visualise in a few seconds the spelling of the noun) and Production Effort are far greater.

---

7. Daniel Gile (C) "L'interprétation de conférence et la connaisance des langues", *Méta*, vol. XXX, no. 4, 1985, p. 324.

8. Daniel Gile (C), ibid. p. 326.

Rather than spell out a name or a term, there is always the possibility to remain on neutral ground and initialise the first letter of the French word by adding oralisation. This technique is the most economic in terms of production time, but its efficacy is uncertain, even dubious, in the case of conference interpreting. It can be employed with more relevance when the word has already been spelled out and understood.

2.2.2   Vocabulary conventions

Access to post-secondary education for Deaf students has encouraged the creation of a large number of neologisms in Quebec Sign Language interpreting over the past ten years. Some of these signs have passed easily into the vernacular and are generally known by a large number of LSQ speakers. For example, the technical signs for syntax, iconicity, morphology and parallel encoding can be used during a linguistics conference. This is not the case with the technical signs for occlusive, affricate or diphthong, which are also concepts in linguistics. In addition, several signs created for a particular programme of study can remain unknown to other Deaf people in the community or be modified when they become adopted into LSQ.

For the interpretation of a particular term, in point 2.2.1 the recognised equivalent in sign language was discussed. This is the second specificity of sign language interpreting which concerns vocabulary: the interpreter may know a technical sign which is unknown to the Deaf recipient, or he or she may even suggest a technical sign for it and the Deaf person prefers to use another sign. This situation has direct consequences for the balance of efforts. At the first appearance of a technical term in French for which the interpreter knows a sign, he or she must first spell this word then produce the technical sign. The production effort is therefore much greater.

Extremely rare in spoken language interpreting, the interpreter and the Deaf person can even hold a brief conversation in parallel during the interpreting performance to agree a sign to use. This private conversation can take place in a few seconds, but it leaves the interpreter faced with a fourth effort, which is completely non-existent in spoken language interpreting: the perception and decoding effort of a linguistic signal coming from the visual-spatial channel. We shall call this new element the Viewing and Analysis Effort. This new effort is added to the others while the maximum capacity remains the same.

2.2.3   Paraphrases

The use of spelling and/or of a technical sign during the interpreting performance depends on the context, the oratory purpose (teaching, informing, advising, congratulating, etc.) and on the Deaf person to whom the message is addressed. With the exception of teaching situations, the specific concepts in French can generally be transmitted from their meaning, without regard for their precise denomination in the source text. For example, during a fundraising event, the term *sponsor* will not be spelled out while it probably would be during a history of art class. In this example, the interpreter will consider the meaning of the word *sponsor* and will produce an equivalent paraphrase. We could therefore expect to see the production of three signs associated with the following semantic categories: person, wealth/money and help/protection. It goes without saying that the production time of a paraphrase exceeds that of a single sign. We note, however, that spoken language interpreters also employ this strategy: "(…) terms that do not exist in the target language, are unknown to the interpreter or momentarily out of his or her grasp are replaced by explanations or paraphrases (…)".[9]

In the case of spelling or technical signs, it is up to the interpreter to decide whether to resort to this or not, taking into account the information that they have depending on the context, the theoretical field and the Deaf recipient. However, using paraphrases is widespread and occurs in all interpreting situations in Quebec Sign Language because the role of the interpreter is to enable communication and ultimately, understanding between two speakers and different cultures. On this point, the specificity of interpreting in Quebec Sign Language resides not so much in having recourse to paraphrases but in its systematic use. It is evident that: the production of a single sign is more economical from the point of view of production time but if this is not understood, the interpreter may be required to add a paraphrase followed by spelling and finally repeating the sign initially produced. The risk of interpreting errors is therefore very high.

2.3   Cultural differences

In all scenarios, the Listening and Analysis Effort is at its maximum when it concerns idiomatic expressions. One has to immediately recognise the connotation of the expression in the source language and identify the cultural equivalents in the target language, or at least give a formulation that captures the tone, the style effect and the meaning of the expression employed, which is a sociocultural problem regularly encountered in interpreting because a all languages underlie a specific culture.

Interpreting in Quebec Sign Language has another sociocultural specificity: the transmission of information that refers to the news. The Deaf community does not have the same cultural behaviours as the hearing community and in particular, they do not have widespread access to electronic media (only through subtitles for television and nothing for the radio). Therefore, news events are often encoded without the name of the protagonists. This has the effect of forcing the interpreter to paraphrase. The sign language interpreter must then be very up to date with current affairs. He or she must be able to immediately identify the situation and succinctly evoke the relevant elements that it composes in order to then specify the names of the people involved. Take as an example a speaker referring to the case of Sue Rodriguez. The interpreter must immediately situate the speech in relation

---

9.   Daniel Gile (B), "Les termes techniques en interprétation simultanée", *Méta*, vol. XXX, no. 3, 1985, p. 205.

to the events to which it refers and then spell the name said by the speaker because the Deaf person will recognise the situation but not necessarily the name of the person. The Listening and Analysis Effort as well as the Production Effort are considerably greater.

Conclusion

Quebec Sign Language has specific characteristics that must be taken into account in order to understand the interpreting process and the efforts required to transmit the message by French-sign language interpreters. The syntax and vocabulary of Quebec Sign Language as well as the cultural differences between the Deaf and hearing communities directly influence the interpreting balance and can explain a number of errors on the part of interpreters.

But still, the sign language interpreting performance demands linguistic skills and an additional effort for spoken language interpreters. This concerns the need to have an active and unprompted knowledge of the written code and Viewing and Analysis Effort.

Currently, research on Quebec Sign Language is in the early stages. This article is only one of the possible exercises to compare and integrate this discipline into the broader field of interpreting in general. The author has so far only touched upon the specificities of sign language interpreting. The issue of proxemics, speech acts, intercultural mediation and interactionist perspectives are also points that must be examined. For now, I simply propose to conclude this article with a discussion of the options for sign language interpreters to reduce the difficulties with regard to the balance of efforts. We will see that Quebec Sign Language, which seemed up to now to be the source of our downfall, is also one of the keys to our salvation.

References

Dubuisson, Colette and Nadeau, Marie, eds., *Études sur la langue des signes québécoise*, Montréal, Presses de l'Université de Montréal, 1993, 226 p.

Gile, Daniel (A), "Le modèle d'efforts et l'équilibre d'interprétation en interprétation simultanée", *Méta*, vol. XXX, no. 1, 1985, pp. 44–48.

Gile, Daniel (B), "Les termes techniques en interprétation simultanée", *Méta*, vol. XXX, no. 3, 1985, pp. 199–210.

Gile, Daniel (C), "L'interprétation de conférence et la connaissance des langues: quelques reflexions", *Méta*, vol. XXX, no. 4, 1985, pp. 320–331.

The specificities of French-Quebec Sign Language interpreting

Second part: How to maintain the balance in interpreting

Danielle-Claude Bélanger

This article follows the presentation of Daniel Gile's Effort Model in the previous issue of *Le Lien*. Firstly, a summary of the factors that cause a fluctuation in the different efforts during the interpreting performance will be presented. Following on from this, the resources that French-Quebec Sign Language (*Langue des signes québécoise (LSQ)*, from now on LSQ) have at their disposal to facilitate the distribution of efforts and to preserve the balance during the interpreting performance will be identified. This article ends with a discussion of the impact of the Effort Model on the judgements about interpreting situations and on the attitudes adopted towards French-LSQ interpreters.

A.   Factors causing an imbalance

Daniel Gile[10] offered a new perspective on the conditions required to carry out the interpreting act by identifying the different types of efforts required for its achievement. We saw in the first part of this article that the interpreter must simultaneously deploy a variety of efforts to accomplish his or her task: the Listening and Analysis Effort, the Memory Effort and the Production Effort. In addition, sign language interpreters must on occasion employ a Viewing and Analysis Effort, which arises from the fact that LSQ is a visual-spatial modality.

Table 1 is a summary of the factors affecting the balance during the interpreting performance. An asterisk indicates those which are particularly significant for sign language interpreting. Note that all the factors impacting on the interpreting performance are not necessarily found in all situations. Added to this is the fact that other factors can intervene at certain moments. This includes physiological factors (fatigue, stress, etc.), which also

---

10.   The presentation of Daniel Gile's Effort Model of Interpreting was presented in detail in the previous issue of *Le Lien*. The three texts by Daniel Gile presented in the references served to explain his model.

influence the interpreter's performance because these modify the maximum level of energy available to accomplish the task.

B. Maintaining balance in interpreting

The question of balance in the interpreting performance is linked to the inescapable problem of time; more precisely, the lack of time. All balancing strategies considered must be justified by the time they save and the most efficient use.

However, all measures are not acceptable: one would not think about telling the client to read the conference poster to avoid interpreting the title of the session. The interpreter must balance ethics and pragmatics: respecting the clients and ensuring the integrity of service whilst at the same time adopting strategies to provide a full and faithful interpretation, despite the constraints that arise from the simultaneity of the process. It is at the juncture of these two imperatives that the interpreter must sometimes interrupt traffic because it is not about finding strategies to continue interpreting at all costs. It is about avoiding the situations that cause an imbalance whilst still providing an intelligible interpretation.

I propose to classify the balancing strategies in simultaneous interpreting into two groups. The first group concerns prevention strategies because these are anticipatory strategies employed in advance of the event. Those strategies implemented during the interpreting performance are considered to be preservation strategies.

1. Prevention strategies

Certain strategies may be deployed before the event to prevent imbalances during the interpreting performance. Automatic language operations and preparation belong in this category. This first case is a long-term measure which involves expanding the interpreter's knowledge in order that he or she can respond naturally and immediately during the interpreting performance. The second case involves employing a strategy occasionally in accordance with the anticipated nature and characteristics of the interpreting performance.

1.1   Automation of expression

The first prevention strategy consists of perfecting the working languages and in particular of *developing automation of expression in the target language.*[11] The acquisition of automation of expression reduces the Memory and Production Efforts. Certain points merit further attention when working from LSQ-French: classifiers, LSQ expressions, qualifiers

---

11.   Karla Dejean Le Féal, *L'enseignement des méthodes d'interprétation*, p. 89.

Table 1. Factors that increase difficulties in interpreting

Type of effort / Category	Listening and analysis effort	Memory effort	Production effort	*Viewing and analysis effort
Context	Auditory interferences Delivery Pronunciation Time lag	Time lag	Time lag Intraspecific feedback (self-correction)	*Visual interferences *Feedback from deaf clients
Speech	Gaps in knowledge of working languages Density of the message	Gaps in knowledge of working languages Technicality of the message	Density of the message	
Syntax		Syntactical differences between the languages (increases the time lag)		
Vocabulary	Interpreter's lack of active knowledge Proper nouns Numbers Lists Foreign words	Interpreter's lack of active knowledge *Proper nouns (spelling)	*Technical terms (spelling – paraphrases) *Proper nouns (spelling)	*Conventions of signing
Sociocultural Level	Impromptu interventions from the audience	*References to the news (reconstruct the event) Idiomatic expressions	*References to the news (paraphrases – explanations)	*Impromptu interventions from deaf clients

Note: The elements in this table were defined in the first part of this article, *Analysis of Efforts and Balance of Interpreting.*

Definition of the categories:

The contextual level includes extra- or para-linguistic information related to the communicational situation (conference, interview, etc.), to the physical environment or to specific characteristics related to the personality of the speakers, and even the interpreter.

The speech level includes general information about the message (style, level of language, logic of the argumentation, etc.). It relates more to the speech in its entirety or to general knowledge of the languages rather than grammatical peculiarities.

The syntactical level concerns the position of the constituents in the sentence, which is the specific order of the words in the working languages.

The lexical level corresponds to specific terms (proper nouns, technical terms, etc.). Note that lists have been classed in this category; they could also be found at the syntactical level. This choice can be explained by the fact that in the case of lists it is the words to be understood and memorised that are of interest, rather than the form that the sentence takes.

The sociocultural level includes linguistic or extra-linguistic information related to the specificities of cultural behaviours and references.

and adverbs. These elements are extremely rich on a semantic level and may even be combined with other signs in the case of classifiers, adjectives and adverbs. It follows that their interpretation takes the forms of a complete sentence, which cases an increased Production Effort. In other LSQ-French interpreting situations, simple and obvious qualifiers can leave the interpreter speechless due the great many options in the choice of French words. Added to this is the problem of the level of language. To interpret a sign indicating swollen cheeks, would you say large? Fat? Plump? Portly? Overweight? Chubby? Obese? It requires rapid analysis of the language level and of the situation in order to find the right word, neither insulting nor inappropriate. It is here that the Memory Effort is mobilised. A simple technique for acquiring automation of expression is to draw up then study bilingual lists of correspondents. For example, making lists, using specific words and considering the different levels of language can help to remember and reactivate the lexical possibilities available to the interpreter when describing LSQ adjectives in French. This means that when person appears, we would gamble on a nose being aquiline, pointed, an eagle's beak, a trumpet, flat, squashed, prominent, hooked, etc. In order to make this vocabulary immediately accessible to the memory it is important to enrich the vocabulary and consider using these words in everyday life to generate automations during the interpreting performance. Using lists of equivalents also clarifies our understanding of terms and expressions, and is especially true for LSQ expressions. Therefore, this is a long-term measure that is not driven by any particular one-off need. Automation of expression saves time during the analysis and transmission of the message, reduces the need for paraphrasing and accumulates different terms to express one single idea, so they impact on the Production Effort.

1.2 Preparation

The aim of preparatory work is to make the event predictable, to the extent that that is possible. It is about reducing the time lag between the speakers and the interpreter, who is not part of the reference group and who, in general, does not share the same behavioural and cognitive references. It is in this sense that preparation is a balancing strategy in simultaneous interpreting, even if it takes place before the event, because this preparatory work enables the interpreter to anticipate the events and the speech to follow during the interpretation. On this topic, Daniel Gile notes that "anticipation reduces the Listening and Analysis Effort without loss, and so more energy can be devoted to Production and Memory".[12]

To grasp the impact of a lack of preparation during an interpreting performance, imagine that you must do a jigsaw without having seen the image to complete. You would continually feel doubtful and apprehensive, you would tend to display excessive caution and you would prefer to draw on information immediately recognisable – the pieces of

---

12. Daniel Gile, 1985 a, p. 46.

the outline – hardly daring to manipulate the central pieces, which are the essence of the process. Transposed to an interpreting performance, it is easy imagine the repercussions of a lack of preparation, or the problem of not having the full picture of the situation in which you are to interpret.

With regard to the Listening Effort, a lack of preparation will cause difficulties in recognising the terms uttered.[13] For example, in a chemistry class you will need more time to recognise the expression *les ions,* which should not be confused with *lésion,* a much more usual term, which in our analogy represents an easily identifiable piece of the outline. In French-LSQ interpreting, doubt and apprehension caused by a lack of preparation will result in lost time: spelling out words more frequently, more redundant messages (for example, by continually adding the spelling of reference points in the space) and a hesitant attitude, which taints the value of the message and may lead to questions for clarification or requests for confirmation on the part of the deaf client.

It is not enough to have read the available texts for the event in order to prepare well. With regard to the Efforts Model, it requires preventative work at different levels. Firstly, it is imperative to ensure maximum overall energy by reducing the risk of interference, which will be possible by preparing psychologically and physically. Secondly, it is important to make sure that conditions are optimal for the effective use of the Listening, Memory and Production Efforts during the interpreting performance through good lexical and cognitive preparation (knowing the translation of terms but also understanding the network of concepts attached to it).

2.   Preservation strategies

Preservation strategies to safeguard the balance in the interpreting performance are deployed during the interpreting act. It is up to the interpreter to analyse the situation at all times and to choose one or several strategies that allow him or her to consciously act on the distribution of interpreting efforts. The key is to be aware of what is happening within us during the interpreting performance, which is no easy task.

Cognitive, communicational and linguistic resources allow us to implement different strategies that will impact on the Listening Effort, the Memory or Production Effort at different times.

2.1   Cognitive resources

The idea that it is important to have some awareness of the interpreting process in order to be able to balance the efforts was introduced. The capacity to accumulate and to retain information then to react later – the time lag – is a cognitive resource which allows this

---

13.   Karla Dejean Le Féal, p. 77.

analysis on a second level, the analysis of the (same) process of interpreting itself. It is important to maintain a distance from the pace set by the person speaking to be able to control the efforts during the interpreting performance. The time lag is not only used to take the necessary time to grasp the concepts and to choose an adequate formulation in the target language. It also allows the prospective analysis of the interpreting difficulties presented in the message, to review the status of the efforts at any given moment (Do I have enough of a delay behind the speaker? Is my message clear? etc.) and to choose the strategies that will counteract the possible errors.

The time lag is the starting point which allows the communicative and linguistic strategies to be used wisely. Paradoxically, it has the immediate effect of burdening all the effort categories, but it coincides with a moment of speech where the difficulties are still relatively easy to manage. Once the time lag is established, it is a *motus operendi*. Its favourable consequences for the interpreting performance become all the more apparent with the need to have a delay in which to choose the type of balancing strategies to utilise during the interpreting performance in accordance with the fluctuation of efforts. In addition, it is felt that this factor must be included in this section because its absence most often has disastrous effects on the interpreting performance: false starts, confusion over terms, poor prediction of the message, syntactical errors, etc. Therefore, its presence is crucial. Denis Cokely[14] confirms its importance in a comparative study of English-ASL interpreters with two, four and six second delays. The interpreters employing a delay of two seconds produced an encoding error in sign language in every 1.2 sentences and those employing a delay of four seconds produced one in every 4.3 sentences. In all cases, a delay of six seconds reduced the occurrence of errors by more than 50%. To give a concrete example, six seconds is the time elapsed from the first ring of the telephone until the second. The reflex to respond to the telephone immediately resembles that which leads the interpreter to begin from the first words spoken. Taking the time to look at the telephone and wait for the second ring before answering… you will see that the time elapsed is quite long. It is all the more long in simultaneous interpreting as this time lapse is not filled with silence!

2.2 Communicational resources

Communicational resources relate to the fact that simultaneous interpreting is an act anchored in a specific context at a specific moment, and the form of the exchange is determined by the environment. This means that the message to be interpreted does not really exist in itself, as an object independent of the situation. For example, in a class I interpreted the simple sentence *Does it bother you?* by signing *Does the overhead projector prevent you from seeing?* Given the circumstances, the interpretation was correct. Very often, the message is backed up and even specified by the elements in the context.

---

14. Daniel Cokely (1986) "The Effects of Lag Time on Interpreter Errors" Stokoe, pp. 341–375.

In the example above, I am part of the meaning by specifying the object of the message with the help of the elements in the situation. Yet it is possible, and sometimes desirable, to go do the opposite and to replace the specific words in French by the designation of the visual elements in the situation. However, this strategy is unsuitable for concepts to be studied in a learning situation. Daniel Gile notes that among interpreters of spoken languages there is a similar strategy, simplification, which consists of replacing an expression by a less precise but sufficiently clear word given the situation (for example the word *amplification* for *push-pull amplifier*).

He adds that "this tactic requires little time and little effort, but involves abandonment of a portion of the information. This abandonment may, however, not result in any loss to the listener, if the context or visual aids (slides, transparencies, diagram) are sufficiently precise".[15] In the case of French-LSQ interpreting, it is not simplification but indexing. The French term is interpreted by an LSQ term itself closely related (physically or semantically) and accompanied by pointing, which specifies the indicated object and the association with the message.

During the symposium on biculturalism and bilingualism which took place at the *Institut Raymond Dewar* last spring, we, the interpreters, used a sign resembling *list in two columns* to indicate the word *paradigm*. This choice was justified because throughout his full presentation on paradigms the speaker used transparencies – which had the title *Paradigms* and was found to be a list in two columns. In a linguistics course I used the expression *Green exercise book* (and pointed) to avoid having to repeat the very long spelling of *Catherine Kerbrat-Orrechioni,* the author of the articles in the exercise book. On another occasion, instead of repeating the names of the participants in a round-table, I signed them by using distinctive sign chosen according to a characteristic of the people: man with a beard, blonde woman, etc. Of course, this last strategy is not used during the presentation of the participants but only for the subsequent speech turns.

These examples demonstrate how visual indicators that are unique to the situation can be used in encoding a message in sign language and, in doing so, free up an enormous amount of time for Listening and Memory Efforts. This technique is much more justified when linked to the cultural phenomenon of names signed in LSQ. On this topic, Jules Desroisiers states that "[the] names [signed] are not only labels (…) they reflect the cultural values and **the models of social interaction**".[16]

2.3   Linguistic resources

Simultaneity and use of space are specific to sign languages. These are very important linguistic resources in maintaining the interpreting balance. These options permit the

---

15.   Daniel Gile, *Les termes techniques en interprétation simultanée,* p. 204.

16.   Dubuisson, Nadeau, ed., p. 172. (*emphasis added*).

message to be synthesised[17] when it is encoded and avoid redundancies, therefore freeing up the Production Effort at the expense of the Listening and Memory Efforts. Yet it could be said that it is about using sign language effectively, that the working languages must be mastered: one could respond that these are not specific strategies. However, the expression of the message by the interpreter is the result of a series of personal choices, from the choice of words to the construction of sentences. A sentence such as *Success is not achieved without effort* could very well be interpreted as follows: *without effort there is failure* or *with effort there is success* or even *success how? effort, effort...* The choices in the expression of a message are, to a certain extent, associated with the interpreting strategies of the interpreter. Some of these strategies are more beneficial to the balance of efforts. This concerns the option to use role-plays and topicalisation of space. These will be presented briefly.

a. Role-play

I am of the opinion that in an interpreting situation, the interpreter can choose to use role-play to transmit the message even when this mode of expression is absent in the source language. For example, in the sentence: "He told me to go away and I responded that I would stay" can be expressed very well by a role play, without distorting the intentions of the person who is speaking, even if direct speech has not been chosen (he told me: "go away", etc.). Yet this choice saves an enormous amount of time during the encoding of the message and also decreases the production effort. In this example, if the speakers have been specified beforehand, it will suffice to use two signs accompanied by two referential movements of the body to express the whole sentence.

Role-play has different functions: the relation between speech, thoughts, actions, experiences and states.[18] Its use frees up the Memory and Production Efforts because, while descriptions in French are linear, role-play can indicate the subject, actions and states at the same time. It has the effect of synthesising the encoding of the message in sign language without loss of information. Like role- play, classifiers are an excellent means of synthesising the encoding of the message in LSQ; however, some are difficult to master during the interpreting performance because they require lots of creativity at a time when our cognitive resources are already heavily burdened. In these situations, it is important to be able to employ automation of expression, and to integrate these factors into our natural expression in LSQ.

---

17. Note that the term *synthesise* is never used in the sense of *summarise*. It concerns to possibility of rendering simultaneously a variety of information.

18. Christiane Poulin, *La réalisation de la référence en langue des signes québécoise: une question de point de vue,* p. 53.

b.   Topicalisation of space

Included in this section are all the procedures unique to LSQ which consist of associating a reference to a given place, whether this is placed on our body (like in a list)[19] or in the surrounding space. In French-LSQ interpreting, the advantage of these methods resides in the fact that they decrease redundancies and repetition of spellings considerably. Also, in the case of a list where three people have been named – let us say Catherine, Lucie and Francine – each digit will be attributed to a particular person. Thereafter, these names will no longer have to be spelled out: it will suffice to point that finger at the corresponding person.

The topicalisation of space allows the efficient use of verbs that can be inflected (to look, to give, to order, to sit down, etc.), which, once again, allows information to be synthesised: subject, verb and complement. The topicalised use of space is not only an economising factor but also one of clarity of message. However, this factor increases the Memory Effort because it becomes necessary to retain the designated placement for each of the referents.

Summary

Below is a table summarising the resources available to reduce the Listening and Analysis Efforts, the Memory Effort and the Production Effort. The effects of decreasing (↓) or increasing (↑) the corresponding efforts are indicated for each type of strategy.

The use of this table is particularly interesting when compared with that of the difficulties during the interpreting performance – Table 1. It is possible and quick to research the strategies that can counter the encountered obstacles in the majority of situations.

These tables can therefore be useful for preparing for an interpreting performance: you research lots of technical terms in your preparatory documents knowing that these elements have the effect of increasing the Production Effort (Table of difficulties), and you will also know that this effect can be counteracted by strategies linked to communicational and linguistic resources (Table of strategies).

These tables are also tools for retrospective analysis: while the interpreter felt overwhelmed because of a large number of proper nouns, knowing that these factors would increase the Listening and Memory Efforts (Table of difficulties), he or she also knew that the prevention strategies could have helped (table of strategies). Obviously, the use of these tables only gives a pointer, avenues for investigation. It comes down to the interpreter to take things into account given the situation as actually experienced. For example, in the case of proper nouns, communicational strategies can also be effective depending on the

---

19.   For more on lists, see the tape produced by the LSQ research group, *Ébauche d'une description de la LSQ series*, "L'énumération".

situation. It remains less that these tools surpass the confusing and inaccurate feelings about having interpreted well or badly.

Strategies	Efforts	Listening effort	Memory effort	Production effort
Prevention Strategies Automation of expressions			↓	↓
Preparation		↓	↓	
Cognitive resources		↑	↑	↑
Preservation Strategies Communicational resources				↓
Linguistic resources			↑	↓

To conclude, it must be said that all the considerations with regard to the most effective strategies in a particular situation do not suppose in any way that these are the only relevant factors. It is important to remember that this is a movement that fluctuates between the different efforts continually sought. Even with the best preparation, the interpreter will never be removed from the present moment to be able to allow him or her to be aware of what is required to succeed in interpreting well!

Conclusion

Daniel Gile's Effort Model of Interpreting is an excellent tool for understanding the complexity of our task. It is possible to identify the most suitable interpreting strategies to avoid errors using this model. The model also reveals the difficulties that are experienced by interpreters but difficult to express in an intuitive way. This now leads to us conclude with a reflection on the vision and attitudes that our clients and the people with whom we engage often have when faced with sign language interpreting.

It is important to be aware that the difficulties of interpreting are not necessarily correlated with the difficulties anticipated in interpersonal communication. In a fluent conversation between speakers of the same language, specialised terms can sooner or later create an obstacle to mutual comprehension and cause a communication failure, which is not the case for lists of common words. Yet for the interpreter, both demand specific efforts and can trigger imbalances and errors during the interpreting performance.

We can with difficulty, even rarely, determine in advance the difficulty of an interpreting situation. How do we know if a particular situation will be difficult to interpret? The technicality of the message is only one of the factors to consider. Too many factors are unpredictable. The delivery, accent, effects of style, language levels, etc. are as much factors that depend in a large part on the personal use that a person makes of their language, outside of any consideration about the topic of the presentation.

Demystifying sign language interpreting involves identifying the real task of the interpreter. Yet we are often in contact with people who plainly do not grasp the difficulties of our task because, from the outside, they only see what they themselves know how to do very well: listen and speak. Hearing clients are often under the impression that it is enough to master some signs to be able to offer the services of an interpreter. This apparent simplicity leads certain people to evaluate our requests (preparatory materials, breaks, group work…) with an attitude that verges on indifference.

To do our job, collaboration with speakers, organisers and participants is essential. Too often we do not receive the preparatory texts, not even summary plans. Too often, Deaf people think that we want to steal their ideas and avoid giving us their texts. Too often, those in charge of interpreting agencies and services neglect to ask for all the information and are happy to reassure us: you are capable. Too often interpreters themselves do not hold their ground and insist. They end up thinking: too bad for them! But it is their deception because, at the end of the day, it is on these skills that the interpreter will be judged. Danica Seleskovitch[20] said "I do not want to know how may lawyer, my dentist, my plumber does his job, I want them to fix my problem, that is all". This position, for the least radical, does not take into account the fact that we depend on the collaboration of the participants to succeed in satisfying their needs. Between the interpreters occupied with the "technical" difficulties inherent in the interpreting process and the speakers reconciling their modes of communication, respect still seems the best attitude.

References

Cokely, Denis (1986). "The Effects of Lag Time on Interpreter Errors", Stokoe, William, ed., *Sign Language Studies,* no. 53, Lanstok Press Inc., pp. 341–375.

Dejean Le Féal, Karla, "L'enseignement des méthodes d'interprétation" in Delisle, Jean, ed. (1981). *L'enseignement de l'interprétation et de la traduction,* Ottawa: Éditions de l'Université d'Ottawa, 294 p, pp. 75–98.

Dubuisson, Colette, Nadeau, Marie, eds., *Études sur le langue des signes québécoise,* Montréal, Presses de l'Université de Montréal, 1993, 226 p.

---

20.   Danica Seleskovitch, *Fundamentals of The Interpretive Theory of Translation,* Waubonsee Community College, videotape.

Gile, Daniel (1985 A) "Le modèle d'efforts et l'équilibre d'interprétation en interprétation simultanée", *Méta,* vol. XXX, no.1, pp. 44–48.

Gile, Daniel (1985 B), "Les termes techniques en interprétation simultanée", *Méta,* vol. XXX, no. 3, pp. 199–210.

Gile, Daniel (1985 C), "L'interprétation de conférence et la connaissance des langues: quelques réflexions", *Méta,* vol. XXX, no. 4, pp. 320–331.

Poulin, Christine (1992). *La réalisation de la référence en langue des signes québécoise: une question de point de vue,* Mémoire de maîtrise, UQAM, 108 p.

Videotapes

Pinsonneault, Dominique (1992). "L'énumération", *Ébauche d'une description de la LSQ* series, VHS videotape, Montréal, LSQ research group, UQAM.

SELESKOVITCH, Danica (1992). "Fundamentals of the Interpretive Theory of Translation", Waubonsee Community College, Video-class, 1h30.

4.4 Turner, Graham. H. 1995. "The bilingual, bimodal courtroom: A first glance." *Journal of Interpretation* 7(1): 3–34.

Graham H. Turner came to the field of sign language interpreting studies from a linguistics (and particularly applied linguistics) background. He began his career working with deaf people as a research assistant at the Deaf Studies Research Unit at the University of Durham, U.K. in 1988. During his time at Durham he worked on the BSL Dictionary project and the Access to Justice for Deaf people project. In 1995 he took up a post with the Deaf Studies team at the University of Central Lancashire, where he taught in Deaf Studies courses, managed various research projects related to sign language, Deaf culture and sign language interpreting, and established the Postgraduate Diploma in BSL/English Interpreting. In 2005 he became Professor and Director of the Centre for Translation and Interpreting Studies in the Department of Languages and Intercultural Studies at Heriot-Watt University in Edinburgh. He served as Director of Research in the School of Management and Languages from 2009 to 2013.

Turner has been an invited speaker at many interpreting and sign language interpreting-specific conferences, and his publications include peer-reviewed journal articles and book chapters on a range of applied linguistics and interpreting studies related topics such as the role and ethics of interpreters, research methods, Deaf people and interpreting in performance, medical and political spheres, and sign language policy and heritage.

The bilingual, bimodal courtroom

A first glance

Graham H. Turner*

Introduction

In this initial exploratory paper, I aim to take a closer look at features of interaction between signing and speaking people mediated by a BSL/English interpreter. The spotlight will be on interaction in an area that many interpreters refuse to touch because of its inherent complexity, i.e. the courtroom. The paper can be seen, rather than as a detailed analysis of the scenario in question, as initial broad-brushed background material identifying certain issues to be considered in the course of more detailed analysis.

In the longer term, such study should not only provide valuable information to feed back into training and awareness programmes, but also offer insights into what goes on in the course of bilingual, bimodal (that is, signed and spoken) talk-in-interaction. To borrow a phrase from Deborah Cameron's keynote paper (Cameron 1994) to the British Association for Applied Linguistics conference, it's a case of "putting practice into theory": analysing practices as a potentially fruitful way of grounding and developing theory.

The tension that is felt within applied linguistic circles between 'doing theories' and 'doing practices' comes into very sharp focus throughout sign linguistics, and it is always worth trying to keep in mind what language researchers are aiming to achieve in this context. In keeping with the valuable critique of research practices that is set out in Cameron et al. (1992), an 'empowering' approach to this study has been adopted wherever possible. The study is, for instance, informed to a considerable degree by practitioners' own beliefs about their interpreting practices.[21]

---

* Graham H. Turner is currently a Research Fellow at the Deaf Studies Research Unit in the Department of Sociology and Social Policy, University of Durham. He is a member of the team which compiled the first Dictionary of British Sign Language/English for the British Deaf Association.

21.   Under the direction of Dr. Mary Brennan and Professor Richard Brown, the author is currently engaged in such a programme of research. Entitled Access to Justice for Deaf People in the Bilingual, Bimodal Courtroom, the programme is supported by the Leverhulme Trust.

Patsy Lightbown's opening plenary at the recent American Association for Applied Linguistics annual meeting (Lightbown 1994) counseled that we must (a) continue to admit what we do not know and (b) refrain from making premature pronouncements. Sign linguistics is a young field, but the applied issues are – after many decades of oppression of signed languages – urgently in need of attention. As a consequence, we frequently find ourselves torn between two goals. On the one hand, as scientists, we want to assert our right (and indeed our duty) to be ignorant and naive and to explore questions to which we do not yet know the answers. On the other – knowing the positive effect linguists' work can have in terms of empowering signing communities – we want to fulfil our role as agents for change by the application of what little we know. Within the sign linguistics field, this position, and the stance of engagement-beyond-the-theoretical which this paper implicitly adopts, has been most clearly articulated by Mary Brennan (1986: 14–16).

Firstly, then, I shall try to put my remarks into some kind of context, and then go on to indicate some dimensions or themes that seem worthy of attention.

Context

Why is the courtroom a particularly important area to study in the UK? After all, article six of the European Convention on Human Rights already includes the instruction that criminal suspects have the right to be informed in a language which they understand about any accusation made against them, and also to have free assistance of an interpreter in court. A December 1993 judgement of the European Court of Human Rights – the Kamasinski case of a US citizen imprisoned in Austria – also stressed that the institution responsible for providing the interpreter is subsequently responsible for the standard and competence of the actual service (Polack & Corsellis 1990).

Is there any reason to be concerned about that standard? The general legal interpreting field in the UK has come under some scrutiny lately – notably through the work of the Nuffield Interpreter Project (Nuffield Interpreter Project 1993) – and a number of cases have been quite well publicised. In 1981, for example, a woman who had come from rural Pakistan to an arranged marriage in Birmingham, England went to prison having killed her husband with an iron bar. She pleaded guilty and served four years of a life sentence before the Court of Appeal acknowledged that the interpreter – an accountant – had spoken to her in Urdu, while her preferred language was in fact Punjabi and she spoke very little Urdu. She probably grasped virtually nothing of what was going on, and certainly not the distinction between murder and manslaughter crucial to her life sentence (Parker 1993).

In a case involving BSL-English interpreting some years ago, a Deaf man was expected to stand trial for rape with interpretation provided by the holder of a Stage 1 certificate in BSL skills – a language skills certificate, not an interpreting qualification. It is required by the regulatory body (the Council for the Advancement of Communication with Deaf People) that a Stage 1 course involve 60 hours of teaching (CACDP no date:2). The exam takes approximately 15 minutes. In fact, the situation with respect to BSL-English interpreting is in many respects markedly better than for most linguistic minorities in the UK (Nuffield Interpreter Project 1993). There are official registers of signing interpreters, and police forces keep their own lists for police station work.

One source of pressure that impacts upon this type of situation is from the interpreters themselves, who are struggling towards notions of increased professionalisation (see Scott Gibson 1990, 1994). "Call me mercenary," wrote then-trainee interpreter Mohammad Islam in a recent issue of the Association for Sign Language Interpreters magazine (Islam, 1993: 31):

> "but I am not getting up at two in the morning, driving for an hour to the police station, working for two hours, spending another hour driving home – all for £26. Would you?"

An impossible situation?

One conclusion that might be drawn from all this is that there is a fundamental problem in a judicial process that requires interpreting. The system is full of holes which can add spin in any direction. In fact, there are those – such as the Canadian Freedom of Choice Movement – who have concluded (Berk-Seligson, 1990: 215) that the presence of an interpreter is actively prejudicial to the interests of the minority-language-using defendant. The group has argued that the defendant has a right to a trial conducted entirely in his or her preferred language. The Supreme Court of Canada has disagreed.

If interpreters must be used, then perhaps it is most advantageous to consider this a tactical strategy, just another part of the legal 'contest'. This kind of perspective has been quite convincingly articulated by the Australian Kathy Laster (1990: 17):

> "The law, while formally assigning only a narrow role to interpreters, in practice makes ambiguous and contradictory demands of them. As a result, non-English speakers are not necessarily always better off when an interpreter is used. The issue whether to use an interpreter in individual cases therefore is best conceived of as a tactical one rather than as an abstract question of 'rights'. The advantage of this approach is that it focuses attention on the aspects of the legal system itself which militate against social justice for non-English speakers rather than allowing interpreters to be regarded as 'the problem' requiring 'reform'."

This proposal clearly requires greater attention, since the implications are considerable. As Ruth Morris concludes from her case study of the Ivan Demjanjuk trial, it seems minimally to be the case that interpretation of legal proceedings has "a persona of its own" (1989a: 36).

Perceptions

What are the sources of the problems in legal interpreting? It seems that one set of problems derives from various participants' perceptions of norms and practices relating to this setting.

There are general perceptions to do with Deaf people[22] and signed languages that are as likely to be held by legal professionals as by other members of the public. Deaf communities all over the world are still struggling to escape the oppressive weight of pathological or medical models of what it means to be Deaf, in favour of cultural and linguistic models (see Lane 1992; Padden & Humphries 1988). Non-Deaf participants in the court are as likely as non-Deaf people in any other walk of life to expect someone else to be speaking 'on behalf of the Deaf person – the 'does he take sugar?' syndrome. This can result in a great deal of confusion over the role of the interpreter. Many people doubt the interpreter's impartiality, or indeed assume partiality. The result (as reported by a number of practitioners) is that interpreters are frequently instructed by the court to 'just relay everything verbatim'. Such an instruction serves only to underline (a) the court's lack of awareness of, or trust in, interpreting procedures, and (b) a lack of appreciation of what must occur in the very nature of the process of interpreting.

The visual-gestural nature of BSL also raises problems of perception of at least three kinds. Firstly, many other participants in the process may have the sneaking feeling that they understand, perhaps quite clearly, what's being signed. Lochrie (no date:5) gives an example from a situation involving a late colleague of his:

> "The Advocate asked the deaf witness … 'Are you single?', the interpreter changed the question to 'Are you married?' which signs easier. The witness shook his head vigorously. The interpreter speaks and says 'Yes, I am single'. The Advocate is nonplussed and says 'But the witness shook his head'. The interpreter then explained that the words are you single would not be easy for the witness to understand, so I asked him 'Are you married?'. The Judge, while understanding the situation, cautioned the interpreter."

Secondly, there is an issue of awareness concerning perceptions of the adequacy of court records. Court records – and records in police stations, where audio recording is standard practice – are kept as written English text, with no further checks and balances built into the system for being assured of interpreting accuracy. BSL does not have a conventional

---

22.   It must be clearly stated that this study could not have come together without the co-operation of organisations in the field, including the Association of Sign Language Interpreters (ASLI), the Scottish Association of Sign Language Interpreters (SASLI), the Council for the Advancement of Communication with Deaf People (CACDP), the British Deaf Association (BDA) and the Royal Association in aid of Deaf People (RAD). Individual correspondents, and persons named in examples of court interaction, are not identified for reasons of confidentially.

writing system comparable to that for English.[23] Keeping a written record of the signing itself would be impracticable under current constraints.

Thirdly, it is widely believed that signed languages are modelled on and run structurally parallel to the spoken languages with which they co-exist (though attempts have been made to create artificial systems organised along these lines, or to adapt natural signed languages to accommodate spoken/written linguistic structural principles – see Anthony 1971; Bergman 1979; Bornstein et al. 1975; Gustason et al. 1975). It is therefore widely, and entirely erroneously, believed that the interpreter's job is therefore a simple matter of adjusting the modality from speech to sign and back.

BSL-English interpreters are no different from any others in many respects, though, such as the outsider's perception that then-task is a straightforward matter of input and output, a simple 'conduit' task. Many lawyers, judges and other legal professionals indicate (Butler & Noaks 1992) that they are not in the least concerned with the need for competent interpretation, assuming instead that interpretation is an entirely mechanical task requiring negligible analytical skills. That lack of concern is itself part of the problem, because (a) it means that any time the interpreter becomes obtrusive for any reason, that will automatically be viewed as something going wrong; and (b) because it is indicative of the fact that, as long as the interpreter is producing something that looks and especially sounds plausible, there is nothing to worry about. I shall come back to this point.

What about the interpreter's own perception of his/her role? Here, too, there is potential for conflict. It is not unusual for the interpreter to be expected to be, and thus to get drawn into being, an agent of the court. One result of this is the interpreter finding him/herself taking on the interactional patterns of the court instead of merely facilitating their flow. Susan Berk-Seligson (1990: 62) provides a clear example of this in the Spanish-English courtroom in the USA. A long exchange is reproduced in which the judge and attorney are trying to get the defendant to state her plea, guilty or not guilty. The defendant keeps answering 'yes' (meaning 'guilty'). Finally, the attorney tells the interpreter "So she's gotta say it, tell her to say it", and the interpreter takes on an instructing role, herself saying (in Spanish), "That is, you have to say it. Say it! What are you?" Anecdotal reports tell us that such exchanges are not uncommon in the BSL-English courtroom.

Conversely, consider this (Nusser, 1993: 4), especially point three:

> "The facts are clear: (1) Though Americans believe that all people should be treated equally, hearing people have more power (i.e. employment and educational opportunities, role models, language recognition, status, etc). (2) In a mixed group of individuals, such as in an interpreting assignment or professional conference, relational power dynamics also exist because of differing values and stereotypes. (3) Hearing interpreters must try as much as possible to act as allies among members of a linguistic and cultural minority."

---

23. The capital 'D' here is adopted – following a convention proposed by James Woodward (1972) and developed by Carol Padden (1980) – to refer to members of the sign language using cultural minority group.

It is absolutely true that BSL-English interpreters are trained to know about Deaf people's lives and Deaf community and cultural issues. Models of interpreting are changing
(McIntire & Sanderson in press; Roy 1993a; Witter-Merithew 1986). But I think one can
clearly see where this statement might be perceived to lead – in respect of its effect on the
neutrality, or otherwise, of the interpretation – if followed through in a courtroom situation. Other professionals in the courtroom can feel threatened by interaction taking place
in a language which they do not understand. 'Interpreter as ally' is a position which must
be treated, especially in public fora, with the greatest of care, and will doubtless be a point
of considerable debate in the near future.

And the interpreter also knows that it is part and parcel of his/her role to be a cultural broker or mediator, smoothing over gaps in cultural knowledge. Learning to do
that effectively is part of the training. But again there seem to be lines to be drawn. The
point is very well made by Jon Leeth, one of Berk-Seligson's interviewees (Berk-Seligson,
1990: 40), who said:

> "The Court Interpreter's Act is not designed as an intercultural tool to integrate people
> into American society. It is an Act designed to bring justice to these individuals just as
> if they were English speaking. It is not designed to give them an advantage…only to
> prevent miscarriages of justice. They have the same responsibilities as anybody else…
> to say 'I don't know what you're talking about. Could you make that clear?'"

One BSL-English interpreter I interviewed recently made a similar point. This person said:

> "I interpreted a case once where the judge and the clerk went into a heated exchange
> on some technical detail. As I tried to convey something of it to the Deaf defendant,
> his counsel said to me, 'Don't bother! It's too technical. He won't understand it'. To
> which I replied, 'That's okay: he has a right not to understand.'"

Some features of court talk

If there are problems for interpreters of a linguistic nature, where are they? There is – as
there has long been in the wider sphere (e.g. Crystal & Davy 1969) – a strong feeling that
the particular vocabulary used in the courtrooms is the real problem (Caccamise et al.
1991; in the UK, the point is also implicit in the recent Royal Commission's recommendation (HMSO 1993) that glossaries of technical terms be developed for minority languages).
And even those whose first language is English would acknowledge that the specialised
and somewhat arcane formal language of the court can, in itself, cause major problems of
comprehension.

Powerless speech

The lexical problems are certainly an issue, but there are others, more disturbing for the
fact that they are not widely appreciated. A whole host of issues are raised in connection

with work done by William O'Barr and associates (O'Barr 1982), demonstrating that the features of what has been dubbed 'powerless speech' can play a significant role in court-rooms. Bear in mind that, in court, participants seek to appear honest, trustworthy, and so on, and that judges and juries use these impressions in framing their decisions. Powerless speech is associated – in the court setting – with weakness, indecision and evasiveness.

These features include, for example, the group of items known as hedges – 'kind of', 'sort of', 'I guess', 'you know' – which sound non-committal, cautious, hesitant, uncertain or indecisive. Observation confirms that they are sometimes introduced into the simulta-neous, unscripted language produced as BSL-to-English interpretation. Other features of powerless speech can also be heard being introduced as a kind of by-product of the inter-preting circumstances.

These points are addressed with respect to the work of interpreters in considerable detail by Susan Berk-Seligson (1990: 148ff). It is beyond the scope of the present paper to draw detailed parallels between Berk-Seligson's findings, relating to Spanish/English inter-pretation, and the situations under scrutiny here. One can, however, begin to see that one not unlikely effect of the interpreter's intervention between the overt conversational partic-ipants is that the contributions of the signing person are rendered more or less 'powerful' than the original texts. In other words, the impact of testimony given by a Deaf person in court can be altered for better or worse in the interpreted rendition. No analysis of 'power-less signing' has ever been done to date, and so it is impossible to say whether the reverse effect is also occurring.

Progress of discourse

The progress of the discourse is an additional matter for attention. O'Barr (1982: 76–83) compares 'narrative style' as a discourse pattern in court – i.e. longer, more elaborately con-structed sections of talk – against 'fragmented style', whereby the discourse is broken up into shorter turns, for instance in rapid question-and-answer exchanges. 'Narrative style' has the appearance of being credible and confident, and is encouraged by lawyers asking open-ended questions to their own witnesses: 'fragmented style' is almost inevitably the result of tightly constrained, quick-fire questioning. Thus, as Berk-Seligson makes abun-dantly clear (1990: 178), if interpretation renders the message more or less fragmented than the original utterance, it has altered the effect of what was signed or said. Such alterations, though their effects may not be immediately apparent, are unlikely to be inconsequential, particularly when they accumulate throughout the duration of a section of testimony.

Of course, question-and-answer as a mode of exchange is very typical of courtroom interaction, and so it matters greatly that interpreters are aware and in control of the effect of how they present questions (cf. Eades 1988, 1992 for discussion of cultural differences in patterns of questioning and their effect on the non-interpreted courtroom). Brenda Danet (Danet 1980) has shown that questions vary in the extent to which they coerce or constrain the answer.

– "You left the pub at midnight….", a declarative that does not ostensibly even ask a question, but leaves the witness to challenge if he/she wishes, is maximally constraining.
– "Did you do it?" or "Did you leave at 7pm or 8pm?" – any kind of question that gives a limited number of choices is still clearly constraining: it is very difficult, for instance, to challenge the premiss upon which a question is founded when all the court is interested in is 'just answer the question: yes or no?'.
– "Where were you on the night of the twelfth?" – WH-questions like this are much more open, giving the respondent more scope to tell things their own way.
– "Can you tell the court what happened?" – this kind of 'requestion' is typically used by lawyers to let their own witnesses tell the story comfortably, in their own words.

Danet shows that the more coercive the question, the greater the tendency for short, fragmented, powerless answers. Clearly, then, the interpreter's control of exactly how these questions can be interpreted is crucial.

Linguistic manipulation

The adversarial contest that the court engages in is also characterised by a degree of linguistic manipulation to control testimony. I will briefly mention two classic examples. The first shows that a skilled questioner can introduce presuppositions that constrain witnesses' answers – and which the interpreter must somehow faithfully maintain. In an experimental study, in which subjects were first shown a short film as evidence, Loftus and Zanni famously showed that the query "Did you see the broken headlight?" produced affirmative responses more frequently than "Did you see a broken headlight?" (Loftus & Zanni 1975). The second example (Loftus & Palmer 1974) showed that asking "About how fast were the two cars going when they smashed into each other?" produces higher speeds in answers than "About how fast were the two cars going when they hit each other?" These examples seem quite clearly to demonstrate the degree of absolute harmony the interpreter must achieve between source message and interpretation in order to be truly unobtrusive or non-distorting in the courtroom.

Linguistic image

I would like to mention one additional issue to do with linguistic image, i.e. the impression one gives simply through one's own vocal presentation. Matched guise testing – in which listeners are asked to rate various voice styles, without realising that they are actually hearing the same person using different 'guises' – has shown admirably that dynamic delivery, fast speech rate, lack of pauses and repetitions and 'normal', steady voice quality are all associated by hearers of English with notions of competence, trustworthiness and likeability(Berk-Seligson, 1990:147). Simultaneous interpretation is not the best place in the world to look for examples of such vocal presentation: it is in the nature of the task – given the cognitive processing being done incessantly by the interpreter, for instance – that these qualities are going to be difficult to achieve.

Linguistic image also comes into play here in connection with our lack of knowledge about how different varieties of BSL are viewed and perceived by other users of the language. Are there signed accents associated with, for instance, boredom and lack of inspiration just as there are amongst spoken varieties? We do not know. On the other hand, we do know from accounts of hearers' attitudes to accents of English (see, for instance, Giles 1970, 1971) that the interpreter who happens to have a strong West Midlands accent may be giving out a potentially misleading and damaging impression of the Deaf person whose comments they are giving voice to.

Issues in 'Deaf Courts'

In the following section, I will briefly identify some issues directly related to bimodal interpreting in legal settings. I use the term 'Deaf court' as a shorthand for 'court in which a Deaf person and an interpreter are active participants'.

Eyegaze

As Diana Eades has found in her very illuminating work in courts with speakers of Australian Aboriginal English (Eades 1988, 1992), averting your eyegaze from the court looks evasive. But it is in the nature of signed languages that Deaf people will do so. They will, for instance, be looking at the interpreter when the cross-examining barrister wants to look them in the eye at the point of the crucial question.

And it is in the nature of signed languages that Deaf people will, as far as the court is concerned, lose their eyegaze almost at random into the middle distance if they are ever given an opportunity to launch into any kind of complex narrative answer (the effect of role shifting and use of eyegaze to locate referents, et cetera).

Exchange norms

Anecdotal accounts from Deaf people suggest that question-and-answer is not a typical form of exchange within the Deaf community, and that longer, more narrative contributions are more common. The constraints of a courtroom system managed in such a manner may serve to disadvantage BSL users (cf. Eades 1988, 1992).

Secondly, because there will usually be one interpreter relaying messages in both directions during any one exchange, at any point where there is overlapping talk (i.e. two or more signed or spoken utterances being made simultaneously), the interpreter is forced to decide whose talk to represent (Roy 1993b). Because there may be two modalities being used at once by two participants, it is perfectly possible for speakers and

signers to overlap each other for seconds at a time with no-one feeling uncomfortable –
except the interpreter!

Slow Interaction

There will always tend to be a moment between the end of the Deaf person's signed answer,
and the start of the next spoken question during which only the interpreter talks. Since
the interpreter's presence will introduce a time lag, it will be difficult to aggressively cross-
examine the Deaf witness. Of course, no one is supposed to harrass the witness anyway,
but attempts are nevertheless made to do so, and the interpreter's presence introduces a
discrepancy between what happens otherwise and what happens in a Deaf court.

As Emmanuel Schegloff (Schegloff 1994), Adam Jaworski (Jaworski 1993) and others
have been showing recently, silence plays no small part in everyday spoken interaction,
and reactions occurring or not occurring (i.e. silences) at any point in the interaction are
a significant element, contributing to the patterns of discourse. In response to a comment
about how late one is for work (made in the hope that an offer of a lift might be forthcoming), for instance, a silence can be extremely eloquent. In a 'Deaf court', there are both
unusual silences in the lagtime where the Deaf person signs and the interpreter has not
yet begun to voice over; and there are 'delayed reactions' by both parties to each other's
contributions (i.e. the reaction time is conditioned by the lagtime).

Politeness

Firstly, if, as Berk-Seligson demonstrates (Berk-Seligson, 1990: 154–169), politeness is a
favourable strategy in court, then interpreters need to know a great deal more than is presently known (precious little) about politeness marking in BSL. Signed languages tend not
to have direct person-to-person forms of address. Interaction typically does not begin until
eyegaze is established: once it has been established, identifying the addressee by name is
superfluous. So when the court is addressing the judge as 'Your Honour', what is the interpreter to do?

Secondly, one aspect of the impersonal nature of much legal interaction is the use of the
full names of witnesses and other individuals named in testimony. In a recently observed
trial, the interpreter reduced these forms to first name terms. "Did you see Arthur Jones
enter the premises?" became "Did you see Arthur enter the premises?" The testimony has
been altered, and native-user intuitions at least suggest that the latter utterance is considerably less formal and forbidding. Does this constitute cultural bridging – on the basis that
Deaf people would not use full names – or a subtle but significant adjustment in the court
procedures? Certainly this is a question of a type worthy of further attention.

Thirdly, I would like to mention here another phenomenon noted by Diana Eades
(1992: 8–10) that she refers to as 'gratuitous concurrence' – i.e. answering 'yes' or 'no' to

questions without understanding them, just in order to get the business over with. This practice is encapsulated in a BSL sign which might be glossed as nod indiscriminately. This sign relates to a practice widely commented on in Deaf-hearing relations – pretense of understanding of, or wilful disregard for, a message conveyed incomprehensibly, typically due to poor signing skills on the part of a hearing person attempting to communicate with Deaf people – and it seems very likely that it occurs in court as elsewhere.

Anticipating questions

It is appropriate in BSL interaction to use headshake and nod in anticipation of certain answers when asking questions: but the interpreter who does this without great care will be leaning into or presuggesting the expected answer. Other questions can become problematic due to the unaddressed assumption, even among interpreters, of word-to-word equivalence between BSL and English. Translating the English question "How did you feel about that?", in a sentence using the sign commonly glossed as how, to many BSL users actually means "By what process did you feel about that?"

Indirect questions

It is commonly reported by BSL-English interpreters that when they interpret English indirect questions – "They asked who was in the shop, and you explained, is that correct?" – into BSL, they are treated by default as if they were in fact direct questions of some sort. This can cause all sorts of problems in question-and-answer exchange: the response "Sally was in the shop: I've already told you this!" would be the kind of response an interpreter often finds him/herself giving voice to in such a situation.

Visual encoding

Many people manage, surprisingly frequently, to overlook the fact that signed languages encode meaning visually. Of course, fingerspelling exists, and many Deaf people are quite happy to see interpreters using fingerspelling when no conventional BSL sign is available to them (Sutton-Spence & Woll 1990, 1993). Many other Deaf people, however, are not sufficiently fluent in English to access meaning via fingerspelling in this way.

And BSL is fundamentally a visual language, a point that is made most clearly and followed through most profoundly by Mary Brennan (Brennan 1992). The result of this is that, for instance, in a recent murder trial, the interpreter needed to know how the murder was perpetrated – it was a stabbing – and to render the English word 'murder' with the sign that might be glossed as stab.

BSL is a language that tends not to use umbrella terms like 'vehicle', 'weapon' or 'assault'. Any weapon one could mention in BSL has a lexical form that is consonant with its visual image: any form of assault likewise, and so on. It is impossible to give coherent visual form to the concept of 'weapon' as a category.

BSL is also a spatial language. So if English says "the two cars crashed", the form taken by the signed interpretation will be influenced by the spatial layout – whether the cars crashed head-on, side-on, et cetera. Interpreters are trained to become adept at using the spatial domain – as native signers do – to establish points of reference and to maintain these points throughout a chunk of discourse. In fact, of course, the interpreter, in attempting to process at incredible speed the information coming across to him/her will make what he/she hears or sees fit to his/her mental model of the scenario. This can cause problems. Observation of an interpreted trial dealing with a violent attack revealed a situation in which it was not until the third day of the trial that the interpreter realised they had consistently reversed the positions of the defendant and the victim. In this instance, it did not become significant, but one day it may.

It is a common strategy among interpreters to solve the problem of visual ambiguity in the English wording (which cannot be sustained in BSL) by offering a series of alternatives. So the interpretation of the English question "How did you get into the factory grounds?" might take the signed form more literally equivalent to "Did you get into the factory grounds by climbing over the wall, through a window, breaking in the door, or what?" The question (specifically in respect of the possible answers it foregrounds) has been altered in the interpretation.

Once again, lack of awareness on the part of the court as to the fundamentally visual nature of the language means that any time when the interpreter has to come out of his/her normatively non-participatory role in order to clarify on grounds such as those noted above, the court is reminded that the interpreter is there and is not a robot undertaking a mechanical task unaffected by the possibility of human error. The interpreter runs the risk of looking incompetent, but the real problem is others' lack of appreciation of differences in the nature of the languages being used.

Co-Construction

One of the interactional issues that is beginning to come to the fore in work on this project is to do with the necessarily multiparty nature of interpreter-mediated interaction. A typical model of 'the best of all interpreted worlds' would have the interpreter utterly unobtrusive and the dialogue continuing as if it were monolingual. But since this is not the case, what are the implications of the interpreter's presence for this as talk-in-interaction in which there are, in fact, minimally three co-actors (Roy 1989; Wadensjö 1992)?

The concept of co-construction, or 'discourse as an interactional achievement', is currently enjoying attention from scholars such as Charles Goodwin (1994), Marjorie Harness Goodwin (1994) and Emmanuel Schegloff (1994) as a central process in social life. Co-construction is conceived as a joining together of participants in the joint production and interpretation of utterances, ideas, and so on. One of the central implications of the idea is that meaning in talk is necessarily not something one person does by themself: meaning is created between producers and perceivers, speakers and hearers. In the interpreted situation, therefore, meanings are in a sense developed and distributed between producer, conveyor and perceiver. What happens if we look into the bilingual, bimodal courtroom for evidence of co-construction?

Well, first of all, there are instances in which the interpreter overtly takes on his/her own persona in what is ostensibly a two-sided exchange between two other people. (Does this affect Deaf people's access to justice? Well, remember, it suits the court to believe that the interpreter is an input-output robot. And remember, the interpreter would not be there but for the Deaf person. So if the interpreter has a problem and becomes 'present', i.e. the robot fails, then in the court's eyes, the root of the problem is somehow connected to the Deaf person.)

Instances in which the interpreter becomes present may include the following (cf. Berk-Seligson, 1990: 55–96).

Direct address

Someone may address the interpreter directly – e.g. "Please ask him how many books he stole."

Anticipating interjection

The interpreter may interject to anticipate a misunderstanding – e.g. "I don't think I made the question clear" – or to block an irrelevant answer – e.g. "The defendant has responded, but he doesn't understand the question, so his answer doesn't make sense."

Clarification request

The interpreter may interject to clarify what someone is saying – e.g. "Could you be more specific about the weapon, because it is hard for me…" This may easily be seen as incompetence, an attempt to criticise the speaker's lack of clarity, or an unwarranted taking control of part of the exchange.

Explanation for approval

The interpreter may interject to explain his/her interpretation: in effect, a way of seeking approval or confirmation from the court that his/her behaviour is acceptable – e.g. "I asked him if he was in contact with his extended family, and I added 'aunts, uncles, grandparents, et cetera.'"

Signed asides

The interpreter may address 'side comments', in a language that the court as a whole cannot access, to the witness/defendant – e.g. when the witness interrupts a rambling section of explanation by the lawyer, signing not true, not true!, and the interpreter responds (in the midst of signing the lawyer's words) tell him, not me!

Indicating direct address

The interpreter may draw attention to what is happening if the witness makes comments directly to the interpreter – e.g. by saying "He says he doesn't understand the question, and he asks me if I understand it."

Unless some strategy (e.g. switching to consecutive interpreting) is found to ensure otherwise, these points are significant because they mark clear instances where the proceedings are absolutely not parallel for both linguistic groups. The co-construction of the discourse is therefore altered: linguistically, something with considerable 'spin' is happening here.

In considering extreme examples of instances where the interpreter makes a self-generated contribution to the interaction, there emerges a sense of the interpreter as the very antithesis of robotic. It becomes apparent that the interpreter is pivotal to the interaction, and in a very real sense is in fact holding the entire conversation alone! After all, it is the interpreter's question that gets answered, and the interpreter's answer that prompts and conditions the next question. Everyone else is left to assume – and they do assume – that they are all engaged in a dialogue with each other, and that they both have access to the same dialogue. This may or may not be the case. In a setting such as a courtroom, where the whole event and its entire process consist of talking, the contribution the interpreter makes towards deciding the direction of the whole undertaking should not be underestimated. The implications of this deserve careful attention.[24]

Conclusions

The 1990s have seen something of a surge in attention to issues relating to language and the law. The first issue of a new journal, Forensic Linguistics, has appeared and commences with a valuable synthesis of some of the field's concerns (Levi 1994). A number of major collections have recently been made available (Levi & Graffam Walker 1990;

---

24. See Brennan et al. (1984) and Brien (1992) for explanation of the researcher's notation system which is used as a tool of linguistic analysis; and Thoutenhoofd (1990, 1992) for comparison of writing systems and notation systems.

Rieber & Stewart 1990; Gibbons 1994) which are likely to become primary resources. However, it has also been noted (e.g. by Tiersma 1993) that linguistic research on the law may remain underused by the legal profession because linguists are not always attuned to issues that other professionals find significant. Perhaps it is therefore worth attempting directly to highlight some of the practicable implications of the preceding discussion.

A number of pointers towards addressing some of the issues raised in this paper can briefly be set out here. These strategies will not be put into practice overnight: in fact – at least in respect of some of them – one would be wary if they were. The pressure to act now – to get more interpreters quickly, to make everyone aware of what it means to use an interpreter quickly – is so intense that the trade-off of speed against care favours short-cuts and feel-good solutions. This is a false economy: the fact that you can measure its effects in the short term does not mean that an answer is the best available. Instant remedies to profound problems may have propaganda value at best, whilst at worst papering over architecturally fundamental cracks. This point has been unequivocally made by Laster (1990: 30):

> "One political danger of quick-fix solutions is that they create the illusion that a problem has been 'fixed'. Yet, in practice they allow government to abdicate responsibility for often more important reforms. Interpreting may be necessary for the community to see that justice is done but the presence of an interpreter will not guarantee that justice is in fact achieved. To ignore this does serious injustice to interpreters and non-English speakers."

The plain truth is that we do not yet know how best to face all of the challenges outlined above. We may have to accept that some of the issues pose insoluble problems. In discussion of bilingual spoken language courtrooms, Morris (1989a: 31) argues:

> "The basic dilemma of court interpretation results from the double need for on the one hand dynamism in interaction, and on the other the utmost accuracy in rendering material."

This seems to present as much, if not even more, of a dilemma in the situations dealt with in the present volume. It may simply be necessary to stop trying to navigate around the cartography of the bilingual, bimodal courtroom as if one could use the same old map: perhaps this is a fundamentally different landscape. It would seem from the accounts in this volume alone that essential features of any programme of improvements to the status quo in this field should include the following:

Awareness

It does seem vital from the foregoing that participants in bilingual, bimodal courtroom interaction should be made aware of the possible outcomes of the linguistic situation that brings the interpreter into the picture. Amongst many possible elements, this should include anticipation, in instructions to participants, of any unavoidable properties of the interpreter's input which might unduly influence decisions: Kathy Laster cites a number of studies arguing that the court system as a whole needs much greater awareness of the linguistic problems inherent in the process of interpretation (Laster, 1990: 19). It should also include attempts to ensure that discipline (in the sense of Morris, 1989a: 33) is maintained over turntaking and delivery. Thirdly, it is crucial that allowances are made for the additional preparation required by all parties if the interpreting is to be maximally effective.[25] Overall, justice will only be served by a wider understanding that this is a hugely complex set of issues.

> "Legal training needs to be expanded beyond simply 'recipe-like' formulae on 'how to work with an interpreter' to incorporate a self-conscious awareness in lawyers of their objectives in questioning witnesses and the impact which an interpreter might have on their approach."
>
> (Laster, 1990: 29)

Provision, recording & monitoring

In a number of countries, calls for legislation regarding statutory provision of interpreting services where necessary have now been heeded. Of course, in the absence of official recognition of national signed languages as equivalent in all relevant respects to spoken languages, it may be a moot point as to whether such legislation can be made to apply in the case of Deaf people. Together, these thus become primary goals for any attempt to address apparent shortcomings in the system of provision. Where these are in place, the secondary goal must be to press for certain guarantees of competence in the interpreting. Berk-Seligson reports (1990: 216) that, with a failure rate of 96%, no test in the USA is as stringent as the federal certification exam for court interpreters: this is surely laudable. An appropriately comprehensive general education in interpreting may be a first stage: a demand for specialist situation-specific training should not be far behind. Attention ought also to be paid to working conditions for interpreters, covering such matters as the length of time for which one interpreter can reasonably be expected to work alone without mental fatigue detrimental to the functioning of the court.

Due process of law, in the event of an appeal concerning interpretation, cannot be guaranteed by an accurate record of court proceedings, but it is unquestionably impossible in its absence. Only if original testimony in both languages being used in the courtroom is recorded can material be compared, analysed and verified so as to ensure that honest and effective work has been done. As yet, however, not only is there no record whatsoever of any original signed material in the bimodal court in England, Wales and Northern Ireland, but the 1981 Contempt of Court Act actively disbars video-recording equipment from the

---

25. Some initial attempts to draw out these implications can be found in Turner & Brown (forthcoming).

courtroom. In the current climate of fair concern over standards as sign language interpreting emerges as a profession, this is a dangerous state of affairs that serves nobody well.

Recording of proceedings is imperative in order to substantiate any subsequent claims or appeals: as Berk-Seligson notes (1990: 217), the provision of checks of this order can be seen as one test of the seriousness of the commitment the system is prepared to make to due process for the non-English speaking. At the actual time of trial, too, the introduction of basic checks and balances would contribute greatly to the cause of justice. No interpreter should be expected to work in a court of law in which he or she alone is able to gauge the accuracy and efficacy of his or her contributions. However competent that interpreter may be, he or she is also human and may make errors. Monitoring is a vital safeguard and must be carried out by trained persons able to recognise the difference between a finely judged question of interpretation and one of genuine and potentially significant mismatch between an original and an interpreter's rendition.

Training

As Morris (1989b: 10) makes most explicit:

> "legislation dealing with the provision of interpretation does not necessarily of itself guarantee the high-quality interpretation which is a sine qua non for the exercising of the rights thus recognized".

High-level education and training of bimodal interpreters is a relatively recent phenomenon.[26] From the foregoing discussion, it can be seen that the ability to attend to detail and know how to respond appropriately in the complex legal milieu cannot become firmly rooted overnight. To function with anything like truly adequate competence, interpreters must be expected to have the greatest possible general command of the two languages involved, and to know the cultural ground in which they are embedded inside out, as well as possessing knowledge of the stylistic and content norms of the courtroom. Understanding of the operational patterns of the court's business must also be developed so that the interpreter is comfortably familiar with the events unfolding around him or her. Such understanding must be genuinely profound: as Laster (1990: 29) puts it:

> "Interpreters need to be made aware of the complexities of the legal system itself, not just the procedures and practices which they are likely to encounter."

In addition, whilst interpreting roles are clearly undergoing reassessment in this field, interpreters should be trained in such a way that they know as well as can be what is required

---

26. A key example of this requirement being taken seriously would be the European Court of Justice where (Heidelberger, 1994: 3–4) interpreters are allowed "ample study time to ensure that [they] are well prepared and familiar with the facts of the individual case, the legal issues involved and the working of the court in general."

of them, how they should aim to conduct themselves, and the limits of the flexibility and responsiveness to circumstances available to them.[27]

Research

Finally, in the context of a field acknowledged to be so well-endowed with unknowns, primary research of all kinds must continue to be a priority. Approximately 35 years of sign linguistic research have produced a number of major analyses yielding a great deal of significant information concerning the elements and structures of signed languages. Nevertheless, the gaps in understanding and codification continue to be wide and much rests on scholars' collective ability to generate accounts of grammar, lexis and patterns of usage which can form the basis for other types of progress.

Research into interpreting as a process and a practice is also vital in order to expand understanding of both internal (cognitive) and external (interactional) strategies which can produce optimal performance of interpreting duties in the intense, multi-layered environment of the courtroom. Controlled experimental research, ethnographic work and action research can all be seen to have considerable contributions to make to the evolution of ever richer and more detailed descriptive and explanatory accounts. These should in turn provide suitable material for application to address the issues identified above.

Acknowledgements

This paper owes much to contributions from Susan Berk-Seligson, Mary Brennan, David Brien, Richard Brown, Ester Chu, Diana Eades, Kyra Pollitt, Maureen Reed, Cynthia Roy, Douglas Silas, and Cecilia Wadensjo, as well as all of the contributors to this volume and individual interpreters interviewed in the course of research. Nobody but the author bears any responsibility for the finished product. The project acknowledges the continuing support of the Leverhulme Trust, ASLI, SASLI, CACDP, BDA and RAD and the generous co-operation of Glasgow and West of Scotland Society for the Deaf, Strathclyde Regional Council and St. "Vincent's Society for the Deaf in Glasgow.

References

Anthony, D. (1971). *Seeing Essential English, vols 1 and 2.* Anaheim CA: Educational Services Division.

---

27.   In the UK, the first postgraduate course in British Sign Language/English Interpreting was established at the University of Durham in 1988.

Bergman, B. (1979). *Signed Swedish*. Stockholm: National Swedish Board of Education.

Berk-Seligson, S. (1990). *The Bilingual Courtroom: Court Interpreters in the Judicial Process*. Chicago IL and London: Chicago University Press.

Bornstein, H. et al. (1975). *The Signed English Dictionary for preschool and elementary levels*. Washington DC: Gallaudet College Press.

Brennan, M., Colville, M., Lawson, L.K. and Hughes, G.S.M. (1984). *Words in Hand: A Structural Analysis of the Signs of British Sign Language (second edition)*. Edinburgh: Moray House College of Education.

Brennan, M. (1986). Linguistic Perspectives. In B. T. Tervoort (ed.), *Signs of Life: Proceedings of the Second European Congress on Sign Language Research*. Amsterdam: NSDSK/Institute of General Linguistics, University of Amsterdam/Dutch Council of the Deaf. 1–16.

Brennan, M. (1992). *The Visual World of BSL: An Introduction. Dictionary of British Sign Language/ English*. London and Boston MA: Faber & Faber. 1–133.

Brien, D. (ed.) (1992). *Dictionary of British Sign Language/English*. London and Boston MA: Faber & Faber.

Butler, I. and Noaks, L. (1992). *Silence in Court? A Study of Interpreting in the Courts of England and Wales*. School of Social and Administrative Studies, University of Wales College of Cardiff/ London: Nuffield Interpreter Project.

Caccamise, F., Oglia, D., Mitchell, M., DeGroote, W. and Siple, L. (1991). *Technical Signs Manual Eleven: Legal*. New York NY: RIT/NTID.

Cameron, D. (1994). Putting our Practice into Theory. In D. Graddol and J. Swann (eds.), *Evaluating Language*. Clevedon, Avon and Bristol PA: British Association for Applied Linguistics in association with Multilingual Matters. 15–23.

Cameron, D., Frazer, E., Harvey, P., Rampton, M.B.H. and Richardson, K. (1992). *Researching Language: Issues of Power and Method*. London and New York NY: Routledge.

Council for the Advancement of Communication with Deaf People (no date). *Curriculum and Assessment Procedures – Stage 1*. Durham: CACDP.

Crystal, D. and Davy, D. (1969). *Investigating English Style*. London: Longman.

Danet, B. (1980). Language in the legal process. *Law and Society Review*, 14: 445–564.

Eades, D. (1988). Sociolinguistic evidence in court. *Australian Journal of Communication*, 14: 22–31.

Eades, D. (1992). Australian Aborigines and the Legal System: A Sociolinguistic Perspective. Paper presented at Sociolinguistics Symposium 9. University of Reading, England.

Gibbons, J. (ed.) (1994). *Language and the law*. London and New York NY: Longman.

Giles, H. (1970). Evaluative reactions to accents. *Educational Review*, 22: 211–227.

Giles, H. (1971). Ethnocentrism and the evaluation of accented speech. *British Journal of Social and Clinical Psychology*, 10: 187–188.

Goodwin, C. (1994). Narrative co-construction in the family of an aphasic. Paper presented to the American Association for Applied Linguistics 'Co-Construction' Colloquium. Baltimore MD.

Gustason, G., Pfetzing, D. and Zawolkow, E. (1975). *Signing Exact English*. Los Alamitos CA: Modern Signs Press.

Harness Goodwin, M. (1994). Co-constructed participation frameworks in a multi-ethnic classroom. Paper presented to the American Association for Applied Linguistics 'Co-Construction' Colloquium. Baltimore MD.

Heidelberger, B. (1994). Legal Interpreting: The Example of the Court of Justice of the European Communities. *The Jerome Quarterly*, 9/3: 3–15.

HMSO (1993). *Report of the Royal Commission on Criminal Justice.* London: HMSO.

Islam, M. (1993). Read, Hear, See… "See Hear!" Read…! *NEWSLI,* 14: 30–31.

Jaworski, A. (1993). *Power of Silence: Social and Pragmatic Perspectives.* London: Sage.

Lane, H. (1992). *The Mask of Benevolence: Disabling the Deaf Community.* New York NY: Alfred A. Knopf.

Laster, K. (1990). Legal interpreters: conduits to social justice? *Journal of Intercultural Studies,* 11/2: 15–32.

Levi, J. (1994). Language as evidence: the linguist as expert witness in North American courts. *Forensic Linguistics,* 1/1: 1–26.

Levi, J. and Graffam Walker, A. (eds.) (1990). *Language in the judicial process.* New York NY: Plenum.

Lightbown, P. (1994). Teachers and Researchers: Both Oars in the Water. Plenary Paper to the American Association for Applied Linguistics. Baltimore MD.

Lochrie, Rev J. S. (no date). Notes for Interpreters for the Deaf in Courts of Law in Scotland. Edinburgh: Moray House College of Education.

Loftus, E. and Palmer, J. (1974). Reconstruction of automobile destruction: An example of the interaction between language and memory. *Journal of Verbal Learning and Verbal Behaviour,* 13: 585–589.

Loftus, E. and Zanni, G. (1975). Eyewitness testimony: Influence of the wording of a question. *Bulletin of the Psychonomic Society,* 5: 86–88.

McIntire, M. and Sanderson, G. (in press). Bye-bye, bi-bi: Questions of empowerment and role. In *Proceedings,* 1993. RID Convention.

Morris, R. (1989a). Court Interpretation: The Trial of Ivan Demjanjuk: A Case Study. *The Interpreters' Newsletter,* 2: 27–37.

Morris, R. (1989b). *Eichmann v. Demjanjuk: A Study of Interpreted Proceedings.* Parallèles: Cahiers de L'Ecole de Traduction et d'Interpretation, Université de Genève. 9–28.

Nuffield Interpreter Project (1993). Access to Justice: Non-English Speakers in the Legal System. London: The Nuffield Foundation.

Nusser, P. (1993). Acting upon your beliefs. *TBC News,* 63: 4.

O'Barr, W. (1982). *Linguistic Evidence: Language, Power, and Strategy in the Courtroom.* New York NY: Academic Press.

Padden, C. (1980). The Deaf Community and the Culture of Deaf People. In C. Baker & R. Battison (eds.), *Sign Language and the Deaf Community: Essays in Honour of William C. Stokoe.* Silver Spring MD: National Association of the Deaf. 89–104.

Padden, C. and Humphries, T. (1988). *Deaf in America: Voices from a Culture.* Cambridge MA: Harvard University Press.

Parker, D. (1993). Mixed-up sentences. *The Guardian.* London. February 2nd.

Polack, K. and Corsellis, A. (1990). Non-English speakers and the criminal justice system *New Law Journal,* November 23rd: 1634–1677.

Rieber, R. and Stewart, W. (eds.) (1990). *The language scientist as expert in the legal setting: Issues in forensic linguistics.* New York NY: New York Academy of Sciences.

Roy, C. (1989). A Sociolinguistic Analysis of the Interpreter's Role in the Turn Exchanges of an Interpreted Event. Unpublished dissertation. Washington DC: Georgetown University, University Microfilms DA064793.

Roy, C. (1993a). The Problem with Definitions, Descriptions, and the Role Metaphors of Interpreters. *Journal of Interpretation,* 6/1: 127–153.

Roy, C. (1993b). A sociolinguistic analysis of the interpreter's role in simultaneous talk in interpreted interaction. *Multilingua,* 12/4: 341–363.

Schegloff, E. (1994). On the co-construction of discourse: The omnirelevance of action. Paper presented to the American Association for Applied Linguistics 'Co-Construction' Colloquium. Baltimore MD.

Scott Gibson, L. (1990). Sign Language Interpreting: An Emerging Profession In S. Gregory & G. M. Hartley (eds.), (1991). *Constructing Deafness.* London/Milton Keynes: Pinter Publishers in association with the Open University. 253–258.

Scott Gibson, L. (1994). Open to Interpretation: The Cult of Professionalism. Keynote paper presented at the 'Issues in Interpreting' Conference. University of Durham, England.

Sutton-Spence, R. and Woll, B. (1990). Variation and recent change in British Sign Language. *Language Variation and Change,* 2.:313–330.

Sutton-Spence, R. and Woll, B. (1993). The Status and Functional Role of Fingerspelling in BSL. In M. Marschark and M. D. Clark (eds.), *Psychological Perspectives on Deafness.* Hillsdale NJ: Lawrence Erlbaum Associates. 185–208.

Thoutenhoofd, E. (1990). The link between calligraphy and notation, or: why type-designing is a job for type-designers. *Signpost,* 3/1: 12–13.

Thoutenhoofd, E. (1992). Trans-scribing and writing: What constitutes a writing system? *Signpost,* 5/2: 39–51.

Tiersma, P. (1993). Review article: Linguistic issues in the law. Language, 69/1: 113–137.

Turner, G.H. and Brown, R.K. (forthcoming). Interaction and the role of the interpreter in court. In Brennan, M. & Brien, D. (eds.) *Issues in Interpreting: Conference Proceedings.* Durham: University of Durham.

Wadensjö, C. (1992). Interpreting as Interaction. Linkoping: Linköping University.

Witter-Merithew, A. (1986). Claiming our destiny. (In two parts). *RID Views.* October: 12 & November:3–4.

Woodward, J. (1972). Implications for sociolinguistic research among the deaf. *Sign Language Studies,* 1: 1–7.

CHAPTER 5

Challenging perceptions of profession and role

Introduction

As the 1980s and 1990s progressed, questions about role, power, and professionalism began to surface. The role of interpreters, relationships to consumers, and responsibilities in light of the changing perceptions are the crux of the articles below. They situate the role in worldviews, discourse, and relationships with our consumers. Although some articles are based on research, others are presented as a pulse on the issues of the time written by leading practitioners and educators at that time.

Since the publication of the first sign language dictionary in America (1965), researchers have established sign languages as syntactically complex languages with distinctive phonological, morphological, and syntactic features that are distinct from spoken languages (Liddell 1980, Klima & Bellugi 1979). It was becoming widely accepted by linguists, anthropologists, and sociologists alike that Deaf people belong to a linguistic and cultural minority group and identify with one another on the basis of using the natural sign language of their country (Brennan 1992).

Alongside these linguistic and social developments, came political changes. During the 1980s, more national associations of the Deaf were established than at any other time period in the history of the World Federation of the Deaf. Deaf people were gaining power and demanding basic rights as citizens of their countries. Sweden became the first country in the world to recognize sign language as the first language of Deaf persons. In 1988, the parliament of the European Community, noting that there are 500,000 profoundly Deaf people in member states whose first language is their national sign language and not the dominant spoken language of their country, recognized, as legitimate languages, the indigenous sign languages of the twelve member states.

Also in 1988 a huge student protest movement at Gallaudet University forced the resignation of a newly hired president who could hear and installed a Deaf president. This protest, now called Deaf President Now (DPN), drew national and international attention and inspired Deaf people everywhere to increase their political involvement within their own countries regarding civil rights and language policy. Countries began to recognize sign languages as the natural language of Deaf persons and provide increased educational opportunities for Deaf children, for studying sign languages, and for training sign language interpreters. All these changes inspired the call for SLI services and training programs in more countries.

But as Cokely (2005) has pointed out, through the 1980s and 1990s in the U.S., people who were not deaf and who did not live or work with the Deaf community began to hire interpreters in large numbers. Interpreting became a professionally paid position, jobs came from the public and private sectors, and often interpreters earned more than most Deaf people. The Deaf community lost its authority in determining who would be an acceptable and effective interpreter. At the same time, academic programs recruited and graduated more and more young people with little or no knowledge of the community and culture, not only to interpret, but also to learn sign language in unrealistic time frames. And, during this same time, Deaf people were expected to "volunteer" their time and energies to share their language, culture, wisdom, and experiences with these newcomers to their world. Inevitably, issues around power, role, and professionalism emerged. Volunteer interpreting fell away, although still performed, but in fewer and fewer circumstances, and most interpreting became paid, professional work.

The profession began to witness what has been described as a 'pendulum swing' to another extreme (Scott-Gibson, 1992) whereby sign language interpreters modeled their role on spoken language interpreters in an attempt to appear more professional. This swing led to what is referred to as the *conduit model* of SLI. Interpreters were expected to adhere to a code of ethics, maintain impartiality and confidentiality, interpret faithfully and accurately, and uphold a professional distance. Metaphors were frequently used to describe interpreters as telephones, bridges or channels to communication (Frishberg 1986/1990; Neumann Solow 1981).

Interestingly, the professional values adopted by sign language interpreters were modeled on conference interpreters who perform their work in a booth at the back of a conference venue, and are rarely seen by their consumers. These interpreters are able to maintain professional and social distance as they can function with minimal contact with the people relying on their services. Obviously this is not the case for sign language interpreters, who need to be physically present and visible in order to provide an interpretation for Deaf consumers.

Before too long, practitioners, consumers, academics and educators began to question the endorsement of a conduit model. People argued that, by adopting certain 'professional' traits, sign language interpreters had lost their connection to the values of the Deaf community (McDade 1995), and that use of a conduit metaphor was neither realistic nor helpful in explaining the role of an interpreter (Roy 1993). Deaf people in particular began to explore what kind of interpreters they really wanted (Heaton & Fowler 1997) – practitioners who were linguistically skilled, professional and ethical, but who also appreciated the cultural values and communication needs of members of the Deaf community. In this sense, this is where SLI debates have been groundbreaking and led the way for spoken language interpreters, as essentially they recognized that sign language interpreters are at the forefront of community (not conference) interpreting practice. Thus the role of the interpreter, and the relationship with consumers, is different. Discussions on the interpreter role in the SLI sector continued for many years before notions of community interpreting as a professional (and not inferior) practice emerged in the spoken language interpreting literature (Pöchhacker, 1999).

As the debates about the conduit model progressed, new terminology and metaphors about roles in interpreted encounters appeared. **Anna Witter-Merithew's** 1986 essay in the RID newsletter *Views* described four 'models' that are also metaphors for the interpreting role – helper, conduit, communication facilitator, and bi-lingual, bi-cultural – metaphors whose labels persist and which spotlight the interpreter. Since the publication of this article, there has been an ongoing discussion of the interpreter's role and these four metaphors are constant themes in that discourse.

In a 1993 paper (now reprinted in the *Interpreting Studies Reader*), **Cynthia Roy** suggested that while these metaphors had different labels, none of them accounted for the ways in which face-to-face conversations required more from an interpreter than a simplistic transfer of a message. Her dissertation study in 1989 examining a naturally occurring, interpreted interaction with three speakers was a new conceptual and methodological approach to the study of interpreting. Up to this point, most investigations of SLI had either been experimental or quasi-experimental, and typically focused on the accuracy of source and target texts as interpreters worked in conference-like settings. But sign language interpreters do the bulk of their work in face-to-face, private meetings with three participants: two primary speakers and an interpreter.

Roy's findings focused on both the structure of the turn-taking (Sacks, Schegloff, & Jefferson 1974) in the three-way conversation, and on the participants' intentions and interpretations about the turns that were taken (Bennett 1981; Tannen 1984). Roy demonstrated that, although many turns are exchanged smoothly through the interpreter, there are also turns that are problematic, and interpreters are in a position to manage and direct the interaction. Her findings revealed that the speakers took turns with the interpreter, the interpreter took turns and resolved overlapping talk, and that this activity establishes that the interpreter, rather than being a neutral conveyor of messages, is an active participant who influences the direction and outcome of the event. Her paper in this Reader focuses on what happens when all the participants speak at the same time, which causes the interpreter to make decisions about who should have the turn. Although it was a case study of one situation, likely the first face-to-face interpreted event to be filmed in SLI, this finding was direct, empirical evidence that interpreters are not conduits and are, in fact, actively engaged in the management of the process.

Marina McIntire and **Gary Sanderson**'s essay, which was originally presented as a paper at the 1993 RID Convention, is about the changing and challenging perceptions of role. Although their discussion centers on the situation in the U.S., their observations were also evident elsewhere in other countries. Essentially, as the interpreter role models changed, relationships between Deaf consumers and interpreters became somewhat contentious. In this paper, McIntire and Sanderson continue the discussion of a continuum of models that had emerged, from helper, to conduit, to facilitator of communication, to the model (of the time): the bilingual-bicultural mediator. They discussed the nature of power relations between Deaf people and interpreters, and how each model has impacted on those power relations. In effect they were the first authors to suggest that sign language interpreters should consider themselves as 'allies' of the Deaf community. This was a controversial suggestion at the time, as although the community of Deaf people and SLI practitioners were beginning to recognize that the conduit model of 'interpreter as invisible non-participant' was not feasible or realistic, they still struggled with the idea that interpreters could actively support the Deaf community without 'taking over' and disempowering them. McIntire and Sanderson explored these ideas further in a later 1995 paper featured in the *Journal of Interpretation* specifically in relation to interpreting in court.

Nadja Grbić's paper, originally written in German, examines the role of sign language interpreters in society, in research and in professional practice. The paper begins by addressing the community settings in which sign language interpreters work most frequently in Austria. At that time, sign language interpreters were only resorted to in "emergency cases", while the communicative needs of the Deaf community in everyday life were being ignored. Grbić then highlights that the "strong culture" decides what role the Deaf community should play in society and that this decision has less to do with integrating the Deaf community and more to do with political, economic and ideological interests. She notes the attention given to SLI in research and points out that existing studies of interpreting focused primarily on cognitive, neurological and psycholinguistic aspects of conference interpreting, while studies devoted to community interpreting are a growing area. The author suggests addressing non-professional interpreting in research as friends or relatives of Deaf people often do SLI. In terms of the professional practice of sign language interpreters, Grbić points out that some interpreters take the role of benefactors, while others the role of linguistic conduits. The author engages critically with those roles and the conflicts arising from them.

Kyra Pollitt's essay presents, humorously, two examples of the models that highlight the problems, benefits, and consumer relationships that arise from the different perceptions of an interpreter's role. Pollitt's essay points to the SLI field's attempts to model themselves after the spoken language conference interpreters who serve an entirely different audience in different circumstances. She describes the work of community interpreters and their lack of clear career path in the U.K. urging interpreters to re-think what professional behaviors are needed in their work.

From R.B.W. Anderson's (1976) pioneering essay on the interpreter's role and continuing today, the discussion of an interpreter's role dominates both polemic and research writings (Napier 2012). As research investigations began to focus on the dialogic nature of community interpreting (Roy 1989a, Wadensjö 1992; Metzger 1995), aspects of role performance increasingly informed the descriptions and explanations of roles and models. The examination of the role of the interpreter still dominates much of the spoken and sign language interpreting studies literature (Pöchhacker 2004). Shaffer (2013) and Napier (2013) note that shifting perceptions of role are often aligned with introductions of different linguistic theories to the examination of the interpreting process and product. Previous role definitions were more aligned with psycholinguistic constructs, that is, the language transfer process. Later models adopted a sociolinguistic approach and considered the interpreter as participant and co-constructor of meaning in the interaction. Shaffer's (2013) work considers the interpreter role from a cognitive linguistic point of view, and how interpreters need to respond to contextualization cues (also reported in Wilcox & Shaffer 2005). The most recent theory from Lee and Llewellyn-Jones (2011) and Llewellyn-Jones & Lee (2014) explores the concept of the interpreter's 'role space' through a combination of psycholinguistic, sociolinguistic and pragmatics theories to suggest that interpreters 'enact' their role to align and converge with participants in different ways; and Robyn Dean is expanding her work on ethical decision-making to challenge the construct of interpreter role in terms of reflective practice (Dean forthcoming).

5.1   Witter-Merithew, Anna. 1986. "Claiming our Destiny, Parts 1 and 2." *Views*, October, 12 and November, 3–4.

Anna Witter-Merithew, who grew up with Deaf parents, has had a long career both as a practitioner and educator in SLI. She holds numerous certifications from the Registry of Interpreters for the Deaf, and earned her Masters degree in Education from Athabasca University in the area of instructional design and technology. Witter-Merithew was the Chairperson for the Department of Interpreter Education at the National Technical Institute for the Deaf (NTID), and a co-founder of the Conference of Interpreter Trainers (CIT), a professional association of interpreter educators, and she has served two terms as the association's Vice-President during 1996–2000. Between 1983 and 1989, Witter-Merithew served as the Vice-President (2 terms) and President (1 term) of the Registry of Interpreters for the Deaf. Two current publications include co-authorship of *Toward Competent Practice: Conversations with Stakeholders* with Leilani Johnson, and *The Dimensions of Ethical Decision-Making* with colleague Kellie Stewart. Witter-Merithew serves on the Board of Editors for the CIT *International Journal of Interpreter Education*.

Witter-Merithew taught in the Interpreter Training Program at Central Piedmont Community College in Charlotte, North Carolina, and became responsible for the instructional programs of the DO-IT Center in Colorado, contributing through the Mid-America Regional Interpreter Education Center (MARIE) to the National Consortium of Interpreter Education Centers (NCIEC) – a federally funded collaborative.

Claiming our destiny

Anna Witter-Merithew

"…It is well for a man to respect his own vocation whatever it is, and to think himself bound to uphold it and to claim for it the respect it deserves" (Dickens).

The Registry of Interpreters for the Deaf was established over 20 years ago, in order to establish sign language interpretation as a profession and to perpetuate standards that validate our ability to provide professional interpretation. We owe much to those individuals who had the foresight and commitment to bring our organization into being. As is true with any organization or relationship, RID has been changing ever since. The dynamics associated with our evolution are complex and fascinating. Let us look at one aspect of change, defining the models we have used to describe ourselves and relating these models to some of the challenges we presently face as an organization. The models I discuss are: the Helper, the Conduit, the Communication Facilitator, and the Bi-lingual/Bi-cultural Models.

It is well-known and well-documented that, prior to the existence of RID, individuals who provided interpretation services were untrained, often unqualified. Their primary goal was to provide help to their deaf relatives, neighbors, students or parishioners. The injustices perpetuated during this era of the "Helping Model" stimulated recognition of a critical need for an organization to establish and maintain standards; thus, the birth of RID.

With the advent of professional standards, a set of ethical practices were defined. These were based on the primary concepts of impartiality, integrity, confidentiality and discretion. These concepts will be found in any professional code and have remained consistent in ours, though our view and understanding of them have been periodically revised.

History shows us that social evolution frequently involves a radical shift from one position to another, in an effort to establish a new identity. Just so, the first model to challenge the view of "interpreter as helper," after the establishment of RID, was the Conduit. In this model, interpreters perceived themselves as "machines," whose sole responsibility was to transmit information between people. This narrow perception was the result of our wish to dissociate ourselves from the "helping" view of the task.

The legislative mandate for interpretation services increased during the late 60's and early 70's. Many short-term educational programs tried to respond to the need. The Conduit Model was carried to the workplace. In our effort to avoid being identified as Helpers, in which interpreters assumed responsibility for everything, we denied responsibility for anything.

Conflicts, however, came from the extreme behaviors stimulated by this view of the task. Interpreters denied responsibility for unsuccessful interpreted events and clients began to perceive interpreters as cold and self-serving. Desperately, some practitioners resorted to the Helper Model to gain acceptance and some success during the interpretation event. At the same time, the academic arena of the profession was exploring alternatives to the extremes of the Conduit Model.

In the mid-70's, a new view emerged; we can call this the Communication Facilitator Model. In this model, interpreters were encouraged to assume responsibility for meeting with clients beforehand to discuss role and responsibilities, and for planning positioning, lighting, dress, professional growth and remuneration. Classes in interpretation began to include discussion of communication models, strategies for effective communication, public speaking and other topics associated with the field of communication in general.

Within this model, some professionals felt that oral facilitation services could appropriately be accommodated. A new dimension to our association's activities was introduced with the advent of oral certification. The internal political and social ramifications of this decision were more intense than were anticipated.

Concurrently, American Sign Language had become the focus of linguistic research and recognition; a strong social movement began as the Deaf Community established its own validity and demanded recognition. This movement, along with the growing body of research and the birth of the Conference of Interpreter Trainers (CIT), continues to stimulate our examination of how we define interpretation and transliteration, and how we view the languages with which we work.

The clarification of the interpretation (and transliteration) task has helped us to realize that the one thing we have historically claimed the least responsibility – the interpreted message – is the very thing over which we have the most control. Our intentions have always been to deliver quality interpretation, but we have lacked the body of research and academic standards necessary to understand what we do. {See Lane's closing address in the new Proceedings for some cogent comments on this issue. ED.} Recent years have seen the growth of a new model: the Bi-lingual/Bi-cultural Model. This places the highest emphasis on the integrity and accuracy of the interpretation, and requires the practitioner to recognize that language and culture are inseparable.

In the past, we have allowed Deaf Education and Vocational Rehabilitation to define our destiny. Our field has embraced many new challenges and RID has begun to focus on internal functions: defining our purpose, clarifying our standards, examining our working conditions, delineating organizational roles, responsibilities and authority. We have been working hard to take ownership of our own field and of the marketplace. Yet we still struggle, face obstacles and experience setbacks. This is in the nature of change and transition.

{The second part of this article will appear in next month's *VIEWS*. ED.}

Claiming our destiny, Part Two

Anna Witter-Merithew

We are an organization which exists to promote the standards and employment of qualified interpreters. Our members are our purpose; we exist to serve our clients and ourselves. We have members who work within each of the models previously identified [Helper, Conduit, Communication Facilitator, and Bi-lingual/Bi-cultural. **See October VIEWS, p. 12, ED.**]. Therefore, we collectively "own" all these models and need to strive towards a collective consciousness. We do not and should not agree on everything, lest we become myopic in our perspective; we do, however, need to agree on our general direction and organizational goals. We as members are obligated to assume the ownership given to us by the By-Laws.

There are several practical ways that we, as members, can begin to assume ownership of the RID. These recommendations are not new and they are not difficult; they are age-old and simple. They warrant repetition, though, as we often neglect then-effectiveness.

First, Elect Responsible Leadership: Each certified and associate member of our organization has a vote. This vote enables us to act in favor of those candidates who represent the values and positions most closely associated with our own. We have a duty to seek out and to support individuals who will respond to positions of leadership with integrity, active involvement and accountability. If our involvement in the nomination and election process is nil, we must be prepared to deal with an outcome that is less than satisfactory. We have gone beyond electing representatives on the basis of "name recognition." Electing responsible leadership should occur at all levels of RID: local, state and national.

Second, Remain Informed: We are fortunate to have many ways of being informed about what transpires within our organization. The *VIEWS* is now monthly and provides a wealth of information, including Board meeting minutes, reports from regional reps, articles, and announcements. The annual Journal of Interpretation provides thought-provoking and current discussions of issues facing our organization. State, regional and national meetings and conventions provide us with an opportunity to participate in policy-making processes. National Board members can be contacted directly, as can committee chairs, for discussion of specific issues or concerns. We are fortunate to have a full-time home office staff that continues to grow and respond to our need for support and information. The mechanisms are in place for frequent communication with members. We need only to choose to access that information and to exercise our authority in holding each other accountable for the process and for the information itself.

Third, Become Involved: One of the greatest rewards I have experienced as a Board member during the past three years has been the opportunity to work with committees. The committee structure of our organization has provided the membership with specific ways to become involved and to effect change. Over 200 members are actively involved in one or another of 27 different committees. Members are working on: a statement of organizational philosophy, name change, standards, convention program, certification standards and implementation, and a host of other critical aspects of operation.

Making a contribution fosters a sense of ownership and as members we desire that sense. We should actively find ways to contribute our talents to the organization through service. Committee involvement is one way. There are a host of others, including: contributing to the newsletter or the journal, volunteering at the home office, serving as an evaluator, serving as a local, state or national Board member, recruiting new members and actively promoting the purposes of the organization. No one individual contribution is more significant than another. It is important to recognize the contributions of individuals, but it is the collective effect of our contributions that moves us forward. Service is the key to involvement. Find new and creative ways to become involved!

Claiming our destiny is the challenge that faces us. We can do so by examining our history, regaining a sense of ownership and by collectively determining our direction. Our organization has rapidly moved from an autocratic system of government to a membership-directed system. We find ourselves in the midst of transition. With a spirit of fair- mindedness, mutual respect and enthusiasm, we can move forward, claiming for ourselves a future in which we recognize the opportunity to work as true professionals. Winston Church ill stated to a group of college graduates: "Never give up, never give up, never give up – in matters great or small...except in honor and good conscience." The same challenge is ours to embrace.

5.2   Roy, Cynthia. B. 1992. "A sociolinguistic analysis of the interpreter's role in simultaneous talk in a face-to-face interpreted dialogue." *Sign Language Studies*, 74: 21–61.

Cynthia Roy has worked as an interpreter, educator, and researcher in SLI for thirty years. She began her work as a community interpreter, completed a Masters degree in Linguistics at Gallaudet University and a Doctorate in Sociolinguistics from Georgetown University. Oxford University Press published her 1989 dissertation entitled 'A sociolinguistic analysis of the interpreter's role in the turn exchanges of an interpreted event' as a book, *Interpreting as a Discourse Process* in 2000.

Roy began her university teaching career in 1985 at Gallaudet University in Washington, D.C. where she taught in the AA SLI program and then, with Robert E. Johnson, created and co-wrote the curriculum for the first U.S. Masters degree in SLI in 1988 and taught there until 1989. Roy moved to New Orleans, LA, and taught writing and linguistics at the University of New Orleans for ten years. In 1999, Roy accepted a position as director of a BA SLI program at Indiana University Purdue University (IUPUI) in Indianapolis, and then in 2003 joined the faculty of Gallaudet University where she is a Professor in the Department of Interpretation. She is the series editor of the Gallaudet University Press *Interpreter Education* series, and the editor of the first three volumes.

A sociolinguistic analysis of the interpreter's role in simultaneous talk in a face-to-face interpreted dialogue

Cynthia B. Roy

Historically, a common but inaccurate assumption of interpreting has been that interpreters serve as nearly robotic conduits of information, who have little or no impact on the communicative situation in which interpretation is taking place. An interpeter is an active participant when simultaneous or overlapping talk occurs. When primary speakers talk simultaneously, the interpreter recognizes the overlap and makes linguistic choices to resolve the overlap, deciding who will get the turn. Many of the decisions made by the interpreter reflect an understanding and interpretation of the social situation of a meeting between student and professor. The interpreter's role is active, governed by social and linguistic knowledge of the entire communicative situation, requiring not only competence in the languages but also competence in the appropriate "ways of speaking" and in managing the intercultural event of interpreting.

Introduction

The world over, people come together who do not speak a common language and who need the services of an interpreter. Historically, the resultant interaction has been perceived as a rather mechanical event in which a speaker encodes a message, an interpreter transforms the forms of one language to the forms of another language, and a receiver decodes the message. A common assumption has been that interpreters serve as nearly robotic conduits of information, who have little or no impact on the communicative situation in which interpretation is taking place. This is an inaccurate perception.

In this paper I will show that a unique feature of interpreted conversation occurs around simultaneous talk. When the primary speakers talk simultaneously, the interpreter recognizes this overlapping talk and makes linguistic choices to resolve the overlap by deciding who will get the turn. For instance, in this study the interpreter resolved overlapping talk by stopping one primary speaker and not the other. Many of his choices exemplified his understanding and interpretation of the social situation of an interview between student and professor. I will demonstrate that the interpreter in this meeting is *not* a neutral conduit, an implicit assumption behind much training and testing of interpreters.

Instead, the interpreter's role is active, governed by social and linguistic knowledge of the entire communicative situation, including not only competence in the languages, but also competence in the appropriate "ways of speaking" and in managing the intercultural event of interpreting.

The main issues

To assist outsiders in understanding the practice of the profession, professional interpreters often describe their role – in the middle – by using metaphors such as 'bridge' and 'channel,' which suggest the link or connection that they make between people who do not speak a common language. Interpreters themselves find it difficult to explain their role without resorting to conduit metaphors, and this explanation then leads to the perception of interpreters as passive, neutral participants, whose job it is mechanically to transmit the content of the source message in the form of the target language.

This perspective developed, in part, from the consistent and unremitting attention of practitioners, educators, and researchers to the work of interpreting in public contexts for one speaker at a time. In public forums interpreters usually interpret for single speakers, who are talking to non-responding audiences whose role in the event has historically seemed unimportant. An interpreter's role in this event does appear conduit-like, passive and non-involved.

Another reason for the persistence of this perspective originates in the research on interpreting, done, for the most part, by cognitive psychologists and psycholinguists who have focused on the cognitive phenomena of language processing and transference. The researchers, fascinated with the complexity of the task of listening, understanding, and speaking simultaneously, have produced detailed models of the psycholinguistic stages of transfer based on errors revealed in the target language production (Gerver 1976; Moser 1978; Cokely 1992). While these models provide an appreciation of the mental complexity of interpreting activity, their very nature reinforces the conceptual model through which interpreting is viewed. Unfortunately, the force of this perspective is such that most of those involved in training and professional testing have devoted their efforts to the details of the interpreted message and its form.

Although the conduit metaphors developed partially in response to a particular role performance and to the direction of research studies, they are also used because of ordinary perceptions about the nature of language and communication. Reddy (1979) explains how normal language use frames language as a conduit for the exchange of thoughts and feelings, thus molding our perceptions about communicative processes. Conduit metaphors, which abound in the fields of communication, psychology, language, and information processing, have naturally been borrowed by those in the field of interpreting, because the primary focus of practitioner, educator, and researcher alike has been on the form and content of the message that interpreters convey. It is easy to see how a communication process involving a supposedly neutral third participant can accept a conduit-type metaphor as a way of defining itself.

However, while public, single-speaker events are the most visible, most publicized, and most accessible to public notice, scrutiny and research studies, they do not represent archetypical interpreting situations. Since public settings have received the bulk of such attention, they are also the standard against which theoretical models and practical concerns are judged. Contrary to these perceptions is the fact that most interpreters work in settings that involve face-to-face interaction among the participants. It is this kind of setting that provides a more realistic object of study through which to understand the linguistic and social acts an interpreter is performing. Interpreters work frequently in settings where fewer than five people are involved. The prototype of this setting consists of three people, two primary speakers and an interpreter. This interpreting situation is not highly visible nor open to public scrutiny because of the personal and private nature of many of these situations in which sensitive issues may be discussed. Many of these situations are confidential; thus, they are difficult to observe as well as difficult to examine openly.

In such settings the two primary speakers are not only active speakers but they are also active listeners. No one is passive in the exchange of messages and flow of conversation. While previously much attention has been given to the message of one speaker, there has been little study of the listener in spite of Nida's call (1969) for such studies; and virtually no attention given to subsequent replies. In a face-to-face setting, these factors are as important as the original message.

Moreover, two primary speakers present their ideas not only using different linguistic structures, but also by following different automatic and unconscious conventions for using those structures (Gumperz & Tannen 1979). For example, inherent in language use are systems for organizing talk, such as openings and closings, turn-taking, pauses, signalling continuing thoughts, interruptions, and the presence or lack of understanding. In a context in which two primary speakers do not know each other's language, the only participant who can logically maintain, adjust, and if necessary, repair differences in structure and use is the interpreter. Because interpreters are the only bilinguals in these situations, the knowledge of different linguistic strategies and conversational mechanisms resides in them alone. This means that the interpreter is an active, third participant, with the potential to influence both the direction and outcome of the event, and that event itself is intercultural and interpersonal rather than simply mechanical and technical.

Studies to date of interpreting are not accounts of interactive events, with descriptions of the participants, their interaction, and their relationships. It is not possible to understand the event of interpreting fully by studying only the interpreter or by studying one speaker and the interpreter. To understand the event requires examining the naturalistic behavior of all the participants. Consequently, this study of interpreting is about the nature of interpreting as a communicative event. It is founded, first, on the notion that live, simultaneous interpreting is a negotiation of two different communication systems and, second, on the observation that the task of managing those systems is largely the work of the interpreter.

The study: An assumption of success

The focus here is a specific conversational phenomenon, that of simultaneous or overlapping talk. It represents part of a longer study, a sociolinguistic description and analysis of a videotaped meeting between a university professor, a doctoral student, and an interpreter (Roy 1989). The videotape and its transcript were used to analyze the exchange of turns among the three participants and the role of the interpreter in that exchange.

My method in that, following Tannen's (1984) study of conversational style, was to record, transcribe, and analyze the tape and the transcript. I analyzed the exchange of turns both as to how they were accomplished and as to how the participants understood the turn-taking exchange. Turn-taking is one of the basic organizational activities of conversation; so it was important to know how turns are organized through a participant who does not initiate them. This analysis was also a way to explore the participation of the interpreter for the purpose of defining and describing such activity.

After a preliminary analysis of the turns, I interviewed the three participants separately for insight into their own actions as well as their understanding of what was going on. After each participant had seen the entire event, I played the tape again, showing them specific sequences that involved turn exchanges. I asked them to observe their own actions as well as the actions of the other participants. I chose the sequences and guided the viewing, because in this relatively brief situation each sequence – the changing of turns and occurrence of other features like pauses and overlapping talk – happened very quickly. I had to show each sequence several times, and as I showed it, I asked each participant to concentrate first on what his or her own actions were. Then I showed the sequence again and asked the participants to comment on the actions or talk of the other participants.

This study, then, is based primarily on the sociolinguistic analysis of the videotape, the transcript, and the participant playback interviews. It is based secondarily on my own observation of the event (I recorded the meeting) and my years of experience as a professional interpreter.

Interpreters are confronted, both verbally and in writing, with their mistakes during interpreting. In addition, much of the research on interpreting has been a comparison of an interpreter's output, the target-language message, with the source (or original) message. This results in a categorization of interpreter errors – breakdowns that pinpoint the psycholinguistic states of information processing. In short, the research points out what the interpreter has done wrong.

My approach here is to adopt the perspective of studying a successful interpreting event and to inquire how such an event took place, based on the understanding that successful communication requires a great deal of effort and energy on the part of all participants, and especially on the part of an interpreter. After asking the participants in this study if they thought everything went smoothly and that the meeting was successful and finding that they did, I explained to them that because of the traditional tendency to criticize interpreters, my goal was, in part, to examine, describe, and explain this event in terms of its success.

Related literature

The study of interpreting is emerging from the study of translation in a number of different disciplines, and to date it has only a small and limited body of research to substantiate its claims. The major focus of these studies has been to describe cognitive processes, whereby the forms of the source language are transformed into the forms of the target language. The primary thrust of interpreting research has been to investigate the simultaneous processing task of listening, interpreting, and speaking. Gerver (1976) provides an extensive review of two categories: (1) temporal measures of input and output rates, speech and pause times, ear-voice spans, words correctly interpreted under different listening conditions, and (2) analysis of errors in the target language production. In addition, cognitive psychologists and psychologists have concentrated on three complex aspects of simultaneous interpreting: time lag, probability prediction, and memory (Benediktov 1974, Oléron & Nanpon 1965; Chernov 1978; Cokely 1984; Gerver 1974; Lambert 1983; Ingram 1985). Based on these studies, theoretical models of the cognitive processing stages have been generated to account for the findings (Gerver 1976; Moser 1978; Ingram 1980, and Cokely 1984). Because much of this literature is reviewed extensively elsewhere (Cokely 1984; Ingram 1985), I will move on to other aspects of interpreting research.

While these models inform us of the cognitive domains of interpreting, this domain is only one part of the complexity that is interpreting. Other important interactional features and strategies that occur when an interpreter is working need the same kind of attention. Anderson (1976, 1978) took a different approach to studying interpretation. As a sociologist he analyzed essential elements that constitute an interpreting situation and discussed the role of the interpreter as "the man in the middle." He noticed that the interpreter can be a powerful figure because the participants lack access to each other's language. He suggested two kinds of typologies for studying interpretation: a typology of situations, and a typology of interpreter's roles. While these studies, published some years ago, established some basic directions for an analysis of the role of the interpreter, research in this direction has not been pursued.

Interactional approaches to language & social life

In choosing to pursue this research direction, the role of the interpreter, I then turned to research in interactional approaches to language and social life. In that vein, a number of studies and theoretical frameworks are important. Because the interchange of interpreting has yet to even be described fully, Hymes (1974), in his now-famous call for adequate descriptions of social interactions, provides a framework, a starting point, from which to describe the complex event of interpreting.

As conversation is the basic material of human interaction and interpreters are an integral part of such interaction, the work of conversational analysts is the foundation of this study. Applying Gumperz's notion of contextualization cues (1982) – prosodic and lexical/phrasal choices that co-occur with the surface content of a message and signal an interpretive frame for the listener – Tannen (1984) further developed the analysis of conversation by identifying and explaining the use of those linguistic and paralinguistic features that constitute a person's conversational style. Tannen, building also on the work of R. Lakoff (1973) who introduced the notion of stylistic strategies, suggests that speakers choose linguistic devices which when used as a larger part of style, serve the paradoxical human needs to be involved with each other and to be independent of each other. Her work resulted in the idea of "conversational style," whereby speakers who vary in ethnicity, regional background, gender, and other respects will vary in their expectations about talk and in their interpretations of another's intentions. One of the demonstrable ways in which people vary is in their assumptions and expectations for turn-taking in conversation.

Turn-taking

One basic, specific conversational activity that can be recorded and described within any event is turn-taking. Turns can be analyzed in two ways: as structural entities, and as natural developments in a discourse event in which the participants come together to accomplish a goal. Both of these approaches form the analysis below. Sacks, Schegloff, and Jefferson (1974) wrote the seminal work on the organization of turns in conversation. The system, as they describe it, consists of two components and an ordered set of rules that operate on those components. Much of their analysis rests on the assumption that, in general, one person speaks at a time and that turns are signalled by syntactic unit-types. However, other analysts (Bennett 1981; Edelsky 1981; Tannen 1984) have pointed out that some of the "rules" postulated in Sacks et al. are not necessarily the way conversation works. They argue that, not only can there be more than one speaker at a time, but that many people do not interpret speaking at the same time as interruption. Tannen (1984), in her study of a Thanksgiving dinner among friends, found that overlapping speech was both comfortable and well-received when used with participants of similar conversational styles. She also showed that these participants did not describe such talk as interruption, but rather as showing interest and involvement.

Bennett (1981) cautions against the use of structural definitions of simultaneous talk because it can lead to false conclusions. Rather, he too suggests that simultaneous talk be labelled as "overlap," which is a descriptive term, because interruption is a judgment that conversational participants make in deciding speaking rights and obligations within a situation.

Others have noted that what counts as a turn is problematic for researchers. Edelsky (1981) found that trying to define a turn by mechanical definitions did not offer as much insight into conversational behavior as did defining turns by assessing a participant's intention to convey a message. In fact, she found that it was possible to take a turn without being the speaker who "has the floor." Tannen (1989), in discussing the research of conversational analysts (i.e. Zimmerman & West 1983), argues that research on interruptions that is based on experimental designs counts the number of occurrences. But counting does not take into account individual and social differences in attitudes toward overlapping speech and whether participants feel they have been interrupted or not. She argues that overlapping speech is often not intended or perceived as interruption, and that perceived interruptions are often neither the fault of intention of any speaker but rather the result of style difference, the interaction of two differing turn-taking systems.

Overlapping (simultaneous) speech is a significant conversational occurrence in interpreting. Interpreters have to make decisions about who has to stop speaking and whose turn it is.

The interpreted event

In the fall of 1987, at a major university in the Northeast a professor, a doctoral student, and an interpreter met for fifteen minutes on a Wednesday morning. The meeting was held in the professor's office, which contained one wall of bookshelves, a desk, two chairs, and five file cabinets, making the office somewhat crowded. The professor sat behind the desk, and the student sat to one side of the desk facing the professor. The interpreter sat beside the professor on a makeshift chair. I stood with my back against the office door and filmed the meeting. Because the interpreter was also the interpreter for the student in class, he was more readily available on the days when the class met. Consequently, this meeting occurred thirty minutes before class.

The student was taking a class entitled: Discourse Analysis-Narrative, which focused on narratives told in conversation. Every student was required to record a conversation, and select a story told by one of the conversationalists. Then students were to transcribe the narrative and use it for analysis during the semester. The professor had to approve every student's narrative selection, so this student had requested a brief meeting with the professor to ask if the transcribed section was an appropriate story and to see if it was acceptable in its present form.

During the analysis I refer to each participant by role (professor, student, interpreter). Given the nature of the interaction, their roles are one of the most important factors in this interaction. Professor of linguistics, Deborah Tannen (director of the dissertation study on which this paper is based) is in her early forties and is the author of six books and numerous articles on sociolinguistics. In one of her books, she analyzed her own conversational style as using cooperative overlap (a feature whereby speakers talk together to show involvement rather than to interrupt), latching (a feature whereby one speaker's utterance follows immediately at the finish of a previous speaker, quick expressive responses, and persistence in a conversational topic.

The student is a Deaf[1] man, in his middle thirties, a doctoral student, and an instructor at another university across the city. He has a Master's degree in linguistics and is actively involved in linguistic research on American Sign Language (ASL), the natural language of Deaf persons in the U.S. and Canada, and a language autonomous in structure, with features shared among all languages as well as unique features well-shaped to the constraints of a visual modality. The student teaches ASL and its structure to undergraduate students at his university. The student is bilingual in the sense that he speaks ASL and can also read and write English. This type of bilingualism in the deaf community is well-documented in the literature (Stokoe 1969; Woodward 1982; Grosjean 1982; Kannapell 1985).

The interpreter is a young, white male in his late twenties who was pursuing a bachelor's degree at a university in an adjoining state. He is the son of deaf parents and a graduate of an Interpreter Training Program (AA degree), and is a popular interpreter in the area. He is a member of the Registry of Interpreters for the Deaf (RID) and was awarded the highest level of professional certification, Comprehensive Skills Certificate (CSC), from this organization in 1983. The student had taken a class from Dr. Tannen before, and the interpreter had also interpreted previously for this student in Dr. Tannen's class; so the three of them knew each other, had held teacher-student conferences previously, and were acquainted, in differing degrees, with interactions involving interpreters.

Turn exchanges

The rest of this paper has an approach that is dual in nature. There are two basic questions to be asked about turns and overlapping talk within interpreted events. One deals with the linguistic structure of the turn-taking mechanism itself; i.e. What happens linguistically when overlapping talk occurs in interpreting? The other asks what sociolinguistic factors influence the interpreter's decisions about overlapping talk within interpreted events. Hence, the analysis is twofold: first, to describe what happens and what decisions

---

1. Upper case is used here to indicate membership in the linguistic and cultural group, more or less regardless of hearing acuity.

the interpreter makes, and second, to investigate sociolinguistic factors that determine the choices made by the interpreter.

My approach in the original study was to test the claims and predictions that might be made by a conduit model of interpreting through the description of a specific conversational feature, turn-taking, to see if the model's claims adequately explained the organization of turns. Although conduit assumptions do not explicitly address turn exchanges, it is possible to address the underlying assumptions that a conduit notion makes about conversational exchanges and from those assumptions deduce implicit claims.

Central to such a model is the claim that the two primary speakers are talking directly to each other. If that were true, turns would be exchanged directly between speakers, and if speakers were exchanging turns then they would be the only participants who manage turns. Another claim is that conversational phenomena such as silence (or gaps) and overlapping talk represent breakdowns in the exchange of words; thus, speakers would have to stop talking and indicate to each other who should go on speaking. In this way, the primary speakers would be repairing the breakdown and reorganizing the exchange.

The analysis of the transcription of the meeting between the professor, the student and the interpreter revealed, however, that turn exchange in interpreting is a complex and complicated event and that, organizationally, the conduit-model's claims about turn-taking are false. What is immediately apparent from the transcript is that although the content and intent of the turn originates with each primary speaker, these two speakers are not talking to each other in the sense of exchanging the direct surface signals of their respective languages. In interpreted events, turns are not exchanged directly across speakers. In fact, each speaker exchanges speaking turns with the interpreter, and in his or her own language. This is the only way the turns can occur.

For instance, if one speaker talks and then stops, and after a slight delay the other speaker starts talking, the surface appearance, or illusion, is that a smooth, uncomplicated exchange has taken place between the two primary speakers. In actuality, a smooth exchange *has* taken place, but it has taken place first between the first speaker and the interpreter, and then between the interpreter and the next speaker, who after hearing the end of an interpretation from the interpreter, has taken a turn to speak. The exchange has worked smoothly between the interpreter and each speaker, not between the two speakers.

Overlap in interpreting

In face-to-face interactions within one language, when another speaker decides to talk, she can do so at any transition-relevant moment in the talk of the other speaker. Sometimes these relevant moments come at the end of the other speaker's talk, but the potential exists for overlap with the current speaker who may not be finished speaking. The potential also exists for simultaneous decisions to take a turn, resulting in two speakers beginning to talk at the same time. Overlapping talk also occurs when one speaker is talking and the listener indicates, verbally or non-verbally, that understanding occurs or has not, or indicates agreement or disagreement. This kind of talk is usually brief in nature and has been termed back-channel (Yngve 1970). This kind of talk is potentially important because it can direct the talk of the speaker.

In interpreting, one kind of overlapping talk is constant; that is, interpreters begin interpreting several seconds after a primary speaker has begun. In interpretation between a signed language and a spoken language, there is not the actual sound of two speaking voices as there would be in interpretation between two spoken languages.[2] With one of the languages being a signed language, however, the "voice" of the interpreter does not interfere, because as the English speaker is talking, the interpreter is signing. And in the other direction, as the signer is using ASL, only the interpreter produces vocalized utterances. Speakers can easily determine that the interpreter is talking, whether signing or vocalizing, from either the head or arm movements of the interpreter or mouth movements of the interpreter. Usually, speakers can also determine that the other speaker is talking by looking at each other, although this is not always the case.

This kind of overlap, then, between speaker and interpreter, which can also seen or heard by the two speakers, is a marker of the unusual nature of an interpreting event. This overlap, due to the necessary lag of interpreting, is also why turns may not operate in expected or ordinary fashion from the perspective of the primary speakers. This interpreting overlap becomes the norm in this unusual event. This interlingual overlap is regular and expected, and when it does not occur, speakers are surprised and may stop speaking. If the overlap lasts too long, speakers again tend to be surprised and can be observed turning their attention towards the interpreter. Overlapping talk between primary speaker and interpreter, then, is an accepted norm of this face-to-face encounter, and is not the kind of overlap to be discussed here.

There is another kind of overlap that occurs in interpreted encounters, however, which requires the interpreter to intervene. This is overlapping talk which occurs between the two primary speakers. This overlap can be easily understood, as turns can be self-generated and/or two participants can engage in simultaneous talk. When interpretation occurs between a signed language and a spoken language, a person who can hear and speak English may not know how one "begins" to speak in ASL, and likewise, a person who cannot hear and uses a visual language cannot always know when speech is occurring.

---

2. Thus we find a primary reason for the extensive development of electronic equipment in spoken language interpreting: to mask the interpreter's voice, or get it "hidden." This equipment makes possible the removal of interpreters from the place where the face-to-face meeting is happening. They are secluded in glass booths where they can see but they cannot be seen or *heard by* the primary participants.

Although both participants can hear when interpreting is between spoken languages, they cannot know what kind of response is occurring.

This is not to say that primary speaker overlap is a customary occurrence. In fact, it appears that the participants in an interpreting situation are, for the most part, aware that something unusual is going on and adjust their usual habits of talking. They may be more cautious about taking a turn, and many times are not quite sure sure if it is their turn or just a pause by the other speaker. However, the occurrence of overlap between the two primary speakers is of particular interest, because when it occurs, the interpreter can, potentially, become the active arbitrator of the turn. Overlap is an interesting phenomenon within interpreted events because the overlap itself cannot be translated, and because the interpreter literally cannot interpret two speakers at the same time. Thus this overlap has a different impact than when it occurs in one-language conversations. In any language there can be overlapping talk without resort to an outside party to stop one or both speakers. But with interpreting, if two speakers overlap, there are potentially *three* people talking, both speakers, and the interpreter. The question then becomes, what does the interpreter do or, rather, what choices are available to the interpreter?

Interpreters have four options when overlap occurs, (a) The interpreter can stop one or both speakers and, in that way, halt the turn of one speaker, allowing the other speaker to continue. If the interpreter stops both speakers, it is possible that one of the primary speakers will decide who talks next, not the interpreter, (b) The interpreter can momentarily ignore one speaker's overlapping talk, hold the segment of talk from that speaker, continue interpreting the other speaker, and then produce the "held" talk immediately following the end of the other speaker's turn. Decisions about holding talk in one's memory lie within the interpreter's ability to do so and the interpreter's judgment regarding the importance or impact of the talk that was held, (c) The interpreter can ignore the overlapping talk completely, (d) The interpreter can momentarily ignore the overlapping talk, and upon finishing the interpretation of one speaker offer a turn to the other primary speaker or indicate in some way that a turn was attempted.

Stopping a speaker

In order to stop a speaker, an interpreter has to do something, verbally and/or non-verbally, within microseconds of the start of overlapping talk. Although there are many strategies for stopping speakers, an interpreter has to choose a strategy that will work in a specific situation with a specific speaker. It is not extraordinary for an interpreter to choose wrong; it is, rather, extraordinary that interpreters choose correctly so often. Examples below will indicate when and where in overlapping talk the interpreter makes one of the decisions listed above and present the sociolinguistic knowledge behind those decisions. Remember that ASL is a language that marks grammatical relationships with the face and by movement in space and in print must be represented by glosses that are *literal* English translations of some *part* of the corresponding ASL lexical item. Therefore the meaning represented here will necessarily seem somewhat skewed or simplified.

The first example below has two instances of overlap within seven seconds of talk. In this example, the professor has been discussing the reasons why the student's work is good but needs some corrections. As the example begins the professor has switched to a new topic, transcribing stories in conversation, which she introduces with the word *chunking*. The example begins with the professor (P) saying, "Chunking," the interpreter (I) rendering an interpretation of what the student (S) says in the next line.

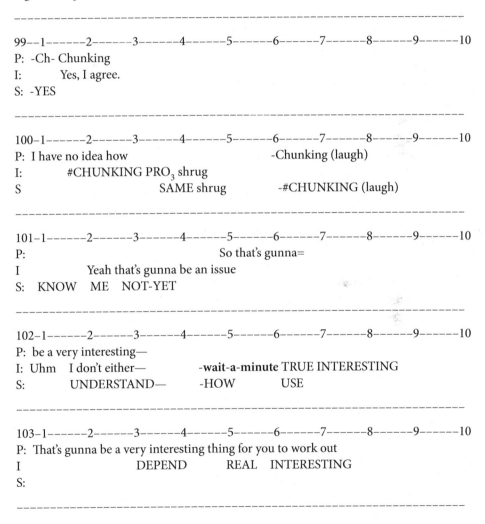

```
-----------------------------------------------------------------------
99--1------2------3------4------5------6------7------8------9------10
P: -Ch- Chunking
I:       Yes, I agree.
S: -YES
-----------------------------------------------------------------------
100-1------2------3------4------5------6------7------8------9------10
P: I have no idea how                    -Chunking (laugh)
I:          #CHUNKING PRO₃ shrug
S                    SAME shrug          -#CHUNKING (laugh)
-----------------------------------------------------------------------
101-1------2------3------4------5------6------7------8------9------10
P:                              So that's gunna=
I           Yeah that's gunna be an issue
S:  KNOW   ME   NOT-YET
-----------------------------------------------------------------------
102-1------2------3------4------5------6------7------8------9------10
P: be a very interesting—
I: Uhm   I don't either—         -wait-a-minute TRUE INTERESTING
S:          UNDERSTAND—          -HOW          USE
-----------------------------------------------------------------------
103-1------2------3------4------5------6------7------8------9------10
P: That's gunna be a very interesting thing for you to work out
I                    DEPEND        REAL  INTERESTING
S:
-----------------------------------------------------------------------
```

The conventions used in the transcription for the professor's and interpreter's speech are from Tannen (1984):

. marks sentence-final falling intonation;
? marks yes/no question rising intonation;
, marks phrase-final intonation, signals more to come;
brackets between lines mark overlap 2 or more speaking;
bent brackets mark 2nd utterance latched onto 1st.

The student's signing is transcribed using conventions for showing ASL utterances from Baker and Cokely (1980).

\# indicates fingerspelled word;
\+ indicates repetition of a sign;
hd nod indicates up-and-down positive head signal;
PRO$_1$ indicates first person;
PRO$_2$ indicates second person.

At the beginning of this example, the student's response (99.1) YES is a response to the interpretation of the professor's prior utterance, which was: "the translation is not exactly idiomatic." Simultaneously, however, the professor continues with her turn and introduces a new topic, chunking. In these two segments, "chunking" is said twice (99.1 and 100.6) by the professor and said the same way both times. There is stress on the first syllable as well as a rising then falling to mid-level intonation, and, when said as /**chunk**-ing/ in English, it also bears the information of "here's what I want to talk about next."

The professor begins with, (99.3) "Ch- Chunking (100) I have no idea how …(101)." The student receives the interpretation of this utterance as "Chunking, it (and the interpreter shrugs)" and then almost immediately begins a response that consists of more than just an acknowledgement. He says, in essence, that chunking is something he wants to discuss (and shrugs as the interpreter did), but he has not yet figured out where the chunks are. The professor, although she has not received the interpretation of these utterances by the student, seems to catch on to the student's puzzlement about chunking and its difficulty, some of which is communicated non-verbally by head-shaking, and the two speakers laugh together. There is overlap as the professor and the student (in fingerspelling) both say "chunking" at the same time, but there is no interpretation taking place at this point. This one word overlap does not receive any resolution by the interpreter. Both speakers seem to know, because they are looking at each other, that the other has said something, although they cannot know what the other has said. Both could be assuming a response has been made by the other that does not require that they give up their turn. The interpreter chose to interpret neither speaker. This is significant, because although the professor can see that the student has said something and is saying more that just 'oh' or 'yeah,' the student cannot know nor guess that the professor's contribution was not only more than an acknowledgement or a response, but a second attempt at opening this topic as well as having more to say about it.

This first instance of overlap happens quickly and just as quickly both primary speakers go on with their turn. The student continues talking sooner than the professor, and the interpreter interprets the student's utterances. As the interpreter produces a translation for the student's talk, the professor begins to speak again (101.5). While the interpreter is producing the last part of his interpretation, the student continues to talk. Now, all of a sudden, there are three speakers, at 102.3: the interpreter, who renders an interpretation for the student; the student, who continues to talk; and the professor, who begins to talk. It is at this point that the interpreter's hand comes up and produces a gesture that results in the student's shifting his eye gaze from the professor to the interpreter and discontinuing his talk. The gesture, understood as '(you) wait-a-minute', functions to stop a person's turn.

The interpreter stops the student from continuing with his turn, whether or not he had any intention of doing so, and begins to interpret for the professor. From the first overlap of a single lexical item by the two speakers, the interpreter continues to interpret the student's remarks, apparently because the student continues with his turn and the professor seems to have stopped (100.8–101.5). The student says KNOW, which is interpreted as 'Yeah, that's gunna be an issue' and continues with NOT-YET, which is rendered as 'Uhm, I don't either.' During the first part of the interpretation (101.5) the professor begins to talk again, "So that's gunna be a very interesting…." Then at 102.3 all three are speaking. As the interpreter produces 'wait-a-minute,' the student's eye gaze is drawn from the professor to the interpreter and he stops talking. Thus, the interpreter stops the student from continuing his turn, and begins an immediate interpretation of the professor's utterances. On the next line of transcript (103.0) the professor restarts her utterance, and the interpreter continues to interpret the professor.

The gesture, 'wait-a-minute,' used by speakers of many different languages including English and ASL, is a powerful strategy used by interpreters. Immediately upon viewing it, the student's hands go down to a resting position and he makes no further attempt to speak. In order to demonstrate how powerful this 'stop' signal is, thirty seconds later when the student has begun to talk, the interpreter reaches out towards the student with an open palm, not the standing index finger, as if to say, 'hold up a second and let me catch up.' The student pauses but does *not* allow his hands to fall to a rest position, and he resumes signing when the interpreter's hand is withdrawn.

At first, it might seem that the interpreter has made an arbitrary choice, choosing the professor over the student. However, the topic "chunking" was begun by the professor at 99.0 and it's clear that she has not finished talking about it. She re-starts her topic, and continues to elaborate on this topic. Even though the professor does pause for a moment, when she begins to talk again, she is continuing with comments about chunking. The next example is another instance of overlap between the two primary speakers in which the interpreter again uses the gesture 'wait-a-minute,' that stops the student's turn. This example occurs after the professor has finished talking about chunking and the student has been talking about potential comparable cues in ASL. The student has been talking for almost 33 seconds at this point when the professor begins to take a turn by saying, "yeah," and then makes two attempts at starting an utterance. As the professor attempts the second start, the student is still talking and the interpreter produces 'wait-a-minute'.

```
124–1------2------3------4------5------6------7------8------9------10
P:
I:  then I'll try to look for
S:  SAME—BETWEEN—TWO—THINGS
```

```
125–1------2------3------4------5------6------7------8------9------10
P:
I:  uhm    something that's                       equal to that
S:  #IF      NOT HAVE                     "WELL" THAT POSS (it's)
```

```
126–1------2------3------4------5------6------7------8------9------10
P:
I:                    within          uhm   spoken language
S:  DIFFERENT   DIFFERENT   LANGUAGE,   PRO3
```

```
127–1------2------3------4------5------6------7------8------9------10
P:                                        —Yeah
I:                           cues. ------
S:  THEN PRO₁ FIND   hd nod   "WELL"            DONT-KNOW
```

$$S:\ \text{THEN PRO}_1\ \text{FIND}\quad \text{hd nod}\quad \text{"WELL"}\qquad \text{DONT-KNOW}$$

```
128–1------2------3------4------5------6------7------8------9------10
P:        —It must be—            —if-
I:  uhm                    —wait a-minute,     HAVE-TO HAVE
3:  BUT    —PRO₁ ANALYZE   —REQUIRE            REQUIRE MUCH
```

$$3:\ \text{BUT}\quad -\text{PRO}_1\ \text{ANALYZE}$$

```
99--1------2------3------4------5------6------7------8------9------10
P:                        Or just thinking about it maybe
I:  I mean it's gunna take a lot of time (laugh)
S:  TIME   TIME (nodding------------)                    YES YOU
```

The student has been talking here about searching for comparable discourse cues in ASL that will help him determine where to chunk the ASL narrative. The professor responds (127.6) with "Yeah," and then starts to talk. The professor begins to talk even though the interpreter has said "uhm," a vocalization in English that can hold a turn at talk by implying there's more to come. But "uhm" can also signal a turn-transition moment in English, at which another speaker can self-select to take a turn. In addition, the interpreter's immediately prior utterance was "spoken language…cues," said with a falling intonation. In fact, the professor starts her response at the end of the interpreter's talk with "yeah."

Although the student continues to speak (127:7), the interpreter's next rendition is "uhm," (128.1), which does not indicate that the student has said something of substance; thus it does not substantially interfere with the professor's continuing turn. So, when all this comes together, the student and the interpreter have been talking for several seconds, the interpreter's prior utterance is said with falling intonation, and "uhm" with a pause does not offer anything of substance, the professor starts to talk. More importantly, the interpreter has constructed all these surface conditions that provide the opportunity for talk by the other speaker. Although "wait-a-minute" is signalled to the student, the professor does not continue either and the interpreter uses the pause to complete an interpretation of the student's utterance. At the professor's utterance, "It must be–," the student is still talking (128:0–3). Perhaps, as the professor utters "if–," the accumulation of the student's continued signing and the interpreter's "uhm" has registered with the professor that the student is still talking. When the student sees "wait-a-minute," he repeats REQUIRE. Since this sign is usually not used with repetition nor inflected, the conclusion we are left with is that something affected the flow of talk, and quite clearly, it seems to be the "wait-a-minute."

In any case, the student finishes his utterance and stops completely, because he lowers his hands. Interestingly enough, the interpreter signs "wait-a-minute" simultaneously with HAVE-TO- HAVE; this can be done because a sign language has separable articulators, the two hands. Thus the interpreter can tell the student to hold his turn while simultaneously starting to interpret what the professor is saying. Then the interpreter drops his hands, an indication that he will not be signing any more. But the student also stops and the interpreter renders an interpretation for REQUIRE MUCH TIME, but does not provide an interpretation for PRO$_1$ ANALYZE, which came before REQUIRE MUCH TIME. Memory studies have shown that the human memory can store chunks of information unless something happens to interrupt the chunk of information. I suggest that having to intervene in an overlap and make a decision has interrupted the flow of information coming from the student, and the interpreter remembers only what he has seen after the overlap was resolved.

Momentarily ignoring a turn, "holding," and delivering later

Next, I present examples of overlap where the interpreter "holds" the talk until he has a chance to interpret it. His ability to "hold" the talk happens for several reasons: the interpreter perceives that the talk is not critical at the moment, the overlapping talk is short, simple, and easy to remember, or the interpreter can project that one speaker is either finishing or will finish soon. Knowing that a speaker is nearing the end of a stream of talk, or at least coming to a turn-relevant moment, is a combination of both grammatical, paralinguistic, and discourse knowledge in both languages (which is knowing how speakers present ideas, make their points, and do summary kinds of talk). The following occurrence of overlap is the first one in this interview between the two speakers. The professor has just finished talking on the phone and is looking at the answering machine near the phone and re-setting it to record telephone messages. The student begins talking as the professor's gaze is still on the machine. The interpreter has not yet begun an interpretation, so as the professor turns back to facing the student, she and the student begin to talk simultaneously, with the student repeating his initial utterance. As they near the completion of their respective utterances, the interpreter also begins to talk, interpreting what the student has said.

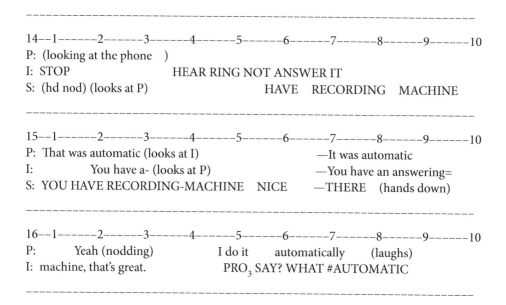

One convention interpreters seem to obey is that if someone has said something, and, in fact, said it two or more times, there is an obligation to get that message out even if it has to wait. As the interpreter successfully completes his second attempt to interpret the student, he is also aware that the student is finished talking because the student's hands go down and rest in his lap. The student has seen the professor talk, once in his direction, and once towards the interpreter. The professor persists with her turn, repeating the same propositional information three times. Before the third attempt, she responds to the interpretation from the interpreter, and, for the third time, repeats her utterance. The interpreter renders an interpretation of the student's talk, "holds" what the professor says, and immediately upon completion of the professor's third try, interprets what the professor has said.

In this segment of talk, the interpreter has made two attempts to interpret the student's utterances, the last one being successful. He then immediately renders an interpretation for the professor. During the interpreter's second attempt to render the student's message, he sees the student's hands do down, which, in ASL, is a clear signal that one is finished talking. Thus he knows that quickly he will be able to render an interpretation for the professor. In this segment the interpreter can hold for an accumulation of reasons; the professor is repeating herself, the content of her utterance is ambiguous yet simple, and he can predict that one speaker will soon stop talking. In the second example, the professor has been discussing Chafe's theory that chunking is a result of a speaker's consciousness focusing on one piece of information at a time. She suggests that if this is true of a spoken language, then it should also be true of a sign language. She suggests that there is a corollary in sign for chunks and then says that if there is none, it would disprove Chafe. Towards the end, the professor pauses and then starts talking again. During her pause, the student makes a response to the interpretation and then, as the professor begins talking again, the interpreter is interpreting the student's response, which consists of only two more signs. In addition, the student's hands go down, a clear signal that he will not say more.

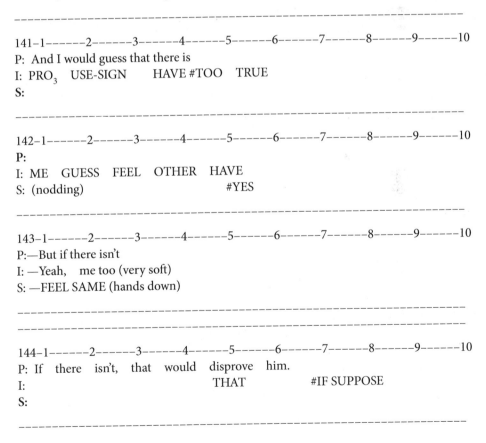

```
141-1------2------3------4------5------6------7------8------9------10
P: And I would guess that there is
I: PRO₃   USE-SIGN      HAVE #TOO   TRUE
S:
```

```
142-1------2------3------4------5------6------7------8------9------10
P:
I: ME   GUESS   FEEL   OTHER   HAVE
S: (nodding)                    #YES
```

```
143-1------2------3------4------5------6------7------8------9------10
P:—But if there isn't
I: —Yeah,   me too (very soft)
S: —FEEL SAME (hands down)
```

```
144-1------2------3------4------5------6------7------8------9------10
P: If   there   isn't,   that   would   disprove   him.
I:                               THAT            #IF SUPPOSE
S:
```

In segment 143, all three participants overlap. The interpreter is giving an interpretation of the student's response, "Yeah, me too." The professor, meanwhile, has begun speaking again, "But if there isn't." As the overlap ends, and the interpreter sees that the student will not continue, he waits for the professor to continue and begins interpreting her remarks (144.5). The interpreter has heard the professor stop talking, and his experience suggests that she will start anew. His experience in this conversation alone has proven that the professor will persist in what she has to say. Consequently, the interpreter appears to be "holding" what the professor has said, knowing there will be another opportunity to interpret her talk because the student has stopped talking.

The interpreter has also recognized the student's contribution as the kind of backchannel, brief response that a listener contributes without necessarily meaning to take a turn. By uttering his interpretation in a soft, lowered voice, he renders this back-channel response from the student appropriately.

In this section I have shown that a unique feature of turn transitions happens around the occurrence of overlapping talk. When the primary speakers talk simultaneously or all three participants begin to speak simultaneously, the interpreter recognizes and acts on resolving overlap, unless he chooses to ignore a speaker's contribution. In this corpus, the interpreter stopped the student through the use of a gesture, labelled as 'wait-a-minute,' which functions to get speakers (of both English and ASL) to hold their turns. I also showed that the interpreter held overlapping talk momentarily and delivered it later because he knew that one of the primary speakers was coming to the end of a turn. Thus the interpreter is again active at a level previously unacknowledged. In stopping the overlapping talk of a speaker, the interpreter is actively making decisions about the emerging conversation, and the obligations of its participants as well as influencing the direction, which, in turn, influences the outcome of the event.

The sociolinguistics of turn exchanges

This section examines the sociolinguistic factors that influence turns around overlapping talk and the way those factors contribute to the interpreter's active participation and decisions about turns within this interpreted event. I begin again with a discussion of the implicit claims that the conduit model would make about sociolinguistic factors influencing turns and overlapping talk. Here it is once again necessary to address the underlying assumptions that the model makes about the participants' and the interpreter's roles in resolving overlap. First though, the meeting of the professor, the student, and the interpreter is a social situation. In it the two speakers are not equal in status and power, and the messages exchanged by the speakers carry social meaning that is embedded in their linguistic nature. To understand the interpreter's role fully, this social situation needs more explication. Next we will see how turns with overlap happen and how primary speakers take or keep turns based on their own sense of when is a turn. Finally, I discuss the reasons behind the interpreter's decisions about overlapping talk. Through-out this section I dis-cuss the active participation of the interpreter and the reasoning behind decisions about the exchange of turns.

A conduit model of interpreting, as has been said, claims that turns are exchanged directly across primary speakers and implies that the primary speakers organize the turns. While primary speakers are not talking to each other in the sense of exchanging messages in the physical signals of their respective languages, they *are* talking to each other in the sense that the content of their respective messages is meant for each other and the goal of their discourse is to accomplish the task which brought them together.

It is important to mention first that the primary problem with the conduit model is that it does not explain nor account for interaction *between* participants. It accounts only for a one-way communication process, in which a sender creates a message and a receiver receives it. It does not concern itself with the nature of exchange in discourse. In addition, it focuses primarily on the form and meaning of the structures that are a part of the mes-sage as well. Consequently, when an interpreter is inserted into a communicative process, the interpreter becomes idealized as a conduit through which a message simply passes. Following this reasoning, of course, speakers would have as their sole purpose the packag-ing of information, and interpreters would have as their purpose its unpackaging, repack-aging, and delivery. This also assumes that the primary participants are equal interlocutors with equal rights and obligations, a situation that we know does not always obtain.

A second claim the model implies is that the types of turns are created by the two primary and equal participants and that overlap, if it occurs, will be dealt with purely as a breakdown in communication between the two primary speakers. Thus the model does not recognize the sociological and pragmatic aspects of the occurrence and management of overlap.

Though this conversation between the professor and the student might seem ordi-nary and straightforward, in some ways it is quite unlike other conversations that occur in everyday life. It is not a casual chat between acquaintances, nor a conversation between colleagues who work together. Within this meeting, communication is in the foreground of attention because the presence of an interpreter puts the focus on the communication.

This kind of meeting is an encounter between relative strangers, who are unequal in authority and unequal in experience with the conversational routines of such a meeting. It is an essential task of the professor to provide information as well as direction and correc-tion by learning about the student's work. It is also practically important for the student to find out who the professor is, but that importance is unofficial. Officially, it is essential that the professor make some determination as to the student's accomplishment of an assigned task in order to give advice or information that makes sense and will help him pass the course. The professor may be accustomed to a set of conversational means of providing information and giving advice to students. But because the student speaks a language other than English and has limited experience in the setting of a large university graduate program, he may or may not be familiar with university graduate program, he may or may not be familiar with these patterns of interaction. It is also possible that the student, although experienced in interpreted meetings, may not be skilled at having a conversation or asking for help from a professor. Of equal importance, the professor and student have considerably differing degrees of experience in situations involving the presence of an interpreter.

In this sort of meeting the teacher acts as an institutional gatekeeper (Erickson & Schultz 1982). She has the responsibility and the authority to make decisions, not only about the outcome of the student's work within a specific course, but also with regard to his forward progress within a doctoral program. Thus the professor is tending a gate of mobility, not only in terms of the outcome of the program, but also as those outcomes influence the student's future life.

The meeting between the university professor and the adult student is a delicate balance between treating each other as equals because of closeness in age (there is only five years difference) and professional status (they both teach at universities, although their levels of degree and position are different), and maintaining the social roles of professor and student. As a teacher, the professor has the information and the knowledge to help a student complete work that is new, while the student's main goal is to learn the material of the course and to do well so that he can continue to progress in the program. Thus for the conduit model neither to account for nor to explain social and interactive processes as they affect interpreting is both unrealistic and simplistic. The messages of each speaker are not strictly for the purpose of packaging information, but are instead complex entities containing equally important messages about relationships between participants, displays of abilities, displays of perceptions, and other messages. Moreover, the professor and the student are not equal interlocutors, but complex human beings who possess different rights and obligations for speaking at different times and for different reasons.

Turns with overlap

Choosing to see communication as requiring effort, and studying its success, leads to the notion that overlap, rather than being viewed as a breakdown, is a natural and expected phenomenon produced by speakers, for either cooperative or uncooperative reasons, and may be understood by listeners as either cooperative or uncooperative. Because turns can also begin at any moment, they can also come about at a moment that ill produce overlapping talk.

The next example takes on a whole new light when the professor and the student elaborate their reasons in playback interviews for persisting with a turn and taking a turn, respectively, both of which created overlap. As the example begins, the professor has switched to a new topic, which is about transcribing stories told in conversation. She introduces the topic with the word *chunking*. Within this segment, the professor is talking, the student overlaps her, and the interpreter resolves the overlapping talk.

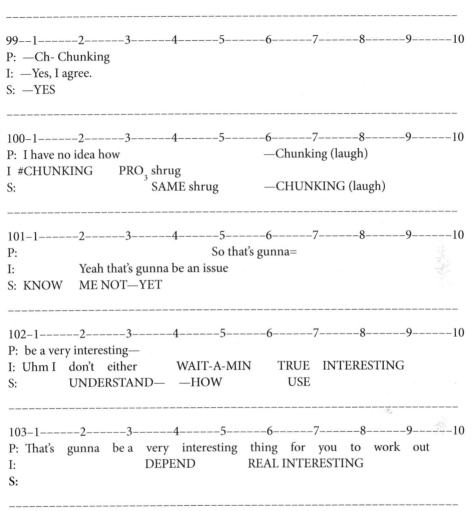

```
99--1------2------3------4------5------6------7------8------9------10
P: —Ch- Chunking
I: —Yes, I agree.
S: —YES
```

```
100-1------2------3------4------5------6------7------8------9------10
P: I have no idea how                    —Chunking (laugh)
I #CHUNKING      PRO₃ shrug
S:                    SAME shrug         —CHUNKING (laugh)
```

```
101-1------2------3------4------5------6------7------8------9------10
P:                              So that's gunna=
I:           Yeah that's gunna be an issue
S: KNOW     ME NOT—YET
```

```
102-1------2------3------4------5------6------7------8------9------10
P: be a very interesting—
I: Uhm I  don't  either       WAIT-A-MIN    TRUE  INTERESTING
S:             UNDERSTAND—  —HOW            USE
```

```
103-1------2------3------4------5------6------7------8------9------10
P: That's  gunna  be a  very  interesting  thing  for  you  to  work  out
I:                      DEPEND          REAL INTERESTING
S:
```

The student begins talking at 100.4, as the professor pauses after "I have no idea how–" He begins quickly and not at a relevant moment during the interpretation. The interpreter has said, in essence: 'She (shrug)' which might mean 'who knows' or 'I don't know.' This is not a complete utterance, it is just a pronoun and a non-verbal gesture. The student begins at 100.4 by saying SAME (shrug) CHUNKING, meaning roughly 'I had the same thought – chunking," which he later explained by giving his reason:

> I said SAME because I wanted to talk about the same thing chunking! And I was glad she brought it up. I didn't really understand it and hadn't remembered to ask her about it. I wanted her to talk about it.

The student, in the example, begins his turn in an enthusiastic, cooperative way, because he was glad the professor brought up the topic he wanted to discuss. In this sense, he collaborates in her shift to a new theme, and takes a turn to contribute to that flow. When the professor says "chunking" once again and pauses (100.6), the student continues with his contribution, and the interpreter, not hearing more from the professor, begins to interpret the student's utterance. However, at 101.5, the professor suddenly begins again, eventually creating overlap with the student and the interpreter, which the interpreter resolves by stopping the student. When the professor begins to talk by saying (101.5), "So that's gunna be a very interesting," she too does not enter at a turn-transition moment in the interpreter's talk. She begins talking for another reason, quite different from the student's reason (from later examination of the record):

> When I'm talking about chunking I think I clearly feel that what I have to say takes
> priority ... and I want to get it out. [The interpreter] starts talking but I don't want to
> hear it. I think I'm not sure whether [the student] was trying to take a turn or give
> a back channel but I'm going to treat it like a back channel because I want to keep
> talking. I wasn't ready to yield the floor.

Not only does the professor give a reason for her persistence in keeping her turn, but this reason reinforces that taking or keeping a turn is not based on surface structure signals alone. She affirms her perception of her role in the event which emerges in her discourse as persistence on the topic and her own sense that the turn is hers. The professor ignored the talk of the interpreter even though she knew the student was talking because she had more to say and felt, since it was her turn, that she could ignore overlap and continue. Moreover, the student wants her to talk about chunking, it is part of the reason he has come to meet her. Thus, both speakers produced turns that involved overlapping talk, but for reasons that are complementary.

This, then, is an indication that primary speakers are also actively involved in creating turns that have motivations to be found in the situated context. Thus, they are as active in regards to turn decisions as the interpreter is in the choice of the form of the turn.

Interpreter decisions about overlap

The next example returns to the example of overlapping talk between primary speakers that the interpreter resolves by stopping the student. Overlapping talk poses a dilemma for interpreters. Whether the talk is simply of a back-channel nature or will become an attempt to take a turn does not deny its meaningfulness in conversational activity. Moreover, at the start of overlapping talk, predicting the intent or purpose of the talk, as a back-channel or as an attempt to say more, is a difficult prediction. The interpreter in this study explained that most of time he judged the purpose of a new utterance by simultaneously considering what had been said, what the topic is, and by waiting until the first parts of an utterance are produced to see if it is going to be brief or continue longer. In interpreted conversations involving a signed language, the interpreter is usually the first to realize that overlap has begun, and in any interpreted conversation the participant who must determine a resolution is the interpreter.

In these situations the interpreter must determine the impact of the overlapping talk, its importance, and its ability to be conveyed. Because the two primary speakers can hear or see each other, they may have some sense that both of them are speaking at the same time, but they cannot know what is being said. The interpreter is the only person who knows at once that a dilemma can develop with overlap and that it may be more than a back-channel from a speaker. In this brief meeting the interpreter has to make eleven decisions regarding overlap. First, a brief summary of the decisions made and their differences:

–   When the student is speaking and the professor overlaps, the interpreter stops the student twice, holds the talk of the student four times and delivers it later;
–   When the professor is speaking and the student overlaps, the interpreter holds the talk of the professor once and ignores the student's talk four times;
–   The interpreter never stops the professor.

This summary would seem to indicate that the interpreter is making decisions which favor the professor and are probably made out of deference to her and her position, while the student is treated less favorably. The interpreter stops the student or ignores his contributions while he holds the professor's talk, but he never ignores her talk and never stops her. The interpreter's knowledge that this is the professor's "territory," along with her persistence on some topics, and the student's willingness to stop, makes it appear reasonable to suggest that the interpreter does decide that the professor's talk is more important than the student's talk. No doubt there is some truth in this reason, but like all discourse events with human beings, the complexity of factors is greater than a single reason. There are ways to understand how the student is also being treated favorably.

In this interpreted event, during overlapping talk, the interpreter uses "wait-a-minute" towards the student twice, and the student stops. The first time the interpreter stops the student is during the "chunking" example. The professor opens the topic of chunking, pauses, and when she begins again, the interpreter realizes she has more to say. The interpreter could be stopping the student because he realized that the professor who started the topic has not finished with her remarks. The interpreter could have decided (based on the student's own reasons for coming) that anything the professor had to say was important, and that it was important for the student to know what she was saying. Moreover, one could argue that the student concurs in the stop request by stopping. The student wants to hear the professor talk about chunking, so he stops talking because he feels that what the professor had to say was more important than anything he had to say.

Thus it can be said that the decision to stop has been made jointly by both the interpreter and the student. It can also be argued that such a decision, which allows the professor to talk, actually favors the student. The student has come to ask for help from the professor, consequently it benefits him to let her talk.

During the playback interview, both the student and the interpreter were asked what 'wait-a-minute' means to them. Interestingly, both said it was a signal to let the student know that the professor had begun talking. However, their actions do not seem to conform to their sense of what 'wait-a-minute' means because both times it was used, the student stopped talking. Moreover, there is other evidence that 'wait-a-minute' functions in a way that gets speakers to stop or hold their turn. At one point, the student himself uses this gesture to signal that he will pause but has more to say, and the professor does not take a turn. Likewise, when the professor indirectly asks for a pause, the interpreter uses the same gesture to the student, and the student does not take a turn. For example, during the first few seconds of talk in the interview, when the phone rings and the professor touches the interpreter's arm and says, "The phone's ringing," the interpreter uses 'wait-a-minute' to stop the student's turn. The student stops mid-sentence. Consequently, it seems to indicate that the gesture 'wait-a-minute' means 'hold your turn'.

With the professor, the interpreter uses "uhm" (which, during playback, he said he used to try to hold the turn), or continues to talk during the professor's overlapping talk; but neither of these actions stops the professor from taking a turn or continuing to talk in quite the same way the student is stopped.

We must also make note of the fact that the interpreter holds the professor's talk four times and delivers it as soon as he is finished interpreting the student. This is interesting, because it means that when the interpreter is interpreting for the student, he does not stop the student but judges that there will soon be an opportunity to deliver the professor's most recent talk. The interpreter also never ignores the professor's overlapping contributions, regardless of whether they are back-channel responses or not.

On the other hand, the interpreter ignores the student's overlapping back-channel responses and holds the student's talk only once. One reason for this may be that when the student makes agreement responses the professor can see for herself the student's nodding head. On the other hand, of course, when his response is more than a 'yes,' the professor cannot know what else the student has said.

During the playback interview, I asked the interpreter about his decisions when over-lap occurs. First, he mentioned that if the two primary speakers begin at the same time, he interprets what he hears, literally:

> I think I am more inclined to go with the voice than I am with signs, I have to be honest. So if they both start at once, I will start signing [interpret what I hear in English]. The Deaf person stops and I continue.

When asked if there could be any other reason other than hearing the English language, he replied:

> Is it a matter of equality?...This is her office, her territory. So he [the student] is the outsider coming in; so I think that [her being the insider] takes a lot of rein too.

Although he views an imbalance, in the sense that where they are meeting is "her territory," it is also interesting that he views the student as an "outsider." Framing the interview in this way, immediately provides the interpreter with a set of conventions for how this type of interaction works.

In the playback interview, the student explained that he wanted to hear what the professor had to say and that he felt that what the professor had to say was more important than anything he had to say. The interpreter arrived at the professor's office with the student and knew that the student was coming for help and information. Moreover, one could argue that the student concurs in the stop by stopping. Thus it can be said that the decision to stop has been made jointly by the interpreter and the student.

The interpreter's knowledge that this is the professor's "territory" (his words), that she is persistent on some topics, and of the student's willingness to stop, makes it appear reasonable to suggest that the professor's talk *is* more important than the student's talk. And it can also be argued that such a decision, which allows the professor to talk, actually favors the student. The student has come to ask for help from the professor; consequently, it benefits him to let her talk.

Undoubtedly, all these factors play a role in the interpreter's decisions about turns with overlap. To what degree the role of teacher and student, the prestige or status of their languages and cultures, or any other factors contribute to the interpreter's decisions remains a subject for future study.[3]

Historically, interpreters have tended not to acknowledge publicly, or instruct new interpreters, that the two primary speakers in interpreted dialogue may have different rights and obligations in talking, nor how this knowledge can influence the interpretations they are rendering. What they miss in not acknowledging these dynamics is that they do successfully interpret the pragmatic meanings of situations intuitively, and, perhaps unconsciously, and that, subsequently, these situations turn out much as they would if the two primary speakers spoke a common language.

Summary

The foregoing analysis of the meeting of the professor, the student, and the interpreter reveals that overlapping talk and the consequent decisions pose a complex task for interpreters. To explain interpreting as a one-way process – as a conduit that is presumed to work back the other way automatically and in exactly the same manner – is insufficient and unrealistic. All communication is an interactive process, and the insertion of an inter-

---

3.   Somehow, though, when we place this one event in the larger context of American universities as gatekeeping institutions, we know that it is very likely that interpreters will stop not the professors but the students who speak a language other than English.

preter can only be understood in terms of the interchange of communication. Communication is an interactive exchange, and when interpreters are used, they are a natural part of the interaction. The point is not their neutrality but rather what is or can be their active participation in the interaction.

The participants interact in complex ways. This paper shows that both speakers and the interpreter create unique kinds of overlap and turns resulting from overlap. Taking and relinquishing turns have been shown to be a mixture of the interpreter's decisions as well as the primary speakers' tacit agreement to accept those decisions. Moreover, by interpreting the pragmatics of this scene, the interpreter aids the minority speaker in behaving in ways acceptable to the larger society and in understanding how such scenes should play out.

Of greater significance, however, is that the interpreter is active in receiving and understanding a message which has social meaning beyond what is found in the surface form. The choice of an equivalent form, which will not only elicit an expected response, but which will also convey the intended social meaning, will be made for reasons other than its surface rendition and must be based on knowledge other than grammatical knowledge. Choosing the right form is dependent on such factors as the relative status of the interlocutors and the desired outcome for the situation.

Interpreters are active members of interpreted conversations. Contrary to the traditional ideology of interpreting, interpreters are involved in interpreting conventions for language use and in creating turn exchanges through their knowledge of the linguistic system, the social situation, and how each participant uses language to say what they mean.

In the meeting examined here, the interpreter exchanged turns with each speaker, and resolved turn problems caused by overlap. In particular, the interpreter recognized overlap quickly, and made linguistic choices to resolve the overlap by deciding who would get the turn. Many of his choices exemplified his understanding and interpretation of the social situation of a meeting between teacher and student.

The interpreter, formerly assumed to be a passive participant, is shown to be an active one – a competent bilingual who possesses not only knowledge of the two languages but also knowledge about the social situation, the "ways of speaking" of both languages, and strategies for the management of the communication event. This study has also shown that the interpreter is not solely responsible for either the success or failure of an interpreting event. All three participants jointly produce this event, and all three are responsible, in differing degrees, for its communicative success or failure.

References

Anderson, B. 1976. Perspectives on the role of the interpreter. In *Translation: Applications & Research,* Brislin ed. NY: Gardner. 208–225.

Anderson, B. 1978. Interpreter roles & interpretation situations. In *Language Interpretation & Communication,* Gerver & Sinaiko eds. NY: Plenum Press. 217–230.

Benediktov, B. 1974. The Psychology of Mastering a Foreign Language. Minsk: Vyshejshaya Shkola.

Bennett, A. 1981. Interruptions & the interpretation of conversation, *Discourse Processes* 4: 2,171–188.

Chernov, G. 1978. Theory & practice of simultaneous interpretation. Moscow. (Translated by J.R. Myers, M.A. thesis) Monterey Institute of International Studies, 1980.

Cokely, D. 1984. Towards a sociolinguistic model of the interpreting process: ASL & English. Ph.D. dissertation. Washington: Georgetown University.

Cokely, D. 1992. *A Sociolinguistic Model of the Interpreting Process.* Burtonsville, MD: Linstok Press.

Edelsky, C. 1981. Who' s got the floor? *Language & Society* 10,383–421.

Erickson, F. & J. Schultz 1982. *The Counselor as Gatekeeper: Social Interaction in Interviews.* New York: Academic Press.

Gerver, D. 1974. Simultaneous listening & speaking & retention of prose, *Quarterly Journal of Experimental Psychology* 26. 337–342.

Gerver, D. 1976. Empirical Studies of Simultaneous Interpretation: A review & a model. In *Translation: Applications & Research,* Brislin ed. N Y: Gardner Press, Inc.

Gumperz, J. 1977. Sociocultural knowledge in conversational inference. In *Linguistics & Anthropology, GUFtTLL, 1977,* Saville-Troike ed. Washington: Georgetown University Press. 191–211.

Gumperz, J. 1982. *Discourse strategies.* Cambridge: Cambridge University Press.

Gumperz, J. & D. Tannen. 1979. Individual & social differences in language use. In *Individual Differences in Language Ability & in Language Behavior,* Fillmore et al. eds. NY: Academic Press. 305–325.

Hymes, D. 1974. Models of Interaction & Social Life. In *Directions in Sociolinguistics: Ethnography of Communication,* Gumperz & D. Hymes eds. NY: Holt, Rinehart and Winston.

Ingram, R. 1980. Linguistic & Semiotic Process of Interpretation. Unpublished training materials. American Sign Language Associates.

Ingram, R. 1985. Simultaneous Interpretation of sign languages: semiotic & psycholinguistic perspectives. *Multilingual* 4: 2, 91–102.

Lakoff, G. & M. Johnson. 1980. *Metaphors We Live By.* Chicago: Univ. of Chicago Press.

Lakoff, R. 1973. The logic of politeness, or minding your p's & q's. *Papers from the Ninth Regional Meeting of the Chicago Linguistics Society.* Chicago: University of Chicago. 292–305.

Lakoff, R. 1975. *Language & Women's Place.* New York: Harper and Row.

Lambert, S. 1983. Recall & recognition among conference interpreters. Ph.D. dissertation, University of Stirling.

Moser, B. 1978. Simultaneous interpretation: A hypothetical model & its practical application. In *Language Interpretation & Communication,* Gerver & Sinaiko eds. NY: Plenum Press. 353–368.

Oteron, P. & H. Nanpon. 1965. Research on simultaneous interpretation, *Journal of Psychology & Pathology* 62, 73–94.

Reddy, M. 1979. The conduit metaphor: a case of frame conflict in our language about language. In *Metaphor and Thought,* Ortony ed. Cambridge: Cambridge Univ. Press. 284–324.

Roy, C. 1989. A Sociolinguistic analysis of the interpreter's role in the turn exchanges of an interpreted event. Ph.D. dissertation, Georgetown University, Washington, D.C. University Microfilms, Inc. DA064793.

Sacks, H., E. Schegloff & G. Jefferson. 1974. A simplest systematics for the organization of turn-taking in conversation, *Language* 50: 4, 696–735.

Tannen, D. 1984. *Conversational Style: Analyzing Talk Among Friends.*

Norwood, NJ: Ablex Publishing Co. 1989. Interpreting interruption in conversation. *Proceedings of the 25th Annual Meeting of the Chicago Linguistics Society,* Chicago, IL, April 28, 1989. Chicago: University of Chicago.

West, C. & D. Zimmerman. 1983. Small insults: A study of interruptions in cross-sex conversations between unacquainted persons. In *Language, Gender & Society,* Thome et al. eds. Rowley, MA: Newbury House. 103–117.

Note: The author thanks Professor Deborah Tannen for her time, attention, and encouragement, the student and the interpreter, whose participation made this and the larger study possible, and Robert E. Johnson, Chair of the Gallaudet University Department of Linguistics & Interpreting.

5.3 **McIntire, Marina and Gary Sanderson. 1995. "Bye-Bye! Bi-Bi! Questions of empowerment and role." In *A confluence of diverse relationships: Proceedings of the 13th National Convention of the Registry of Interpreters for the Deaf, 1993*, ed. by J. Plant-Moeller, 94–118. Silver Spring, MD: Registry of Interpreters for the Deaf.**

Marina McIntire has been a linguist, interpreter and educator for over 40 years. She holds a Ph.D. in Linguistics from the University of California Los Angeles (UCLA), and has taught interpreting and linguistics at California State University at Northridge (CSUN), Northeastern University in Boston, Western Maryland College, Durham University, and Gallaudet University and in numerous workshops and colloquia. McIntire is known for her editorship of many RID and CIT conference proceedings and the *Journal of Interpretation*, and has published widely about American Sign Language, linguistic aspects of interpreting, and language acquisition. She has consulted extensively on curriculum for both ASL and Interpreting Programs and was the director of the ASL Program at Northeastern from 1993–1996. She has also served on national and international boards and committees of interpreting.

Gary Sanderson, who grew up with Deaf parents, was a part of the community at California State University at Northridge (CSUN) since he was a child. His father, Robert Sanderson, was a student in the National Leadership Training Program, and Gary attended CSUN as a student while working as an interpreter. He then worked at CSUN full-time as a coordinator of interpreting services and an outreach coordinator. He served as interim director of the CSUN National Center on Deafness for two years. His career at CSUN spanned 38 years and he was known nationally and internationally as "Mr. CSUN." Sanderson received awards and recognition from national organizations such as the Registry of Interpreters of the Deaf, the National Association of the Deaf, and others. Gary retired from CSUN in 2009 due to health complications from which he passed away in May 2011.

Who's in charge here?

Perceptions of empowerment and role in the interpreting setting

Marina L. McIntire* & Gary R. Sanderson**

Introduction

We have prepared this paper not from an academic approach, but as practitioners and interpreter educators with an interest in addressing certain issues that we deal with on a daily basis. The issues we examine here are those surrounding: (a) power and empowerment in the interpreting situation; (b) gender and power; and (c) the sense of disempowerment with which most interpreters address the task of working in legal settings.

When D/deaf people and interpreters work together, each comes to the situation with a set of expectations about the distribution of power, e.g. the interpreter's role and the D/deaf person's responsibility regarding the communication task. Over the years, however, interpreters' views of our own roles have shifted; these shifts have resulted in a considerable lack of trust between the Deaf community and interpreters.

We believe that the models of interpretation, as described by Witter-Merithew (1986), reflect a great deal about power and how power is distributed in the relationships we have with our consumers, both D/deaf and hearing. The helper model withholds power from the D/deaf consumer; interpreters in this model, in our view, often believed and therefore acted as though D/deaf people were powerless, incompetent, and unable to get what they needed on their own. D/deaf people, in this view, had to depend on interpreters.

In shifting to the machine/conduit model, we rejected any responsibility for what happened to D/deaf people, became 'invisible' behind the skirts of the newly adopted Code

* Marina L. McIntire, Ph.D., CSC, CI, CT, is Associate Professor and Director of the American Sign Language Program at Northeastern University in Boston. She teaches ASL linguistics and ASL-English interpretation and conducts research into the normal acquisition of ASL.

** Gary R. Sanderson. CSC, BA, is the Coordinator of the Regional Outreach Program at the National Center on Deafness. California State University Northridge. He has been certified since 1975. He has published on educational interpreting and repetitive motion injuries among sign language interpeters.

of Ethics and refused to 'step out of role', ever. Moreover, we avoided responsibility for the message – as Witter-Merithew (1986) pointed out, the part of the transaction which we absolutely must be responsible for! For a variety of reasons, we soon shifted to a somewhat gentler approach – the communication facilitator. This move began the process of allowing interpreters to empower themselves to ask for things they needed to make the communication process go more smoothly. As facilitators, we recognized that we had some responsibility for the message, and possibly even for the success of the communication exchange. Realizing we had an effect on the communication process, we began to empower ourselves, as well as D/deaf people. In this model, interpreters occasionally 'slipped' and took on behaviors and apparent responsibilities that we now see as appropriate: specifically, we served as cross-cultural mediators. But because most of us had been trained to believe in the machine model, we experienced a great deal of guilt when we did so.

Having arrived at – or more aptly, now approaching – a bilingual and bicultural model, we have the opportunity to view our consumers as co-equals and as human beings who have both the rights to and responsibilities for their own destinies. The bi-bi model recognizes that interpreters work between members of (at least) two cultures and that interpreters bear the responsibility for successfully managing and negotiating the communication event. Moreover, we can consciously choose which 'model' we work in for a particular situation. For example, suppose we appear in a situation in which a highly experienced D/deaf consumer informs us: "I want every word she says, exactly as she says it. Do not change a thing!" In other words, "Please be a machine." The most empowering response – the most appropriate response – is surely to accommodate that consumer's preference. We have then put them in charge.

In the past, these models were rarely formally laid out for us; rather they represent shifting views and beliefs about the relationships between interpreters and the D/deaf people they work with. The problem for the last twenty or so years has been that there is little or no consistency in our approach. D/deaf and hearing consumers never know what they're going to get: a consummate conduit or a humane helper.

What do we mean when we say the models are about power? The graphic in Figure 1 below may help.

This configuration allows us to see that each model relating to the power distribution between interpreters and D/deaf people has an influence on each of the other models.

Power and People

What is power? According to one dictionary, power represents the ability or capacity to act or perform effectively. That doesn't seem such a bad thing to have. We believe that interpreters and D/deaf consumers alike experience a great deal of confusion between

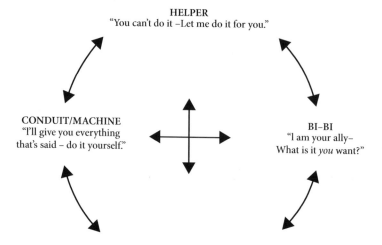

HELPER
"You can't do it –Let me do it for you."

CONDUIT/MACHINE
"I'll give you everything
that's said – do it yourself."

BI-BI
"I am your ally–
What is it *you* want?"

COMMUNICATION FACILITATOR
"I am your advocate–I'll help you do it."

power and control. Control is defined (as a verb) as follows: to exercise authority or dominating influence over; to direct; to regulate. Surely this is what we didn't want when we shifted from helpers to machines. Rather than denying personal power, however, we should have been concerned about avoiding behaviors and attitudes that were aimed at controlling D/deaf people's lives. For example, in group discussions, interpreters normally operate on the assumption that it is inappropriate to interrupt a hearing person's turn in order to get the D/deaf person's comments in. So we in effect cede control to the hearing consumer; but to the D/deaf person, we appear to be controlling. The same thing is true when interpreters are apparently inactive in their 'lag' or 'thinking' time: D/deaf people feel they are being discounted and left out, while hearing people are getting information in a timely fashion. We suggest that interpreters have allowed our deference to hearing consumers to control us, thus disempowering ourselves and indirectly oppressing D/deaf consumers.

As interpreters, we need power. Because most of us are female (male RID membership is outnumbered 6:1), most of us start at a disadvantage. We are not saying that it is necessarily a disadvantage to be female in any absolute sense. Rather, in US society in general, being female means one enters most situations as a relatively disempowered person. In addition, although D/deaf people increasingly view themselves as a cultural minority, society in general views deaf people as 'handicapped' and therefore lacking power. Moreover, it will be a long time yet before all D/deaf people view themselves as completely empowered. As a result, when any D/deaf person walks into a legal situation with a female (and young) interpreter, the two of them are entering an uphill battle.

A recent demographic profile of RID members shows the following information: 16% are male and 84% are female; nearly two-thirds of us are under forty years of age; and we have levels of formal preparation in interpretation as follows:[4]

a. no formal preparation   15%
b. one year   19%
c. two-year program   39%
d. BA degree in interpretation   9%
e. MA degree in interpretation   0.6%

In sum, more than one-third of those responding to this particular question in the survey have either no formal preparation or around one-year's worth of preparation.

Implications

What are the implications for the interpreted situation? Let us look at characteristics of women's language (from Lakoff 1975):

1. Hedges: sort of, kind of, guess, seems like
2. Superpolite forms: would really appreciate it if, would you please…if you don't mind
3. Tag questions: question structures which suggest their own answer, such as isn't it and weren't you
4. Speaking in italics: intonational emphasis on words like so and very
5. Empty adjectives: these convey no substantive information, but mainly express the speaker's feelings – for instance, divine, charming, cute, sweet, adorable, lovely
6. Hypercorrect grammar and pronunciation
7. Lack of a sense of humor
8. Direct quotations, rather than paraphrasing
9. Special lexicon: e.g. vocabulary relating to colors
10. Question intonation in declarative contexts: i.e. answering a question with a question-like response (…around 6 o'clock?), indicating that the response calls for approval by the questioner.

O'Barr (1982) refers to this dialect as 'powerless', rather than as women's language. In examining courtroom transcripts, O'Barr found that this usage is neither characteristic of all women nor limited only to women. While more women use it, all the women who

---

4. Percentages given here are as proportions of the entire population responding to the survey: of these, some 17.4% did not answer the question about their level of formal preparation.

have low scores for it have unusually high social status. Those men who used powerless language in their sample held subordinate, lower status jobs. O'Barr's conclusion is that it appears that the tendency for more women than men to use 'powerless' language is due to the greater tendency of women to occupy relatively powerless social positions.

Many, even most, male interpreters have learned ASL and interpretation from women instructors. When going into various interpreting assignments, these male interpreters have faced comments such as "You sign like a woman." Many also have the habit of using typical powerless/women's language learned from their instructors when interpreting from sign to English.

In the courtroom

What does all of this mean for the interpreter in the legal setting? Let's start by seeing how many interpreters have been certified for work in such settings. The following figures are the latest numbers from the RID:

	SC:L–97	CLIP–27
Region I:	14	1
Region II:	23	3
Region III:	15	3
Region IV:	13	5
Region V:	32	15

SC:L interpreters were, in all likelihood, trained in a conduit model; that was the most current and acceptable model for many years. The CLIP group are the few who have trained in the now acceptable, 'best practices' model. It would be unfair of us to pass judgment on what was acceptable twenty years ago. Rather, we simply note that a change is in the works. In the last three years, the CSUN Legal Interpretation summer program has prepared 27 people, both Deaf and hearing, to work in legal settings. This is the first program in the US to address the issues of legal work in a thorough and appropriate fashion, fully informed by the bi-bi model. We regard this as salutary but recognize the inadequacy of these numbers to relieve the need felt around the nation for competent interpreters in legal settings, whether civil or criminal, whether juvenile court or police station procedures. The simple fact is that even in regions 'rich' in interpreters qualified for this sort of work, there is a desperate lack of interpreters and D/deaf people are being ill-served in probably 90% of the instances when they face legal proceedings of any sort. Only sensational cases, such as murders and rapes, get adequate service, and then often only after the damage has been done.

The majority of legal situations are likely to be handled by relatively young, relatively inexperienced female interpreters. Their experience and knowledge of both courtroom language and protocol are likely to be based on a one-day legal interpreting workshop and, like most mainstream Americans, on television versions of the legal process, such as LA Law. As Lakoff (1990:101) points out:

> "Legal language is intended for clarity, but that aim often renders it particularly opaque. It is a language devised for and by professionals, but its most important users, the jurors, are amateurs".

In this case, we would suggest that the typical interpreter in legal settings is at least as ill-prepared for legal language as the jurors are.

Most interpreters with this level of qualification cannot feel comfortable in the courtroom setting. The formality of the setting, the unfamiliarity of the procedures, and the seriousness of the consequences will impel interpreters into one of at least two directions/reactions. Some – those who are perhaps more experienced in general interpretation – may take the courtroom in a somewhat casual fashion, insisting that if one is qualified to interpret, there are simply a few little extras to be worked out (where to stand, for example) and from there on, it's nothing special. A second group – we suspect the majority of us, including many who are even more experienced – have a very different sense: we are terrified of the court and terrified of the responsibility. When faced with interpreting in such settings, these interpreters are not at all comfortable nor secure in how to manage such a difficult situation. These interpreters are likely to fall back on the model which relieves them of the responsibility: the machine/conduit. This is the model under which the interpreter can simply transmit the information and allow any further complications to be 'handled' by the consumers: "If you don't understand me, you'd better talk with your lawyer. I've done my job."

Language and power

In both cases, certain issues remain the same: those of language and power. In his work on metanotative qualities of interpretation, Cokely (1983:16) points out what we all know from experience: "...the way messages are expressed is often coupled with stereotypic judgments of the speaker's social status, educational level...and so forth". These remarks are in harmony with Berk-Seligson's (1990) and O'Barr's (1982) experiments in which they showed (O'Barr, 1982:75) that for jurors in a mock trial:

> "the use of powerless style produced consistently less favorable reactions to the witness... [T]he style... strongly affects how favorably the witness is perceived, and by implication [this] suggests that these sorts of differences may play a consequential role in the legal process itself.

That is to say, typical women's style (that which is most unconscious and most comfortable for women) has a measurably negative impact on juries, and presumably everyone else in the room, including judges. Also, D/deaf people are viewed by society in general as 'handicapped' and therefore relatively powerless. The combination of a handicapped person along with a woman interpreter puts both of them at a disadvantage within a context that is based on power relationships.

We have stated that the interpreter is likely, in this situation, to revert to a machine model of behaviors and decision-making. Alternatively, if the interpreter has a strong sense of how absolutely helpless the D/deaf person is in this setting, she may take on old helper behaviors, feeling that she is the only person who can 'save' the D/deaf consumer. We know that there were and are interpreters who would lie, change testimony, or lead the witness, all in the service of 'helping deaf'.

One other factor impinges on all of this: where is the D/deaf consumer in her own empowerment process? Most of the model changes that interpreters have made have been made unilaterally – without any consultation between interpreters and D/deaf consumers. Other social changes have begun to affect this working relationship. Some D/deaf people's views regarding their own place in the world have shifted. The success of the 'Deaf President Now' movement was the flashpoint of the D/deaf power movement; along with various state and federal laws and regulations, this has given many D/deaf people a burgeoning sense of power in their daily business. When working in a legal setting, interpreters may find themselves with someone who wants total control over her situation. Or they may find someone who has never worked with an interpreter before and has no idea what it means to have mediated communication. In each case, the D/deaf person's sense of her own power should have an impact on the interpreter's decision-making and other behaviors. But not all interpreters are equipped for this. The interpreter who has retreated to a conduit model will be of no help to the D/deaf person who has no experience working with an interpreter. The helper interpreter who sees the D/deaf consumer as helpless will soon be brought up short by a seasoned, empowered consumer.

What are the implications of all these complex factors?

Passive males

D/deaf males may – because of female interpreters' use of powerless language – appear overly passive or powerless in the eyes of the court and the jury in particular.

Aggressive females

D/deaf females may be portrayed as overly aggressive by male interpreters using powerful language.

Homosexual people

D/deaf people may be viewed as homosexual because of cross-gender interpreting and the use (or absence) of powerless language.

Powerless testimony

According to Berk-Seligson (1990), interpreters' language behaviors – many of them simply the result of language processing – will lead them to present testimony in powerless style. These include the addition of hedges, polite forms of address, and hesitation forms where they did not exist in the original source message.

Intrusion

Our very presence in court – not only an "extra" body, but one who "waves her hands" – represents an intrusion and can disrupt the normal flow of courtroom business.

Distraction and disempowerment

Again according to Berk-Seligson (1990), the interpreter's behavior – the need to interrupt, the need to consult with a witness and the like – not only distracts the attention of the court, but can disempower the attorneys.

Embittered deaf people

Interpreters who are confused about their own empowerment can conflict with D/deaf people who are becoming clearer about their own, leading to embittered feelings on the part of the Deaf Community.

Embittered interpreters

Likewise, D/deaf people who are confused about their own empowerment can have conflicts with interpreters, leading to embittered feelings among some interpreters.

Impact not transmitted

Participants, both D/deaf and hearing, will be generally unaware that the interpreter may be skewing not just the content of their message, but also the metanotative sense of the proceedings. That is, the intended impact of witness testimony in all likelihood will not be transmitted accurately.

Suggested remedies

As with all other professional issues we face, the first steps toward resolution are recognition and identification of the problems. The issues we have addressed here regarding power and control, as well as the use of powerless language, require that we understand – as a community – the power imbalance that we create and that we buy into. Next, the interpreting community must open up these discussions with D/deaf consumers so that changes can be made. The relationships that have gone sour will never be improved until we discuss these questions openly and freely.

Some other possibilities are as follows:

General training & recruitment

Firstly, interpreter education programs need to include modules on metanotative qualities and the presentation of affect. Interpreters need to be aware that deaf and hearing consumers alike are judged as a result of the interpreter's use of language. Secondly, qualified D/deaf interpreters should be working in tandem with qualified hearing interpreters. This means establishing programs which truly prepare D/deaf people for the realities of interpretation. Finally, we should consider recruiting more men into the field, in order to alleviate the issues around powerless language usage.

Research & specialist training

We need additional research into interpreters' use of powerless language and its actual impact on the interpreting situation. Interpreters in the court setting must be prepared to work there. If they are comfortable, then they won't fall back into the trap of powerless language so readily. In addition (taking advantage of the Certification Maintenance Program requirements of RID), interpreters and RID chapters could dedicate learning time to linguistic, sociological, psychological, and cross-cultural topics which would help us resolve issues of power and control.

Activities in the wider sphere could also be beneficial: RID could ally themselves with spoken language interpreter organizations around court interpreting and legal issues. In any case, we must advocate both on state and federal levels to limit work in courtrooms strictly to interpreters who have been trained and certified for work in these settings.

Court awareness

Following the example of the Los Angeles Superior Court, courts around the country should have at least one full-time staff member who is both knowledgeable about Deaf Culture and interpreting and who is comfortable and knowledgeable about the courts. (In Los Angeles, she is Deaf and a qualified interpreter.) Such a staff member could prepare judges and other officers of the court for cases involving D/deaf people and interpreters. Advocates who are similarly knowledgeable could be dispatched to work with attorneys in assisting them with preparation of a case.

RID chapters and the national RID representatives could and should be making presentations at Bar Association workshops, judges' conferences, and the like to help educate hearing consumers. Court interpreting offices need to know about the use of D/deaf interpreters and they need to know about what qualifies interpreters to work in court. Once the court begins its business, instructions from judge to jury should include information about processing time, the fact that interpreters are an 'intrusion', the need for extra time which arises out of the need for accuracy, and the importance of watching the witness rather than the interpreter.

Just recently, conversation has re-opened between the NAD and the RID. This is the beginning at a national, organizational, and official level. Individuals have responsibilities as well, however; each of us can act on our own, trying to build rapprochement with the D/deaf people we work with and trying to develop our own understanding of the bi-bi model and the others which preceded it.

Elsewhere in this volume, you will find other suggested remedies for the larger problem. These are just the beginning. We challenge RID chapters, federally-funded Interpreter Education Projects, interpretation programs in colleges and universities, D/deaf people and interpreters to indulge in some introspection and then to find workable solutions for the problems we all face.

References

Berk-Seligson, S. (1990). *The bilingual courtroom: Court interpreters in the judicial process.* Chicago IL: University of Chicago Press.

Cokely, D. (1983). Metanotative qualities: How accurately are they conveyed by interpreters? *The Reflector,* 5 (Winter): 16–22.

Lakoff, R. (1975). *Language and women's place.* New York NY: Harper & Row.

Lakoff, R. (1990). *Talking power: The politics of language.* New York NY: Basic Books.

McIntire, M. and Sanderson, G.R. (in press). Bye-bye, bi-bi: Questions of empowerment and role. In *Proceedings.* 1993 RID Convention.

O'Barr, W. (1982). *Linguistic evidence: Language, power, and strategy in the courtroom.* New York NY: Academic Press.

Witter-Merithew, A. (1986). Claiming our destiny. (In two parts). *RID Views.* October: 12 & November: 3–4.

5.4   Grbić, Nadja. 1997. "About Helpers and Experts: The changing social practice of sign language interpreting." In Text – *Kultur – Kommunikation: Translationals Forschungsaufgabe. Festschrift aus Anlaß des 50jährigen Bestehens des Instituts für Übersetzer- und Dolmetscherausbildung an der Universität Graz*, ed. By Nadja Grbić and Michaela Wolf, 293–305. Tübingen: Stauffenburg.

Nadja Grbić has studied linguistics and Slavic languages and is an Assistant Professor at the Department for Translation Studies at the University of Graz, Austria. She teaches translation and interpretation studies and is preparing her post-doctoral dissertation (Habilitation) on the construction of sign language interpreters as an occupational group in Austria. Research topics include sign language interpreting, sociological issues of translation and interpreting, translation history, feminist translation, and scientometrics. She has conducted several research projects on sign language interpreting and sign language lexicography and developed a full time training program for sign language interpreters at university level, which started in the autumn of 2002 in Graz. While she publishes much of her work in German, some of her publications are also available in English, including "Where do We Come From? Who Are We? Where Are We Going? (2007), a bibliometric analysis of writings and research on sign language interpreting. She is a co-editor of Routledge's *Encyclopedia of Interpreting Studies*.

About helpers and experts

The changing social practice of sign language interpreting

Nadja Grbić

In the United States there is an online discussion group by and for sign language interpreters which has existed for some time. It addresses theoretical issues as well as issues pertaining to the practice of intersemiotic interpreting.[5] In June 1996 it was possible to follow one of the discussions of the so-called "TERPS-list" whose members – momentarily weary of the recurring problems in their profession – sent anecdotes about the "most unusual interpreting settings" to cyberspace:

> I've thought about this all week and have finally come to the conclusion that the most unusual assignment that I've had was with a student/client who was doing a summer internship at the local zoo [...] The gorillas and orangs were being moved from the vet barn to their new quarters in the primate building, so while the vets were checking their ears, eyes, teeth, under the hood, etc. the student was smearing their hands with this goo that was supposed to harden and become mold etc. It didn't work (too much hair), but it was interesting to feel how much their hands felt like ours, and just fun being that close to the animals. I mean, sit on the floor with a 300-pound gorilla resting in your lap and interpret!   (George 1996)

The discussion also included anecdotes about interpreting for people with minimal proficiency in English and ASL (American Sign Language); an assignment for a deaf-blind woman who had taken a skydiving course; a medical examination where the patient was lying prone, while the interpreter had to be lying on the floor of the examination room, so that she could be seen by her deaf client; assignments in gay bars, swimming pools, dance studios, etc.

The examples are entertaining. However, they primarily serve as an illustration of the social practice, the space which a society is willing to grant to the members of a particular form of discourse. As compared to international standards and in light of the human right to information and knowledge, the social practice of sign language interpreting in Austria has proven to be assigned a highly marginal, albeit not always openly undesired, role.

---

5. Tweney/Hoemann (1976:138) expanded Jakobson's term "intersemiotic translation" and applied it to sign language interpreting.

The present article aims to outline the role of sign language interpreting in three contexts: society, research and professional practice. From the asymmetries presented, clear implications for research, pedagogy and practice can be derived. They are to be understood as an incentive to review old thought patterns so that in future and on the basis of concrete research questions and corpora, the multifacetedness and dynamics of the influencing variables, which govern action initiation, action process and action product, can come into view.

1.   A case for emergencies

In their extensive study published in 1989 Ebbinghaus/Heßmann refer to the "emergency service character" of sign language interpreting in Germany.

> When a deaf person has to appear before the court as a party to the case, capturing his/her statement in standard language is granted through the presence of an interpreter. The same applies to police investigations (…). Beyond those settings the necessity of resorting to interpreters is hardly recognized. How to manage the most urgent communicative necessities of everyday life remains solely the concern of the individual deaf person who has to rely on his/her ingenuity, organizational talent and wallet. Deaf people who require an interpreter find themselves faced with the choice of either going through tedious administrative procedures to have their limited and not clearly defined legal rights acknowledged or digging deep into their pockets. In most cases they would try to manage without interpreters.
>
> (Ebbinghus/Heßmann 1989: 119 et seq.)

This description of sign language interpreting as a case for emergencies holds true in Austria even today. Wiesinger (1996) conducted a survey in which she asked 68 deaf people from all over Austria about their personal experiences with interpreters. One of the questions was about the settings for which interpreters are most frequently brought in. The answers are represented in the following figure (ibid. 159–161):

The categories "driving school", "public authorities", "court" as well as "other" were rated as "frequently". However, it is important to note that "frequently" – as evident in the table – is a relative rating. The rating that is represented much more strongly is "never". The results of this small-scale study largely echo the findings of a survey conducted by Grbić (1994) where 34 sign language interpreters were asked to name the most frequent interpreting domains. "Public authorities/agencies" were ranked first; "court/police" as well as "everyday situations" (which Wiesinger refers to as "other") were rated second; and "driving school" took third place (ibid. 170 et seq.).

Yet even when a public authority acts as a translation service initiator, i.e. brings in interpreters to work for the "strong culture" with a view to satisfy first and foremost the communication needs of the dominant majority, professional practice shows that

Resorting to interpreters

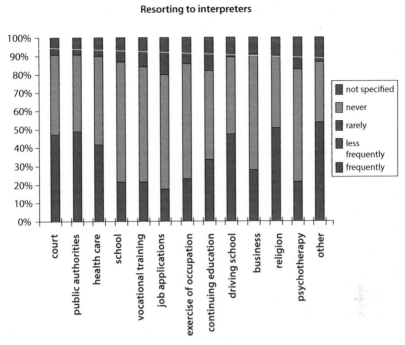

ignorance and disinterest often determine the social action. Below is an example case[6] to illustrate that:

Venue: Court
People: Judge (J)
          Deaf person (D)
          Lawyer (L)
Interpreter (I)
J: I hereby open the hearing.
I: (interprets into sign language)
J: (interrupts) I, what are you saying to him?
I: I hereby open the hearing.
J: You can't speak to D. You have to interpret to me what you are signing.
I: I only interpret what is being said.
J: (continues) Present in the court room are…
I: (interprets)
J: (interrupts again) Tell me what you just signed. You can't do that!
I: What I just interpreted was: Present in the court room are… I have to interpret into sign language, because everybody else who is present can hear what is being said and I was called in specially for D, so that he too can understand everything.

---

6.   The example case was kindly made available to me by sign language interpreter Christina Gruska-Mikulasek.

J: Oh OK, I understand. The accident happened on…
I: (interprets)
J: (interrupts yet again)
L: (jumps up) Your Honour, this can't go on. The I interprets what is being said. If we continue like that, we'll be here till tomorrow.
J: OK, I understood. Let's move on.

Historical investigations, as well as recent studies on social interactions with deaf people, reveal that the primary aim of the so-called inclusion of deaf people into society is driven by assimilative, remedial motives rather than integrative interests (cf. Lane 1993 on the USA). The decision about what role deaf people should be playing in society is made by the "strong culture" for whom various political, ideological and economic interests are forefronted. This reflects the fundamental collective thought patterns of strong cultures or societies which produce disparities in intercultural (migrants vs. locals), but also in intracultural (deaf vs. hearing) contact, all of which leads to social stratification. To what extent this constitutes conscious or unconscious behaviour can only be speculated and will thus not be discussed any further. Sociological and historical studies on deafness in our cultural area are urgently needed, particularly as they would shed light on significant factors that greatly affect individual interpreting behaviours.

Empirical studies, for instance, on interpreting situations in the context of the socially disadvantaged groups of migrant laborers, refugees and asylum seekers can benefit to a considerable degree from sociolinguistic studies, which have been carried out in the German-speaking world since the seventies. However, it has not been possible for the discipline of "Deaf Studies" (cf. Andersson 1997) to gain a foothold at our universities – with few exceptions[7] – as yet.

Despite the lack of empirical data, a preliminary model of deafness needs to be developed as a basis for further discussions. This model would, on the one hand, draw on research findings from other countries, such as the USA or Great Britain. Of course, these findings would not be one-to-one applicable to the situation in Austria, but they would certainly be a valuable contribution. On the other hand, the model would rely on observations of the deaf community in Austria in the course of the past five years. On this basis, we would set out from a cultural model of deafness which does not factor out disability, but contrary to the widespread medical-pathological model, also accounts for cultural factors which shape the deaf community as a diaculture and holds it together. The focus is not on deficiency, but rather on difference (cf. Grbić 1997a).

---

7.   See studies conducted by the Centre for Sign Language at the University of Hamburg, series *Internationale Arbeiten zur Gebärdensprache und Kommunikation Gehörloser* (International Studies on Sign Language and Deaf Communication). Hamburg: Signum Publishing.

2. Research as indicator for societal interests

During the years which Gile (1994:151 et seq.) referred to as the Renaissance of the discipline, Interpreting Studies as a sub-discipline of Translation Studies produced a series of findings that could only be operationalized for sign language interpreting in a restricted thematic area. This might be attributable, on the one hand, to the relatively short history of the discipline from a history of science perspective, as it is still in the process of defining the fields of research and developing methods or examining the relevance of methods from other disciplines to the field. On the other hand, the research community of this sub-discipline seems to have been self-restrictive for a relatively long time by postulating that the scope of research is sufficiently covered by addressing primarily simultaneous conference interpreting. Consequently, the prevailing research focus revolved around translation processes during simultaneous interpreting. Studies have employed predominantly cognitive-psychological, neurophysiological and psycholinguistic approaches. As a result, other factors such as status, prestige, power, identity or culture were largely disregarded, although Anderson already noted in 1979 that in establishing their situation-specific role, interpreters in the booth are too driven and limited by the social structure of the network of interaction. This, in turn, could have implications on the quality of their output.

On closer consideration, the postulated "standard case of simultaneous conference interpreting" fails to stand up to scrutiny. Even in the absence of empirically generated figures one can formulate a preliminary hypothesis that the grey zone of interpreting outside of large conferences constitutes, in all likelihood, a significant field of work, although it is not yet clearly defined in Austria at the moment. Neglecting this field in research might be due to the fact that the majority of interpreter-mediated interactions are of non-professional nature, i.e. they are carried out by people who are not formally trained and are more or less bilingual, such as acquaintances, relatives, social workers, teachers and the like.

Studies on non-professional interpreting were therefore not established in Interpreting Studies for a long time. They emerged, for instance, in German linguistics where the discursive structure of interactions mediated by non-professional interpreters was analyzed as part of larger studies in Intercultural Communication (cf. inter alia Rehbein 1985 or Knapp-Potthoff/Knapp 1987). In the English-speaking world Harris (1977) had already pleaded at the end of the seventies to not neglect what he referred to as "natural translation" in the framework of academic research on interpreting.

It was only recently that studies on *community interpreting* increasingly found their way to relevant publications and specialist conferences. Community interpreting cannot be regarded nowadays as a special case, possibly by way of the postcolonial discussion in Translation Studies which is increasingly bringing into focus the interplay between translation and power. Instead of pleading for drawing a demarcation line between expert translators/interpreters on the one hand and non-professional everyday interpreters on the other hand (cf. Pöchhacker 1991:41), as it was the case a few years ago, today it is necessary to develop models on the basis of observational and experimental studies which adequately describe both fields of action and their prototypical sub-categories in order to obtain findings which can serve the professionalization of interpreting practice on the long-term. Countries in which interpreting for linguistic minorities has been institutionally and legislatively anchored (cf. for instance Wadensjö 1992 or Gentile et al. 1996) provide valuable impetus to a field, which have thus far been treated as a stepchild and is slowly starting to lose the nimbus of the peripheral.

> [it] is a fact that in Austria [...] the world of community interpreting is necessarily looked at (or even down upon), if it is looked at all, from within the well-established world of conference interpreting and university-level interpreter training. With community interpreting in such a 'peripheral position' vis-à-vis the central concern with conference interpreting, the voice of its representatives or practitioners is not likely to be heard. I would therefore like to take advantage of my position in the First World' of interpreting to [...] draw attention to the current practices and needs in the 'Third World' of interpreting in Austria.   (Pöchhacker 1997:215)

Research on sign language interpreting per se developed primarily in the United States in similar hermeneutic circles as "Deaf Studies". Findings from Interpreting Studies received little attention. By the same token, Interpreting Theory has only started in the mid-nineties to take cognizance of interpreting for the deaf (discussed extensively in Grbić 1997b). The development in the training sector, at least in the USA, progressed differently to that in research. The long tradition of training programmes in sign language interpreting set a frame which allowed for the development of curricula for *community interpreting* (cf. Downing/Helms Tillery 1992:2).

These developments in research history prompt us to rethink traditional approaches and orientations. It is an integrative, multi-perspective approach to research, which Snell-Hornby (1989:12) called for in Translation Theory in general, that would be expedient in the long term for the field of sign language interpreting which combines the domains of *community interpreting* and conference interpreting. The necessity to overcome the habit of thinking in terms of camps, which is advocated here, is not meant to be a call for an uncontrolled pluralism of methods. It rather serves to create new possibilities to take more heed of interdisciplinary points of intersection on the basis of an open system of self-regulating usefulness mechanisms.

3.   About Von Übermenschen [Superhumans] und Nichtpersonen [nonpersons]

As stated at the beginning of this article, the demand for professional sign language interpreters in Austria is high. At the same time, the profession is undergoing a significant change. In addition to the classical settings "public authority/agency", "court/police" and "driving school" the education sector is increasingly becoming a workplace. While in Grbić's (1994) study the education sector was only represented marginally, a small-scale survey conducted in 1997[8] revealed that almost one fourth of assignments occur in the domains of basic education, vocational training and continuing education. The demand put forward by Deaf Organisations for recognition of sign language and with it equal opportunities in education (by bringing in interpreters among other things) is already having an initial impact in Austria.

This real expansion of the profession can be clearly illustrated in reference to the change of the notion of role, which provides practitioners with an inexhaustible pool of topics to discuss. Although we believe that a social role per se is not definable, but rather acquires its meaning in the interplay with other individuals or groups in certain situations, from time to time certain "role trends" can be detected, which correlate with the development of social interests. The role perceptions of sign language interpreters are retrieved or established by all participants in the action scheme in a specific situation. In addition to regional and temporal parameters role perceptions are affected by group expectations, i.e. conventions and norms, and also by individual, i.e. motivational, emotional or cognitive, interests. The questions which arise are the following:

–   What roles are assigned to deaf people by the "strong culture" and what are the connections to the existing social practice of interpreting that can be drawn?
–   What role is assigned to sign language interpreters in the hearing society?
–   What role do they assume in the deaf community?
–   What is sign language interpreters' self-perceived role?

In what follows we aim to abstract from concrete action situations or actions schemes and focus on two prototypical role metaphors which in our view played a key role in shaping the social practice of sign language interpreting in the past years, and successfully counteracted the process of professionalization through their simplistic perspective.

---

8.   This survey was conducted at the Institute for Translator and Interpreter Training at the University of Graz in the context of the HORIZON-project which was funded by the European Social Fund and Austrian Federal Ministry of Labour and Social Affairs. As part of this project a one-year university course among other things was developed as continuing education for practicing sign language interpreters who had not undergone formal training. The course (which took place between March 1997 and February 1998) was advertised for the whole of Austria. The 24 participants, who were selected based on their language competence and interpreting experience, filled out a questionnaire in which they were asked, among other things, about the settings in which they work.

3.1 Interpreters as benefactors

Family members, friends and acquaintances have always been interpreting for deaf people, just as children of migrants do for their parents (Kohn 1996). A similarly emotionally motivated group of interpreters was made up of social workers, teachers and clerics who felt obliged to help their fosterlings linguistically as well. As representatives of society ("strong" culture) and of their profession they are authorized to give advice and make decisions on behalf of the deaf. They take on the most active role in the triad of deaf person – interpreter – hearing person. Although they seem to be standing up for the interests of the vulnerable group, in reality they are at the top of the pyramid of power. Their actions express the paternalistic notion that without their help deaf people would not be able to take responsibility for their personal, social and professional affairs. I will refer to this as "pseudo-loyalty". At the same time their actions reflect their mistrust towards society and its members who are not familiar with deafness. This is why they consciously or unconsciously, as a result of their partiality, undermine the normative system of the dominant, stronger culture. Related metaphors are: adviser, advocate, helper and the like. In our survey of 1994 (Grbić 1994) 36% of the interpreters who participated in the study stated that they also act as advisers; 36% also regarded themselves as social workers (multiple answers possible). Merely 10% of the deaf respondents (Wiesinger 1996) took the view that interpreters should be "neutral". To fulfil their purpose interpreters should take the side of their ("weak") culture.

3.2 The interpreter as conduit

In the course of the emancipation of the deaf community on the one hand and the professionalization aspired by practitioners on the other hand, a second, widespread metaphor was established, that of the conduit. Interpreters convey content from one language to another, and as such they are not to engage emotionally in order not to go beyond their scope of responsibility. Instead, they should be impartial, objective and neutral. They adopt the naive premise that language is a neutral, transparent transmitter of content and depose themselves from actively participating in the process of interaction. They seem to be at the bottom of the pyramid of power. They regard themselves as *non-persons* and are not aware of the manipulative potential of the role they chose. I would like to refer to their ostensible neutrality as "double pseudo-loyalty". The spread of this role metaphor in Austria is underpinned by the adoption of ethical codes for interpreters from professionally and socio-culturally different contexts without reflection.

3.3 Role conflicts

Since sign language interpreters work for two clients in face-to-face interactions, who in many cases want to further different interests, problematic role conflicts emerge from a socio-psychological point of view. There is no clearly defined outline of the role and ascriptions are objectively inadequate and incommensurable. The multiple expectations forecast conflicts of interests, power and culture:

> The interpreter, like the foreman, is occupationally vulnerable to counter pressures from his two clients. No matter what he does, one of them is apt to be displeased.
> (Anderson 1976: 217)

This conflict potential is further intensified as a result of the often discrepant self-perception of sign language interpreters. Being between the Scylla of the benefactor and the Charybdis of the language transcoding machine, they overload their role to such a degree that is almost evocative of personal conflicts. In the already cited study (Grbić 1994) 13 out of the 36 interpreters stated that they assume a double function and also act as advisers; 13 regarded themselves also as social workers, 7 felt they acted as advocates for deaf people. At the same time, 16 were of the opinion that interpreters had to remain neutral and confine themselves to linguistically conveying the message. The numerous multiple answers were not surprising and confirmed the hypothesis formulated in advance which predicted the incompatibility of the tasks which they set for themselves.

4. Conclusion

Sign language interpreting is a form of social practice which is governed by certain aims. Although actions, as is the case with other processes, present themselves to us as individual instances, one can still extrapolate certain action schemes. A sociology of interpreter behaviour as well as a framework for analysis which is methodologically adequate for different interpreting settings are, however, yet to come.

The roles of sign language interpreting in society, in research and in professional practice, which were outlined in this article, provided insight into the formation of judgments, prejudices and myths and their own reproductive dynamics. Applied, pragmatic research, which aims to gain knowledge that can be made to serve training must allow for a broad starting base whilst taking into account these social processes. In so doing, light can be shed on the multi-layered communicative system of interdependency in all its facets. With this in mind, empirical studies on prevalent interpreting settings, which address the interplay between the relevant influencing variables, would be desired.

Vermeer's Skopos Theory and Holz-Mänttäri's Theory of Translational Action seem suitable as theoretical frameworks. Their point of departure is an interactional pragmatic definition of translation and they account for various extra-textually relevant factors in the translation process as well as the active role of translators and interpreters. In addition to Vermeer's factors, other parameters pertaining to interpreting such as time pressure, specificities of the spoken/sign language, non-verbal communication and the like need to be examined in terms of their relevance to the action process. Since in sign language interpreting we are mostly dealing with interactional situations characterized by a distinctly asymmetric constellation of interests and power which result from an extreme disparity between a "strong" and a "weak" culture, it seems appropriate to also adopt a critical approach, similar to that integrated in the methods of *critical linguistics* and the *Manipulation School*[9] and applied to discourse analysis and literary translation respectively. In this way we bring to the forefront influencing variables such as social status, prestige, power, conventions, norms and ideology and the like.

Bibliography

Anderson, R. Bruce, W. (1976). "Perspectives on the Role of Interpreter", in: R. W. Brislin (ed.), 208–228.

Anderson, R. Bruce, W. (1978). "Interpreter Roles and Interpretation Situations: Cross-Cutting Typologies", in: D. Gerver/H. W. Sinaiko (eds.) *Language Interpretation and Communication.* New York: Plenum Press (NATO Conference Series: III, Human factors 6), 217–230.

Andersson, Yerker. (1997). "Deaf Studies – A New Academic Field". Lecture at the University of Graz, Institute for Translator and Interpreter Training, April 1997. Unpublished manuscript.

Brislin, Richard W. (ed). (1976). *Translation. Application and Research.* New York/London: Gardner Press.

Downing, Bruce T. /Helms Tillery, Kate (1992). *Professional Training for Community Interpreters. A Report on Models of Interpreter Training and the Value of Training.* Minneapolis: Center for Urban and Regional Affairs.

Ebbinghaus, Horst/Heßrnarm, Jens. (1989). *Gehörlose Gebärdensprache Dolmetschen. Chancen der Integration einer sprachlichen Minderheit.* Hamburg: Signum (Internationale Arbeiten zur Gebärdensprache und Kommunikation Gehörloser 7).

Gentile, Adolfo/Ozolins, Uldis/Vasilakakos, Mary. (1996). *Liaison Interpreting. A Handbook.* Melbourne: Melbourne University Press.

George, Paula. (1996). "REPLY: Most unusual interpreting settings", in: TERPS-L.

Gile, Daniel. (1994). "Opening up in Interpretation Studies", in: M Snell-Hornby/F. Pöchhacker/K. Kaindl (eds.) *Translation Studies – An Interdiscipline.* Amsterdam/Philadelphia: Benjamins (Benjamins translation library 2), 149–158.

Grbić, Nadja. (1994). *Gebärdensprachdolmetscben als Gegenstand einer allgemeinen Sprach- und Translationswissenschaft unter besonderer Beriicksichtigung der Situation in Österreich.* Graz: Dissertation.

Grbić, Nadja. (1997a). "Academic Acceptance of Sign Language: From Hearing Loss to Deaf Culture", in: *The Right to Knowledge for the Deaf. Proceedings of the International Conference, 3–5 October 1996, Brdo pri Kranju* (in preparation).

Grbić, Nadja. (1997b). "Gebärdensprachdolmetschen", in: Salevsky, Heidemarie (ed.) *Sachwörterbuch der Translationswissenschaft.* Heidelberg: Groos (in preparation).

---

9. See Schjoldager's (1994) examination of the *Manipulation School* for Interpreting Studies.

Harris, Brian. (1977). "The Importance of Natural Translation", *in: Working Papers on Bilingualism* 12, 96–114.

Knapp-Potthoff, Annelie/Knapp, Karlfried. (1987). "The man (or woman) in the middle: Discoursal aspects of non-professional interpreting", in: K Knapp/W. Enninger/A. Knapp-Potthoff (eds.) *Analyzing Intercultural Communication.* Berlin/New York etc.: Mouton de Gruyter (Studies in Anthropological Linguistics 1), 181–211.

Kohn, Fay. (1996)."Migrant children interpreting for parents – an ethnographic study", in: *New Horizons. Horizons nouveaux. XIV World Congress of the Fédération Internationale des Traducteurs (FIT), Proceedings Volume 1.* Melbourne: AUSIT, The Australian Institute of Interpreters and Translators, 366–385.

Lane, Harlan. (1993)."Die Medikalisierung des Kulturgutes Gehörlosigkeit", in: R Fischer/H. Lane (eds.) *Blick zurück. Ein Reader zur Geschichte von Gehörlosengemeinschaften und ihren Gebärdensprachen.* Hamburg: Signum (Internationale Arbeiten zur Gebärdensprache und Kommunikation Gehörloser 24), 563–584.

Pöchhacker, Franz. (1991)."Einige Überlegungen zur Theorie des Simultandolmetschens", in: Textcon Text 6/1, 37–54.

Pöchhacker, Franz. (1997). "Is There Anybody out There? Community Interpreting in Austria", in: S. E. Carr/R. Roberts/A. Dufour/D. Steyn (eds.) *The Critical link. Interpreters in the Community.* Amsterdam/Philadelphia: Benjamins (Benjamins translation library 19), 215–225.

Rehbein, Jochen. (1985). "Ein ungleiches Paar – Verfahren des Sprachmittelns in der medizinischen Beratung", in: J. Rehbein (ed.) *Interkulturelle Kommunikation.* Tübingen: Narr (Kommunikation und Institution 12), 420–446.

Schjoldagers, Anne. (1994). "Interpreting Research and the 'Manipulation School' of Translation Studies", in: *Hermes* 12, 65–89.

Snell-Homby, Mary. ([1]1986, [2]1994). "Übersetzen, Sprache, Kultur", in: – (ed.) *Übersetzungswissenschaft. Eine Neuorientierung. Zur Integrierung von Theorie und Praxis.* Tübingen: Francke (UTB 1415), 9–29.

Tweney, Ryan/Hoemann, Harry. (1976). "Translation and Sign Language", in: R. W. Brislin (ed.), 138–161.1.

Wadensjö, Cecilia. (1992). *Interpreting as Interaction. On dialogue-interpreting in immigration hearings and medical encounters.* Linköping: Linköping University.

Wiesinger, Karin. (1996). *Probleme des Gebärdensprarhdalmetschens.* Graz: MA Thesis.

5.5   Pollitt, Kyra. 1997. "The state we're in: Some thoughts on professionalization, professionalism and practice among the UK's sign language interpreters." *Deaf Worlds* 13(3): 21–26.

Kyra Pollitt has been a practicing interpreter/translator and educator for over 25 years. Pollitt qualified as a BSL/English interpreter under the examination system of the Council for the Advancement for Communication with Deaf People (CACDP, now known as Signature) and after working for the Royal National Institute for Deaf People in London (now known as Action on Hearing Loss), she became an interpreting fellow in the Deaf Studies Research Unit at Durham University, and later worked as an in-house interpreter for the Channel 4 Deaf community program 'Sign On." Pollitt has taught interpreters across the U.K., at the University of Central Lancashire, the City Lit, and for SLI Ltd, as well as delivering professional development workshops. She was one of the pioneers of formal sign language translation (SLT) work in the U.K., and is also a well-known theatre interpreter.

Pollitt's publications have discussed the role of the sign language interpreter and interpreting models, theatre interpreting and sign language translation. After graduating with an MSc in Interpreting and Translating in a European Context (EUMASLI), Pollitt has recently completed an arts-based Ph.D. study to tie together art, performance and sign language to explore dimensions of sign language poetry, which she has termed 'Sign Art.'

The state we're in: some thoughts on professionalism and practice among the UK's sign language interpreters

Pollitt, Kyra

This paper evolved from a presentation entitled 'Professionalism in interpreting: it may look good but is it good practice?' given to the Issues in Interpreting (2): international perspectives conference, Durham University, Durham (19–22 September, 1995).

A version of this paper was published in Deaf Worlds, Issue 3, Volume 13, 1997.

Introduction

I have been working as a British Sign Language/English interpreter for a number of years now. In my daily professional life I am coming across an increasing number of interpreting colleagues who can be categorised as belonging to one of two distinct types. Allow me to introduce you to an example of the first, who we'll call Annabel (I should stress here that no direct reference to any individual interpreter is intended). Annabel is a nice woman. She regularly attends her local deaf club, and any deaf social event that she can. She often works unsociable hours to help her Deaf friends, regularly expecting no financial reward. She does not allow the fact that she holds only a Level I (basic) Certificate in Sign Language Skills deter her from her mission to help those less fortunate than herself.

In contrast, let's introduce Betty, our type B interpreter. Betty would not dream of compromising the independence of her 'clients' by offering her services on a voluntary basis. She is an efficient, professional businesswoman with a mobile phone, fax and designer suit to prove it. Having achieved a Level III (advanced) Certificate in Sign Language Skills and undergone a rigorous three weeks of interpreter training, Betty ranks herself amongst the skilled elite of the employment world. Betty measures her success by market share and profit margin, and sees 'nothing unethical about making money'.

How do two so diverse practitioners come to occupy the same field at the same time? In the U.K. the last fifteen years or so have seen great changes in the personnel undertaking the sign language interpreting task. As practitioners moved away from charitable practice (Annabel) and Social Work, so the Thatcherite ethos began to influence the field (Betty). By 1991, Liz Scott Gibson was able to describe the cardre of interpreting practitioners as constituting an "emerging profession" (Scott Gibson 1991: 257), which later came to define itself through an American-born theory which placed the interpreter as the invisible, dispassionate 'conduit' of other peoples' communications.

In attempting to liberate Deaf people from the yolk of paternalism and care, there is no doubt that the move to establish interpreting on a professional basis was both a positive and a significant step. However, by 1994, Scott Gibson was describing "the cult of professional expertise" as "one of the most fundamental difficulties experienced by Sign language interpreters today". Her sentiments were echoed, in the same year, from across the Atlantic where Marie Philip was calling for less "business" and greater "togetherness" between interpreters and the Deaf community (Philip, 1994). So what went wrong?

What went wrong?

I suggest that the crisis was and is one of self-identification for the interpreting profession. Given the lack of established Deaf professions, interpreters looked to established hearing professions for role models. This, I suggest, entailed a number of problems.

Firstly, in seeking to adopt the professional values of the hearing majority, interpreters were seen to eschew the precious cultural values of the Deaf community who, in their own terms were not clients, but teachers, mentors, family members and friends. The wider cultural conflict between the individualistic, Thatcherite values of hearing Britain in the '80s and '90s, and the collectivist, reciprocity-driven values of the Deaf community was reinforced in microcosm in every interpreted event. It is little surprise, then, that Deaf people continued to use Annabels in preference to Bettys.

Secondly, the hearing profession which sign language interpreting chose to emulate most closely was that of the spoken language interpreter. The argument went something like this: spoken language interpreters interpret between languages; (British) Sign Language is now fighting for recognition as a language; therefore if we fight for the same working conditions and professional rewards as spoken language interpreters, we will be doing our bit to further the cause of sign language recognition, and ultimately the liberation of Deaf people.

This would be all well and good if the spoken language interpreters that were being emulated were those who worked in community settings. They were not. Despite considerably less expertise, education and training, and without an appropriate market, sign language interpreters began to agitate for the same working conditions and rewards as those who interpret in spoken languages at international commercial and political conferences.

The third problem entailed in striving to create a profession was and is a lack of clear career structure. This produced the anomaly that those who had only recently qualified were afforded the same status and, perhaps more importantly, given the same financial rewards as those who had been interpreting for many years. The system of training and qualification that was put in place recognised only that individuals were 'safe to practise' in a general sense. The qualification was ostensibly valid for a period of only five years; in reality, this condition was never observed and interpreters were not required to retrain or resit the examination. Further, specialist certificates (qualifying individuals to work in legal or medical situations, for example) were oft vaunted but failed to materialise. In their absence, many interpreters began to claim 'specialisations' without having had sufficient -or often *any* – further training. They awarded themselves the right to charge more on the basis of these spurious specialisations, and advertised their services to those outwith the field who had little reason to question their integrity.

A rock and a hard place

It would seem that we are caught between a rock and a hard place; whilst Annabel is unacceptable to those wishing to improve the quality of interpreting services, and cut the paternalistic bonds, Betty is unacceptable to large numbers of Deaf individuals and many other professionals working between the hearing and Deaf worlds. So what can be done? I suggest that we begin by re-examining the theoretical models we have come to accept as underpinning our practice and our goals.

Let's start with theories of what a profession is and should be. Those of us who have been around long enough remember being bombarded with lists of desirable attributes, or traits, which we needed to secure in order to establish ourselves as a profession. Here is an example taken from Fenton (1993) which lists thirteen traits taken from the work of twenty one writers:

- Professionals adhere to a professional code of ethics
- Professions are organised occupations
- Professional skills are based on a theoretical knowledge
- A profession requires training and education
- Competence is tested
- Professions stress altruistic service
- Skills are applied to the affairs of others
- Professionals provide indispensable public service
- Professionals are licensed or registered
- There is a definitive professional-client relationship
- The best impartial service is given
- There is a definite fee
- Professionals have strong loyalty to colleagues

All of these traits could be said to apply, at least in theory, to the field of sign language interpreting, and therein lies the rub. *Trait theories* are widely recognised by sociologists in this field (Crompton, 1990; Fenton, 1993) as being so over-simplified as to yield false results. Control theories, on the other hand, concentrate more on the process and dynamics of professionalization and consequently, I suggest, may prove more valuable to our field.

Here's an example charting the development of spoken language interpreting in Taiwan by Tseng (cited in Fenton, op cit): *Figure 1.*

The conditions described in phase one of Tseng's model will be instantly recognisable to those familiar with the field in Britain. Whilst many practitioners are involved in competition and price cutting (or in our case, bizarrely, price-raising), still others are working for no fee. Consumers become confused and fail to recognise the complexity of the task and the high level of skill required to perform it adequately. Although they want a good quality service, they don't know where to go to get it and, as a result, begin to lose confidence in the service.

Eventually some good practitioners meet to decide how to professionalise the field. This leads to a demand for training institutions, although as these begin to compete with each other there is little quality control of the variety of training on offer. Fortunately some training institutions produce good practitioners, heralding phase two. There are now a number of trained, inadequately trained and untrained practitioners working as interpreters (cf. Annabel and Betty). The trained interpreters band together to protect themselves and the consumers, and they force further development within training institutions. This ushers in phase three, when a Code of Ethics is formulated and enforced, and a publicity campaign is mounted to inform the public, consumers and statutory authorities about the standards they should expect and demand. Thus we witness the beginnings of market control and the censure of unprofessional practice, which are pre-requisites for phase four. Now all sides know what constitutes good practice, can begin to recognise interpreters as professionals, and can work together to campaign for state recognition and licensure.

Although Tseng's model seeks only to accurately describe the process of professionalization for a certain group of spoken language (community) interpreters in Taiwan, there are many parallels with the state of the art amongst sign language interpreters here in Britain and consequently many lessons that can be drawn (this is a useful classroom exercise in interpreter training). Above all, we need to abandon our self-serving tendency to simply attribute various desirable traits to ourselves and concentrate more on the true difficulties and dynamics of the process of professionalization if we are ever to gain valuable and realistic insights into what has happened, what is happening and what is likely to happen. It is only with such insights that we can begin to plan and attempt to control the development of the profession.

New breed, new models

To my mind one of our most pressing needs is that of re-evaluating our role models. The vast majority of BSL/English interpreters are not, and will never be, interpreters of international conferences. We are, for the most part, what have become known as community interpreters (and are elsewhere sometimes termed *dialogue* interpreters). Using either the term dialogue or community allows us to recognise the differences in role and function between ourselves and those interpreters of international conferences who, in the past we have so desired to emulate. It should also allow us to recognise that models of function and codes of practice/ethics designed for conference interpreters cannot hope to accurately describe or prescribe what we can do. In the main we are there to assist members of the community who are not native speakers of English to gain full and equal access to statutory services. We should not be ashamed to be the poor relations of those grand individuals who occupy the wine bars of Zurich, Geneva and Brussels. Rather, we should take pride in doing what we do well.

We must recognise, too, that we cannot look to the spoken language community/dialogue interpreting field to provide a role model because we are already at the forefront of that field. We are contributing much to the debate that is currently developing in wider interpreting circles on the role and function of community/dialogue interpreters. We have vast experience, drawn from a constant and stable minority language community requiring access to many domains of civil and social life, and we can draw upon that for the benefit of all.

Rather than assuming that we are individual failures because we have cause to transgress the Code of Practice/Ethics, we should be openly discussing why such transgressions are sometimes felt to be necessary. Tate and Turner (this volume) have done valuable work in identifying what they term the "conspiracy of silence" over the gap between theory and practice, and Hull's (1995) candid analysis of her own educational interpreting practices has blazed a trail for all of us to follow. For my part I offer the notion, explored more thoroughly elsewhere (Pollitt, forthcoming and b), that we should view our role more as arbitrators at sites of discoursal conflict than either robotic conduits or paternalistic advocates, including the works of Wadensjö and Roy alongside those of Seleskovitch and Lederer in the curriculum.

Such a theoretical approach is able to take into account the desires of all parties engaged in the interpreted interaction, and negates the need to unthinkingly adopt general patterns of 'professional' behaviour from other (hearing) arenas. In order for it to be successful, however, we must be willing to work alongside the Deaf community to forge an understanding of what constitutes professional behaviour according to the cultural mores of the Deaf world. This is a thorny issue for most British Deaf professionals and non-professionals, since the recruitment of white collar workers from the Deaf community is a recent phenomenon. Yet for interpreters to conduct themselves in a way which is regarded as both professional and acceptable by the Deaf community we must first identify acceptable and unacceptable professional Deaf behaviours.

Career structure

To outlaw the practices of the self-proclaimed experts who command vastly inflated fees, and thus further secure quality and safeguard the interests of all consumers, we must seek to establish a clear career structure for interpreters working with sign languages. This begins, I would argue, with not only standardised assessment (e.g. NVQs), but of a core national curriculum for interpreter training which demands, alongside language competencies, interpreting skills and an understanding of theory and ethics, some competency in the fields of legal, medical, educational and social services as pre-requisites to qualification. Interpreters should also be required to undergo refresher training every five years, in addition to any further specialist training they may wish to undertake. The advantages of such a system would be;

- That the threshold of 'safety to practice' is raised for legal, medical, social services and educational interpreting
- That the barriers between 'old' and 'new' interpreters are broken down by retraining, which offers the opportunity of cross-fertilisation of experience and fresh perspectives
- And that retraining becomes a gateway to further career development.

After successfully completing retraining, individuals could become eligible to train as mentors. This would involve being introduced to counselling and training skills, as well as more in-depth work on understanding practices and ethics. After a certain number of years as a mentor, the individual interpreter would then become eligible to undertake training to become a trainer. This would require the development of skills in the teaching of adults, as well as further interpreting theory and some linguistics.

Voice of the profession

All of the above relies, of course, on the ability of the profession to effectively regulate its members, and the willingness of the market to sustain mentors. This is where the professional association comes into its own. In the UK, the Association of Sign Language Interpreters of England and Wales (ASLI) has recently sought to broaden its membership base in order to increase its lobbying power. This I see as a vital step in beginning to establish a 'voice' for the profession. Unfortunately ASLI does not yet hold either the register of interpreters or the Code of Ethics in this country. It is, therefore, unable to censure the activities of its members. Nonetheless, if ASLI is successful enough in attracting ever larger numbers of practitioners into its folds, it will begin to wield the necessary power to effect change. One of the most exciting prospects being mooted at the time of writing involved the merging of ASLI with ABSLT (the Association of British Sign Language Tutors), a move which can only be positive in effecting some of the changes called for in this paper.

That interpreting with British Sign Language has begun to emerge as a profession in the U.K. is without doubt, and this should be celebrated. It is my hope that the field has now matured sufficiently for it to take stock of its condition, draw upon its experience, and have the courage to realign itself in anticipation of future development. We have the potential to create a positive force for change, not only for ourselves, but for the Deaf community and the wider body of dialogue interpreters who work with spoken languages. It's in our hands.

References

Crompton, R. (1990). *Professions in the current context.* Work, Employment and Society, May 147–166.

Fenton, S. (1993). *Interpreting in New Zealand: An emerging profession.* Journal of Interpretation, 6: 1 155–165.

Hull, S. (1995). *Changing the message? Communication support and educational interpreting.* Paper presented at Issues in Interpreting II conference, University of Durham, 19–22nd September, 1995.

Philip, M.J. (1994). *Professionalism: From which Cultural Perspective?* Keynote paper presented at Issues in Interpreting conference, University of Durham, 17–20th April, 1994.

Pollitt, K. (forthcoming a) *The death of the ethic? The crisis facing sign language interpreting in the U.K.* Keynote paper, internet conference, Northeastern University, Boston, U.S.A.

Pollitt, K. (forthcoming b) *This thing is bigger than the three of us* (tentative title). In Roy, C.B. (ed) Innovative Practice in Interpreter Education. Gallaudet University Press, Washington D.C.

Scott Gibson, L. (1991). *Sign language Interpreting: An Emerging Profession.* In Gregory, S. And Hartley, G.M. (eds) Constructing Deafness. Open University Press, Milton Keynes. 253–258.

Scott Gibson, L. (1994). *Open to Interpretation: The Cult of Professionalism.* Keynote paper presented at Issues in Interpreting conference, University of Durham, 17–20th April, 1994.

CHAPTER 6

International perspectives on the emerging profession

Introduction

This chapter offers essays on how the international profession of SLI evolved over time and features papers that describe simultaneous interpreting, accreditation processes, descriptions of role models that were prevalent in the field; contrasting SLI with spoken language interpreting, and its emergence as a profession. Included in this group are interpreting specialists from different parts of the world, including Australia, the United Kingdom, Germany, Belgium, and South Africa. All of these articles were published from the mid-1980s to the late 1990s. Before that time, the U.S. dominated in the development of the profession in many ways, through the development of guidelines, establishment of a professional association, organization of conferences, and the production of publications (as documented in Chapters 1–4). Nevertheless, it can be seen that other countries were also working hard at developing their own professional practices.

In the 1990s there was a sudden emergence of a range of publications describing the SLI situation in various countries across the world. We recognize that many other countries were also seeing the emergence of SLI in their own contexts, but very little has been written about them that we could find. The purpose of this chapter is to highlight the fact that, although discussions of SLI in the U.S. and U.K. tend to dominate the literature (not surprisingly given most publications are in English), we wanted to acknowledge that key shifts were also happening in the profession elsewhere. Not all countries have followed the model developed by the U.S., as they had to take local contextual, linguistic and cultural considerations into account, and other countries have a closer allegiance between spoken and sign language interpreting (see for example, Napier 2005; Hein 2009).

In Australia, **John Flynn** is regarded as the person whose work led to a major shift in the recognition of SLI in the country. Initially Flynn approached the National Accreditation Authority for Translators and Interpreters (NAATI), which is the national regulatory authority for testing in all languages, and was instrumental in getting them to agree to set up a panel to examine interpreting tests in 'Deaf Sign Language.' Many years later the nomenclature was changed to Australian Sign Language (Auslan) to reflect the linguistic research conducted by Trevor Johnston, that identified lexical and grammatical features of the language and led to the publication of the first Auslan dictionary (Johnston 1989).

Flynn's paper documents the initial establishment of NAATI accreditation testing for SLI in Australia.

Since the first tests were conducted, over 1,000 NAATI accreditations have been awarded: 154 at Professional Interpreter level, and 880 at Paraprofessional level (Robert Foote, NAATI Accreditation Manager, personal communication, August 2012). ASLIA was established in 1991 and the Interpreter Trainers Network held its first workshop (now a symposium) in 2003, which was inspired by the CIT conferences held in the U.S. For an updated overview of the Australian situation, see Bontempo & Levitzke-Gray (2009), Napier, McKee & Goswell (2010). In this paper, Flynn outlines the very early development of the NAATI Auslan interpreter tests.

Liz Scott Gibson is one of the most well known sign language interpreters in the world. Although her work as a sign language interpreter practitioner, educator and advocate has had a worldwide impact, her roots began in the U.K. and she was one of the first people to acknowledge that SLI was an emerging profession in that country. In this paper she discusses the shift away from a paternalistic welfare-based model of interpreting and the professionalization of the interpreter role, which had a major influence on the discourse around SLI at that time. The central thrust of her argument is that although the U.K. SLI profession at that time (early 1990s) was becoming more established, it was still an emerging profession and attention needed to be paid to the needs of consumers, standards, policies, provision and education and training.

This paper by Scott Gibson is widely cited in the literature and the SLI profession continues to be described as 'emerging' as recently as 2007 (Bontempo & Napier 2007). Napier (2011) has argued that compared to the study of translation studies, it is legitimate to refer to SLI professionalism and scholarship as emerging, even nearly twenty years after Scott Gibson used the term. In fact, in relation to the U.S-based SLI profession, which has been established as a profession for nearly 50 years, Winston and Cokely (2009) still refer to SLI as an 'emerging field' in their overview of the National Consortium of Interpreter Education Centers. For an updated overview of the SLI profession in the UK, see Stone (2010).

In her paper about the SLI profession in Germany, **Andrea Schulz** refers to the fact that people had been effectively working as interpreters with the Deaf community in Germany for over 200 years, but had never achieved any official recognition. She mentions a reference about 'transmission for the deaf-mute' in 1785, which demonstrates that SLI work has indeed been around for a lot longer than the formally recognized structures of the last 40–50 years. This is also confirmed in the U.K., where reference has been made to 'interpreters' for Deaf people in London courts as early as 1771 (Stone & Woll 2008).

Schulz acknowledges the particular difficulties for the German Deaf community in maintaining their language and culture through the Nazi era, a situation experienced by other Deaf communities that have lived through turmoil when their countries are at war, or experiencing revolutions, invasions or separatist policies (see also for example Kosovo, Hoti & Emerson 2009). One thing that Schulz, and Hoti and Emerson have noted respectfully is that when the Deaf community struggles through this kind of experience, it significantly slows down the development of the profession. Schulz in particular notes the attrition experienced in Germany when people leave the profession due to lack of career pathways, opportunities and recognition. This attrition is still an ongoing problem in the current day, but more often due to occupational overuse syndrome (also known as repetitive strain injury), where sign language interpreters cannot sign due to severe pain in their arms (Madden 2005; Fischer & Woodcock 2008).

In the remainder of her chapter, Schulz discusses attempts to develop a formal SLI training program at the University of Hamburg, and notes that there is still much work to be done. For an update, De Wit (2005) gives an overview of the SLI situation throughout Europe, including Germany.

Sweden was one of the first countries to establish SLI as a profession and to provide interpreter training, thus **Anna-Lena Nilsson** discusses the historical development of the sign language interpreting programs in that country, with the first organized (short) inter- preter training course taking place in 1969, and the Swedish Association of Sign Language Interpreters established in the same year. The first 4-year interpreter training program began in 1996 at a community college (folk school). Sweden is often regarded as a leader in the sign language interpreting world, in terms of well-established working conditions for interpreters (for example, they were one of the first countries to bring teams of interpreters to work at the World Congress of the World Federation of the Deaf, rather than just one interpreter). As well as talking about different domains of SLI (education, community, con- ference), Nilsson specifically compares the similarities and differences between spoken and sign language interpreting. Like Australia (see Bontempo & Levitzke-Gray 2009), Sweden has a uniform approach to spoken and sign language interpreting (Hein 2009). Nilsson also notes that the responsibility for training sign language interpreters was transferred to the Institute for Translation and Interpreting at Stockholm University, which recently established a new Bachelor's program in the university and created an academic faculty member position at professorial level to run that program. In addition, mechanisms were being put in place to require sign language interpreters to be certified through the National Judicial Board for Public Lands and Funds, alongside spoken language interpreters. This requirement came in to force in 2004 (Hein 2009).

The paper included in this chapter by **Akach** and **Morgan** gives an overview of the status of the SLI profession in South Africa at the time – 1999. Given the situation of apart- heid in SA, the interpreting situation has always been complicated. There are now 11 offi- cial languages in South Africa. South African Sign Language (SASL) is recognized in the constitution, although there is still debate about what the official sign language looks like. Afrikaans and English – speaking Deaf people use different varieties of SASL (Aarons & Akach 2002). Nonetheless, sign linguists began producing systematic research on SASL in the 1990s (see for example, Penn 1990, 1992; Penn & Reagan 1994) and thus South Africa has made great strides in SLI profession. The testing/accreditation system is aligned with spoken languages, but not much formalized training is available. SLI provision is happening in the community, on television, and in some higher education institutes, but is still on an ad hoc basis and not standardized.

There is now an emerging body of research on SLI in South Africa, for example, Swift (2012) completed her Masters dissertation on educational interpreting, Selzer (2010) completed her Masters dissertation on SASL interpreting in parliament, and Wehrmeyer (2014) has investigated the comprehension of SASL interpreters on television. Greater numbers of students are undertaking Masters and Ph.D. research through UniSA and WITS, working closely with spoken language colleagues (led by Kim Wallmach). Other discussions of the SASL interpreting situation can be found in Lotriet (1998), and Deysel, Kotze, & Katshwa (2006).

Like South Africa, Belgium has a complicated situation for sign language interpreters, as there are actually two different sign languages that are used, which mirror the situation for spoken languages. Belgium is divided into Flemish speakers who live in Flanders, and French speakers.[1] Therefore one sign language allies with the Flemish (Flemish Sign Language), and the other with the French (Belgian French Sign Language). In a later paper, Van Herreweghe & Vermeerbergen (2006) discuss the fact that Flemish Sign Language interpreting has actually been provided since the early 1980s, but that systematic research into Flemish Sign Language (VGT) has had a major impact on the recognition of the need for SLI. Interestingly, another publication explores the same situation for Belgian French sign language interpreters, and the fact that the profession is still struggling to make gains in terms of developing formal interpreter training (Haesenne, Huvelle & Kerres, 2008).

Since the publication of the articles featured in this chapter, which led the way for a global picture of the SLI profession, we continue to see the further emergence of professionalization of SLI, for example, in former Soviet Union countries (Ojala-Signell & Komarova 2006), the Asia-Pacific region (Takagi 2006), Palestine (Alawni 2006), Kosovo (Hoti & Emerson 2009), Fiji (Nelson, Tawaketini, Spencer & Goswell 2009), and Kenya (Mweri 2006, Okombo, Mweri & Akaranga 2009). The establishment of the World Association of Sign Language Interpreters (WASLI) in 2005 has been an integral part of the internationalization of SLI as a profession, with regular conferences, publication of proceedings, and information available on their website; which also builds on the work of the European Forum of Sign Language Interpreters (efsli), which was established in 1993.

---

1.   See http://www.ethnologue.com/show_country.asp?name=be

6.1   Flynn, John. 1985. "Accreditation of interpreters in Australia." *Journal of Interpretation* 2: 22–26.

From a deaf welfare worker background (originally qualified through the British DWEB examination route, see Chapter 1), John Flynn worked with the Deaf community for many years when ad hoc interpreting was a part of his role. In the 1980s when the paradigm shift began, he was one of the first to lobby for recognition of the status and role of sign language interpreters as professionals. In fact, the Australian Sign Language Interpreters Association has an annual oration named after him (*The JW Flynn Oration*), for which members nominate a leading figure in the Australian SLI profession who has made a significant contribution to the Australian SLI profession through their work. The oration is held at the annual national conference, and orators are asked to explain their journey through the SLI profession and provide insights and inspiration to novice and experienced interpreters alike.

Accreditation of Interpreters in Australia

John W. Flynn

This paper was first presented to the IXth World Congress of the World Federation of the Deaf, State University of Palermo, Sicily.

The quality of interpreting services for deaf people and the means of testing and accrediting interpreters have doubtless been of concern to deaf people of the world since interpreting services were first available. In this respect, Australia is no different from other countries. Speaking now of Australia, various attempts have been made to evaluate the skills of interpreters in deaf sign language for over 100 years, but perhaps none is as likely to succeed as a recent action.

A move has been made to arrange for the National Accreditation Authority for Translators and Interpreters (N.A.A.T.I.) to accredit deaf sign and deaf oral language interpreters. Before explaining how they do it, however, I ought to say what N.A.A.T.I. is. It is an Australian government Authority established on December 14, 1977, by the then Commonwealth Minister for Immigration and Ethnic Affairs. There are thirteen members of the Authority drawn from senior administrators, academics, and practicing translators and interpreters throughout Australia. The work of the Authority is funded by the Australian government and is served by a Secretariat within the Department of Immigration and Ethnic Affairs.

The principal objectives of the Authority are: (1) to establish the standards and conditions leading to professional status, and in so doing develop translating and interpreting in Australia to meet community needs; and (2) to develop the basic infrastructure for the emergence of a national self-regulatory professional body, in the expectation that this body would, within five years, assume responsibility for the profession, including accreditation.

To clarify the need for accreditation, I should explain that in Australia, access to most public services and facilities is possible only through the English language. Indeed, most of these services and facilities are geared to cater only to the English-speaking public. Because of a very large flow of immigrants into Australia in the post-war years, there are many Australian citizens and residents for whom English is used, at best, as their second language. Because of these citizens' inadequate knowledge of English, they face the risk of misunderstanding and exploitation. Many experience serious difficulties in gaining access to public services and facilities.

Although the Authority has received applications for accreditation or recognition in approximately 80 languages, accreditations have been granted in eighteen languages and recognitions in 33 languages. With respect to testing, the Authority recognizes four categories, ranging from high to low demand.

To achieve its ends, N.A.A.T.I. determines levels of skills for translators and inter-preters appropriate to Australian conditions, taking into account the 1973 recommenda-tions of the working party and of the committee on Overseas Professional Qualifications. N.A.A.T.I. provides advice and guidance on course content to tertiary institutions conduct-ing or planning courses in Translation and Interpretation, so that gradually such courses will be eligible for accreditation at the level determined for that course by N.A.A.T.I. N.A.A.T.I. also develops tests and any other procedures necessary to assess and provide a means of accreditation for those who, with or without formal qualifications obtained in Australia or elsewhere, are practicing or wish to practice as translators or interpreters in Australia. Such procedures may include study or supervised field training approved by the Authorities.

N.A.A.T.I. provides a means of accreditation for those who have successfully com-pleted courses at various levels, based on standards of competence established by the Authority. It monitors changing Australian needs for interpreter/translator services and it advises on the development of training programs throughout Australia to meet these needs. It encourages employers to require accreditation by N.A.A.T.I. as a prerequisite for appointment. It maintains a public register of translators and interpreters who meet the standards established by the Authority. It reports annually to the Minister for Immigration and Ethnic Affairs on the work of the Authority.

You will see from the foregoing material that the reason for the establishment of N.A.A.T.I. is the very reason for establishing registrys and accreditation procedures in deaf sign languages in other parts of the world.

We in Australia were wanting to establish an Australian accreditation system for deaf sign language. Therefore, it was put to N.A.A.T.I. that there was a need for them to acknowl-edge deaf sign language as a language and expand the scope of N.A.A.T.I. to include it. Unknown to us, there was also a similar move from the Aboriginal languages. Therefore, the Australian Federation of Deaf Societies pushed the case and, after at first rejecting our contention that deaf language came within the scope of N.A.A.T.I., the Minister for Immi-gration and Ethnic Affairs determined that the deaf sign and deaf oral language should be accepted within N.A.A.T.I. Subsequently, I was appointed to the Authority and attended my first meeting in early 1982. As a member of the Authority, I have responsibility, together with my colleagues, for all languages, but naturally I concentrate specifically on deaf sign and deaf oral language interests.

And now some specifics about the methods N.A.A.T.I. uses. It tests on five levels of competence. It establishes language panels to write the tests for those levels. It has in each state a panel which actually conducts tests. As far as Aboriginal and deaf languages are concerned, the language panel itself is also the panel which conducts the testing in line with N.A.A.T.I. standards for all other languages. Prior to the establishment of the deaf panel, the chairman of N.A.A.T.I. called a meeting of officers and of the department, deaf people and representatives of organizations serving deaf people. At those initial dis-cussions, there was some question as to whether there should be separate accreditation in signed and spoken language. It was agreed to have separate testing. A number of people take both tests.

The administration of the tests is rather complex. The panel has been treading uncharted paths. Nevertheless, to date we have written Level I (Language Aide) tests and conducted them in Melbourne, Sydney, and Adelaide (the capital cities of three states of Australia). The first of the Level II tests in Melbourne attracted nine candidates for testing in deaf oral language and eight for testing in deaf sign language.

The format of a Level I test is as follows. First, we conduct free conversation in both languages, possibly involving discussion of a subject or subjects such as job function. Five or six minutes is allowed for this. In the second segment, the candidate is required to converse in the language being tested (signed or oral) with an actor, from whom the candidate will obtain the information sought in a simple form. The form has from ten to twelve questions, which the candidate will be required to fill in, using English. One of the questions on the form involves a full sentence answer. Ten minutes is allotted for this. The third segment of seven minutes is where the candidate is asked to explain in both signed and oral language how to get from point A to point B. Seven minutes is allotted for this.

Level II is regarded as more complex. It is the first level at which the person accredited is called an interpreter. It represents a level of ability for the ordinary purpose of general business, conversation, reading, and writing. This level is generally suitable for those who use sign language or deaf oral language as an important part of their principal duties. The test runs for approximately forty minutes. The first Part is an introductory conversation which is not graded. Then there are two dialogues of 250 to 300 words each, between an English speaker and a speaker of the deaf language being tested (signed or oral). Then there are some questions on cultural and social aspects of hearing loss.

We could have established a separate testing and accreditation system solely for purposes of serving the deaf and hearing-impaired populations. If we had done that, there would not be much point in writing this Paper, because in the United States particularly, there is considerable experience operating such a system. The step we took in Australia is significant in one major respect: interpreting needs for deaf and hearing-impaired people are being met in parallel with the interpreting needs in many other languages. Therefore, deaf persons' interpreting needs are being seen to along with those of the hearing community. This is one more way of bringing deaf people's needs to the surface in such a way that they may walk equally with their fellows.

6.2   Scott-Gibson, Liz. 1992. "Sign language interpreting: An emerging profession." In *Constructing Deafness*, ed. by Nadja Grbić and Michaela Wolf, 253–258. London: Milton Keynes Open University Press.

Based in Scotland, Liz Scott Gibson has worked as Director of Interpreting Services for the British Deaf Association, and later as Chief Executive Officer for Deaf Action, a Deaf community service provider organization in Edinburgh. She has worked as a British Sign Language interpreter and an International Sign interpreter; was instrumental in the establishment of three professional interpreting associations, and went on to serve as President of the Scottish Association of Sign Language Interpreters (SASLI), the European Forum of Sign Language Interpreters (EFSLI), and the World Association of Sign Language Interpreters (WASLI). Scott Gibson has taught in various university programs, including the Masters in BSL-English Interpreting at Durham University and the European Masters of Sign Language Interpreting at Heriot-Watt University, and has also been involved in projects to deliver introductory SLI training in many African and European countries, and is frequently invited as a keynote speaker to SLI conferences internationally.

Sign language interpreting

An emerging profession

Liz Scott-Gibson*

Introduction

In 1989, the United Nations General Assembly, as part of its World Programme of Action concerning Disabled Persons for the decade 1983–1992, issued a set of 'Guidelines' to promote effective measures to enable 'full participation and equality for persons with disabilities';[2] the 'Guidelines' recognize that 'disabled persons are agents of their own destiny rather than objects of care', and refer to the need for educational provision to be made available through interpreters who are 'proficient in the indigenous sign language', as well as more general access to information by means of sign language interpretation.

Whilst there are those members of the British Deaf community today who continue to feel uncomfortable bearing the label of 'disabled person', it is true that the Community welcomes the recognition that their specific linguistic needs may be met by the provision of sign language interpreters, by such prestigious bodies as the United Nations General Assembly, and, nearer to home, as contained in the resolution unanimously accepted by the European Parliament in Strasbourg in 1988, calling for the official recognition of sign languages. However, whilst it may be accurate to say that sign language interpreting is indeed an emerging field, it is, in addition, one which is not only under-resourced, but one which has struggled with its identity.

In order to examine this more closely, it is necessary to look at the development of this fledgling profession.

Historical development

Sign language interpreters have been present in the Deaf community for generations. Traditionally they were perhaps religious workers or teachers who had acquired some

---

* Director of Sign Language Services, British Deaf Association, Carlisle.

2.   The Tallin Guidelines for Action on Human Resources Development in the Field of Disability, UN, 1969.

knowledge of sign vocabulary by association with Deaf people, but more frequently it appeared that they were people who had grown up in a family with at least one Deaf member, who had reasonable fluency in both sign language and English, and who had thereby assumed the role of the 'go-between' in a variety of settings between the Deaf and hearing communities. Such people had been brought up to share the values of the Deaf community, were perceived by them as less likely to threaten or try to change it, and were, accordingly, highly valued.

Such individuals were, for many Deaf people, the only channel to wider hearing society, and this often resulted in their acquiring positions of power and influence, either informally, or more formally, as the 'missioner' for the many clubs and societies for the Deaf which were founded in the late nineteenth and early twentieth centuries. These missioners not only offered sign language interpretation when needed, but acted as the brokers between one community and another, providing advice and support as necessary to enable Deaf people to, for example, find employment, seek medical treatment, hold religious services, and enjoy leisure activities. However, by the mid-twentieth century, Britain was beginning to become aware of the existence of a range of minority groups – including that of the Deaf community – in its midst: there was a growing belief that such groups should be enabled to become part of mainstream society, and not continue in what was a perceived ghettoization of service delivery. This liberal philosophy regarded the missioner, with his monopoly of power (albeit at times unsought) over the Deaf community with horror.[3] Local authorities began to take over the welfare services offered by the missions and societies, and workers were increasingly encouraged to seek professional social work training, and to clarify their own roles and responsibilities.

Whilst this professionalization was welcomed by many Deaf people, there was some sadness at what was thought to be a decline in sign language skills, as many social workers, being removed from the hub of Deaf community and cultural life, found difficulty in developing and maintaining a minimum competence in sign fluency. There were others who, whilst recognizing that there were members of the Deaf community who were less advantaged and in need of the specialist help that a trained social worker could give, began to articulate a resentment at being labelled a social work client when all that was necessary for them to function independently in most situations was access to appropriate interpreting assistance.

In an attempt to respond to this, the British Deaf Association established a major project (funded by the DHSS) in 1977 to examine the whole area of sign language learning, interpreter training and assessment. It became clear that, for many Deaf people, to have to rely on a friend, neighbour or relative to 'help out' with interpreting support when

---

3.   See, for example, 'Hearing Impaired or BSL Users? Social Policies in the Deaf Community', by P. Ladd in *Disability, Handicap and Society* vol. 3 no. 2, 1988.

required, was an anathema; it implied that Deaf people were incapable of taking care of their own affairs, and because this type of interpreting assistance was provided on a voluntary basis, Deaf consumers felt unable to complain if dissatisfied with the service provided. In addition, there was no guarantee that such an individual was performing the task adequately, far less that the 'interpreter' was aware of the rights of the client to expect impartiality and confidentiality. Deaf people wanted to have access to a pool of people who would be competent, aware of their professional responsibilities, and thereby paid professional rates. From this initiative evolved the two Registers of Interpreters in existence today (that for **the** Council for Advancement of Communication with Deaf People, established in 1980, and that for Scotland, presently maintained by the Scottish Association of Sign Language Interpreters, which was founded in 1981). The work being done to expand the numbers of interpreters available to function in a wide range of settings – medical, educational, legal, religious, political, employment related, on television and in the theatre, and at meetings and conferences – coincided with the work being done by research teams at the University of Bristol and Moray House College in Edinburgh in the late 1970s, into the structure of British Sign Language (BSL). This established that the sign language used by deaf people was not, as it had been labelled, 'inferior' and 'ungrammatical', but rather should be viewed as a fully fledged language, with its own grammatical rules and structure. It therefore was necessary to ensure that sign language interpreters were fully fluent in both this (and not merely some manually coded form of English) and English. Efforts were accordingly made (with both greater and lesser success) to implement these research findings into sign language courses, and Deaf native users of BSL were trained to teach the language.[4] The number of sign language courses increased, helped in part by the funding of a number of full-time 'Communicators' courses around the country by the Training Agency, who were beginning to recognize that there was a desperate need for communication support for Deaf people in employment training, but such courses in themselves were insufficient to provide the level of skills required by interpreters.

Current situation

To function as an interpreter it is necessary to not only have good BSL skills, and, as stated by Koser,[5] '… the ability to intuit meanings, the capacity to adapt immediately to the subject, speaker, public and conference situations, the ability to concentrate, a good short and

---

4. The British Deaf Association sponsored the Deaf Studies Research Unit at the University of Durham, which has to date trained 143 people to teach BSL at foundation level and is currently offering the opportunity for Deaf people to take an Advanced Diploma/MA in BSL teaching.

5. Quoted by Liz Scott-Gibson, British Deaf Triennial Congress. Rothesay, 1986.

long term memory, a pleasant voice, above average endurance, and very good nerves ...', but excellent English language skills. Interpretation is not merely comprehension of a message, but is the process by which one is able to express those thoughts understood in one language in a second language, in the same way that a native speaker would express him- or herself, in style, and in intent. It is an understandably complex process, and one which requires additional high level training (presently being offered by the Universities of Bristol and Durham). In addition to being bilingual, interpreters must also strive to become bic. ultural, for accurate transmission of information may take place only if based on a deep knowledge of both languages, both cultures, and the cultural differences involved, and it is this awareness that current training seeks to provide.

Over and above this, however, is the requirement stated by Deaf people (based on observation and anecdotal evidence in this country, and the results of a survey conducted in the USA in 1988)[6] as having prime consideration – something labelled 'attitude'. In an attempt to ensure that consumers of an interpreting service receive a professional service delivered by interpreters with the right 'attitude', a Code of Conduct and Practise was established for registered sign language interpreters to adhere to, which embodied principles of impartiality (to assist interpreters – said to apply to particularly to children of Deaf parents – overcome the impulse to be helpful, and possibly controlling), responsibility and confidentiality. The former was also especially intended to enable a clear distinction to be drawn between the perceived advice giving, counselling, advocacy role of the social workers with Deaf people, and that of the interpreter as a mechanism to enable information exchange between two languages and cultures to take place.

Whilst some clarity is now developing about the respective roles and responsibilities of social workers and interpreters, there continue to be problems. In the apparent absence of sufficient numbers of independent interpreters, Social Workers with Deaf People are still obliged to carry out the function of interpreter, accompanying Mr/Mrs Smith for a job interview, and Mr/Mrs Smith to the doctor. Not only does this lead to confusion in the minds of the consumer of such a service, but it would also appear to result in a certain amount of resentment and frustration from trained social work personnel who are unable adequately to utilize their skills and knowledge with this particular client group, as an inordinate amount of their time has had to be expended on non-social work tasks, such as interpreting for people who should not be termed 'clients', and who, by so doing, are performing a task for which they may have received no training whatsoever. (Indeed, it is in fact possible to become a specialist social worker without ever having been assessed in one's ability to communicate with one's client, far less interpret for them.)

---

6.   From *Sign Language Quarterly*, Sign Language Associates, Inc., Silver Spring, MD, USA, 1989. Quoted by Betty Colonomos in Bi-Cultural Seminar held at University of Durham, October 1989.

The situation is far from satisfactory, and it is not helped by the insistence of some employing authorities that interpreting is an integral part of the social work task. It is inappropriate to expect that all sources of information should be channelled through a Social Worker with Deaf People in this way, and it is to be welcomed that there are now some more enlightened authorities which are beginning to differentiate these functions and establish separate interpreting services to promote equality of access and opportunity for the Deaf community. Nevertheless, such developments are by no means widespread, and, apart from particular and individual negotiated provision made by the Training Agency, some employers, organizations and individuals, Deaf people have neither access to, nor the means to pay for, an interpreting service.

Future trends

It is encouraging, nevertheless, to see that the Deaf community is becoming more sophisticated in its approach to interpreting services: there is a move away from the insistence on the 'interpreter as machine' image – the 'non-person' – which assumes that any two people involved in a dialogue are equal, to a recognition that sign language users are employing a minority language in an interaction with people who are using the language of a dominant, power holding majority. It is therefore essential that an interpreter recognizes this and the cultural differences involved in order to ensure that successful dialogue takes place. The extreme swing away from the former benevolent/paternal interpreting of the traditional 'missioner' or other 'helper' to a rigid interpretation of the Code of Practise on issues of neutrality and responsibility, is being tempered by a more mature move towards a humanistic model, involving greater cultural awareness and respect.[7]

The Deaf community is also developing to become much more politically active and to be aware of the need to lobby to have its demands met. Thanks to on-going consumer education programmes, Deaf people are increasingly knowledgeable about the standards of service delivery which they can expect from social workers, interpreters and other professions, and are prepared to articulate any dissatisfaction. The Deaf community, therefore, has a major responsibility to press for more and better trained social workers, and an increase in the number of, and the means to pay for, professional sign language interpreters.

Regrettably, this growing awareness on the part of the Deaf community is not always matched by parallel enthusiasm in other spheres. Although the recent *Say it Again* report,[8] published by the Social Services Inspectorate, recommends that local authorities should

---

7.   *Rebuilding Bridges to the Deaf Community*, by M.J. Bienvenu in *TBC News*, no. 4, June 1988.

8.   Social Services Inspectorate, *Say it Again*, Department of Health and Social Security.

consider the provision and funding of interpreter services, it makes no clear statement about the nature of such services, and there is no government funding available to pay for interpreter training. Furthermore, as long as Social Workers with Deaf People continue to perform interpreting tasks outside the remit of their professional role, they continue to paper over the cracks in the system and deny Deaf people the opportunity for greater and improved access to a wider hearing society.

It is true that there is still a very small number of registered sign language interpreters throughout the UK (some seventy in England, Wales and Northern Ireland, and twenty-one in Scotland); even fewer are functioning exclusively as interpreters. However, there is within this emerging profession a wish to work to improve the type and standard of service they can offer. Professional associations of sign language interpreters have been established (in 1981 in Scotland and in 1988 in England, (Wales and Northern Ireland) which it is hoped can provide support and access to information and on-going training for interpreters, as well as working to promote knowledge about the profession. Links are being forged with sign language interpreters in other countries (for example, through the European Forum of Sign Language Interpreters) in order to learn from different experiences. Whilst it is undoubtedly the case that sign language interpreting in this country is indeed an emerging profession, it would appear to be one which is ready to respond to the challenges which will be presented to it in the coming years. For the consumers of such a service, this can only be welcome news.

6.3 Schulz, Andrea. 1997. "Sign language interpreting in Germany on the way towards professionalism." *Meta* 42 (3): 546–549.

Coming from a teacher of the deaf background, Andrea Schultz has played a key role in the SLI profession in Germany and on a European level, with heavy involvement in the European Forum of Sign Language Interpreters (efsli). She was the first Secretary of efsli when it was constituted in 1993, and remained on the board for many years. Schulz was instrumental in establishing the first university SLI training program in Germany at the University of Hamburg, which she describes in this paper. One of her most remarkable contributions has been the translation (with Dina Tabbert) of a popular German music album composed by Wolfgang Müller, to create 'soundless music' for deaf people.[9]

Although Schulz no longer works there, the University of Hamburg continues to train interpreters, and has also provided training to Deaf interpreters working between different sign languages, led by Deaf Professor Christian Rathmann in the Institute for German Sign Language and Communication of the Deaf. Things have changed dramatically in Germany since Schulz's 1997 article, and there now also exists quality standards for the training and examination of sign language interpreters, as endorsed by the Deutscher Gehörlosen-Bund (German Deaf Association) and the Berufsverband der Gebärdensprachdolmetscher Innen Deutschlands (Association of German Sign Language Interpreters).

---

9. See http://www.kroethenhayn.com/?cat=products&subcat=&id=149

Sign language interpreting in Germany on the way towards professionalism

Andrea Schulz

Afin de répondre à la nécessité de former des interprètes en langue des signes, l'Université de Hambourg a implanté, en 1993–1994, en collaboration avec des linguistes, des interprètes et des professeurs du Centre for German Sign Language and Communication of the Deaf, un programme menant à un diplôme universitaire. Cet article rend compte de ce programme et en décrit la structure et les composantes.

Responding to the need to provide formal training and certification for sign language interpreters, in 1993–94 the University of Hamburg in a collaborative effort by linguists, interpreters and deaf lecturers of sign language, implemented a program leading to the "Diploma in Sign Language Interpreting" This article describes the structure and components of the program of studies.

Anyone who – due to professional reasons or personal interest – takes a closer look at the development of the occupation of "Sign Language Interpreter" will find that it is tightly interwoven with the varying history of the deaf community in Germany.

The earliest known source in the German language which mentions a "transmission for the deaf-mute" dates back to 1785. Between this early testimony and today, quite a few references to this kind of activity and/or to the people pursuing it can be found. Such reports have been everything else but systematically collected in archives, nor were they always produced on the basis of professional interest – in most instances remarks on the context discussed here can be found in marginal notes only –, but nevertheless they very clearly reveal that the reputation of these people and of their activity is always bound up with the standing of sign language and of the language user group, i.e. the deaf community. In times which could be characterized as "the blossom of deaf culture" (when deaf people were known, recognized, and represented in any occupational group, including academic professions), we find far more and clearly more positive descriptions of sign language interpreting than in the very dark times of this language community. Under the rule of the Nazis in Germany, e.g. deaf people were among those affected by the attempts to systematically decimate and eradicate anything of different nature by compulsory sterilization and other forceful methods. In these times there obviously was no room for individuality, which would have been expressed by an independent language and culture. Even less needed were persons who might have acted as communicators between the cultures of the deaf and of hearing people. Despite numerous attempts to rob the deaf of their own cultural identity, this community has continued to exist until the present moment, and undeterred by many interventions of so-called benefactors and carers, the deaf community has managed to preserve and steadily develop its own language and culture. Consequently, the activity of transmitting spoken language into sign language and vice versa has been preserved as well. It is quite intentional that I call this *the activity of transmitting* rather than the occupation or the professional practice of sign language interpreting. The concepts of "occupation" and "professionalism" imply a consensus about skills and competence as well as the provision of places (of thought, experience, and work) for the acquisition of these capabilities.

In defiance of all insights and suppositions, however, the interpreters of sign language have so far been denied the status of an independent occupational profile. An interpreter is nowadays defined as somebody whose occupational practice consists of translating utterances from one language and culture to another and thus establishing communication between two or more persons. But the interpreters of sign language were lacking appropriate opportunities. For more than 200 years they have been unable to obtain an occupational qualification, i.e. to complete a course of studies for sign language interpreters which would even have come close to other qualification programmes.

Partly due to ignorance, partly against better judgement, the field of so-called "sign language interpreting" offered rich opportunities for paternalistic attitudes towards the language community and for enhancing the image of the "interpreters", etc. Selfish interests were often pursued behind a "mask of benevolence," while the clients were unable to notice what was going on and/or had no chance of preventively eliminating certain people. Thus there were (and still are) many cases, in which the own helper syndrome or an "image neurosis" was satisfied instead of pursuing an activity within the defined scope. This negative picture also included some rather questionable practices on the part of some individual "interpreters" who were distinguished by crass profiteering rather than excelling by high-quality work.

At the same time there were always other people who, in the absence of an opportunity for obtaining a qualification somewhere, just gave their best and tried to perform their task as well as possible, especially as the demand for interpreting services appeared to be growing larger and more urgent. The pressure on this particular group of people kept increasing. They were getting caught up in the most difficult contexts without having an exact definition of tasks and responsibilities, and they were even held personally responsible for positive or negative outcomes. This was a burden which many of them could or would no longer bear. Highly motivated people with an excellent background who appeared to be predisposed to the profession of sign language interpreter moved away from it.

The language community of the deaf suffered from this development. In their struggle for the recognition of their language and culture, deaf people were, on the one hand, dependent on bilingual, bicultural people who could establish communication between their deaf community and the hearing community by way of translation. On the other hand, it was recognized time and again that this very bilingual and bicultural knowledge granted incredible power to the owners of such skills. This led the deaf to try and take some controlling measures. Their regional representations issued interpreter ID cards which were granted to those candidates who had taken an "examination" and whose performance had been considered adequate. Such examinations have been implemented in the German federal states of Hamburg (at the end of a "makeshift training course") since 1983, in Bavaria since 1983, in North-Rhine Westphalia since 1987, and in Schleswig-Holstein since 1991.

From today's perspective, these arrangements may appear to be provisional, especially since there was no training concept and hardly anything like a consensus on skills testing criteria. However, these efforts in the early 1980's generated an impulse: For the first time in more than 200 years, interpreting from and into sign language began to be considered as an activity which is not carried out on the basis of vague talents, but requires factual and technical qualifications. This triggered a heated debate on the definition of tasks and responsibilities of sign language interpreters, which were and still are extremely different in the various regions of the country. But everybody agrees that there is a steadily growing demand for sign language interpreter services, and that a training course is both necessary and indispensable.

Since the early 1990's an attempt has therefore been made at the University of Hamburg to respond to the aforementioned problems and deficits in an open-minded, competent and creative manner. Within the scope of a model experiment, the first – and so far the only – course of university studies for a "Diploma in Sign Language Interpreting" has been developed since the Winter Semester 1993/94 in a cooperative effort by linguists, interpreters and deaf lecturers of sign language at the Centre for German Sign Language and Communication of the Deaf. After the successful completion of the model experiment in July 1996, the course was firmly established as of the Winter Semester 1996/97. In the future, twenty study places for first-year university students will be made available in each winter semester.

In the following, I should like to give a brief outline of the structure and concepts of the course of studies for a diploma in sign language interpreting.

The standards of admission to the University of Hamburg have to be met as an entrance requirement. The course ends with a diploma examination for the academic degree "Diploma in Sign Language Interpreting." The successful completion of compulsory seminars and periods of work experience is required for admission to the diploma examination, which then consists of a diploma thesis as well as a theoretical and practical final examination. The focus of this course is on learning interpreting techniques in theory and practice on the basis of comprehensive linguistic competence in the German language, German Sign Language, and visual-tactile communication systems (manual alphabet, signed and sign-supported German, lip-reading, oral interpreting, tactile interpreting for deaf-blind people, and others). Moreover, skills are taught for interpreting in specific life situations and service environments of the deaf (authorities, health care, etc.), in education and training, including vocational training and continuing education, as well as social, cultural and political life.

The course in Sign Language Interpreting consists of eight major sections:

Language Competence: This area is designed to provide the basic practical language requirements for later work as an interpreter in the German language, German Sign Language, and visual-tactile communication systems. Students need to acquire a high level of language competence, and become familiar with the culture and social structure of the sign language community. In a contrastive relationship to German Sign Language, German Spoken Language has been included as a second language of reference.

Theory of Interpreting: Studying the rules of professional conduct and practice related to interpreting is an important part of this section. The historical development of "Sign Language Interpreting" as a profession is studied in national and international contexts. Attention is focussed on individual elements of the process of interpretation against the background of the state of the art in translation studies.

Interpreting Techniques: This section includes memory training as well as an introduction to the theory and practice of consecutive interpreting and note-taking techniques. It serves as preparation for the consecutive interpretation of face-to-face conversations, lectures and group discussions. This is followed by an introduction to simultaneous interpreting. Additional aspects are written translations, the sight translation of printed texts, telephone interpreting as well as team-specific interpreting activities such as shadow and relay interpreting.

Rhetoric: Starting from the linguistic basics of text production, knowledge is provided about specific techniques related to the various practices of spoken and sign language in German-speaking countries as well as the visual-tactile communication systems used in this geographical area. Specific forms of expression within various age and social groups as well as among dialect users will also be considered.

Sociology and History of the Sign Language Community: Focuses on the social situation of the sign language community as a sign language minority, with due consideration of the history and development of the international deaf community.

Linguistics: Deals with the linguistic analysis and description of German Sign Language and German Spoken Language. The translation and scientific notation and transcription of sign language, including the introduction to relevant computer software programmes, constitute an essential part of the capabilities in linguistics.

Subject Areas: Technical introductions to various subject areas and scientific disciplines (medicine, psychology, law, computer science, education, linguistics, sports, theology, tourism, and theater) are compulsory for all students. This is intended as an important content-oriented foundation for proper interpretation in these areas. It includes in particular the teaching of crucial subject-related terminologies and the required vocabularies of signs for technical terms.

Administrative Procedures: This section seeks to provide basic information on administrative procedures. It deals not only with the administrative contexts of specific government authorities, but also with business management issues which are related to tax regulations, insurance, contracting, and the like. This knowledge is intended not only as a prerequisite for interpreting assignments in these fields, but also as practical assistance to interpreters who usually work on a freelance basis.

Although the course of studies is no longer in a model stage, the deaf and hearing members of the faculty still consider it as work in progress in many ways. They have a strong interest in an exchange of experience with representatives from other countries inside and outside of Europe. In the future, it is hoped that this course will stimulate interest and encourage contact between students in various countries. Last but not least, the practical orientation of this course demands that the study performance should steadily be measured against the requirements of day-to-day work. This calls for a continuous effort to try and close the gap between scientific theory and the real needs of society.

6.4   Nilsson, Anna-Lena. 1997. "Sign Language Interpreting in Sweden." *Meta*, 42(3): 550–554.

Anna-Lena Nilsson became a qualified professional sign language interpreter after completing the Swedish Sign Language interpreter training course in 1981. Between August 1981 and August 1986 she was a full-time sign language interpreter in teacher training colleges in Stockholm. In August 1986 she began working in the sign language section of the Department of Linguistics at Stockholm University, where she was initially hired as an interpreter, but gradually become more involved in teaching and research in sign language linguistics and interpreting. Anna-Lena completed her Ph.D. on Swedish Sign Language in 2010. In 2014 she took up a position as Professor of Sign Language and Interpreting Studies at Sør-Trøndelag University College in Norway. Her publications range from descriptions of Swedish Sign Language to explorations of Swedish Sign Language Interpreting. Her main research interests are the linguistics of sign language, corpus-based approaches to sign language research, discourse structure and cohesion, and sign language interpreting.

Sign language interpreting in Sweden*

Anna-Lena Nilsson

Cet article évoque certaines des ressemblances et des différences qui caractérisent l'exercice effectué par les interprétes en langue des signes et par les interprétes en langues orales. Il se termine par un bref historique de l'évolution des services d'interprétation en langue des signes en Suéde et donne un aperçu de la situation actuelle.

Some of the similarities and differences between the work carried out by sign language interpreters and interpreters between spoken languages are discussed. A short description of the historical development of sign language interpreting services in Sweden as well as an outline of the situation today follows.

Similarities

Working as a sign language interpreter at various international conferences, I have had many interesting discussions with colleagues "in the booths." After a day of watching sign language interpreters working, and maybe also doing relay-interpreting from our spoken interpretation of a signed presentation, they have come to a single conclusion: all interpreters do the same job; we interpret between two languages. In an infinite variety of situations the interpreter receives a message in one language and interprets it into another language, simultaneously or consecutively. Knowledge of languages and cultures are the most important tools of the trade for all interpreters. But being bilingual/bicultural is not necessarily enough to make an interpreter of somebody. The skill of interpreting takes training, talent, and time, to master. The basics of interpreting that have been mentioned in the above apply regardless of what the working languages of the interpreter are.

Differences when one language is visual

One (or more) of the working languages of a sign language interpreter is a visual/gestural language, i.e. the natural sign language of a country. Signed languages are not visual representations of a country's spoken language. They are full, natural languages in their own

---

* I would like to thank my colleagues Inger Ahlgren and Brita Bergman for valuable comments on earlier versions of this article.

right, with a structure of their own. Signed languages make use of all three dimensions of the space in front of the person signing, and movement is an essential part of these languages. These essential aspects of the language are by their very nature difficult to render graphically and/or in print. Even though some writing systems have been constructed, most speakers of signed languages have no means of writing that language. This is partly why interpreters working with signed languages have practically no dictionaries to use in their work. Recently, work has been initiated in several countries, though, with the aim of producing dictionaries using the latest computer technology. There is however a more socio-political reason to the lack of dictionaries. This will be mentioned later.

With one working language being auditory and the other visual, it is always practically possible to interpret simultaneously. Many hearing persons find it very disturbing when it is totally silent in the room and a deaf person is signing for several minutes. Therefore there is often a more or less overt pressure on us to interpret simultaneously in all situations. Thus, for sign language interpreters working simultaneously is the norm, regardless of whether we interpret at an international conference or in a dialogue between two people e.g. in a police interrogation.

Since signed languages are visual it is not possible for sign language interpreters at a large conference; for example, to be an "impersonal voice" in the ears of those participants in need of interpreting services. When interpreting into sign language we must always be positioned so that everybody who needs our services can see us. Preferably we should be placed close to the speaker, to make it possible for the deaf participant to look at the speaker too, from time to time, and form an opinion of the situation based on that information as well as on what is said.

Recently discussion has also emerged regarding what possible effects there can be on the intonation pattern of simultaneous interpretation when one language is visual. The problem with anomalous prosody in simultaneous interpreting has been discussed among interpreters and teachers of interpreting for a long time (Williams 1995). The issue of the possible effects of language modality on simultaneous interpretation is discussed e.g. in Isham (1994), Isham (1995), Isham & Lane (1993), and Williams (in press).

Differences due to the fact that one language is a minority language

Acquiring the necessary fluency in a signed language can pose a problem, if you are not a native speaker. There is no "Deaf-country" which you can visit in order to learn its sign language. Moreover, most countries in the world have traditionally not given official recognition to their national sign language as a language. Research in signed languages was not initiated until the late 1960's, and it is still carried out only in relatively few countries in the world. The knowledge acquired is limited and there have been attempts made to describe only comparatively few sign languages. Even the sign languages which have been studied for the longest period of time have only been partially described. As a consequence there are hardly any comprehensive dictionaries published for the signed languages of the world. Most countries offer no opportunity to study sign language at an academic level and the pedagogical issues surrounding the recently emerged task of teaching sign language to adult beginners have only begun to be solved. With the lack of knowledge about signed languages, and the small possibilities offered to study them today, even native speakers of the language (e.g. hearing children of deaf parents) have no opportunity to learn anything **about** their language.

For a language as small as e.g. Swedish Sign Language, there is also a problem due to a lack of qualified interpreters. There are simply not enough native speakers of the language who are interested in, and capable of, becoming simultaneous interpreters. Even though it is often argued that an interpreter working into her/his native language will produce the most idiomatic interpretation, it is frequently not possible to work in accordance with this belief.

Signed languages have not been regarded as real languages and the speakers of signed languages have not been regarded as equals in society. Deaf people are still frequently regarded as "deaf **and dumb**." This situation adds extra pressure to the process of simultaneous interpretation as most sign language interpreters will feel a need to make extra certain that what they produce when they interpret is an adequate spoken version of what the deaf person signed. There is a deep affinity between most sign language interpreters and deaf people which has its roots in the oppression it is felt that society has subjected speakers of sign language to.

The development of sign language interpreting in Sweden

In the following section the development of sign language and its situation in Sweden today are described. It must be emphasized, however, that the situation differs from country to country. It is only in relatively few countries in the world, and quite recently, that it has become possible to earn a living as a professional sign language interpreter. More and more countries are now acknowledging sign language and the need for interpreting services for deaf people, and they are now for the first time planning formal education for sign language interpreters.

Sweden holds a very liberal view of a person's right to an interpreter in a number of situations, when that person does not speak Swedish. This view is largely due to the sizeable number of immigrants that have arrived during the last decades. It is estimated that one million people of the approximately eight million inhabitants in Sweden were themselves born in another country, or have at least one parent who was. During the past twenty-five years we have also seen a radical change in Swedish society as to the view of deaf people and their right to interpreting services. The earliest sign language interpreters were friends and relatives of deaf people, but also professionals in the field of deafness e.g. ministers of the deaf. The first mention of deaf people's right to an interpreter, and legislation regarding their right to an interpreter during legal proceedings, dates back to 1947. Not until 1968 did the Swedish Parliament provide money for interpreting services on an experimental basis, and in 1969 one full-time interpreter was employed. As of 1976 there have been full-time interpreters employed throughout the country, financed by society as part of the public health budget.

Training programs for sign language interpreters have developed constantly over the years. Since the first two-week course in 1969, the basic training for sign language interpreters has expanded to a two-year full time program, with fluency in sign language as an entrance requirement. January 1996 also saw the start of a four-year project with the aim of teaching sign language as well as interpreting to a group of specially selected students. In 1991, responsibility for the training of sign language interpreters was transferred from the Swedish National Board of Education to the Institute for Interpretation and Translation Studies (IITS) at Stockholm University. The decision resulted in the Institute being responsible for the training of all interpreters in Sweden, regardless of working languages and regardless of whether the interpreters were going to work as community interpreters or as conference interpreters. The process of initiating a certification system for sign language interpreters, on par with the existing certification system for interpreters working with immigrants in their contacts with Swedish authorities, has recently begun.

Interpreting services today

Deaf people in Sweden have been acknowledged as bilingual with a right to be "fluent in their visual/gestual sign language and in the language society surrounds them with – Swedish." (Swedish Parliament, 14 May 1981). As of 1993, the legal right of a deaf person to interpreting services in every day life, free of charge, has been expanded. The situations specifically mentioned in the new law include going to the drugstore, the dentist, the doctor, various contacts with authorities, union meetings, information meetings at work, weddings, funerals and other religious services, leisure activities as well as work and activities in various associations. The law also specifically states that interpreting services should not be restricted to those situations listed. There is no upper limit as to the number of hours of interpreting a person is entitled to. When an estimate of the need for interpreters in Sweden was done in 1991 the figures used to calculate the average need of interpreting services were: three hours/week for each deaf person and one interpreter per twelve deaf persons. There are approximately 8,000–12,000 deaf persons in Sweden, and the need was estimated at 750 full-time positions for sign language interpreters. Based on these figures the need is far from met. At the last count (1991) there were approximately 120 interpreters employed full-time by the county councils and approximately another 40 were as educational interpreters. There were also some 300–350 interpreters working on a free-lance basis. The most serious threat to deaf people's legal right to sign language interpreting services today is the serious lack of qualified interpreters throughout the country.

Even though there is no mention of hearing people and their need for interpreting services in their contacts with deaf people a common practice has developed. In many places in Sweden it is perfectly acceptable for e.g. a doctor or a real estate agent to engage an interpreter when they know that the patient/client is deaf. The cost will be defrayed by the county council in these situations as well as in any other situation.

Community interpreting

The interpreting services a deaf person is entitled to in accordance with Swedish law are organized through sign language interpreting units located in approximately 25 cities all over Sweden, and financed by the county councils as part of the public health services. As can be understood from the varying situations where deaf people have a legal right to interpreting services, a sign language interpreter must be prepared to work in practically any situation. Sometimes the topics discussed will be theoretical and highly specialized, and sometimes there may be need for sign language interpreters in very private and emotional situations like child births, divorce proceedings, etc. An advantage of centralized services is that there is a pool of interpreters to choose from, making it easier to send the interpreter(s) best suited for the assignment. Whenever an assignment is estimated to last for more than 1 or 2 hours, or judged to very taxing, the co-ordinator of services can send two or more interpreters. For the interpreters themselves, working with a group of colleagues gives them the opportunity to discuss professional issues frequently. Working in pairs, as happens quite often, adds the extra security of being two persons responsible for the transmission of the message.

Educational interpreting

There is no interpreting in primary schools in Sweden. Deaf children in need of visual communication attend special schools, where sign language is the language of instruction. Practically all deaf youth go on to secondary education which is specialized as well. Only in exceptional cases are interpreters needed in the secondary education. Every deaf person has the same right as any other citizen to enrol in higher education. In tertiary education, however, deaf students attend the same universities and higher education facilities as other students. When a deaf person is accepted as a student, interpreters must be hired to interpret classes, seminars, student discussion groups, etc. Hiring interpreters is the responsibility of the school/university in question and the services are free of charge for the student. Today there are some 50 interpreters employed all over the country as full-time interpreters in tertiary education. Educational interpreters usually work in pairs, except in situations where the students work mainly on their own and get brief instructions from the teacher. Besides interpreting, educational interpreters have part of their working hours scheduled for preparation. They frequently have to study textbooks and other material before interpreting e.g. a lecture physiognomy.

Conference interpreting

For a deaf person to make a career or be active in an association in today's society, attending various conferences is a necessity. Sweden entering the European Union has generated a number of meetings and conferences as well. Sweden is a small country with a small national language and as soon as sign language interpreting is needed at international conferences Swedish sign language interpreters will therefore have to work into/from yet another language (usually English). There are no special training programs for sign language interpreters working at international conferences. When a Swedish deaf person gives a presentation in Swedish Sign Language, there is need for a Swedish sign language interpreter with enough knowledge and skills in English, for example, to do simultaneous interpretation into English instead of into Swedish. Since each country has its own sign language, just as it has its own spoken language, a native speaker of English (e.g. an American sign language interpreter) will usually not be of any use, as she or he is not likely to understand Swedish Sign Language.

Another problem regarding presentations in sign language at conferences etc. stems from the fact that the presenters usually do not write their manuscript in sign language, but in Swedish or English. To produce an adequate simultaneous interpretation of an academic presentation with its highly specialized content and vocabulary, the interpreter needs to prepare thoroughly. To get presenters' papers well in advance of a conference in order for interpreters to be able to prepare is usually difficult. For sign language interpreters, there is an added problem – even if we do get a deaf presenter's paper in advance, what is printed there is **not** what the speaker will say. What is printed is a translation of the presentation into English, Swedish, or another written language. Moreover, that translation may sometimes have been done by somebody other than the presenter. On a number of occasions, Swedish sign language interpreters and deaf Swedish presenters have worked together in a very fruitful manner. The presenter and the interpreter(s) have met and worked together beforehand, rehearing the presentation and the interpretation in order to find where potential difficulties are and finding solutions. The result has been very encouraging and this approach has more or less developed into common practice.

The future

With the transfer of the responsibility of training sign language interpreters to the Institute for Interpretation and Translation Studies, a more integrated view on issues regarding interpreting has emerged. We are hoping to be able to use our common knowledge and our experiences from various aspects of interpreting to develop both the training and practice of all kinds of interpreters.

References

Isham, W. P. (1994): "Memory for Sentence form after Simultaneous Interpretation: Evidence both for and against Deverbalization", Lambert, S. & B. Moser-Mercer (Eds), *Bridging the Gap*, Amsterdam Benjamins, pp. 191–211.

Isham, W. P. (1995): "On the Relevance of Signed Languages to Research in Interpretation", *Target*, *1* (1), pp. 135–149.

Isham, W. P. & H. Lane (1993): "Simultaneous Interpretation and the Recall of Source-language Sentences", *Language and Cognitive Processes*, 8, pp. 241–264.

Williams, S. (1995): "Observations on Anomalous Stress in Interpreting", *The Translator*, 1 (1), Manchester, St Jerome Publishing, pp. 47–64.

Williams, S. (in press): "Prosody and Comprehension in Simultaneous Interpreting", Paper presented at ASLA '95 Symposium om sprakforstaelse, Lund, 9–11 November 1995, To appear in ASLA report 1996.

6.5   Akach, Philemon and Ruth Morgan. 1999. "Sign language interpreters in South Africa." *Liaison interpreting in the community*, ed. by Mabel Erasmus, 67–76. Hatfield, Pretoria: Van Schaik Publishers.

Philemon Akach has played a key role in supporting sign language and SLI teaching and research in Africa, particularly in Kenya (Akach 1991) and South Africa (Akach 2006), and was Chair of the only Department of South African Sign Language (SASL) in South Africa at the University of Free State in Bloemfontein. His research interests focus on sign language linguistics, syntax and sociolinguistics of SASL, and sign language in deaf education in Africa. He has worked extensively as an International Sign interpreter for the World Federation of the Deaf (WFD) and in other contexts, and was also a member of the inaugural board when the World Association of Sign Language Interpreters (WASLI) was established in 2005. He is now retired.

Ruth Morgan is a Lecturer in South African Sign Language and joined the University of the Witwatersrand in July 2010. She has worked in the field of sign languages and Deaf cultural studies for over twenty years. In the late 1980s, after completing her MA degree, she worked with a group of Deaf Namibians to compile a dictionary of Namibian Sign Language. After completing her Ph.D., she returned to South Africa where she did social research. Her postdoctoral research focused on working with a team of mostly Deaf people to collect and analyze the life stories of Deaf South Africans. She then worked for eight years in the lesbian, gay, bisexual, and transgender (LGBT) sector as the Director of the NGO Gay and Lesbian Memory in Action. Morgan's more recent work has focused on the intersection of Deaf, gay and HIV issues. She has also worked in teaching English to Deaf adults.

Sign language interpreting in South Africa

Philemon Akach & Ruth Morgan

Introduction

"Interpretation is not a new phenomenon; it is as old as the human race. It is easily forgotten how old the task of interpreting is, but how new the profession of interpreters is" (Kyle & Woll 1985a: 217). In a multilingual country such as South Africa which also has a constitution guaranteeing language rights for all minority groups, including the right of the Deaf[10] to access the hearing world through the use of sign language, the provision of interpreting services should be taken for granted. However, this is not the case, especially where sign language interpreting is concerned.

In order to put South African Sign Language (SASL) interpreting into context, it is necessary to investigate the historical background of the Deaf, of sign language and of Deaf culture.

First, we therefore consider the Deaf community, their culture, and their sign language. Secondly, we offer a historical survey of the oppression of both Deaf culture and sign language. Lastly, we discuss SASL interpreting: in the past, the present and the future, underscoring the need for training professionalisation.

What is South African Sign Language (SASL)?

South African Sign Language (SASL) is a "visual-gestural" language created and used by Deaf South Africans to communicate with one another. It is a language which, as opposed to a spoken language, is perceived through the eyes (visually) and not through the ears (aurally). That explains the "visual" nature of SASL. What is meant by "gestural"? Gestures as used by Deaf people have usually been dismissed as primitive, uncoordinated and inexplicable movements of the hands in the air. The signs of SASL and all natural sign languages are gestural in nature as they are made up of precise, regular, rule-governed body movements. Words or signs are made up of specific handshapes at precise locations with particular hand orientations and movements. Apart from the most

---

10.   References to the Deaf with a capital "D" are used to denote that Deaf people constitute a cultural group which share common cultural values and a common language, namely a sign language. The capital initial letters in South African Sign Language (SASL) designate a proper noun in the same way as we refer to any users of a language (e.g. French, isiZulu or English).

obvious movements of the hands and arms, the entire face and upper body are used in the formation of signs and the grammar of sign language. Facial expressions and movements of the head and upper body play a central role in the grammar and intonation of sign language.

The long-standing definition of language as a specifically vocal medium of communication (Yule 1986) has always facilitated the dismissal of a language that is visual-gestural. The words of George W. Verditz, a Deaf teacher who went on to become the President of the National Association of the Deaf (NAD) in the United States of America in 1904, negate any such dismissal. He quipped that: "As long as we have Deaf people, we will have sign language" (Baker & Cokely 1980: 1–7).

These words hold true today. Research shows that various countries have their own sign languages created by their Deaf ancestors and still used by Deaf people today. We can refer to American Sign Language, French Sign Language, Chinese Sign Language, British Sign Language, Japanese Sign Language, Namibian Sign Language, Ethiopian Sign Language and South African Sign Language, to mention a few. Even in countries where research has not been carried out, for example in many countries in Africa, sign language exists wherever there are Deaf people. Schools for the Deaf play a key role in the development of sign languages and the maintenance of Deaf culture, as will be shown below, but in the absence of a specialised school, a Deaf child born to hearing parents will always communicate in idiosyncratic signs (known as "home signs"). The lack of a signing environment or community does not impede the development of a few "home signs" to communicate with the immediate family.

Oppression of sign language

Unfortunately, the oppression of sign languages the world over began with the introduction of so-called Deaf education. Most educators (teachers) were hearing people, as the Deaf were not allowed to become teachers. These hearing teachers focused on teaching Deaf children how to speak. This approach proceeds from the view that any Deaf child or person is defective and deviant and therefore needs treatment in order to be (re)habilitated to the norm (speaking). This is the pathological view of Deaf people, as opposed to the sociological view.

The earliest historical record of Deaf education dates back to the sixteenth century. Deaf children of wealthy parents in Spain were given into the care of a monk named Pedro Ponce de Leon who was to teach them how to speak so that they could inherit their parents' wealth. This was tantamount to blackmail, with the parents holding their own children to ransom. Such situations led to a great controversy between oralism (speech) and manualism (sign language) which raged for centuries and is still heated, even in South Africa today.

Despite the fact that this controversy has usually been dominated by the view of the hearing world and by the medical model, both of which advocate oralism, sign language has thrived in many countries in Europe. Until 1880 there were Deaf teachers in schools for the Deaf using sign language as a medium of instruction, thereby imparting knowledge, rather than speech at the expense of knowledge. In 1880, an attempt was made to banish sign language from education. At a conference dominated by hearing educationalists and teachers, and in which Deaf people did not participate, a resolution was passed that the only mode of communication to be used with and by the Deaf was oralism (speech). This attempt to banish sign language did not succeed, as Deaf people continued to use it among themselves. Sign language is part of the Deaf and can never be eliminated as long as there are Deaf people in the world.

However, the infamous Milan resolution forced sign language out of the classroom and out of the sight of hearing people, especially teachers. Deaf students who were caught signing to each other were punished. The invention of hearing aids in the 1940s aggravated the oppression of sign language as amplification of sound facilitated the task of the oralists, who were focusing on speech. However, despite all the technology in the world there are Deaf people today who cannot and who do not want to speak and who choose to use sign language.

In 1960, William Stokoe, an American linguist, published his scientific findings on American Sign Language (ASL) proving that ASL was a visual-gestural language, independent of any spoken language (Stokoe 1960). He showed that the same levels of analysis used in spoken language (i.e. phonology, morphology and syntax) could be applied to the analysis of signed languages. These findings were ridiculed by the proponents of oralism.

Also in the 1960s, a group of hearing educators proposed, without any scientific research, that if Deaf people were to use any form of sign language, the signs must follow the grammar (word order) of spoken language and be accompanied by speech. Groups of educationalists in the USA advocated the idea that Deaf children could learn a spoken language (English) on the hands. They invented a sign system to code English in this way. Moreover, they invented signs for English words such as "is", "are", and "were". (These are all forms of the copula "*to be*". Sign languages do not have copulas and therefore no natural signs exist for this structure.) However, this American idea gave rise to signed exact spoken languages, for example Signed Exact English, Signed Exact Swedish, Signed Exact Danish, Signed Exact isiZulu, Signed Exact isiXhosa, Signed Exact Kiswahili, and many more.

Signing and speaking at the same time, known as Simultaneous Communication (Simcom) and/or Total Communication (TC), was adopted all over the world, especially in Deaf schools. The belief was that if the Deaf used these unscientific modes of communication, they would automatically learn to read and write the spoken language(s) of the various countries. However, this was not to be because Deaf learners left school with only basic literacy skills. This still occurs today (e.g. in the USA Deaf children leave school with a reading level equivalent to that of a hearing child in the fourth grade).

This scenario does not interfere with the development of the natural sign language created by Deaf people themselves. Natural sign language has its own vocabulary and grammar which are completely different from those of any spoken language. It is impossible to sign natural sign language and to speak simultaneously, as the word orders of the spoken and signed languages are different. In addition, a great deal of the grammar of sign languages is depicted on the face by eyebrow movements and head movements, which makes talking impossible.

The South African situation

The situation described above was paralleled in South Africa. Oralism dominated education for the Deaf from the time that the first school was established. The developments and changes in Europe and the USA also affected South Africa. The philosophy of Total Communication gave rise to the publication of a book, *Talking to the Deaf* by Nieder-Heitmann (1980), which described a set of signs used to teach children spoken languages. These signs were based on a manually coded system called the Paget-Gorman system which was developed in Britain to teach children English on the hands. Thus this first book on South African signs advocated the notion of Simcom and/or TC. The second book on South African signs, *The South African sign language dictionary* (Penn et al. 1992) attempted to overcome the problems inherent in *Talking to the Deaf*. However, this text was also problematic in that over ten varieties of signs were identified as corresponding to each English word. There was no detailed linguistic analysis, which gave rise to the misperception that there are many different sign languages in South Africa as a result of variation at the lexical level. Furthermore, the signs in this dictionary are not accepted by Deaf people as representative of the signs they use.

Again, the publication and propagation of these books and their approaches did not impact in any way on the development of SASL, the natural sign language created by Deaf South Africans. From the linguistic point of view it would seem that SASL is one language, despite the social divisions created by the apartheid system. Investigations (Aarons & Morgan, in progress) are being undertaken to document the sign language used by Deaf people across racial lines. Even if the lexicon (vocabulary) is different across racial lines and/or regionally, SASL may have one overall grammatical structure. It has been observed that variation in vocabulary does not prevent coherent communication among the Deaf. Deaf people all over the country watch the same signers on television shows, which will also contribute to the standardisation of SASL across regions and ethnic groups.

SASL is now recognised as a language in its own right and has been endorsed by the Constitution of South Africa as a language to be developed under the Pan South African

Language Board (PANSALB). The South African School Act has also accepted SASL as an official language for learning purposes. The stage is now set for extensive development through both research and usage. All human languages are dynamic. New ideas, concepts and vocabulary come into a language as old ideas, concepts and vocabulary are dropped. Languages are known to develop new concepts as users are exposed to new experiences. With the domain of SASL rapidly increasing, the language should and will flourish.

In order for health services, justice, education, television news, and many other essentials to be accessible to the Deaf in a multilingual society such as South Africa, interpreting services are imperative. Conversely, a good grounding in SASL, its present status and its future development is vital for the training of interpreters.

Who uses SASL?

Approximately 500 000 South Africans use SASL. These are Deaf people who identify themselves as culturally Deaf. There are also an insignificant number of hearing people who can use SASL fluently. On the other hand, many Deaf people do not know or use SASL as their language. These are deaf people who grew up with oralism, and identify mainly with hearing people and attempt to belong to a hearing culture. They do not use SASL and they either speak or use sign-supported isiZulu/English, etcetera.

What is meant by the Deaf community?

The Deaf community is different from other communities which live in a particular geographical area. Deaf communities in any country in the world are not restricted to one geographical area. Before the advent of special schools for Deaf children there were very few Deaf communities, only individual Deaf people living isolated from each other with no means of getting together. However, in some areas where there was a high incidence of genetic deafness, Deaf communities emerged, for example Martha's Vineyard in the USA had a vibrant Deaf community living there in the early part of this century (Groce 1985).

Statistics from the USA have indicated that 90% of the Deaf are born to hearing parents. In their first few years of life they are thus extremely isolated in the hearing world. For a language to be created, develop, and thrive, one needs a community living cohesively together and using that particularly language day in and day out. Schools for the Deaf, which are fortunately residential, play the most important role as a focal point for the formation of the Deaf community and as the place where the Deaf community survives. After school, clubs, associations and sports organisations for the Deaf provide avenues through which these bonds are sustained.

The cultural versus the pathological view of Deafness

There are two views of Deaf people. The first is the clinical or pathological view which takes the behaviours and values of the hearing majority as the "standard" or the "norm". Deaf people are seen as deviating from that norm. Lane (1992: 43) refers to this discriminatory view as "audism". On the other hand, there is the cultural or sociological view which focuses on the language, experiences and underlying values of a particular group of people who happen to be Deaf (Baker &Cokely 1980: 54–58).

The Deaf community generally excludes hearing people, except in the restricted functional interactions needed in order to accomplish tasks. Deaf people generally mistrust hearing people, perceiving them as oppressors of sign language and of Deaf culture. This perception extends to all hearing people until they prove that they can be trusted by demonstrating that they can use natural sign language fluently and spending time socialising in the Deaf community.

The pathological view has been widely held by hearing professionals working for Deaf people. When one analyses the early history of Deaf education, one sees very clearly that the controversy over oralism versus manualism was born out of this pathological view – "the Deaf must talk to be normal". This is identical to the colonial view of indigenous African peoples whose languages were marginalised and oppressed. Until the lifting of the apartheid laws in South Africa, the indigenous African languages were not considered fit for any official communication including education. Denial of one's language may be considered the worst of all oppressions. A world-wide test of the performance of school leavers in science and maths, conducted in 1997, put South Africa at the bottom of the ratings. This was rightly attributed to the fact that the tests were administered in a language that was foreign to the learners. Those who performed well were undeniably speakers of Afrikaans or English.

The cultural view of Deafness in South Africa sees the Deaf as a group of people who share a common language (SASL) and a common, visually-based Deaf culture. In the cultural framework the degree of hearing loss is irrelevant; instead, self-identification as a member of the Deaf community is important.

Sign language interpreting for the Deaf

Sign language interpreting is the single most important window through which the Deaf community can have access to all that is taken for granted by hearing society. Face-to-face community interpreting is needed in the following situations: doctors' consulting rooms, police stations, and courts; when negotiating for a bank loan, or for credit in stores; on television news; at public meetings, and in educational situations. The list is endless. An interpreter plays a key role in making each situation successful.

This service is not only crucial for the Deaf community in South Africa. The hitherto marginalised spoken languages are in the same position as the Deaf as far as the demand for interpreter services is concerned. Multilingualism is taken as a human right in South African society and enshrined in the Constitution. This calls for well-structured interpreter training programmes producing professional interpreters. However, sign language interpreting is not recognised as a profession. There is a glaring lack of training programmes and facilities.

What is interpreting?

According to the *Advanced learners' dictionary of current English* (Cowie 1989), to interpret is to give a simultaneous *spoken* translation from one language to another. An interpreter therefore is one who does simultaneous translation from one language to another. While this definition of interpreting is acceptable, it is crucial that the writers correct the misconception that exists within it. The phrase "spoken translation" is misleading since interpreting can be done from any language into any sign language and vice versa. Sign language is not a spoken language since it is not sound-based but visual-gestural. Although the definition is quite recent, it ignores the fact that sign language exists alongside spoken languages and that a good deal of interpreting involving the two language types is already taking place.

A definition of interpreting which is more agreeable to the concept of sign language outlined in this article is given by Catford (1965: 20):

> Translation is concerned with a certain type of relation between languages and is consequently a branch of comparative linguistics. [...] Translation can be performed between any pair of languages or dialects – 'related' or 'unrelated' and with any kind of spatial, temporal, social or other relationship between them.

Catford's definition highlights the directional relationships existing between languages. Translation is performed in a given direction, that is from source language to target language. Sign language can therefore, in this context, be the source language or the target language or vice versa, thereby forming a translation pair with any spoken language.

For an interpreter to interpret, that is, to work from and into any pair of languages entails training, as any profession demands.

The current South African interpreting situation

Historically, sign language interpreters have usually been present in Deaf communities. The history of the development of sign language interpreting is recorded in Europe and the USA (Gibson 1990: 253–258). Traditionally, children of Deaf adults (CODAs) assumed the responsibility for making communication possible between the Deaf and hearing communities. Religious workers, teachers and social workers who had acquired some knowledge of sign language vocabulary and structure through association with Deaf people also rendered such a service. In retrospect, this was a dangerous situation, in that these people developed the attitude of the helper towards the helpless. They were indispensable and wielded tremendous power.

The Deaf community in South Africa has not been spared this apparently inevitable developmental trend. As has been mentioned, no formal training of sign language interpreters was undertaken in South Africa until 1997. The Deaf community in South Africa are therefore in a situation similar to that of the Deaf in Europe and America many years ago. A few CODAs, social workers, teachers and friends of the Deaf render interpreting services in South Africa. There is, however, a small difference from the European or American situation in that a few skilled, qualified interpreters trained abroad are also operating in the country. Their impact emphasises the importance of training and professionalism.

Interim short-term measures to remedy the situation

The Deaf Federation of South Africa (DEAFSA), an organisation representing the Deaf people of South Africa, has fought for the recognition of SASL. Knowing the need for and the importance of sign language interpreting, DEAFSA put some interim measures into place in collaboration with the Unit for Language Facilitation and Empowerment (ULFE) of the University of the Orange Free State (UOFS). These two institutions ran a four-week interpreters' training course in 1997. The ULFE had by then presented intensive four-week training programmes for interpreters working for the Truth and Reconcilliation Commission (TRC), the provincial legislature, the Department of Justice and the national parliament. DEAFSA requested a course to upgrade the skills of sign language interpreters who interpret on a daily basis or intermittently for the Deaf in various areas of South Africa. The Deaf communities in each province nominated their most skilled interpreters to attend the intensive training course.

The course proved beneficial to the participants as it covered the theory of translation and interpreting, general community interpreting techniques as well as sign language structure, linguistics and SASL enhancement. The participants were subjected to a vigorous theoretical and practical examination before certification. Their certificate can count as a study credit or meet the admission requirements for further courses.

The envisaged future

DEAFSA has approached the departments of translation at various universities with the request that they include SASL in their programmes. The academics need no convincing, in fact are eager to launch such a course, but financial constraints present a major problem. This appeal for a basic human right comes at a time when universities' subsidies are being decreased. If other means can be found to raise funds then these programmes can be established. Human resources are only a problem in so far as the universities do not have sign language experts on their staff. However, the few available sign language linguists and qualified sign language interpreters can be used nationally on a part-time basis to teach sign language theory, sign language enhancement and practical interpreting skills.

In this regard the University of the Orange Free State (UOFS) launched a course in South African Sign Language as an academic subject in January 1999. The course is being phased in over a period of three years. Students can take this course as a major or a minor within the various BA curricula of the University. Over a period of time the course is aimed at generating a number of graduates who will join the interpreting profession with a strong Sign Language combination. UOFS also offers several postgraduate professional courses, such as the Diploma in Legal Interpreting, the Advanced Diploma in Translation/Interpreting, a BA for the Language Professions and an MA in General Linguistics with specialisation in Interpreting. In the latter courses students require a combination of any two languages including the combination of SASL and any official South African language.

Other Universities which have taken action in this regard are the University of the Witwatersrand, which has launched a three-year Diploma in SASL Interpreting and a Deaf Studies Centre. At the University of South Africa (UNISA) an interpreter's training programme is in the planning stage. The University of Durban Westville has indicated that it may offer a winter school for people interested in learning sign language. If this succeeds, they will consider offering a longer and a more intensive course.

Professionalisation of interpreting

Being a professional has to do with the ability to profess to a collective standard of ethics and practice above self-interest. Professionals attain recognition by creating some form of professional body to regulate the ethics and practice of members as well as to regulate interdisciplinary relationships between one profession and another.

From the foregoing, it can be stated that a professional is trained to recognised standards of competence, adheres to a recognised code of practice and enjoys the support and regulation of a professional structure.

While interpreting is taken for granted for hearing people, it is not so for Deaf people. This statement may be qualified even further. In the USA and certain European countries, interpreting for the Deaf has acquired "at par" status with spoken language interpreting. This, however, did not come easily. It was the result of an uphill struggle for sign languages to be recognised as languages in their own right. South Africa today has an advantage with regard to this last requirement in that SASL is not only recognised as a language to be developed but also as an official language for educational purposes. This should give sign language interpreting the necessary impetus for rapid development.

Spoken language interpreting was referred to as a young profession by Herbert (1978 as quoted by Kyle and Woll (1985b: 217)), while sign language interpreting is in its early infancy. In many countries, and especially in Africa, it may be described as yet to be born (Akach 1994: 154). Sign language interpreting is thus a "fledgling" and not a "fledged" profession (Gibson 1990: 153).

The acceptance of sign language interpreting as a profession just like any other profession in South Africa is long overdue, for the simple reason that the demand is quite apparent. In terms of the Constitution of the Republic of South Africa, Deaf people are being discriminated against as their right to access language is being denied. Deaf people do not have access to the spoken languages used in everyday situations, for example educational institutions and the courts. Therefore trained interpreters who can make the language of universities and courts accessible to Deaf people are essential in order to begin to redress the discrimination that Deaf people **have** endured as a result of the oppression of SASL.

Bibliography

Aarons, D. & Morgan, R. (in progress). *An investigation into the linguistic structure of the signed languagels used by the Deaf communities in the Western Cape and Gauteng.* CSD research grant.

Akach, P.A.O. 1994. Interpreting as a profession. In Skjolden, H. & Glad, P. (Eds), *Sign language interpreting for the Deaf.* Proceedings of the 4th East and Southern African Sign Language Seminar (edited). Denmark: Danish Deaf Association.

Baker, C. & Cokely, D. 1980. *ASL: A teacher's resource text on grammar and culture.* Washington, DC: Gallaudet University Press.

Catford, J.C. 1965. *A linguistic theory of translation.* Nairobi: Oxford University Press.

Constitution of the Republic of South Africa, 1996. Act 108 of 1996. As adopted on 8 May 1996 and amended on 11 October 1996 by the Constitutional Assembly. Pretoria: Government Printer.

Cowie, A.P. 1989. *Advanced learners' dictionary of current English.* Oxford: Oxford University Press.

Gibson, L.S. (Ed.). 1990. *Sign language interpreting: an emerging profession in constructing deafness.* London: Printer Publishers, in association with Open University.

Groce, N.E. 1985. *Everyone here spoke sign language: hereditary deafness on Martha's Vineyard.* Cambridge, MA: Harvard University Press.

Herbert, J. 1978. How conference interpretation grew. In Gerver, D. & Sinaiko, H.W. (Eds), *Language interpretation and communication.* New York: Plenum.

Hymphrey, J. & Alcom, B. 1995. *So you want to be an interpreter: an introduction to sign language interpreting.* Amarillo, Tx: H&H.

Kyle, J.G. & Woll, B. 1985a. *Language in sign: an interpretational perspective on sign language.* London: Croom Helm.

Kyle, J.G. & Woll, B. 1985b. *Sign language: the study of Deaf people and their language.* Cambridge: Cambridge University Press.

Lane, H. 1992. *The mask of benevolence: disabling the Deaf community.* New York: Vintage.

Lane, H., Hoffmester, R. & Bahan, B. 1996. *A journey into the deaf world.* San Diego, California: Dawn Sign.

McIntire, M. 1990. *The work and education of sign language research and application.* Proceedings of the International Congress. Hamburg: Signum.

Nieder-Heitmann, N. 1980. *Talking to the Deaf.* Department of Education and Training and SANCD. Pretoria: Government Printer.

Penn, C, Foreman, D.O., Simmons, D. & Forbes, M.A. 1992. *Dictionary of South African signs.* Pretoria: Human Sciences Research Council.

South African Schools Act, Act 84 of 1996. Cape Town.

Stokoe, W.C. 1960. *Sign language structure: an outline of the visual communication systems of the American Deaf: studies in linguistics.* Occasional Papers No. 8. New York: University of Buffalo.

Woodward, J. 1980. Social linguistic research on ASL: an historical perspective. In Baker, C. & Battison, R. (Eds), *Sign language and the Deaf community: Essays in honour of William C. Stokoe.* Silver Springs, MD: NAD, 117–134.

Yule, G. 1986. *The study of language.* Cambridge: Cambridge University Press.

Epilogue

Our focus in this Reader has been on past scholarship not readily available to students and educators. There is still a need for more people to publish their research (Napier 2011b), as many excellent Ph.D. studies remain largely unpublished.

This Reader features papers produced up to 1999, as publications after the year 2000 are a lot more readily accessible via online databases, and also available in wider range of publications. The *Journal of Interpretation*, published by the Registry of Interpreters for the Deaf in the USA, *Das Zeichen* in Germany, and other publications listed in the International Bibliography of Sign Language previously hosted by the University of Hamburg include publications from journals such as the *Journal of Deaf Studies and Deaf Education*, *Deaf Worlds* (no longer published), and *Sign Language Studies,* all of these have featured, and continue to feature, articles on SLI.

Additionally, Metzger and Fleetwood's *Studies on Interpretation* series, published by Gallaudet University Press, is a source of cutting-edge research on SLI. The first volume in the series was published in 2003 (at the time of publication of this Reader the 12th volume had just been issued and the 13th was in press), and the series includes a mix of edited volumes with several contributors, or sole authored books that are typically the product of Ph.D. research.

The papers in this Reader have laid the foundation for the sign language interpreting profession worldwide and for the increasing body of SLI research that is now appearing. Increasingly, we witness discussions of evidence-based research studies of SLI in other journals outside of the sign language and deafness sectors. Articles now often appear in Translation and Interpreting Studies journals, such as *Interpreting: International Journal of Research and Practice in Interpreting, Babel, The Translator*, and *International Journal of Interpreting & Translation Research*; confirming that SLI is more widely regarded as being equivalent to spoken language interpreting, and therefore discussions of SLI can be appreciated by any Interpreting Studies scholars. Furthermore, SLI research can also be found in broader linguistics journals, such as: *Applied Linguistics, Discourse and Communication, Journal of Pragmatics, Multilingua;* and professional domain journals that discuss contexts in which sign language interpreters work, for example, *Family Medicine, Journal of Mental Health Counseling, Law Reform.*

In addition to that broader dissemination, we are also witnessing the growth of international cross-linguistic and cross-modal collaborations in the form of research projects that directly compare different aspects of spoken and sign language interpreters' practice (e.g. Shaw, Grbic & Franklin 2004; Shaw 2011a; Swabey et al. forthcoming), and also in the form of conferences that feature both spoken and sign language interpreting presentations relevant to the conference theme (Napier 2012). Given the advent of technologies, there is greater scope for international collaboration (Shaw 2006), with the outcomes of such research being more readily accessible to interpreter practitioners, educators and researchers.

Given the explosion of SLI research, there is no doubt that emerging areas of study will continue to evolve, including the study of Deaf interpreters (see Adam et al. 2014), the use of video remote technology in the provision of SLI (see Brunson 2011), and the relationship between interpreter education programs and the Deaf community (see Shaw 2011b). Furthermore, it is envisaged that there will be increasing use of corpus and mixed-methods research approaches, as is also expected in Interpreting Studies generally (Napier & Hale 2015).

Leeson, Wurm and Vermeerbergen (2011) note that there are three dimensions to the emerging SLI research field: (1) we have *generation zero research* (earlier descriptive and prescriptive works on SLI practice and profession, as outlined in Chapters 1–2 of this Reader); (2) *first generation research* (which is where, they suggest, we are now and provides theoretical considerations and analyses; which we have covered in Chapters 3–5 of this Reader); and (3) *second generation research* (which is what we need more of – investigation of what students/professionals do with the knowledge gleaned from first generation research, that is, how they actually apply in practice what they have learned). It is our hope that this Reader will enable SLI researchers and educators to foreground their future efforts in producing more first and second-generation SLI research.

Bibliography

Aarons, Debra, and Philemon Akach. 2002. "South African Sign Language: One sign language or many?" In *Language in South Africa*, ed. by Rajend Mesthrie, 127–147. Cambridge: Cambridge University Press. DOI: 10.1017/cbo9780511486692.007

Adam, Robert, Steven Collins, Melanie Metzger, and Christopher Stone. 2014. *Deaf interpreters at work*. Washington, DC: Gallaudet University Press.

Akach, Philemon. 1991. *Kenyan Sign Language dictionary*. Nairobi: Kenyan National Association of the Deaf.

Akach, Philemon. 2006. "Colonisation of sign languages and the effect on sign language interpreters." In *Proceedings of the Inaugural Conference of the World Association of Sign Language Interpreters*, ed. by Rachel L. McKee, 32–43. Coleford, UK: Douglas McLean.

Akach, Philemon and Ruth Morgan. 1999. "Sign language interpreters in South Africa". In *Liaison interpreting in the Community*, ed. by Mabel Erasmus, 67–76. Hatfield, Pretoria: Van Schaik Publishers.

Alawni, Khalil. 2006. "Sign language interpreting in Palestine." In *Proceedings of the Inaugural Conference of the World Association of Sign Language Interpreters*, ed. by Rachel L. McKee, 68–90. Coleford, UK: Douglas McLean.

Anderson, R. Bruce W. 1976. "Perspectives on the role of the interpreter." In *Translation: Applications and Research*, ed. by Richard Brislin, 208–228. New York: Gardner Press.

Angelelli, Claudia. 2003. "The visible co-participant: The interpreter's role in doctor-patient encounters." In *From Topic Boundaries to Omission: New Research on Interpretation*, ed. by Melanie Metzger, Steven Collins, Valerie Dively, and Risa Shaw, 3–26. Washington DC: Gallaudet University Press.

Arjona, Etilvia. 1983. "Issues in the design of curricula for the professional education of translators and interpreters." In *New Dialogues in Interpreter Education, Proceedings of the Third National Conference of Interpreter Trainers*, ed. by Marina McIntire, 1–16. Silver Spring, MD: Registry of Interpreters for the Deaf.

Bélanger, Danielle-Claude. 1995. "Les spécificités de interprétation en langue des signes québécoise. Première partie: Analyse à partir du modèle d'efforts et de l'équilibre d'interprétation." *Le Lien* 9(1): 11–16; [Translated by Lee Williamson].

Bélanger, Danielle-Claude. 1995. "Les spécificités de interprétation en langue des signes québécoise. Deuxième partie: Comment préserver l'équilibre d'interprétation." *Le Lien* 9(2): 6–13. [Translated by Lee Williamson].

Bennett, Adrian. 1981. "Interruptions and the interpretation of conversation." *Discourse Processes* 4: 171–88. DOI: 10.1080/01638538109544513

Bergman, Brita. 1973. "Teckenspråkets lingvistiska status." In *Psykologisk skriftserie nr 4*, ed. by Lars von der Lieth, 211–215. Köpenhamns universitet.

Berk-Seligson, Susan. 1990. *The Bilingual Courtroom: Court Interpreters in the Judicial Process*. Chicago: University of Chicago Press. DOI: 10.1017/s004740450001513x

Bontempo, Karen and Jemina Napier. 2007. "Mind the gap! A skills gap analysis of sign language interpreters." *The Sign Language Translator & Interpreter* 1(2): 275–299.

Bontempo, Karen and Patricia Levitzke-Gray. 2009. "Interpreting Down Under: Sign language interpreter education and training in Australia." In *International Perspectives on Sign Language Interpreter Education*, ed. by Jemina Napier, 149–170. Washington, DC: Gallaudet University Press.

Bontempo, Karen and Jemina Napier. 2009. "Getting it right from the start: Program admission testing in signed language interpreting programs." In *Testing and Assessment in Translation and Interpreting Studies*, ed. by Claudia Angelleli and Holly Jacobson, 247–295. Amsterdam: John Benjamins. DOI: 10.1075/ata.xiv.13bon

Bontempo, Karen and Jemina Napier. 2011. "Evaluating emotional stability as a predictor of interpreter competence and aptitude for interpreting." *Interpreting, International Journal of Research and Practice in Interpreting* 13: 85–105. DOI: 10.1075/intp.13.1.06bon

Brasel, Barbara Babbini, Dale Montanelli, and Stephen P. Quigley. 1974. "The component skills of interpreting as viewed by interpreters." *Journal of Rehabilitation of the Deaf* 7: 20–27.

Brasel, Barbara Babbini. 1976. "The effects of fatigue on the competence of interpreters for the deaf." In *Selected Readings on the Integration of Deaf Students at CSUN #1*, ed. by Harry Murphy, 19–22. Northridge, CA: California State University at Northridge.

Brennan, Mary. 1975. "Can deaf children acquire language? An evaluation of linguistic principles in deaf education." *American Annals of the Deaf*, 120(5): 463–479. DOI: 10.1353/aad.2012.1048

Brennan, Mary. 1992. "The visual world of BSL: an introduction." In *Dictionary of British Sign Language*, ed. by David Brien, 1–133. London: Faber & Faber.

Brennan, Mary. 1999. "Signs of injustice." *The Translator* 5(2): 221–246.
DOI: 10.1080/13556509.1999.10799042

Brennan, Mary and Richard Brown. 1997. *Equality Before the Law: Deaf People's Access to Justice.* Durham, UK: Deaf Studies Research Unit: Durham University.

Brennan, Mary and Richard Brown. 2004. *Equality Before the Law: Deaf People's Access to Justice.* (2nd ed.). Coleford, UK: Douglas McLean.

Brunson, Jeremy L. 2011. *Video Relay Service Interpreters: Intricacies of Sign Language Access.* Studies in Interpretation. Washington, D.C.: Gallaudet University Press.

Carr, Silvana, Roda Roberts, Ann Dufor, and Diana Steyn (eds). 1997. *The Critical Link: Interpreters in the Community. Papers from the First International Conference on Interpreting in Legal, Health, and Social Service Settings (Geneva Park, Canada, June 1–4, 1995).* Amsterdam and Philadelphia: John Benjamins. DOI: 10.1075/btl.19

Cerney, Brian. 2013. "Revisiting Brasel (1976): Should We Switch Every Twenty Minutes?" Accessed April 29, 2013. http://handandmindpublishing.blogspot.co.uk.

Cokely, Dennis. 1982. The interpreted medical interview: it loses something in the translation. *The Reflector* 3: 5–10.

Cokely, Dennis. 1985. "Interpretation: a sociolinguistic model." Ph.D. diss., Georgetown University.

Cokely, Dennis. 1992. *Interpretation: A sociolinguistic model.* Silver Spring, MD: Linstok Press.

Cokely, Dennis. 2005. "Shifting positionality: A critical examination of the turning point in the relationship of interpreters and the deaf community." In *Sign Language Interpreting and Interpreter Education: Directions for Research and Practice*, ed. by Marc Marschark, Rico Peterson, and Elizabeth Winston, 3–28. NY: Oxford University Press.

Davis, Jeffrey. 1989. "Distinguishing language contact phenomena in ASL interpretation." In *The Sociolinguistics of the Deaf Community*, ed. By Ceil Lucas, 85–102.
DOI: 10.1016/b978-0-12-458045-9.50010-0

Davis, Jeffrey. 1990. "Linguistic transference and interference: Interpreting between English and ASL." In *Sign Language Research: Theoretical Issues*, ed. by Ceil Lucas, 308–321. Washington, DC: Gallaudet University Press.

Davis, Jeffrey. 2003. "Cross-linguistic strategies used by interpreters." *Journal of Interpretation* 18: 95–128.

Davis, Jeffrey. 2005. "Code choices and consequences: Implications for educational interpreting." In *Educational Interpreting: From Research to Practice*, ed. By Mark Marschark, Rico Peterson and Elizabeth Winston, 112–149. Oxford: Oxford University Press.

Dean, Robyn. Forthcoming. "Ethics and ethical discourse in community interpreting: Consideration of cognitive and psychological factors." PhD. Diss, Edinburgh: Heriot-Watt University.

De Wit, Maya. 2005. *Sign Language Interpreting in Europe*. ITV Hogeschool Voor Tolkien & Vertalen.

Deysel, Francois, Thelma Kotze and Asanda Katshwa. 2006. "Can the Swedish agency model be applied to South African Sign Language Interpreters?" In *Proceedings of the Inaugural Conference of the World Association of Sign Language Interpreters*, ed. by Rachel L. McKee, 60–67. Coleford: Douglas McLean.

Dickinson, Jules. 2014. *Sign Language Interpreting in the Workplace*. Colchester, UK: Douglas McLean Publishing.

Eco, Umberto. 1976. *A Theory of Semiotics*. Bloomington, IN: Indiana University Press. DOI: 10.1017/s004740450000484x

Fant, Lou. 1990. *Silver Threads: A Personal Look at the First Twenty-five years of the Registry of Interpreters for the Deaf*. Silver Spring, MD: Registry of Interpreters for the Deaf.

Finton, Lynn, and Richard Smith. 2005. "Compression strategies: ASL to English interpreting." *Journal of Interpretation* 8: 49–63.

Fischer, Steven and Kathryn Woodcock. 2008. "A cross-sectional survey of reported musculoskeletal pain, disorders, work volume and employment situation among sign language interpreters." *International Journal of Industrial Ergonomics* 42(4): 335–340. DOI: 10.1016/j.ergon.2012.03.003

Fleischer, Larry. 1975. "Sign Language Interpretation Under Four Conditions." Ph.D. diss., Brigham Young University.

Flynn, John. 1985. "Accreditation of interpreters in Australia." *Journal of Interpretation* 2: 22–26.

Frishberg, Nancy. 1986. *Interpreting: An Introduction*. Silver Spring, MD: Registry of Interpreters for the Deaf.

Frishberg, Nancy. 1990. *Interpreting: An Introduction* (2nd ed.). Silver Spring, MD: Registry of Interpreters for the Deaf.

Gannon, Jack. 1981. *Deaf heritage: A narrative history of deaf America*. Washington, D.C.: Gallaudet University Press.

Gerver, David. 1971. "Simultaneous interpretation and human information processing." Ph.D. diss., Oxford University.

Gerver, David. 1976. "Empirical studies of simultaneous interpretation: A review and a model." In *Translation: Applications and Research*, ed. by Richard Brislin, 165–207. New York: Gardner Press.

Gerver, David and H. Wallace Sinaiko (eds). 1978. *Language Interpretation and Communication* (Vol. 6). New York: Plenum Publishing Corporation. DOI: 10.1007/978-1-4615-9077-4

Gile, Daniel. 1991. "The processing capacity in conference interpretation." *Babel International Journal of Translation* 17(1): 15–27. DOI: 10.1075/babel.37.1.04gil

Gile, Daniel. 1994. "Opening up in interpretation studies." In *Translation Studies: An Interdiscipline*, ed. by Mary Snell-Hornby, Franz Pöchhacker and Klaus Kaindl, 149–158. Amsterdam: John Benjamins. DOI: 10.1075/btl.2

Gile, Daniel. 1998. "Observational studies and experimental studies in the investigation of conference interpreting." *Target International Journal of Translation Studies* 10: 69–93. DOI: 10.1075/target.10.1.04gil

Grbić, Nadja. 1997. "Von Handlangern und Experten. Die soziale Praxis des Gebärdensprachdolmetschens im Wandel." In *Text – Kultur – Kommunikation: Translation als Forschungsaufgabe. Festschrift aus Anlaß des 50jährigen Bestehens des Instituts für Übersetzer- und Dolmetscherausbildung an der Universität Graz*, ed. by Naja Grbić, and Michaela Wolf, 293–305. Tübingen: Stauffenburg. DOI: 10.1075/target.11.1.25van

Grbić, Nadja. 2007. "Where do we come from? What are we? Where are we going? A bibliometrical analysis of writings and research on sign language interpreting." *The Sign Language Translator & Interpreter* 1: 15–51.

Haesenne, Thierry, Damien Huvelle and Patricia Kerres. 2008. "One step forward, two steps back: Toward a new signed language interpreter training programme in French-speaking Belgium." *The Sign Language Translator and Interpreter* 2(2): 177–196.

Hale, Sandra and Jemina Napier. 2013. *Interpreting Research Methods: A practical resource*. London: Bloomsbury.

Harrington, Frank and Graham H. Turner (eds). 2001. *Interpreting Interpreting: Studies and Reflections on Sign Language Interpreting*. Coleford, UK: Dougals McLean Publishing. DOI: 10.1075/intp.6.2.09roy

Heaton, Mark and David Fowler. 1997. "Aches, aspirins and aspirations: a Deaf Perspective on interpreting service delivery." *Deaf Worlds* 13(3): 3–8.

Hein, Anna. 2009. "Interpreter education in Sweden: A uniform approach to spoken and signed language interpreting." In *International Perspectives on Sign Language Interpreter Education*, ed. by Jemina Napier, 124–148. Washington, DC: Gallaudet University Press.

Herbert, Jean. 1952. *The Interpreter's Handbook: How to Become a Conference Interpreter*. Genève: Georg.

Hoti, Selman, and Susan Emerson. 2009. "Beginnings of the interpreter training program in Kosovo." In *International Perspectives on Sign Language Interpreter Education*, ed. by Jemina Napier, 57–76. Washington, DC: Gallaudet University Press.

Hurwitz, Alan. 1980. "Interpreters' effectiveness in reverse interpreting: Pidgin Sign English and American Sign Language." In *A Century of Deaf Awareness in a Decade of Interpreting Awareness: Proceedings of the 6th National Conference of the Registry of Interpreters for the Deaf*, ed. by Frank Caccamise, James Stangarone, Marilyn Mitchell-Caccamise, and E. Banner (eds.), 157–187. Silver Spring, MD: RID.

Ingram, Robert M. 1974. "A communication model of the interpreting process." *Journal of Rehabilitation of the Deaf* 7: 3–9.

Ingram, Robert. 1978. "Sign language interpretation and general theories on language, interpretation and communication." In *Language Interpretation and Communication*, ed. by David Gerver, 109–118. New York: Plenum Press. DOI: 10.1007/978-1-4615-9077-4_11

Janzen, Terry and Barbara Shaffer. 2008. "Intersubjectivity in interpreted interactions. The interpreter's role in co-constructing meaning." In *The Shared Mind: Perspectives on intersubjectivity*, ed. by Jordan Zlatev, Timothy P. Racine, Chris Sinha and Esa Itkonen, 333–355. Amsterdam: John Benjamins. DOI: 10.1075/celcr.12.18jan

Johnston, Trevor. 1989. *Auslan Dictionary: A Dictionary of the Sign Language of the Australian Deaf community*. Maryborough, VIC: Deafness Resources Australia.

Klima, Edward and Ursula Bellugi. 1979. *The Signs of Language*. Boston, MA: Harvard University Press. DOI: 10.1017/s0047404500008575

Lee, Robert and Peter Llewellyn-Jones. 2011. *Re-visiting Role: Arguing for a multi-dimensional analysis of interpreter behavior*. Paper presented to the Supporting Deaf People online conference, 2–13 February 2011. Available: http://www.online-conference.net/sdp2011/programme.htm#lee

Leeson, Lorraine, Svenja Wurm and Myriam Vermeerbergen. 2011. "'Hey Presto!' Preparation, practice and performance in the world of signed language interpreting and translating." In *Signed Language Interpreting: Preparation, Practice and Performance,* ed. by Lorraine Leeson, Svenja Wurm and Myriam Vermeerbergen, 2–11. Manchester: St Jerome.

Li, Shuangyu. 2013. "Co-construction of interpreted conversation in medical conversation." *Applied Linguistics Review* 4(1): 127–149. DOI: 10.1515/applirev-2013-0006

Liddell, Scott. 1980. *American Sign Language Syntax.* The Hague: Mouton. DOI: 10.2307/414075

Llewellyn-Jones, Peter. 1981. "Target language styles and source language processing in conference sign language interpreting." Paper presented at the *3rd International Symposium on Sign Language Interpreting,* Bristol, UK.

Llewellyn-Jones, Peter and Robert G. Lee. 2014. *Redefining the Role of the Community Interpreter: The Concept of Role Space.* Lincoln, UK: SLI Press.

Locker, Rachel. 1990. "Lexical Equivalence in Transliterating for Deaf Students in the University Classroom: Two Perspectives." *Issues in Applied Linguistics* 1(2): 167–195.

Lotriet Annelie. 1998. "Sign language interpreting in South Africa: Meeting the Challenges." Paper presented to the *Critical Link 2: Interpreters in the Community,* Vancouver, July 1998. Available: http://static.squarespace.com/static/52d566cbe4b0002632d34367/t/5347f53ee4b03c03e0 77d949/1397224766516/CL2_Lotriet.pdf

Lucas, Ceil and Clayton Valli. 1992. *Sign Languages in Contact.* Washington, DC: Gallaudet University Press. DOI: 10.1017/s0272263102224055

Madden, Maree. 2005. "The prevalence of occupational overuse syndrome in signed language interpreters in Australia – What a pain!" In *Attitudes, Innuendo, and Regulators: Challenges of Interpretation,* ed. by Melanie Metzger and Earl Fleetwood, 3–70. Washington, DC: Gallaudet University Press.

McBurney, Susan. 2012. "History of sign languages and sign linguistics." In *Sign Language: An International Handbook,* ed. by Roland Pfau, Markus Steinbach and Bencie Woll, 909–948. Amsterdam: De Gruyter Mouton. DOI: 10.1515/9783110261325

McDade, Robert. 1995. What can interpreters learn from professional footballers? Paper presented at the Issues in Interpreting 2 conference, University of Durham, Durham, UK, September 1995.

McIntire, Marina. 1980. "Some linguistic factors in the training sign to voice interpreters." In *A Century of Deaf Awareness in a Decade of Interpreting Awareness Proceedings of the 6th National Conference of the Registry of Interpreters for the Deaf,* ed.by Frank Caccamise, James Stangerone, Marilyn Mitchell-Caccamise, and E. Banner, 189–97. Silver Spring, MD: Registry of Interpreters for the Deaf.

McIntire, Marina and Gary Sanderson. 1995. "Who's in charge here? Perceptions empowerment and role in the interpreting setting." *Journal of Interpretation* 7: 99–113.

McIntire, Marina and Gary Sanderson. 1995. "Bye-Bye! Bi-Bi! Questions of empowerment and role." In *A Confluence of Diverse Relationships: Proceedings of the 13th National Convention of the Registry of Interpreters for the Deaf, 1993,* 94–118. Silver Spring, MD: Registry of Interpreters for the Deaf.

Metzger, Melanie. 1995. "The Paradox of Neutrality: A Comparison of Interpreters' Goals with the Reality of Interactive Discourse." Ph.D. Diss., Washington, DC: Georgetown University.

Metzger, Melanie. 1999. *Sign Language Interpreting: The Paradox of Neutrality.* Washington, DC: Gallaudet University Press.

Metzger, Melanie. 2006. "Salient studies of signed language interpreting in the context of community interpreting scholarship." In *Linguistica Antverpiensia: Taking stock: Research and methodology in community interpreting* (vol. 5), ed. by Erik Hertog and Bart van der Veer, 263–291. Antwerpen: Hogeschool Antwerpen, Hoger Instituut voor Vertalers en Tolken.

Metzger, Melanie and Cynthia Roy. 2013. "Sociolinguistic studies of signed language interpreting." In *The Oxford Handbook of Sociolinguistics*, ed. by Robert Bayley, Richard Cameron and Ceil Lucas, 735–753. New York: Oxford University Press. DOI: 10.1111/josl.12065

Miller, Katrina. 2001. "Access to sign language interpreters in the criminal justice system." *American Annals of the Deaf* 146(4): 328–330. DOI: 10.1353/aad.2012.0188

Miller, Katrina. 2003. "Signs of prison life: Linguistic adaptations of deaf inmates." *Journal of Interpretation*, 5: 129–142.

Moser, Barbara. 1978. "Simultaneous interpretation: A hypothetical model and its practical application." In *Language Communication and Interpretation,* ed. By David Gerver and H. Wallace Sinaiko, 353–368. New York: Plenum Press. DOI: 10.1007/978-1-4615-9077-4_31

Murphy, Harry. 1978. "Research in sign language interpreting at California State University Northridge." In *Language Interpretation and Communication,* ed. by David Gerver & H. Wallace Sinaiko, 87–97. New York: Plenum Press. DOI: 10.1007/978-1-4615-9077-4_9

Mweri, Jefwa. 2006. "Complexities and challenges of interpretation in the Third World: The Kenyan case." In *Proceedings of the Inaugural Conference of the World Association of Sign Language Interpreters,* ed. by Rachel McKee, 134–140. Coleford, UK: Douglas McLean.

Napier, Jemina. 2002. *Sign Language Interpreting: Linguistic coping strategies.* Coleford, UK: Douglas McLean. DOI: 10.1002/dei.171

Napier, Jemina. 2004. "Interpreting omissions: A new perspective." *Interpreting* 6(2): 117–142. DOI: 10.1075/intp.6.2.02nap

Napier, Jemina. 2005. "Training sign language interpreters in Australia: An innovative approach." *Babel: International Journal of Translation* 51(3): 207–223. DOI: 10.1075/babel.51.3.01nap

Napier, Jemina. 2007. "Cooperation in interpreter-mediated monologic talk." *Discourse and Communication,* 1(4): 407–432. DOI: 10.1177/1750481307082206

Napier, Jemina (ed.). 2009. *International Perspectives on Sign Language Interpreter Education.* Washington, D.C., Gallaudet University Press. DOI: 10.1075/intp.12.2.10kel

Napier, Jemina. 2011a. "Signed language interpreting." In *The Oxford Handbook of Translation Studies,* ed. by Kirsten Malmkjaer and Kevin Windle, 353–372. New York: Oxford University Press. DOI: 10.1093/oxfordhb/9780199239306.001.0001

Napier, Jemina. 2011b. "If a tree falls in the forest, does it make a noise? The merits of publishing interpreting research." In *Advances in Interpreting Research: Inquiry in Action,* ed. by Brenda Nicodemus and Laurie Swabey, 121–152. Philadelphia: John Benjamins. DOI: 10.1075/btl.99.09nap

Napier, Jemina. 2012. "Editorial: Community interpreting research: A critical discussion of interpreting education and assessment." *International Journal of Interpreter Education* 4(2): 1–5. DOI: 10.1075/intp.12.2.10kel

Napier, Jemina. 2013. "Examining the notion of interpreter role through a different linguistic lens." In *Evolving paradigms in interpreter education: Impact of interpreting research on teaching interpreting,* ed. by Elizabeth Winston and Christine Monikowski, 151–158. Washington, DC: Gallaudet University Press.

Napier, Jemina. In press. "Not just child's play: Exploring bilingualism and language brokering as a precursor to the development of expertise as a professional signed language interpreter." In *Non-professional Interpreting and Translation: State of the Art and Future of an Emerging Field of Research,* ed. by R. Antonini. Amsterdam: John Benjamins.

Napier, Jemina, and Sandra Hale. 2015. "Methodology." In *Routledge Encyclopedia of Interpreting Studies,* ed. by Franz Pöchhacker. New York: Routledge.

Napier, Jemina, Rachel L. McKee and Della Goswell. 2010. *Sign Language Interpreting: Theory and Practice in Australia and New Zealand.* Sydney: Federation Press.

Napier, Jemina, and David Spencer. 2008. "Guilty or not guilty? An investigation of deaf jurors' access to court proceedings via sign language interpreting." In *Interpreting in legal settings,* ed. by Debra Russell and Sandra Hale, 72–122. Washington, DC: Gallaudet University Press.

Nelson, Kate, Inise Tawaketini, Ruth Spencer and Della Goswell. 2009. "Isa Lei: Interpreter Training in Fiji." In *International perspectives on sign language interpreter education,* ed. by Jemina Napier. Washington, DC: Gallaudet University Press.

Nicodemus, Brenda, and Karen Emmorey. 2012. "Direction asymmetries in spoken and signed language interpreting." *Bilingualism: Language and Cognition.* Available on CJO 2012. DOI: 10.1017/s1366728912000521

Nida, Eugene. 1976. "A framework for the analysis and the evaluation of theories of translation." In *Translation: Applications and Research,* ed. by Richard Brislin, 47–91. New York: Gardner Press.

Nilsson, Anna Lena. 1997. "Sign Language Interpreting in Sweden." *Meta Translators' Journal,* 42(3): 550–554. DOI: 10.7202/003738ar

Ojala-Signell, Raili, and Anna Komorova. 2006. "International development cooperation work with sign language interpreters." In *Proceedings of the Inaugural Conference of the World Association of Sign Language Interpreters,* ed. by Rachel L. McKee, 115–122. Coleford, UK: Douglas McLean.

Okombo, Okoth, Jefwa G. Mweri and Washington Akaranga. 2009. "Sign language interpreting in Kenya: A general overview." In *International Perspectives on Sign Language Interpreter Education,* ed. by Jemina Napier, 295–300. Washington, DC: Gallaudet University Press.

Owens, Andrew. 2012. *Say what you see. Sign language interpreting: Voice-over.* London: The Wakeman Trust.

Pasquandrea, Sergio. 2012. "Co-constructing dyadic sequences in healthcare interpreting: A multimodal account." *New Voices in Translation Studies* 8: 132–157.

Penn, Clare. 1990. "How do you sign 'apartheid'? The politics of South African Sign Language." *Language Problems and Language Planning* 14(2): 91–103. DOI: 10.1075/lplp.14.2.02pen

Penn, Clare. 1992. "The sociolinguistics of South African Sign Language." In *Language and Society in Africa,* ed. by R. Herbert, 277–284. Johannesburg, South Africa: Witwatersrand University Press. DOI: 10.1017/s0041977x00009381

Penn, Clare and Timothy Reagan. 1994. "The properties of South African Sign Language: Lexical diversity and syntactic unity." *Sign Language Studies* 85: 319–327. DOI: 10.1353/sls.1994.0011

Per-Lee, Myra S. 1980. *Interpreter Research: Targets for the Eighties.* Washington, DC: The National Academy of Gallaudet College.

Pöchhacker, Franz. 1999. "Getting organized": the evolution of community interpreting." *Interpreting* 4(1): 125–140. DOI: 10.1075/intp.4.1.11poc

Pöchhacker, Franz. 2004. *Introducing Interpreting Studies.* London and New York: Routledge. DOI: 10.1075/intp.6.2.14gar

Pöchhacker, Franz. 2011. "Researching interpreting: Approaches to inquiry." In *Advances in Interpreting Research: Inquiry in Action,* ed. by Brenda Nicodemus and Laurie Swabey, 5–26. Philadelphia: John Benjamins. DOI: 10.1075/btl.99.04poch

Pöchhacker, Franz and Miriam Shlesinger. 2002. *The Interpreting Studies Reader.* London and New York: Routledge. DOI: 10.1075/bct.9

Pollitt, Kyra. 1997. "The state we're in: Some thoughts on professionalization, professionalism and practice among the UK's sign language interpreters." *Deaf Worlds* 13(3): 21–26.

Poyatos, Fernando. 1987/2002. "Nonverbal communication in simultaneous and consecutive inter-pretation, a theoretical model and new perspectives." In *The Interpreting Studies Reader*, ed. by Franz Pöchhacker and Miriam Shlesinger, 235–252. London and New York: Routledge.

Quigley, Stephen. P. (ed). 1965. Interpreting for deaf people: A report of a workshop on Interpret-ing. Governor Baxter State School for the Deaf, Portland, Maine, July 7–27, 1965. U.S. Dept. of Health, Education, and Welfare, Vocational Rehabilitation Administration: U.S. Govt. Print Off.

Quigley, Stephen P., Barbara B. Brasel and Dale Montanelli. 1973. Interpreters for Deaf People: selec-tion, evaluation, and classification. Final Report HEW. SRS 14-P-55400/5.

Roberson, Len, Debra Russell and Risa Shaw. 2011. "American Sign Language/English interpreting in legal settings: Current practices in North America." *Journal of Interpretation* 13(1): 64–79.

Roy, Cynthia. 1987. "Evaluating performance: An interpreted lecture". In *New Dimensions in Inter-preter Education: Curriculum and Instruction: Proceedings of the Sixth National Conference of Interpreter Trainers*, Marina McIntire (ed.), 139–147 Silver Spring, MD: RID.

Roy, Cynthia. 1989. "A Sociolinguistic Analysis of the Interpreter's Role in the Turn Exchanges of an Interpreted Event." Ph.D. diss., Washington, DC: Georgetown University.

Roy, Cynthia. 1992. "A sociolinguistic analysis of the interpreter's role in simultaneous talk in a face-to-face interpreted dialogue." *Sign Language Studies* 74: 21–61. DOI: 10.1353/sls.1992.0018

Roy, Cynthia. 1993. "The problem with definitions, descriptions and the role metaphors of interpret-ers." *Journal of Interpretation* 6: 127–154.

Rozan, Jean-Francois. 1956. *La Prise de Notes en Interprétation Consecutive*. Genève: Georg.

Russell, Debra. 2002. *Interpreting in Legal Contexts: Consecutive and Simultaneous Interpretation*. Burtonsville, MD: Sign Media. DOI: 10.1075/intp.6.2.10ben

Sacks, Harvey, Emmanuel Schegloff and Gail Jefferson. 1974. "A simplest systematics for the organi-zation of turn-taking in conversation." *Language* 50: 696–735. DOI: 10.2307/412243

Schein, Jerome. 1974. "Personality characteristics associated with interpreter proficiency." *Journal of Rehabilitation of the Deaf* 7: 33–43.

Schulz, Andrea. 1997. "Sign language interpreting in Germany on the way towards professionalism." *Meta Translators' Journal* 42(3): 546–549. DOI: 10.7202/004054ar

Scott-Gibson, Liz. 1992. "Sign language interpreting: An emerging profession." In *Constructing Deaf-ness*, ed. by Susan Gregory and Gillian Hartley, 253–258. Milton Keynes: Open University Press.

Seleskovitch, Danica. 1968/1978 (English version). Interpreting for International Conferences. Prob-lems of Language and Communication. Washington, DC: Pen and Booth.

Selzer, Marsanne. 2010. "*South African Sign Language used in Parliament: Is There a Need for Stan-dardisation?*" Masters diss., Stellenbosch University.

Shaffer, Barbara. 2013. "The notion of meaning and its relationship to beliefs about interpreter role." In *Evolving Paradigms in Interpreter Education: Impact of Interpreting Research on Teaching Interpreting*, ed. by Elizabeth Winston and Christine Monikowski, 128–150. Washington, DC: Gallaudet University Press.

Shannon, Claude. E. and Warren Weaver. 1949. *A Mathematical Model of Communication*. Urbana-Champaign, Illinois: University of Illinois Press.

Shaw, Sherry. 2006. "Launching international collaboration for interpretation research." *Sign Language Studies* 6(4): 438–453. DOI: 10.1353/sls.2006.0028

Shaw, Sherry. 2011a. "Cognitive and motivational contributors to aptitude: A study of spoken and signed language interpreting students." *Interpreting, International Journal of Research and Prac-tice in Interpreting* 13(1): 70–84. DOI: 10.1075/intp.13.1.05sha

Shaw, Sherry. 2011b. *Service Learning in Interpreter Education*. Washington DC: Gallaudet University Press.

Shaw, Sherry, Nadja Grbić and Kathy Franklin. 2004. "Applying language skills to interpretation: Student perspectives from signed and spoken language programs." *Interpreting, International Journal of Research and Practice in Interpreting* 6(1): 69–100. DOI: 10.1075/intp.6.1.06sha

Shunsuke, Ito. 1968. "Interpreting to ensure the rights of deaf people: Interpreting theory." In *Japanese Newspaper for the Deaf*, July 1, 1968.

Siple, Linda. 1996. "The use of additions in sign language transliteration." In *Assessing our work: Assessing our worth: Proceedings of the 11th National Convention of the Conference of Interpreter Trainers*, ed. by David M. Jones, 29–45. USA: Conference of Interpreter Trainers.

Solow, Sharon Neumann. 1981. *Sign Language Interpreting: A Basic Resource*. Silver Spring, MD: National Association of the Deaf.

Stokoe, William C. 1960. Sign Language Structure: An Outline of the Visual Communication Systems of the American Deaf. Studies in Linguistics: Occasional Papers, 8. Buffalo, NY: Department of Anthropology and Linguistics, University of Buffalo.

Stokoe, William C., Dorothy C. Casterline and Carl G. Croneberg. 1965. *A Dictionary of American Sign Language on Linguistic Principles*. Washington, D.C.: Gallaudet College Press.

Stone, Christopher. 2010. "Access all areas—sign language interpreting, is it that special?" *Journal of Specialised Translation* 14: 41–54.

Stone, Christopher. 2012. "Interpreting." In *Sign Language: An International Handbook*, ed. by Roland Pfau, Markus Steinbach and Bencie Woll, 980–998. Amsterdam: De Gruyter Mouton. DOI: 10.1515/9783110261325

Stone, Christopher and Bencie Woll. 2008. "Dumb O Jemmy and others: Deaf people, interpreters and the London courts in the eighteenth and nineteenth centuries." *Sign Language Studies* 8(3): 226–240. DOI: 10.1353/sls.2008.0009

Strong, Michael and Steven Fritsch Rudser. 1986. "The subjective assessment of sign language interpreters." *Sign Language Studies* 15(53): 299–314. DOI: 10.1353/sls.1986.0018

Swabey, Laurie, Marty Taylor, Daniel Gile, Brenda Nicodemus, Jemina Napier and Lorraine Leeson. Forthcoming. "*Cross-linguistic comparison of spoken and signed language interpreters' renditions of a single speech.*"

Swift, Odette. 2012. *The Roles of Signed Language Interpreters in Post-secondary Education Settings in South Africa*. Masters diss., University of South Africa.

Tannen, Deborah. 1984. *Conversational style: Analyzing talk among friends*. Norwood, NJ: Ablex. DOI: 10.1017/s0047404500011830

Takagi, Machiko. 2006. "Sign language interpreters of non-English speaking countries who support international activities of the deaf." In *Proceedings of the Inaugural Conference of the World Association of Sign Language Interpreters*, ed. by Rachel L. McKee, 25–31. Coleford, UK: Douglas McLean.

Tervoort, Ben.T. 1953. "Structurele Analyse Van Visueel Taalgebruik Binnen Een Groep Dove Kinderen." Ph.D. diss., University of Amsterdam.

Turner, Graham. H. 1995. "The bilingual, bimodal courtroom: A first glance." *Journal of Interpretation* 7(1): 3–34.

Turner, Graham H. and Richard Brown. 2001. "Interaction and the role of the interpreter in court." In *Interpreting Interpreting: Studies and reflections on sign language interpreting*, ed. by Frank J. Harrington and Graham H. Turner, 152–167. Gloucestershire: Douglas McLean. DOI: 10.1075/intp.6.2.09roy

Tweney, Ryan and Harry Hoemann. 1976. "Translation and sign language." In *Translation: Applications and Research*, ed. by Richard Brislin, 138–161. New York: Gardner Press.

Valdes, Guadalupe, Cristina Chavez, Claudia Angelelli, Kerry Enright, Dania Garcia, and Marisela Gonzalez. 2003. *Expanding Definitions of Giftedness: The Case of Young Interpreters from Immigrant Communities*. Mahwah, NJ: Lawrence Erlbaum Associates.

Van Herreweghe, Mieke and Myriam Vermeerbergen. 2006. "Deaf signers in Flanders and 25 years of community interpreting." In *Linguistica Antverpiensia: Taking stock: Research and methodology in community interpreting* (vol. 5), ed. by Erik Hertog and Bart van der Veer, 293–308. Antwerpen: Hogeschool Antwerpen, Hoger Instituut voor Vertalers en Tolken.

Venuti, Lawrence (ed.). 2000. *The Translation Studies Reader.* London and New York: Routledge. DOI: 10.4324/9780203446621

Wadensjö, Cecilia. 1992. "Interpreting as Interaction: On Dialogue Interpreting in Immigration Hearings and Medical Encounters." Ph.D. diss., Linköping University. DOI: 10.1075/target.6.1.19mor

Wadensjö, Cecilia. 1998. *Interpreting as Interaction.* London: Longman.

Wadensjö, Cecilia. 2008. "In and off the show: Co-constructing 'invisibility' in an interpreter-mediated talk show interview." *Meta Translators' Journal* 53(1): 84–203. DOI: 10.7202/017982ar

Wehrmeyer, Jennifer. 2014. "Eye-tracking Deaf and hearing viewing of sign language interpreted news broadcasts." *Journal of Eye Movement Research* 7(1): 1–16.

Wilcox, Sherman, and Barbara Shaffer. 2005. "Towards a cognitive model of interpreting." In *Topics in Signed Language Interpreting*, ed. by Terry Janzen, 27–50. Amsterdam/Philadelphia: John Benjamins. DOI: 10.1075/btl.63.06wil

Winston, Elizabeth. 1989. "Transliteration: What's the message?" In *The Sociolinguistics of the Deaf Community*, ed. by Ceil Lucas, 147–164. Washington, D.C: Gallaudet University Press. DOI: 10.1016/b978-0-12-458045-9.50013-6

Winston, Elizabeth and Dennis Cokely. 2009. "The National Consortium of Interpreter Education Centers in the United States of America." In *International Perspectives on Sign Language Interpreter Education,* ed. by Jemina Napier, 267–294. Washington, DC: Gallaudet University Press.

Witter-Merithew, Anna. 1986. "Claiming our Destiny, Parts 1 and 2." *Views* October: 12 and November: 3–4.

Yoken, Carol. 1979. *Interpreter training: The state of the art.* Washington, DC: National Academy of Gallaudet College.

Zimmer, June. 1989. "Toward a description of register variation in American Sign Language." In *The Sociolinguistics of the Deaf Community,* ed. by Ceil Lucas, 253–272. New York: Academic Press. DOI: 10.1016/b978-0-12-458045-9.50018-5

Zimmer, June. 1992. "Appropriateness and naturalness in ASL-English interpreting." In *Expanding Horizons: Proceedings of the Twelfth National Conference of Interpreter Trainers*, ed. by Jean Plant-Moeller, 81–92. Silver Spring, MD: RID.

Subject Index

Page numbers in italics refer to figures and tables.

Name Index